# Revisioning Italy

T0337896

# Revisioning Italy

## *National Identity and Global Culture*

Beverly Allen and Mary Russo, editors

University of Minnesota Press
Minneapolis
London

Copyright 1997 by the Regents of the University of Minnesota

Published by the University of Minnesota Press
111 Third Avenue South, Suite 290
Minneapolis, MN 55401-2520
http://www.upress.umn.edu

Library of Congress Cataloging-in-Publication Data

Revisioning Italy : national identity and global culture / Beverly Allen and
    Mary Russo, editors.
        p.    cm.
    Includes index.
    ISBN 0-8166-2726-6 (hardcover : alk. paper). — ISBN 0-8166-2727-4
(pbk. : alk. paper)
        1. National characteristics, Italian.  2. Italy—Civilization—1945–
3. Italians—Foreign countries—Ethnic identity.  I. Allen, Beverly.
II. Russo, Mary J.
DG455.R48   1997
945.092—dc21                                                      97-20530
                                                                      CIP

Printed in the United States of America on acid-free paper

The University of Minnesota is an equal-opportunity educator and employer.

10 09 08 07 06 05 04 03 02 01 00 99 98     10 9 8 7 6 5 4 3 2 1

In memory of our fathers,
Everett Ernst Allen
and
Leroy Michael Russo

# Contents

Preface     ix

Introduction     1

*Part I: Culture and Place: Italy as a European Country*

The Myth of Backward Italy in Modern Europe     23
*John Agnew*

Italy, Exile Country     43
*Antonio Negri*

They're Not Children Anymore: The Novelization of
"Italians" and "Terrorism"     52
*Beverly Allen*

"Italy" in Italy: Old Metaphors and New Racisms
in the 1990s     81
*David Ward*

*Part II: Impositions, Race, and Colonization*

Italy: Cultural Identity and Spatial Opportunism
from a Postcolonial Perspective     101
*Mohamed Aden*

African Americans and the Italo-Ethiopian War     116
*Ayele Bekerie*

Shades of Black in Advertising and Popular Culture     134
*Karen Pinkus*

Is *Aida* an Orientalist Opera?     156
*Paul Robinson*

*Part III: Immigrations*

Strangers in Paradise: Foreigners and Shadows in
Italian Literature                                          169
*Graziella Parati*

The Preclusion of Postcolonial Discourse in Southern Italy  191
*Pasquale Verdicchio*

Anarquistas, Graças a Deus!: "Italy" in South America      213
*Francesca Miller*

*Part IV: Postmodernity and Global Italy*

Venice, Venice, and L.A.: Cultural Repetition and
Bodily Difference                                          235
*Mary Russo*

Decolonizing the Screen: From *Ladri di biciclette* to
*Ladri di saponette*                                       253
*Marguerite R. Waller*

If the Japanese Are Samurai, the Italians Are *Baka*:
The Multiple Play of Stereotypes                           275
*Antonio Marazzi*

Spaghetti Eastern: Mutating Mass Culture,
Transforming Ethnicity                                     292
*Elaine K. Chang*

Contributors                                               315

Index                                                      319

# Preface

Contemporary cultural studies have come to understand nation, nationhood, place, and identity as volatile entities in a postmodern world. The unprecedented cultural conflicts associated with the much-anticipated observance in 1992 of the Quincentenary of Columbus's voyages to the Americas marked an irrevocable break with the monumentalization of Italian culture and traditional models of cultural influence.

In October 1992, a group of scholars, activists, and statesmen from many disciplines gathered at Syracuse University to investigate how our various fields were addressing contemporary realities of national identity. Our only common characteristic was that, for all of us, Italy was not anymore a given. The place of Italy in history and cultural geography was now in question. Historians and journalists had for some time been speaking of a new Europe, and the economic unification of Europe projected for 1992 raised the issue of the meaning and resiliency of the nation-state in a European context in general. But a European context by itself was far from sufficient. Given recent global demographic patterns, including the new African, Eastern European, and Philippine immigrations to Italy, we had to question the notion of national identity and, in fact, identity in general for the twenty-first century.

As we addressed this radical shift from various perspectives, further questions emerged: if Italy were no longer locatable, neither were our disciplines themselves. A new, more powerful strategy was called for that would cross disciplinary boundaries and explode the category "Italy" from within its traditional regional, peninsular, and European contexts and, from the outside, through its multitudinous occurrences and transmissions in Africa, Asia, and the Americas. The project that emerged is thus linked inextricably to contemporary trends in transnational cultural studies.

The title of the Syracuse conference, "Designing Italy: Italy in Europe, Africa, Asia, and the Americas," has been replaced by a new title, *Revisioning Italy: National Identity and Global Culture*. The rhetoric of "designing Italy" still resonates throughout the manuscript, however, and it is worth explaining briefly the power it had in our conference discussions. "Designing Italy" may suggest a facile identification with fashions and luxury exports. Clearly such associations are earmarks of a current consumerist reception of Italy in a global market. "Designing" seeks to go far beyond this recent cliché, however. "Italy" has been "designed" all over the globe as an identity, a criterion of similarity, that is in fact never the same. It is in a state of flux, up for negotiation, getting handed over, claimed, held up bannerlike to legitimize particular acts or even entire lives, and sometimes even the taking of lives. It is found in great variation within the peninsular and insular territorial boundaries of the nation-state called Italy itself, but it is also found, sometimes to greater effect, in other places where "place" is drawn in the colors of colonialism, postcolonialism, immigration, exile, and the multinational markets and labor relations of postindustrial capitalism. "Italy," a name often associated with great high culture, contemporary design—as in furniture, fashion, and food—now shows up as an image itself "designed" by the forces and powers of cultural determination.

"Design" is also something that the nation-state Italy has or has had on other places than its own territory, on other cultural products than those its in-border residents invent. "Italy" has had designs, for example, on Ethiopia, on Somalia, on Libya. It has had designs on U.S. neighborhoods, on Brazilian politics, on global popular media, on gender and sexuality, on racial and class hierarchies outside its own borders. It has also, of course, had designs on its own peninsular reconstitutions, and on its new politics, as contributors here variously show.

Participants at the 1992 conference are joined in the present volume, *Revisioning Italy*, by other interested scholars. As a group, we recognize the urgency of arriving at ever more adequate strategies for the study of culture. No intellectual considerations of cultural production and national identity are adequate, however, unless they acknowledge both the local and the global aspects of interculturalism and involve a strenuous dialogue between contesting positions. Although the contributors to this volume agree on the importance and urgency of such dialogues, their perspectives on such terms as "identity," "centrism," and "ethnicity" are varied and sometimes conflicting.

The editors wish to acknowledge most gratefully the support of the Humanities Council at Syracuse University and the generous grant that allowed our 1992 conference to occur as the first Smith Symposium in the Humanities. We thank Paul Archambault, in particular, for his early and most generous support of our project, Augustus Pallotta for his constant encouragement and helpful intervention, and Margie May for her energetic, considerate administrative support. Thanks to Hampshire College for research support. Warm thanks also go to our readers at the University of Minnesota Press, to our editor, Biodun Iginla, and his assistant, Elizabeth Knoll Stomberg, for giving us opportunities to improve our book, and to Lisa Freeman and Amy Unger for seeing the project through. Thanks especially to one of the contributors, Ayele Bekerie, who aided notably in the preparation of the book. His editorial and consulting input was very helpful, especially at the early stages of this project. Many thanks to Euan Hague for his adept research and editing contributions and to Sebastian Sobolewski for his guidance in the wide, wide world of word processing. Thanks go also to Maurizio Lazzerato, who videotaped Antonio Negri's presentation in Paris, to Danilo Quinto for some timely readings, and to Dan Warner for his technical expertise, *farfalle ai funghi*, and warm, sustaining presence throughout the entire project.

# Introduction

From 1993 to 1995, while we were planning this book and were considering the status of narrative and metaphor in relation to national identity, many allegories and images of Italianicity came our way via newspaper, telephone, television, radio, fax machines, E-mail, conversation, travel, and other modes of personal experience. In 1993, a monument that Italy symbolically and economically trades on, the Uffizi Museum in Florence, was ripped apart by a bomb. In this bombing, just off the famous Piazza della Signoria, five people were killed. The bombing, later designated by the press as a Mafia-driven event intended to hinder the corruption investigations in Italy, destroyed both human life and paintings and sculptures that have long constituted a significant part of Italy's classical heritage—more ruins in the marble wilderness. The reporting and interpretation of this "tragic event" went back and forth between the United States and Italy in journalistic fragments and non sequiturs.

In the United States, National Public Radio interviewed an Italian man on the street. When questioned about this and other recent bombings in Italy, he replied that the violence made him fear a return of fascism, and terrorism, and further loss of life.

In Florence in 1994, U.S. students on a program abroad gazed at the floral wreaths that had been left at the bomb site and expressed shock that violence like this could occur. Why, they questioned, would a people destroy its own cultural monuments? They could understand such an act only as wanton and meaningless. For these students, social violence is apparently not political.

In the summer of 1994, during an attempted car jacking on an auto-
strada south of Naples, a small boy from the United States was shot to
death. The Italian press associated this new form of violence with the
tradition of southern Italian banditry. In what seemed to the Italian
media a gesture of astounding generosity, the boy's parents donated
his organs to Italian donor banks. Belying their reputation as a con-
sumately generous people, the Italians have the smallest donor bank
of all developed countries. According to press reports, it is simply not
the national custom to will organs. Is there a shared revulsion toward
giving up or receiving parts of the body as "natural symbols" of the
nation?[1]

Similarly, it has not been the historical custom to adopt children or
give them up for adoption. Children who were unrecognized by their
biological fathers were stigmatized socially and legally until after World
War II. They were denied the privileges of full citizenship and treated
almost as if they were immigrants or illegal aliens. Perhaps such stories tell us something about the fragility of national identity when it is
imagined as body politic.

Pushing the metaphor of reproduction as an index of social formation
further, consider the hyperbolic attempts to prolong childbearing age
in Italy. These gained vast television and tabloid coverage when new
reproductive technologies enabled an Italian woman in her sixties to
bear "her own" child and thus set the record as the world's oldest
mother. Significantly enough, the same country has produced state-of-
the-art neonatal care that sets the standard for the world's youngest
babies. Could this extension of the parameters of Italian reproduction
be symptomatic of a crisis of national identity triggered by the new
immigrants from Africa and Eastern Europe?

Not far from the train station in Florence there is an area that has become an African piazza. Over and over again during 1993 and 1994
we heard about intercultural spaces that progressive Italians were providing as acts of reciprocal acculturation. For many Italian youths,
accoutrements of African dress and body ornamentation were fast
becoming fashionable clichés. In clear resistance to the xenophobic
rap of the Northern League, the irredentist politics of the ultranation-
alist fascists, and Berlusconi's glossy portrayal of an Italy made of
Euroyuppies, popular music—even the popular music performed on

television spectacles—sang for tolerance and a multiethnic society.[2] When skinheads beat up an African immigrant on the outskirts of Rome, demonstrations against racism followed. It was almost as if a shudder had gone through Italy, reminding it of the particularly brutal murder of Pier Paolo Pasolini on those same Roman outskirts—Pasolini the homosexual, the Catholic, the communist, Pasolini who paradoxically had tried to film an African Oresteia.

Contemporary cultural studies have come to understand nation, nationhood, place, and identity as volatile entities in a postmodern world.[3] Simultaneously, Italy has come to embody the myriad, contradictory historical forms of modern nationhood. As the *fabulae* above suggest, anyone engaging in a contemporary consideration of Italy, Italianicity, or Italian studies must pay attention to the provisional, multifocal, and potentially violent aspects of cultural practices that reiterate Italian identity. This collection of essays by a diverse group, including scholars from many fields, a displaced African statesman, and immigrant and exiled intellectuals, brings together varying perspectives on historical and contemporary cultural formulations of Italian national identity, both within Italy and abroad, through immigration, colonization, tourism, and global culture markets.

## Exile, Immigration, and Imagined Communities

Recent studies of nationalism and identity have followed the lead of Benedict Anderson in describing the nation as an "imagined community."[4] As many of the papers in this collection indicate, Italy is nothing if not deeply imagined, serving as the Other country for northern cultural tourism. More powerful European nations have dominated and fetishized a "piccola Italia" as weak, effeminate, southern, and exotic throughout its formative modern history. In the nineteenth century, for example, it flourished as an aesthetic and erotic free space where cultural elites from northern Europe and the United States were free to construct and explore alternative identities and lifestyles.[5]

Anderson's study of nationalism as a global phenomenon has given rise to many reconsiderations of that term in specific geopolitical contexts. Two of Anderson's tenets regarding nationalism have had particular importance for this project. First, Anderson's anthropological approach removes nationalism from the sphere of the ideological, where it has been considered either "good" (the Western gift to the rest of the world) or "bad" (in its associations with war, imperialist aggression, domestic violence, "ethnic" hatreds, and the destruction of international movements). If we take nationalism to be closer to a concept like kinship, for example, then we may arrive at more complex, provisional, and inclusive views of Italy and Italianicity than recent framings derived from the debates around "identity politics" in the United States have allowed.[6] Viewing nationalism in this way does not avoid conflict or absolve blame, as the papers here vividly demonstrate. It does, however, leave room for a consideration of "Italians," and by extension members of other national groups, as both subjects and objects of nationalism in all its effects. The anthropological view thus enables scholars to gather together, as we have done, varying perspectives and vastly different kinds of cultural productions in a common analytic project.

Second, Anderson's identification of the major role of print capitalism in instituting specific forms of nationalism has generated new appreciations of the role of representation at every stage of nation building. We are committed to the collective study of different kinds and locations of cultural production, including canonical and eccentric words and images. The novel, opera, poetry, film, photography, popular print media, grafitti, and cartoons as *representational and representative practices* are necessary objects of study in any viable theory of national identity.

## Italy and Ethnicity

> No nation possesses an ethnic base naturally, but as social formations are nationalized, the populations included within them, divided up among them or dominated by them are ethnicized—that is, represented in the past or in the future *as if* they formed a natural community, possessing of itself an identity of origins, culture and interests which transcends individuals and social conditions.[7]

The notion of "natural rights" of citizenship elaborated in eighteenth-century Europe assumes that no essential differences exist among individuals. Nonetheless, this kind of "horizontal brotherhood" (Anderson) always occurs in conjunction with a set of particularizing differences. We might, in fact, claim that any given nation and nationality defines itself largely in relation to differences *within* it, to the "vertical" arrangement of such constitutive categories as ethnicity and "race," class and gender.

The term "ethnicity" is rapidly becoming a euphemism for its discredited precursor, "race." Hidden racist discourse thus constantly repositions Italian identity, like many others, both within and outside a historical congruence of some imagined biological community with the Italian nation and the Italian state. In the geopolitically loosened places of immigration, for example, it can easily be construed as a kind of inherited biological characteristic set, and has been, both from the outside and from within. In the United States, this shows up in the way Southern plantation owners, because they saw Italians as a "black" "race," sometimes used them as slaves.[8] Later, immigration quotas were to perpetuate similar conflations of "race," "ethnicity," and "color."[9]

Within its national context, Italian ethnicity is a shifting variable often perceived from the outside as a seamless surface. Antonio Gramsci did much to change this perception. In addressing the question of the south, he first drew international attention to the hierarchical economic configuration that cast southern Italians as ethnically inferior to northern Italians. This othering, demonizing dynamic still holds sway in peninsular Italy both in such common phrases as "Africa begins just south of Rome" and in the complex, virulent phenomenon of the Northern League. In each example, the south constitutes both the Italian nation and its Other.

Patterns of Italian ethnicity mark the legacies of Italian fascism and imperialism. A spate of controversial Benetton ads, for example, depicting such catastrophes as famine and AIDS, comes from a cultural cauldron that is still negotiating the history of Italian fascist imperialism while postcolonial populations reread that same history for themselves, in Mogadishu as well as Rome.[10]

Recent emigrations map the notions of ethnic difference constituted in Italy onto more heterogeneous transnational terrain. The cultural positionings of internal peninsular migration from South to North, that is, reappear in immigrant communities in northern Europe, Canada, and the United States. As contributors to this volume indicate, such diverse locations as the Canadian metropolis and the countryside in Brazil bear witness to Sicilians, or Genovese, becoming Italians by virtue of their displacement from Italy.

Racial, ethnic, and gender stratification works differently in different locales. In South and North America, for example, both destinations of waves of Italian immigrants, local constraints determine social positionings according to highly varied notions of skin color. Since European colonization occurred in vastly different ways in South and North America, it established contrasting notions of gender and ethnicity in the two hemispheres. As is often pointed out, English settlers in North America, male and female, came with the intention to stay and propagate their culture; they were families escaping religious persecution in Europe who, for the most part, did not produce children with the people who were already living in North America. Thus no well-defined colonial mestizo population appeared in Canada and the United States. In contrast, the Spanish colonizers in South America were men without families along; they intended not to settle in the land they had ravaged but to return to Europe with the spoils of their conquest. When they found themselves stranded in American territories without the wealth they had dreamed of—as often happened—they mated with the women who were already living there and thus contributed to the formation of a long-standing mestizo population and a more highly nuanced color-based racism than exists in North America. Subsequent immigrations of "Italians" or "Italian Americans," and of all other immigrant groups, for that matter, took on ethnic identities in relation to these racial markers.

The Italianicity of Italian immigrants to the United States was and is defined by many institutions, from neighborhood chapters of the Knights of Columbus to the mass media. The U.S. version of "Italy" includes ethnic loyalty, traditional values of family and kitchen, grand opera, stylish imports, and, if the continuing production of Mafia films is a fair indication, male bonding at its most sentimental and pernicious. High style in particular has become a clichéd version of "Italianicity" in fashion, cars, and domestic design: an Italian car, to the American observer, is a Ferrari, a Lamborghini, at the very least an Alfa Romeo; hardly ever does the humble Fiat come to mind. This strategy of marketing by national association works on a transnational scale alongside another marketing strategy based on regional associations. Thus Tuscan olive oil, Milanese fashion, and tourism in Sardinia, rather than "Italian" oil, style, and beaches, are the packaged products. Of the two, the national-referent strategy is the strangest for Italians, whose symbolic culture depends much less on constructions of national icons than does that of the United States.

One of our contributors, for example, recalls a visit by an Italian intellectual to a central New York city. On a trip to the local megasupermarket, the visitor was astonished to find Italian flags just about everywhere: on products ranging from cheeses to vinegar to sparkling water. Since Italy does not espouse the cult of the national flag, this Italian had never in his life seen so many Italian flags in one place.[11]

Offsetting the fact that some of these characteristics of Italianicity correspond to some of the most unstable and contested aspects of "American" society, cultural productions have also designated "Italy" as a reassuring and generally conservative model of identity, culture, and consumerism in the United States in recent decades. Such a designation ignores, of course, the difficult history of immigration, labor struggles, interethnic and interracial relations, and the structural subordination of Italian Americans, all of which make this group an unlikely paradigm of the American Dream of assimilation and economic success.

On the contrary, as Stanley Aronowitz points out in *The Politics of Identity*, Italian Americans continue to be "chronically underrepresented in the professions, in managerial strata, in the political directorate."[12] Furthermore, in the one area where their presence has been historically strong—as semiskilled and skilled workers in the construction and textile industries—jobs are in steady decline.

An interrogation of the class and "racial" components of Italianicity within the United States points in two directions: (1) toward an acknowledgment of Italian Americans as a group marked ethnically and by class, and (2) toward an acknowledgment of the structural position of Italian Americans as a borderland of racialized distinction: the last "white" "racial" category in a sweep from "white" to "black." The films of the African American filmmaker Spike Lee, for instance, acknowledge the intriguing and dangerous nature of this proximity in their stories of racial violence and interracial love.

## Colonization in Africa

Internal differences of "race," class, and gender would seem to disappear in Italian colonial history, where "Italians" unite as nationals and as Europeans against Africans and African "territories." Nonetheless, the long, ignominious history of Italian invasions in Africa is not complete without some consideration of these factors. Without recounting this history in detail, we would signal that Italian nation building corresponded historically to Italian imperialist expansion. Italy came late to both of these modernist endeavors. The "ancient" history of Italy, the "glories of Rome," were resurrected by every imperialist campaign, as were identifications with the great republics of Genoa and Venice, the Christian empire, and the kingdoms of Naples and the Two Sicilies. It was but a short symbolic leap from these ideological mappings of Italian greatness to the military aggressions in Ethiopia, Libya, and Somalia.

Italy had, of course, compelling economic advantages to be gained by invading Africa. Italy's nineteenth-century economic growth, though relatively rapid, could not keep pace with its increasing population. As the economic gap between north and south widened, the united Italy promised by the 1860 constitution failed to materialize. Massive emigration and colonization thus became necessary defining features of the new nation-state.

Having joined in the late-nineteenth-century European imperialist scramble for Africa, Italy became the first modern European power to be defeated by an African state when the Ethiopian army defeated the Italian army at the Battle of Adwa in 1896. By the end of the First World War, Italy's colonial expansion in Africa was behind that of other European powers, three of which (Belgium, England, and France) had already established their domination over some of the most profitable regions in Africa and Asia.

With the fascist seizure of state power in 1922, Mussolini began to envision an expanded Italian future in Africa. To this end, Italy invaded Ethiopia in 1935.[13] By the end of this campaign, Italy had consolidated its posssessions in Libya, Somalia, Eritrea, and Ethiopia.[14] In the years that followed, emigration from the Italian peninsula to northeast Africa continued in spite of the financial disaster the colonies had become, although it remained less significant than Italian emigration to the Americas, Australia, and other arrival countries.[15] Italy's defeat in World War II finally assured its demise as a colonial power.

Italian identity thus increasingly became a necessity for the cultural coherence of Italian immigrant communities on a global scale. Simultaneously, it endured as a vestigial effect of colonialism on populations in the regions of Africa that had spent years under the burden of Italy's colonialism.

## Italy in the New Europe

Italian identity is being reconstituted today not only in relation to the postcolonial metropolis but also within a shifting European context.[16] The current move to European economic unification marks a decisive change in the symbolic space called "Europe" itself. This fin-de-siècle standardization is emblematic of all cultural moments when the symbolic and the real are not distinguishable: currency, like a quark, simultaneously partakes of two natures, and what is symbolic is also what is real. The prospect of an economically unified Europe with a common currency has brought many to question the meaning and the resiliency of the traditionally configured nation-state as a stable, locatable place or a unified "ethnic" or cultural identity, or both. Italy's own highly regional character and its north-south cultural and economic imbalance render it a microcosm of Europe as a whole. Recent immigration patterns have generated new regional and xenophobic political discourses. At the same time, the history of the Italic peninsula can be understood with reference to Africa, Asia, and the Americas as easily as with reference to central or northern Europe. At this demographic juncture, it becomes impossible to understand Italy outside a theory of cultural dispersion.

## Italian Studies

Can we study "Italy," then, and how? We begin here. In the American university, Italian studies has most often been the realm of hybridized departments—French and Italian, Spanish and Italian, for example—that relegate "Italian" to a secondary status in a minimally historically justified coupling. Italian, the national language standardized only recently with national television, the language that is no one's native language, is taught in U.S. colleges and universities to the accompaniment of a flutter of clichés from raucous imitations of Neapolitan songs to meticulous instructions on how to prepare pasta. Presiding over this feast of the superficial, ironically, is the profound figure of Dante, invented over decades in Italy and the United States as the father of Italian national literature. Cultural monumentalization here plays a double role. On the one hand, figures like Dante and Machiavelli protect the prestige of the endangered humanities in an age of shrinking resources. On the other hand, their veneration is a symptom of immigrant "Italy," where the homeland is constantly reinvented in order to institute prestige where none might otherwise obtain.

Recently, however, Italian studies in the United States has benefited from two tectonic shifts. Younger scholars, steeped in critical theory from experiences often outside Italian departments, have begun to engage in a critique of ideology leading to an expansion of the old hagiographic and monographic model of literary studies into cultural literary studies and feminist studies where modes of cultural constitution—production, gender, class, age, and space, for example—are constant contexts and where a figure like Dante never appears lost and alone, outside culture.

It is, in fact, a felicitous paradox of contemporary scholarship that some of the most telling challenges to national identity are coming from locations within the university that depend precisely on that entity for their institutional validity: national language departments. Much of the work now being done by "Italianists" demonstrates a critical understanding that the national entity is clearly a historically constructed unit of the institution and, as such, is open to multiple placements and directions.

The path we have chosen in this collection has led us far from traditional realms of canonical Italian identities. We see the hierarchy of Italian studies in the United States as yet another "design" of Italy, and we have opted to analyze precisely the production and effects of such designs. This book, with its hybrid provenance, is offered as an expansion of Italian studies in the Americas, Europe, Asia, and Africa into contemporary modes of interdisciplinary inquiry. The contributors to this volume come from the university categories of African American studies, anthropology, critical theory, comparative literature, English, feminist studies, film studies, geography, history, theory of the state, and Italian, as well as from national-level politics and transnational political activism.

As diverse in our subject positions as we are in our professional categories, the contributors have engaged in sometimes heated dialogue that has uncovered, reciprocally, some hidden ethnocentrism all around. Our perspectives on such terms as "identity," "centrism," and "ethnicity," for example, are varied and at times conflicting. Variously constituted notions of gender, as another example, have kept us at odds on the role of gender across other identity categories. A term like "nomadism," furthermore, suggests a theoretical and tactical escape from a hegemonic centralizing logic to one contributor and a misappropriation of a culturally specific term, designated by ecological conditions and pastoral practices and determined by the notion, precisely, of a literal center, to another. In spite of these significant differences, our separate works inhabit similar conceptual places and thus constitute a move toward new designs of culture.

## Part I: Culture and Place: Italy as a European Country

The title of Part I indicates an ideological beginning of our project. We aim to displace considerations of culture from a purely temporal metaphor where history seems carved in marble and reigns supreme—thus conveying authority to whomever controls its writing—to a more spatial metaphor where local and more expanded territorial contexts may show cultures in simultaneity rather than in succession. Although it would seem to go without saying that Italy is a European country, the parameters that define Europe are continually shifting, as the papers in this part and others indicate. Europe may be the most familiar place in which to situate Italy and Italian identity, but it is by no means the only place—or the "natural" one.

In the opening essay, the geographer John Agnew interrupts the developmental trajectory of European modernism that plots Italy as the location of mythic backwardness, "an *anomaly* to Europe's destiny with liberal democracy." By redirecting the historical discourse that differentiates Italy as an underdeveloped country in perpetuity—like Pinocchio, always aspiring to but never quite reaching maturity—Agnew demonstrates the instrumental value of this myth of the peninsula for the constitution of a modern Europe.

Writing from Paris, the exiled political philosopher Antonio Negri relates firsthand the disparaging European modernist characterization of Italy as a country without a state. On the contrary, he argues, "Italy is a country with *two* states, with *two* realities . . . on one hand, an eternal Catholic stasis, a cynicism equaled only by boredom or the mild climate, and, on the other, an always overflowing hope, a capacity for building experiences for others, for being, from this point of view, stateless, as they say in France, or internationalists, as Italians say."

Beverly Allen argues for the inextricable relation between contemporary geopolitical identity and the novel. Her study of Italian "terrorism" and novels about it reveals how this historical genre "depicts the kind of individual necessary as a subject in the modern Western European nation-state." The first examples of "terrorist" novels at the onset of the *anni di piombo* (years of lead—the period of clandestine political violence in Italy dating roughly from the late 1960s through the mid-1980s) recast the subject of clandestine political violence as not so much an enemy of the state as an errant child, who could ultimately rejoin the Italian bourgeois family. Later novels, written as the Italian economy began to suffer severely from a radical decrease in foreign tourism, deny all such reconciliation, casting the "terrorist" as perverse and alien to normative national categories and the nation-state as a community that implicitly would not produce such aliens and that would again be safe once they were crushed.

Like Allen, David Ward describes a contested space of Italy within Italy. Recent national Italian political culture (represented here by political speeches, slogans, graffiti, and cartoons) is, in his essay, the site of a polarizing struggle for the moral authority and political advantage of owning the powerful rhetoric of antifascism. Ward argues that the historic failure of Italy to come to terms with its fascist past enables both the right and the left to claim that theirs is the true Italian identity, the one congruent with the modern democratic state. As a consequence of this historical disavowal, racism and xenophobia are now appearing in new forms.

## Part II: Impositions, Race, and Colonization

Part II suggests some of the directions a redressing of historic injuries and a reversal of cultural disavowal might take. "Impositions" in the context of this section refers not only to the forcing of one culture on another that occurs in imperialist expansion and colonization; it also refers to the location and dispersal *within* and *between* cultures of images, artifacts, and events that originated elsewhere.

In "Italy: Cultural Identity and Spatial Opportunism from a Postcolonial Perspective," Mohamed Aden draws on his own experience in colonized Somalia and in postcolonial Somali government. His view of the Italian colonizer, stereotyped as "Mario the African," not only elucidates the class mobility suddenly accessible to Italian peasants turned soldiers but also reflects an ugly image of the colonizer that, by and large, Italians continue to disavow. As an exiled Somali living in Turin, Aden views more recent Italian-Somali relations as replaying many of the cultural insensitivities and economic aggressions of the earlier colonial period.

Impositions are not only rank instances of colonization, however, nor are they merely reducible to cultural looting. Historically, they have also manifest themselves as dynamic interactions in a constantly revalenced intercultural exchange. Ayele Bekerie's essay, "African Americans and the Italo-Ethiopian War," acknowledges the fact that cultural looting, such as the transfer of an Ethiopian stela to a piazza in Rome, flagrantly persists. It also suggests that the Italian invasion of Ethiopia led African American residents of Harlem toward a Pan-Africanism where race transcended national identity, and toward an involvement with interethnic issues between themselves and Italian Americans within the United States. Simultaneously, in a transnational context, Bekerie argues, the writings and activities of African Americans, including intellectuals such as Langston Hughes, Marcus Garvey, W. E. B. Du Bois, and Paul Robeson, encouraged Ethiopians and other Africans to articulate their own identity within a new international context.

Images of black bodies within the burgeoning discourses of Italian modernity—design, fashion, advertising, and mass media[17]—are the topic of Karen Pinkus's "Shades of Black in Advertising and Popular Culture." For Pinkus, the meaning of blackness in Italian culture belongs to a still unwritten history of postcolonial, postmodern Italy. Her study of the iconography of blackness associated with Italian modernism, fascism, and consumerism implicates the present state of racial tension in Italy and complicates models of national identity based on state and race. The distinction she draws between nation-state and nation-race still acknowledges "the fundamental reality existing in both Italy and the United States: the universal subjectivity of whiteness with regard to blackness" within the representational practices she studies.

Paul Robinson intervenes in contemporary debates about culture, race, and imperialism with "Is *Aida* an Orientalist Opera?" In response to Edward Said's reading of Verdi's "Egyptian" opera as yet another instance of European orientalizing, Robinson argues instead that "the ideological import of Verdi's exotic musical gestures in the opera is more complicated." By analyzing Verdi's use of European normative and "exotic" musical idioms, Robinson shows how Verdi's imperial power, Egypt, which seeks to subjugate its African neighbor

Ethiopia, is musically associated not with a generic "Europe" but with a general notion of imperialism, while Ethiopia is musically associated with an Italy subjugated to the Hapsburg dynasty. As an *Italian* opera rather than an orientalist one, *Aida* allegorizes the struggles of the Risorgimento and reveals Verdi's sympathies as being clearly with the Ethiopians. As Robinson insists, "in Verdi's imagination, Italy was always a colonized country."

## Part III: Immigrations

Colonialism is always a two-way street.[18] Colonialism is historically linked to immigration, but, as Pasquale Verdicchio argues in "The Preclusion of Postcolonial Discourse in Southern Italy," postcolonial theory often elides not only the effects of race but also the ambiguous situations where "First" and "Third" World categories are not clearly distinguishable. The unacknowledged colonization of southern Italy by the Piedmontese government at the time of national unification produced a situation in which "southern Italian immigrants to North America, by far the greater part of immigrants from Italy, are among those groups that straddle the borders of nationalism in a continuous identity flux." The subaltern status of such immigrants as second-class citizens admitted under racist immigration quotas but called upon nonetheless to stand for "Italy" makes their case a revealing one.[19]

National identity in immigrant situations has two seemingly contradictory functions that often go unheeded. In the country of arrival, it camouflages differences within the immigrant national identity category, differences, for example, of class, gender, race, politics, or other characteristics that would hold sway in the country of origin. Simultaneously, it polices the national identities in both the country of origin and the country of arrival, excluding people according to racist, classist, and other subjugating criteria that obtain on both sides. Francesca Miller reminds us, however, that national identity in an immigrant community can well be secondary to an international political identity in her "Anarquistas, Graças a Deus!: 'Italy' in South America." Her study of the memoir of Zelia Gattai brings us to the Colonia Cecilia, an anarchist agricultural colony in nineteenth-century Brazil where religious, political, regional, racist, and national identity categories played out against one another over several generations.[20]

In a dramatic reversal of the nineteenth- and twentieth-century pattern of Italy as a supplier of worker immigrants to northern Europe and the Americas, the last fifteen years have seen Italy, like other European countries, become a place of arrival for immigrant workers from Africa, Eastern Europe, and Asia. In "Strangers in Paradise: Foreigners and Shadows in Italian Literature," Graziella Parati addresses how recent literary production by such "foreigners" challenges modernist notions of literature and national life. When Italian is the native language of a second-generation Senegalese Italian woman, for example, to what national literary tradition do her novels belong? Parati argues that these cultural practices have "created representations of the transition from an apparently mono- to a multicultural sense of the Italian nation."

## Part IV: Postmodernity and Global Italy

Although the move of Africa into the Italic peninsula is clearly not historically limited to our own time, the way in which it and other recent immigrations are modulated by historical politics and economic contexts is specifically postmodern; that is, recent immigrations are connected both to histories of Italian imperialism and colonization and to contemporary realities of the global marketplace. These postmodern dynamics are applicable for exported Italy as well.[21] Drawing on Michel Foucault's formulation of repeatable materiality, Mary Russo, in "Venice, Venice, and L.A.: Cultural Repetition and Bodily Difference," argues against a modernist idea of the enduring legacy model of cultural influence and against a prevalent postmodern view of cultural immigration as the free and limitless movement across borders. Instead, she asserts, the actual transposition of images, bodies, political identities, and even cities is a reciprocal process, "one that is complicated by a geography of displacement and refiguration. Interculturalism . . . can be both a communal possibility and a market projection."[22]

The cultural reciprocity and market volatility of immigration and colonization are also themes in Marguerite R. Waller's "Decolonizing the Screen: From *Ladri di biciclette* to *Ladri di saponette*." Waller sees in these neorealist and postmodern film texts a reversal of the familiar model of the encounter between the so-called Old and New Worlds. According to Waller, both of these films investigate "how it feels to be 'discovered' as a potential source of superprofits by corporate, multinational 'Hollywood.'" Postmodern subjectivities are both enabled and impeded, therefore, by "uneven flows of people, politics, money, and media around the world."[23]

Cultural exchange between the Italic peninsula and Asia is, of course, not new. The dialogic reciprocity between Marco Polo and Kubla Khan is one historic example of early modern contact.[24] In "If Japanese Are Samurai, Italians Are *Baka*," the anthropologist Antonio Marazzi studies contemporary versions of such reciprocity as modulated according to the shifting planes of postmodern global markets. His comparative study of the "multiple mirror-like stereotyping processes" according to which Japanese people figure Italians and vice versa finds that creative misrecognitions afford good opportunities for self-analysis. "Each culture has its own internal processes for creating the exotic, the barbarian, and the savage, and an awareness of these processes can stimulate a critique of one's own reactions to the encounter with a real or imagined outsider."

At times such reciprocities, rigidly stereotypical though they be, produce cultural transformations. Elaine Chang has noticed a series of these "transformers" that blends signifiers of Japanicity and Italianicity in popular culture. Her "Spaghetti Eastern: Mutating Mass Culture, Transforming Ethnicity" demonstrates how such vastly popular youth culture phenomena as the Teenage Mutant Ninja Turtles and the Karate Kid provide models of what she calls "mass culture surrogacy." She argues that "although ethnic cultural effects prove highly elastic and portable, their 'free play' is by no means unrestricted. . . . Try as they might, mass culture and its consumers simply cannot mutate fast or effectively enough to keep up . . . with their own contradictions."

Our engagements here with the peninsular and the transnational, the canonical and the eccentric, the metropolitan and the postcolonial productions of Italian national identity relocate such production within a global context and problematize any traditional, "natural," or value-free instances of national identity. We disagree as to what should, or will, happen next. Can progressive politics revalorize national identity as a minimally significant tag for social groups? Will subaltern politics stick with national identity as a stairway to international respect and economic viability? Are demographic changes in Italy, the United States, and elsewhere leading to a flattened multiculturalism, where histories of groups look interchangeable, or to skirmishes of identity politics, where groups vie for recognition and privilege, or something else? Is the notion of national identity itself beginning to fade, as the nation-state gradually abdicates responsibility for the welfare of its citizens on all sides of all divides? Can we imagine social organization with something other than national identity? What would it be?

This collection of essays is a first step toward posing and answering many versions of these questions. The "Italy" offered up here as object of analysis is a paradigm for similar considerations of all other national identities. In an era when global markets have transcended the kind of nationalist divisions that people are still dying for, our task is to continue our analyses, so that as the new formulations arise we shall be able to understand the patterns of dominance and subjugation they bring. *A presto.*

## Notes

1. See Mary Douglas, *Purity and Danger: An Analysis of Conceptions of Pollution and Taboo* (London: Routledge and Kegan Paul, 1966), and *Natural Symbols: Explorations in Cosmology* (London: Pantheon, Penguin, 1970).

2. On music and immigration, see Iain Chambers, *Migrancy, Culture, Identity* (London and New York: Routledge, 1994). See also James Clifford, "Travelling Cultures," in L. Grossberg, C. Nelson, and Paula Treichler, eds., *Cultural Studies* (London and New York: Routledge, 1992).

3. On nationalism, modernity, and culture, see E. J. Hobsbawm, *Nations and Nationalisms since 1780: Programme, Myth, Reality* (Cambridge: Cambridge University Press, 1990); Homi K. Bhabha, ed., *Nation and Narration* (New York: Routledge, 1990); Perry Anderson, "Nation-States and National Identity," *London Review of Books*, May 9, 1991; and Andrew Parker, Mary Russo, Doris Sommer, and Patricia Yaeger, eds., *Nationalisms and Sexualities* (London and New York: Routledge, 1992).

4. Benedict Anderson, *Imagined Communities: Reflections on the Origin and Spread of Nationalism* (London and New York: Verso, 1983). See also Partha Chatterjee, "Whose Imagined Community?" in *The Nation and Its Fragments: Colonial and Postcolonial Histories* (Princeton, N.J.: Princeton University Press, 1993); Renato Rosaldo, "Re-imagining National Communities," *Stanford Center for Chicano Research Working Paper Series* no. 36 (Stanford University, 1991). See also the contributions of Lydia Liu, Mary Layoun, Nalini Natarajan, Kamala Visweswaran, and Norma Alarcón in Inderpal Grewal and Caren Kaplan, eds., *Scattered Hegemonies: Postmodernity and Transnational Feminist Practices* (Minneapolis and London: University of Minnesota Press, 1994). For important discussions of gender and nationalism in the Third World, see Chandra Talpede Mohanty, Ann Russo, and Lourdes Torres, *Third World Women and the Politics of Feminism* (Bloomington: Indiana University Press, 1991).

5. See, for instance, Liana Borghi et al., eds., *Viaggio e Scrittura: Le straniere nell'Italia dell'ottocento* (Florence: Libreria delle donne, 1988); Sergio Romano, *L'Italia scappata di mano* (Milan: Longanesi, 1993); Gian-Enrico Rusconi, *Se cessiamo di*

*essere una nazione: tra etnodemocrazia regionale e cittadinanza europea* (Bologna: Il Mulino, 1993); Giovanni Spadolini, *Nazioni e nazionalità in Italia* (Rome and Bari: Laterza, 1994).

6. An example of the fruitful directions the kinship metaphor can take is provided by Jongwoo Han and L. H. M. Ling in "Masculine State, Feminine Society: A Feminist-Postcolonial Interpretation of East Asia's Capitalist Developmental State" (unpublished paper delivered at the 1995 American Political Science Association meeting, Chicago).

7. Étienne Balibar, *Race, Nation, Class: Ambiguous Identities* (London: Verso, 1991), 96.

8. See Mary Bucci Bush's story "Drowning" for a fictionalized treatment of this historical phenomenon as it came to her in family stories (San Diego: Parentheses Writing Series, 1995).

9. Here see Pasquale Verdicchio in this volume.—*Ed.*

10. Here see Mohamed Aden in this volume.—*Ed.*

11. Italians like flags, however, as can be seen from the plethora of soccer-team flags in bars and stadiums throughout the peninsula and in the widely publicized medieval panoply surrounding such festivals as the Palio Race in Siena. Appearances of the national flag are rare, however, even in international competitions where one might most readily expect them. During the 1994 World Soccer Cup competition, for example, the Italian national team, called "Gli Azzurri" (the blues), took the color blue as its emblem rather than the red-white-green of the national flag.

12. Stanley Aronowitz, *The Politics of Identity: Class, Culture, and Social Movements* (New York: Routledge, 1992), 56.

13. Here see Ayele Bekerie (in this volume).—*Ed.*

14. See, for example, Tekeste Negash, *Italian Colonialism in Eritrea, 1882–1941* (Uppsala: Acta Universitatis Upsaliensis, 1987); and John Wright, *Libya: A Modern History* (London: Croom Helm, 1982).

15. On the post–World War II Italian presence in Africa, see Mohamed Aden in this volume.—*Ed.*

16. See, for example, Romano Ruggiero, *Paese Italia: Venti secoli d'identità* (Rome: Donzelli, 1994); Saverio Vertone, ed., *La cultura degli italiani* (Bologna: Il Mulino, 1994).

17. See also Victoria De Grazia's *The Culture of Consent: Mass Organization of Leisure in Fascist Italy* (Cambridge, England, and New York: Cambridge University Press, 1981).

18. See Mary Louise Pratt's elaboration of "the contact zone" in *Imperial Eyes: Travel Writing and Transculturation* (London and New York: Routledge, 1991).

19. The U.S. Immigration Act of 1924 set the first barriers against immigration, working primarily against southern European immigration (from Italy and Greece) and Asian immigration in general.

20. See the discussion of how nationalism varies in different historical moments and different locations in the introduction to Parker et al., eds., *Nationalisms and Sexualities.*

21. For a fashion-driven model of Italy as a cultural export, see the catalog for "The Italian Metamorphosis" exhibit at the Guggenheim Museum, October 7, 1994–January 22, 1995; see also Beverly Allen, "The Novel, the Body, and Giorgio Armani: Rethinking National 'Identity' in a Postnational World," in Giovanna Miceli Jeffries, ed., *Feminine Feminists: Cultural Practices in Italy* (Minneapolis: University of Minnesota Press, 1994), 153–70.

22. For a key discussion of global culture, see Arjun Appadurai, "Disjuncture and

Difference in the Global Cultural Economy," *Public Culture: Bulletin for the Center of Transnational Cultural Studies* 2 (1990): 1–24.

23. See Homi K. Bhabha's discussion of cultural dissemination in *The Location of Culture* (New York and London: Routledge, 1994); see also the recent anthology edited by Angelika Bammer, *Displacements: Cultural Identities in Question* (Bloomington and Indianapolis: Indiana University Press, 1994), Julia Kristeva, *Nations without Nationalism*, trans. Leon S. Roudiez (New York: Columbia University Press, 1993).

24. In *Invisible Cities* (New York: Harcourt Brace Jovanovich, 1974), Italo Calvino conceptualizes this contact as an actual dialogue whose theme is the cosmopolitical space of the city. Calvino has his character Polo insist on the trope of Venice as the cosmopolitan site par excellence that every other city in some way repeats. [See Mary Russo in this volume.—Ed.]

Part I

Culture and Place: Italy as a European Country

# The Myth of Backward Italy
# in Modern Europe

*John Agnew*

Italy now has by most accounts the third- or fourth-largest economy in Europe and is one of the world's most "developed" societies in terms of levels of consumption, life expectancy, and possibilities for individual expression. But it is not unusual to read in the Italian press with respect to some feature or another of Italian life that Italy is "Lontana dal continente" or "Fuori dall'Europa" (both in *L'Espresso*, December 15, 1991, 20). With the advent of the bribery and corruption scandals in 1991–92 enveloping many of the politicians and the political parties that ruled post-World War II, the sense of geographical alienation from political conditions elsewhere has deepened further. Nor is it rare to find in scholarly writing on Italy recourse to the metaphor of "backwardness" as an appropriate description of the social and political character of the peninsula (and islands) and its population.

For some years I have been fascinated, if somewhat perplexed, by the ease with which Italians and others account for some particular feature of "Italian life" in terms of Italy's generic "backwardness" or "immaturity" in comparison to other European countries. More often than not, invoking backwardness appears to involve situating the phenomenon in question (Mafia, government deficit, economic disparities between north and south) in a simple temporal backward-modern couplet that all who read or hear intuitively understand as meaningful. Yet, if similar phenomena (organized crime, government corruption, public sector debt, etc.) were "explained" the same way in England or the United States, doubts about the sanity of the proposer would immediately arise.

But the Italian case does touch on a more general question in historiography: how to deal with the particular experiences of different territories in relation to a standard account of national development. This is often referred to as the issue of "exceptionalism" and takes its meaning in relation to the dominance of English, French, American, and, sometimes, German experience as norms against which the historical evolution of other national spaces should be compared.

My purpose in this essay is twofold: to explore the roots of the metaphor of backwardness and to attempt to understand why it has come to pervade discourse about Italy. I do this as someone who has tried for some years to understand what I see as the fatal attraction of academics and journalists to simple evolutionary schemas such as backward-modern without paying attention to their intellectual genealogies. This essay can be seen as one exploration in the genealogy of the metaphor of backwardness and its metamorphosis into a myth about Italy. The metaphor fuses a set of understandings about people and their places that are at once analytic and normative. Historically, however, the normative component, or moral judgment, has faded from view and the analytic claim of the metaphor, to *explain* difference, has become paramount.

## Metaphors of Backward Italy

How widespread is invocation of backwardness and the backward-modern metaphor in relation to Italy? As Mason (1988) has pointed out, discussion of modernity and modernization has been central to much contemporary Italian history and social science, but without self-consciousness as to terminological precision or explicit attention to the implication that Italy is somehow "behind" other countries and needs to modernize. Adoption of the vocabulary of backward and modern is not restricted to a particular school or political grouping. Across the political spectrum there is common recourse to the language of "the modern" and "modernization" even though there may be differences over the substantive components of modernity. For example, debate over fascism from both left and right has been dominated by claims and counterclaims as to its "modern" and "traditional" qualities. In other countries this vocabulary has been much more contestable and contested than it appears to be in relation to Italy. In Italy it has become central to *conceptions of the country* and to Italy's place in the world of nation-states.

The vocabulary of backwardness and modernity can be found everywhere. Some arbitrary examples can be provided from both academic and political sources. Discussion of Italy's economy is dominated by the theme of the country's "lagging behind" and "catching up" relative to the economies of northern Europe. To Rossi and Tonioli (1992), for example, "given Italy's relative backwardness around the turn of the century, a higher long-term growth rate might have been expected" (537). A one-volume history of postwar Italy (Ginsborg 1989, 1990), published to rave reviews in Italy and England, is portrayed by its author as "charting the country's dramatic passage to modernity" (1). Although writing from a standpoint sympathetic to the problems of the growing Italian working class, the author has frequent recourse to the language of modernization and backwardness in characterizing Italy (and particularly the Italian south) by its lack of "civic trust" and the "precariousness" of its modernization. A recent book by Settembrini (1991) traces Italy's political backwardness to a prevalent "antibourgeois" ideology that the author finds in both fascism and antifascism. Italy is treated as an *anomaly* to Europe's destiny with liberal democracy when, as Vivarelli (1991) points out in a devastatingly stinging review, Italy symptomatizes the universal dilemmas and difficulties involved in gaining and deepening democratic practices.

A "cultural anthropology" of Italy by Tullio-Altan (1986) provides an extreme example of the use of the metaphor of backwardness. Indeed, from this point of view Italy represents a case study in the total failure of modernization. Tullio-Altan presents Italian national history as a continuous unfolding of "sociocultural backwardness" as patronage politics, anarchistic rebelliousness, organized crime, and lack of civic consciousness have conquered ever larger public spaces. Everything that is distinctively Italian about Italy is backward when compared to the successful countries to the north. What is more, the struggle for modernity is hopeless in the face of the strengthening forces of backwardness. Finally, the sociologist Gallino (1987) sees in Italy the absence of a "fundamental ingredient of modernity . . . the interest of the individual in public action" (76). This is seen as a product of the peculiar "mix" of traditional and modern elements in Italian society rather than the singular victory of backwardness.

In many political circles in the 1970s and 1980s the language of modernization completely replaced older terminologies. This was especially obvious with the Socialists after Bettino Craxi became their leader in 1976. But elements in the Christian Democratic Party, particularly activists close to the former prime minister, Ciriaco De Mita, also adopted this language as a substitute for older "pastoral" and Catholic themes. On the political left there was an appearance of not wanting to be left behind. Alberto Asor Rosa, an intellectual affiliated with the then Communist Party, was quoted (Rasy 1985) as saying that "altogether the left has never had control over innovation and modernization as a value at the core of its project," implying that it now should have such a value. Renato Curcio (1987), one of the founders of the left-wing terrorist group the Red Brigades, reports in an interview from prison that "if Italy has changed and modernized itself in so radical a way, this is due to the social conflict of the 1970s of which the Red Brigades were a component."

On the basis of such a wide range of sources, I would claim, therefore, that the image of a backward Italy struggling (somehow) with modernity is a dominant representation of the country in the eyes of both Italian and foreign commentators. Before turning to the origins of this understanding of Italy, I want to give closer attention to two of the sources mentioned earlier, the books by Ginsborg and Tullio-Altan. I would not claim that these books provide a true sample in a statistical sense of all writing about contemporary Italy. My argument is rather that they represent two leading *genres* of writing about Italy. One is largely English in origin in its reliance on an unfolding historical narrative of a precise historic period; it implicitly compares Italy through the concepts it uses to a reading of English experience. The other, more typically Italian in origin, expresses an exasperation with the failure of Italian institutions to match the perceived success of similar institutions elsewhere.

Ginsborg's detailed narrative account of Italian history from 1943 to 1988 works around a series of oppositions through which movement from backwardness to modernity is interpreted. In order of degree of abstraction these are weak state/strong society, familism/collective action, workers/bourgeoisie, north/south, corrective/structural reform, and militancy/*riflusso* (retreat into private life). Ginsborg operates from a standpoint sympathetic to the condition of workers and peasants in the early postwar period. He sees the period 1943–48 as one in which opportunities to redistribute wealth and power were lost. He subsequently reads history in terms of the consequences of this fateful failure. A British reader cannot but see an implicit comparison between this diagnosis and the typical British reading of what happened in Britain during the same period and its consequences for postwar Britain; the "corrective" reforms of the first postwar Labour government marked a clear watershed with the past and the beginnings of the modern welfare state. Yet, in spite of the road taken, by the 1980s the "nationalization" of values taken for granted for the case of postwar Britain has finally captured even the most recalcitrant of Italians, though Ginsborg is doubtful as to its permanence. This is because Italy's modernity is uniquely fragile, threatened by the persisting possibility of *reversal* of the current balance of oppositions. The path to modernity chosen in the immediate postwar years, therefore, is still subject to unpredictable shifts and pathological turns. Consequently, as Ginsborg concludes on "Italy in the 1980s," Italy remains a country with a "deformed relationship between citizen and state" (421), where "neither from civil society nor from the state has there emerged a new and less destructive formulation of the relationship between family and collectivity" (418), and, more particularly, "the lack of *fede pubblica* (civic trust) continues to bedevil southern society"(417). *True* modernity, in this naturalized discourse of a country changing in spite of its essential self, is always around the corner or elsewhere, not in Italy.

"The cult of modernity," as Mason (1988, 131) suggests, "may grow out of a concern with its opposite." Rather than the drive toward modernity, even if it is precarious, the persistence of backwardness then takes center stage. In his book, Tullio-Altan (1986) sees Italy as condemned to perpetual repetition of a primordial condition of civic immaturity. He attributes this to the temporal persistence and geographical spread of the syndrome of "amoral familism" first diagnosed by the American political scientist Edward Banfield in his *The Moral Basis of a Backward Society* (1958). Banfield was later to gain notoriety for his claim that the riots in American cities in the period 1965–68 were mainly for "fun and profit" (Banfield 1972). Banfield's 1958 book is still widely used in introductory university courses on Italian politics and society in the United States.

To Tullio-Altan, the roots of Italy's backwardness lie in the initial failure at the moment of unification in the last century to overcome the "national dualism" between a developing north and a backward south. He makes much of Mazzini's prophesy that "Italy will be whatever the Mezzogiorno will be" (Tullio-Altan 1986, 16). Two phenomena in particular are identified as responsible for this: clientalism (votes exchanged for favors) and the practice of *trasformismo* (collaboration among politicians by the exchange of favors). As a result of the pervasiveness of these practices, a bourgeoisie with a national orientation capable of overcoming local and regional outlooks failed to develop, and this perpetuated the cultural backwardness of Italy as a whole. It is a strange inversion of Gramsci's argument about *la questione meridionale* that unification failed to produce a true revolution because northern workers and southern (and other) peasants did not make common cause against the unifying northern bourgeoisie. But it parallels arguments common to historians of Germany that when compared (implicitly) to England or France, Germany failed to have a proper bourgeois revolution. The specificity and tragedy of German history is thereby explained by reference to what German history was *not* through comparison with idealized English or French national histories (Blackbourn and Eley 1984).

The fusion of what may be old and/or new in any particular epoch and nation-state is thus reduced by Tullio-Altan to a straightforward manifestation of *absence* put in temporal terms as backwardness. The Italian political class, in particular, is seen as embodying both a culture that is particularistic and a parallel political practice that is clientelistic and transformist. But what if this is not much or at all a heritage of the past? What if they are elements of a "modern and effective system of power designed to integrate into the national society masses of people who are dangerously inclined to claim democratic participation and their own emancipation," in other words, "a modern political culture" (Signorelli 1986, 45)? Both Mason (1988) and Lembo (1988) offer arguments for this reversal of Tullio-Altan's thesis. As Mason (1988, 144) suggests, the "civic maturity" of Tullio-Altan's (absent) modernity would not be popular with the dominant groups in most "modern" polities. Encouraging withdrawal from active participation in politics or the widespread subversion of political institutions for personal gain is not unique to contemporary (and backward) Italy.

The attribution of backwardness only makes sense, therefore, if the "backward" features of Italian politics and society are implicitly compared to some ideal of modernity. For Tullio-Altan, this appears to be defined largely by the *absence* of those features that identify Italy as backward (clientalism, *trasformismo*). But there are some more positive clues as to the essence of modernity. The social conscience based on individual responsibility produced by the Calvinist branch of the Protestant Reformation, and, of course, missing from Italian historical experience, is a concept introduced early in Tullio-Altan's analysis to frame later discussion of the specific features of Italian cultural stasis. In fundamental opposition, a concept drawn from Banfield's report of his fieldwork in one southern Italian village in the early 1950s, Italian "amoral familism," the inability to act collectively for a common good beyond the bounds of a nuclear family, is identified as the conceptual key to understanding Italian difference from the Calvinist's modern conscience.

A more relevant criterion for the thesis of backwardness, however, might be the evidence for the presence of an integrated national bourgeoisie, seeing that this appears to be the critical variable in accounting for the lack of a "modern" society in Italy. Yet, as a comparative analysis of France, Germany, and Italy in the first half of this century has suggested, "the excitement of constructing a true directing class made the Italian elite more compact than the wider and less defined French bourgeoisie" (Maier 1979 [1975], 62). Italy, therefore, had a more homogeneous and integrated bourgeoisie than the presumably more modern France. *Empirical* comparison can sometimes undermine abstract bombast.

## From Metaphor to Myth

This criticism is all very well, one might say, but surely the vocabulary of backward and modern is nothing more than a stock of evocative metaphors that helps to communicate the differences between Italy and two ideal types of society—the backward and the modern. I would argue that the vocabulary is now much more than this; it now organizes and directs thinking about the "nature" of Italy. From this perspective, "backward Italy" has become a *myth*, the idealization involved forgotten as the metaphor has substituted for analysis. This is not to say that the metaphor is necessarily false in all its usages, only that it functions more as a fable than as a mere communicative device.

Kermode (1967, 112–13) makes a distinction between "myth" and "fiction" that may be helpful here. In his view, a fiction is "a symbolic construct ironically aware of its own fictionality, whereas myths have mistaken their symbolic worlds for literal ones and so come to naturalize their own status" (Eagleton 1991, 191). The line between the two is fuzzy rather than hard and fast, as all fictions can become myths once they are established and widely disseminated. This is what has happened to the metaphor of backward Italy.

It is something of a conventional wisdom among European and American intellectuals that modernized societies (Europe—particularly England—and the United States are the paradigm cases at a global scale) are rational and secular to the exclusion of traditional/metaphysical myths about their founding and nature. As is argued later in this essay, this position has become a central element in the backward-modern metaphor itself. Modernity is by definition life without myth. As sensitive a commentator on contemporary American society as Sheldon Wolin (1985) appears to endorse this position. Modernization is seen as destroying the mythology that is necessary for political community. But perhaps it is more that our most cherished European myths, such as backward-modern, are simply ones without eschatological hope of a better world *in its entirety*. Perhaps they are merely naturalized fictions that give meaning to historical and political speculation about the trajectory of particular societies contained by the boundaries of territorial states.

But how has mythmaking been possible in the case of backward-modern? What is it about this particular metaphor that has turned it into myth? My response falls into two parts. The first involves sketching out the origins in European thought of the metaphor of backwardness (and its polar opposite, modernity). The second attempts to offer an understanding of why the metaphor has acquired the status of myth specifically in relation to Italy.

## Spaces of Backwardness

One consequence of Columbus's famous voyage of 1492 was a heightened sense among European intellectuals of a hierarchy of human societies from primitive to modern. It is surely no coincidence that in conventional historiographies "modern" history begins with the era of Columbus. However, the simple juxtaposition of newly discovered and primitive worlds against a familiar and modern "Old World" from which the discoverers came is an altogether too simplistic if currently popular view of what happened (see, e.g., Pratt 1992). All societies define geographical boundaries between themselves and others (Helms 1988). Sometimes the world beyond the horizon is threatening, sometimes it is enticing. But not all engage in portrayals of the others as "backward."

In fact, little has been written of how exactly "early modern" Europeans assimilated "exotic peoples" into their understandings of historical geography. In a major review of scholarship covering the sixteenth and seventeenth centuries, however, Ryan (1981) suggests that the major means was through the assimilation of the exotic into Europe's own pagan and savage past. "In the triangular relationship among Europe, its own pagan past, and the exotic, the principal linkage was between Europe and antiquity" (Ryan 1981, 437). The categories of "pagan" and "barbarian," discovered as an inheritance from the European Ancients, were deployed to differentiate the new worlds from the old (Pagden 1992). Thus, a conception of the *temporal* transition through which the European social order had been transformed was imposed upon the *spatial* relationship between the new worlds and Europe in its entirety. The religious dimension was especially important in reading the new pagan worlds as standing in a relation to the (European) Christian world as that world stood in relation to its own pagan past.

This is not entirely surprising if it is remembered that "discovery" of the new geographical worlds coincided with the rediscovery of Europe's own ancient past. Indeed, as Mandrou (1978, 17) recounts, "The new worlds that fascinated the intellectuals of the sixteenth century were not so much the Indies—West or even East—but those ancient worlds which the study and comparison of long-forgotten texts kept revealing as having been richer and more complex than had been supposed" (17).

Of course, Italy was the center for this new activity, associated as it was with monastic libraries, universities, and the recovery of ancient texts. Ironically, given the challenge to ecclesiastical authority that the rediscovery of the Ancients could entail, it was from within the church that the "new learning" arose: "Italian cities, richer in Churchmen than any others in Europe, and closer to the papal authority, constituted the setting that was most apt to stimulate the study of ancient texts and pre-Christian thought" (Mandrou 1978, 23).

The articulation of spatial differences in temporal terms was reinforced by the "taxonomic lore" that Renaissance-era Europeans

learned from the Ancients. As Said (1978) has suggested, much ancient Greek drama involved demarcating an "imaginative geography"
in which Europe and Asia are rigidly separated. "Europe is powerful
and articulate; Asia is defeated and distant. . . . Rationality is undermined by Eastern excesses, those mysteriously attractive opposites to
what seem to be normal values" (57).

An image of essential difference with roots sunk deeply in the primordial past was used to invent a geography that had no real empirical points of reference (Springborg 1992). In terms of such categories
as race, property, oligarchy, etiology, and economy, the Orient (and
non-Europe in general) was claimed as "the negation of all that was
being claimed for the West, by polemicists knowing, in fact, very little
about it" (Springborg 1992, 20). (This is why Martin Bernal's claim
for a *Black Athena*, a Greece that owed much to the Orient, is so profoundly shocking to both conventional European historiography and
established social sensibilities.) The "Ottoman peril" of the Renaissance period gave particular credibility to the sense on the part of vulnerable Europeans of a profound chasm between the familiar world of
Europe and the exotic world of the oriental Other. In Europe, "The
Turkish threat worked toward reviving a waning loyalty to the *Res-
publica Christiana* and gave new life to the old cry for peace and unity
in a Christendom subject to the pope" (Schwoebel 1967, 23).

As the European states emerged from the dynastic struggles and religious wars of the seventeenth century and embarked on their schemes
of empire building outside of Europe, comparisons of themselves to
the ancient world, especially the "model" provided by Rome, proved
irresistible. Lord Lugard (1926), the British ruler of northern Nigeria,
was to maintain that Britain stood in a kind of apostolic succession of
empire: "As Roman imperialism . . . led the wild barbarians of these
islands along the path of progress, so in Africa today we are re-paying
the debt, and bringing to the dark places of the earth . . . the torch of
culture and progress" (618).

Perhaps the peak of this Romanist historiography is found in the
writing of Hegel, especially in the *Philosophy of Right*, first published
in 1821. On the basis of the relative extent of the absolute sovereignty
of the state and its "ethical substance," the nation, Hegel divided the
world into four historical realms arranged hierarchically, with the oriental (India seems to have figured prominently in his thinking) as the
lowest, the Germanic as the highest (surprise!), and the ancient Greek

and Roman worlds, as the precursors of the Germanic, in between. Effective state sovereignty was a necessary condition for achieving moral identity (Agnew 1993).

Beginning in the late eighteenth century, the resort to classical precedent to understand spatial differences in social order was also put on a scientific foundation. Pragmatic common sense was backed up by explanation in terms of natural processes or by analogy to natural processes. It became increasingly popular to see social change as a transition from one stage or level of *development* to another (Esteva 1992). As the nineteenth century wore on, and in imitation of discourse within biology, this view was elaborated upon as an evolutionary movement from a lower to a higher level of organization. Some parts of the world were at levels of development in terms of economic growth and social and political progress that Europe had experienced previously. The idiom of what Guha (1989, 287) terms "Improvement" came to prevail over that of "Order." The distinction no longer lay primarily in essential difference that could not be transcended but in the possibility of overcoming backwardness through imitation. The future of the backward lay in repeating what Europe had done (Tipps 1973).

By the close of the century, modernity was increasingly conceived of as the form of society in which social interaction is rationally organized and self-regulating. Max Weber's theory of rationalization provided the most important account of this modernity within an evolutionary historiography. For Weber, the rationalization of social life involved the increasing regulation of conduct by instrumental rationality rather than "traditional" norms and values. Weber himself was less than enthusiastic about this process of modernization. But many of his sociological disciples have had few doubts. The version of Weber's theory disseminated in the English-speaking world by Talcott Parsons, as Habermas (1987, 2) notes, "dissociates 'modernity' from its modern European origins and stylizes it into a spatio-temporally neutral model for processes of social development in general." Modernity, often confused with the United States, becomes a social model to which other "less developed" societies can aspire.

A final boost to the designation of areas as backward or modern came from the ideological combat of the Cold War in which the two modern worlds of capitalism and communism struggled for dominion in the backward or traditional Third World (Pletsch 1981). Although later adopted as a symbolic referent for the solidarity of former colonized peoples, the term "Third World" was never a particularly useful empirical designation. Its meaning was premised on the prior existence of two competing models of development that would allow for no alternatives. The backwardness of the Third World was necessary to define the modernity of the other two. *They* are what *we* used to be like. Only by having a backward could there be a modern.

## Why Backward Italy?

Italy is very much part of the Europe that figures in this outline history of the concept of backwardness. But the conceptual grid of which it is a component, figuring spatial differences in temporal terms, has become so universalized, considered applicable in such diverse circumstances, that differences *within* Europe have also come to be thought of in terms of backwardness and modernity. So, although at a global scale Italy is considered modern, within Europe it can be seen as backward. A more poverty-stricken vocabulary for dealing with sameness and difference between places is hard to imagine! Yet, its attractiveness for treating spatial differences in terms of temporal ideal-types has been so great that it has spread from its original global context of use to other scales without much comment.

There are a number of reasons why Italy has become prone to characterization in terms of backwardness. The first is its apparent failure to live up to earlier promise. The signs of an incipient modernity associated with the Renaissance never produced the "universal state" that Hegel would later see as a prerequisite for true modernity. From this point of view, Italy has been plagued by a persisting disunity based on geoeconomic and linguistic fragmentation. Unlike Germany in the nineteenth century, where identification with a *Heimat* (or "homeland") allowed for widening identification with territorial state and nation (Applegate 1990, 13), local identity in Italy has not led easily toward a wider sense of national identity (Lanaro 1989, 28). The very city-states that are associated so intimately with the Renaissance failed to produce the integrated national state that would have taken Italy to the next level of modernity. The variety and density of urban centers in Italy worked against the ready creation of a territorial state with a dominant capital city. Foreign potentates found in Italy almost unlimited possibilities for a strategy of divide and rule. The power of the Universal (but also Roman) Church has continually frustrated attempts at creating a national state in its homeland. The common identity of Italians as Catholics made the achievement of a more circumscribed national identity seemingly redundant for large segments of the population. Not even the pious Manzoni could successfully challenge this paradox. Because of its difficulties with the papacy, the monarchy of unified Italy was not able to fuse religious symbolism with dynastic history in the ways common elsewhere in Europe. Recent Christian Democrats have not really tried to fuse religious with national identity. They look to locality or to "Europe" for their political identity (Lanaro 1989; Forgacs 1990).

The sense of failure to mature as a political entity has deep roots in Italy. The major theme of Machiavelli in such works as *The Prince* and *The History of Florence* was the civic corruption of his epoch compared to the civic excellence of the ancient Romans. Manipulation and penetration from "outside" were indicted as the main culprits. Again, the heroes of the Risorgimento in the early nineteenth century blamed the reactionary Austrian and Bourbon regimes that governed large parts of the peninsula and islands for the pervasive political and economic stasis that they were operating against. The image of subordination to neighboring states became a fixed element in the national consciousness as conveyed through Manzoni's influential novel of the Risorgimento, *I promessi sposi*. Generations of Italians were exposed to the making of Italy by reading this allegory of inner purity and tenacity struggling with external tyranny and exploitation.

The failure of unification to live up to expectations, because it came about through "conquest and subterfuge" rather than popular insurrection and replaced a set of reactionary governments with a single one, added a further blow to the fragile Italian collective identity. A permanent feature of Italian historiography became argument over the "failure" of unification. Each new "failure"—the Liberal governments of the late nineteenth century for failing to match the colonial and economic achievements of the contemporary Great Powers, the failure of the Italian military in both world wars, the failure of fascism as a "developmental dictatorship" to help Italy "catch up" with the rest of Europe—gave rise to new attempts at Risorgimento. As these, particularly fascism, then the antifascist Resistance of 1943–45, and, finally, the student and worker enthusiasms of 1968–72, themselves

failed to deliver an eschatological promised land, further disillusion-
ment has been assured.

Carlo Collodi's *Pinocchio*, first published in 1880, captures in alle-
gorical form the fate of backward Italy always awaiting its true liberation to modernity. Collodi was a disenchanted supporter of the original Risorgimento. The mischievous puppet aspires to true childhood,
but his bad behavior seems to condemn him to perpetual puppethood.
Only after demonstrating human virtue does he become a real boy.
His path of metamorphosis follows the track of Italian history, from
a puppet forced to move to the reflexes of others, to a donkey (a symbol for adherence to church doctrine favored by nineteenth-century
anticlericals), to an autonomous personality (courtesy of a completed
Risorgimento) (Boime 1986, 68).

Comparison with an external standard has been fundamental to the
image of failure. No longer the seat of modernity after the sixteenth
century, lost to either the Germans, English or Americans, Italy became synonymous for Italian and non-Italian alike with the decadence
of a Mediterranean world that had once again turned its back on its
inheritance. The French defeat by Prussia in 1870, the Italian defeat
by Ethiopia in 1896, and the Spanish defeats at the hands of the
Americans at the turn of the century, conspired to produce the idea of
a link between military effectiveness, political development, and ethnicity. This was bolstered by the growth of a positivist sociology based
on environmental and "racial" determinism. Southern Italians were
characterized as particularly primitive—unpredictable, unreliable, re-
bellious, and criminal. They were a "drag" on the development of Italy
as a whole. The image of a tragic Fall from Grace relative to success
elsewhere became rooted in Italian as well as foreign accounts of Italy.
Lanaro (1989), in a brilliant book on the "self-images" of Italians,
notes cynically that "admiration for foreigners has been the principal
ingredient of Italian nationalism" (212). Those who doubt its continuing power among foreigners should try convincing American under-
graduates studying in Italy that there is as much interest in the contemporary society as in what happened there between 1450 and 1580!

The late-nineteenth-century politician Francesco Crispi has been
perhaps the only Italian political leader apart from Mussolini to create
a rhetoric that saw modern Italy in apostolic succession to previous
periods of national "greatness" and as a "body" overcoming its fragmentation. But the danger of pointing to the past was that it served to

remind everyone of the gap that now existed between the noble past and the degenerate present. The massive emigration from the southern regions, the failure to emulate the apparently "effortless" colonial successes of the British and the French (symbolized above all by the military defeat at the hands of the "barbarian" Ethiopians at Adwa on March 1, 1896), and persistent political and military mismanagement were especially galling. When the rhetoric of Roman/imperial reincarnation turned out to be hollow, as with both Crispi's colonial adventures and fascism's claims as a "developmental dictatorship," the conception of Italy as a spiritual idea in the process of becoming realized in a modern form was also discredited (Lanaro 1989, 221).

Some specific influences on thinking about Italy's place on the backward-modern continuum relative to other countries have been particularly important. The influence of Hegel on Italian historiography has reinforced the idea of Italy's "lagging behind" the rest of Europe in the development of a modern political identity. This is not an influence in the straightforward sense of borrowing Hegel's philosophy of history. Rather, it is the peculiar Italian rendering of the Hegelian *Weltgeist*, above all by Benedetto Croce, as the need to abandon sectional material interests for a higher national interest. Croce read German experience in this light as the successful pursuit of interests embodied in the idea of a "culture," of a "common sense" that would inspire people to a new "way of life" (Jacobitti 1981, 7, 162). This vision inevitably pictured Italy as a "pupil" of the more advanced northern Europeans, to whom Italians should look for inspirational models.

The "late" industrialization of Italy and the "persistence" of traditional norms and values (above all, suspicion of the state and its works) have also provided prima facie evidence for a *Weberian* reading of Italian backwardness. In comparison with most other European countries, Italy appears to have retained a greater element of those "nonrational" values associated with ascription rather than achievement, specific loyalties rather than general value commitments that Parsons associated with tradition, especially in the continuing importance of family ties for the economy and the role of clientalism in the national bureaucracy. Gift and redistributive transactions do not easily fit into evolutionary schemes based on the presumed "victory" of market exchange and "economic rationality" (Veyne 1990), yet these have remained of particular importance within the Italian political

economy. What Marcel Mauss named "noble expenditures" that bind
rich to poor in the displacement of class struggle have been an important mechanism for maintaining social order but have worked against
the emergence of an "impersonal" state based on an abstract equal
citizenship as its operating ideal.

The three major social groupings of postunification Italy with possible roles in creating a "breakthrough" to a stronger national identity—
the capitalists, the workers, and the middle class—elaborated alternative institutions (e.g., the Case del Popolo for the workers) and
regarded the state as a client rather than an object of commitment or
affection (Lanaro 1989). Fascism's identification of *la patria* had to
work with a mosaic of identities and expectations rather than an inte-
gral texture based on the prior diffusion of a singular cultural vision.

The absence from the peninsula of the heroic feats and sharp historical breaks that have lain behind so much sociological theorizing, such
as that of Weber and Parsons—the Protestant Reformation, the Revolution of 1789—have also encouraged a sense of an unheroic or even
"cowardly" history that has not escaped from a past of traditional-
local ties and sentiments. The major irony in this hand-wringing is
that many of the social indicators associated with "backwardness"
have deepened as the country has "modernized." For example, the
welfare state has increased the importance of political/family connections as disability pensions have been awarded *increasingly* on a "particularistic" basis (Ferrera 1987). The opposition of backward and
modern thus dissolves as, "we discover continuity in change, tradition
in modernity, even custom in commerce. Still, not all that was solid
now melts into air, as a certain post-modernist reflexive anthropology
has prematurely supposed. There remain the distinctive differences,
the cultural differences" (Sahlins 1992, 36).

Finally, the two political cultures that grew in Italy at the turn of the
century and reappeared after fascism, the socialist and the Catholic-
popular, have been largely without sentiments of national identity and
solidarity. To them Italy has been the site of struggles over grand ideas
that transcend any one national space. In the postwar period, this has
often involved looking outside of Italy for models of social development. On one side, at least until the 1960s, the Soviet Union was seen
as a paragon of modernity. Some of the student revolutionaries of
1968 looked to China and "Maoism" for their model (the conservative Milan newspaper *Corriere della Sera* referred to the student revo-

lutionaries en masse as *i cinesi*). On the other side, if also with increasing uneasiness during the years of the Vietnam War but seemingly without much choice in the context of the Cold War, was the United States. All groups used the United States as their measure, whether as a challenge or as a threat. Rather as in the Third World, there was a "struggle" over the model of modernity in postwar Italy. The major political parties and their associated intellectuals defined their goals largely in terms of Italy's backwardness in relation to the two foreign models of modernity.

Within Italian society and among many intellectuals it is evident that the American model proved the most enticing. American standards became the ones by which Italian performance was measured; they defined the road to follow. As Lanaro (1989, 81) emphasizes "an arsenal of symbols and objects represented by the United States" came to substitute for the absence of an effective "center" within Italian society. The American perspective on modernization (i.e., Americanization) spread widely as the American social sciences, especially a political science of a particularly American provenance, expanded within the Italian universities in the early 1970s (Agnew 1988). The nationalization of values relating to consumption and politics and the achievement of high mass consumption became indicators of Italy's emulation of American modernity. This fit well the imperatives of a political class that put its faith in material progress to neutralize concerns about the contemporary moral order of clientalism and insider dealing that they represented. The persisting failure of significant groups and regions to experience the fruits of material progress and, more significantly given the often explicit comparison with the United States, the lack of an American "civic virtue," popular celebration, and adulation of existing political institutions without much active participation in them, only reinforced the idea that Italy, with its popular contempt for existing institutions yet deeply politicized weltanschuungs, was not only different, it was still backward even after all these years.

## Conclusion

Here is one of Italy's most renowned astrologers (Francesco Waldner) telling Hans Magnus Enzensberger his view of Italy's perpetual political impasse:

The Italian peninsula as a whole may be under the dynamic sign of Aries, but the republic's horoscope is dominated by Gemini. Apart from that, every horoscope consists of four elements: earth, water, fire, and air. But the republic was declared on June 18, 1946, and there were no planets in earth signs on that date. That's why this state lacks authority. It's unable to act effectively. Alternatives exist only for the individual. That makes survival possible. (Enzensberger 1989, 40)

For Enzensberger, in comparison with assorted social scientists, journalists, and pundits, the astrologer emerges as one of the more sober commentators on the Italian condition.

One might note that there is little difference between the empirical analysis of the astrologer and that provided by the discourse of backwardness and modernity. In neither case is Italy the actual object of analysis. For one it is the position of birth signs; for the other it is comparison with ideal types that become confused with empirical referents (such as England or the United States). Yet we scoff at the astrology as "unscientific" while seeing the backward/modern polarity as unquestionably "sound," "scientific," or "commonsensical."

It is precisely the commonsensical quality of the polarity that gives it mythic power. Since Columbus first returned, we have become so used to characterizing geographical differences in idealized temporal terms that we cannot see any problems with this way of thinking. We assimilate empirical information to the polarities. We read the whole world through them. The ultimate irony, given Columbus's own origins in an Italian city-state, is that in a European context Italy has been more readily portrayed as backward rather than modern. Of course, there is not much choice! A temporal metaphor initially applied to make sense of the spatial "gap" between the new worlds and the old has become a preferred way of dealing with Italian differences relative to an idealized European modernity. In so doing, the intrinsically *normative* character of the terms "backward" and "modern" has been obscured. Yet it is their nature as *moral judgments* about people and places that gives them such power. Columbus and his contemporaries at least understood that.

## Works Cited

Agnew, John. 1988. "'Better Thieves Than Reds?' The Nationalization Thesis and the Possibility of a Geography of Italian Politics." *Political Geography Quarterly* 7: 307–21.

———. 1993. "Timeless Space and State-Centrism: The Geographical Assumptions of International Relations Theory." In Stephen Rosow et al., eds., *The Global Economy as Political Space*, Boulder, Colo.: Lynne Rienner.

Applegate, Celia. 1990. *A Nation of Provincials: The German Idea of Heimat.* Berkeley: University of California Press.

Banfield, Edward. 1958. *The Moral Basis of a Backward Society.* New York: Free Press.

———. 1972. *The Unheavenly City.* Boston: Little, Brown.

Blackbourn, David, and Geoff Eley. 1984. *The Peculiarities of German History: Bourgeois Society and Politics in Nineteenth-Century Germany.* New York: Oxford University Press.

Boime, Alberto. 1986. "The Macchiaioli and the Risorgimento." In E. Tonelli and K. Hart, eds., *The Macchiaioli: Painters of Italian Life, 1850–1900.* Los Angeles: Frederick S. Wight Art Gallery, UCLA.

Curcio, Renato. 1987. Interview. *L'Espresso*, January 18: 28.

Eagleton, Terry. 1991. *Ideology: An Introduction.* London: Verso.

Enzensberger, Hans Magnus. 1989. *Europe, Europe: Forays into a Continent.* London: Hutchinson.

Esteva, Gustavo. 1992. "Development." In Wolfgang Sachs, ed., *The Development Dictionary: A Guide to Knowledge as Power.* London: Zed Books.

Ferrera, Maurizio. 1987. "Il mercato politico-assistenziale." In Ugo Ascoli and Raimondo Catanzaro, eds., *La società italiana degli anni ottanta.* Bari: Laterza.

Forgacs, David. 1990. *Italian Culture in the Industrial Era, 1880–1980: Cultural Industries, Politics and the Public.* Manchester: Manchester University Press.

Gallino, Luciano. 1987. *Della ingovernabilità: La società italiana tra premoderna e neo-industriale.* Milan: Comunità.

Ginsborg, Paul. 1989. *Storia d'Italia dal dopoguerra a oggi. Società e politica 1943–88.* Turin: Einaudi.

———. 1990. *A History of Contemporary Italy: Society and Politics, 1943–1988.* London: Penguin.

Guha, Ranajit. 1989. "Dominance without Hegemony and Its Historiography." *Subaltern Studies* 6: 210–309.

Habermas, Jürgen. 1987. *The Philosophical Discourse of Modernity.* Cambridge: Polity Press.

Hegel, G. W. F. 1967. *Philosophy of Right.* Oxford: Oxford University Press.

Helms, Mary W. 1988. *Ulysses' Sail: An Ethnographic Odyssey of Power, Knowledge, and Geographical Distance.* Princeton, N.J.: Princeton University Press.

Jacobitti, Edmund E. 1981. *Revolutionary Humanism and Historicism in Modern Italy.* New Haven: Yale University Press.

Kermode, Frank. 1967. *The Sense of an Ending.* New York: Oxford University Press.

Lanaro, Silvio. 1989. *L'Italia nuova. Identità e Sviluppo, 1861–1988.* Turin: Einaudi.

Lembo, Rosario. 1988. "Il Mezzogiorno tra storia e antropologia." *Studi Storici* 29: 1051–68.

Lugard, F. D. 1926. *The Dual Mandate in Tropical Africa.* Edinburgh: Oliver and Boyd.

Maier, Charles J. 1979. *La rifondazione dell'Europa borghese: Francia, Germania e Italia nel decennio successivo alla prima guerra mondiale.* Bari: De Donato. (Original English edition, *Recasting Bourgeois Europe.* Princeton, N.J.: Princeton University Press, 1975.)

Mandrou, Robert. 1978. *From Humanism to Science, 1480–1700.* London: Penguin.

Mason, Tim. 1988. "Italy and Modernization: A Montage." *History Workshop* 25–26: 127–47.

Pagden, Anthony. 1992. *European Encounters with the New World: From Renaissance to Romanticism.* New Haven: Yale University Press.

Pletsch, C. E. 1981. "The Three Worlds, or the Division of Social Scientific Labor, circa 1950–1975." *Comparative Studies in Society and History* 23: 565–90.

Pratt, Mary Louise. 1992. *Imperial Eyes: Travel Writing and Transculturation.* London: Routledge.

Rasy, Elisabetta. 1985. Interview with Alberto Asor Rosa. *Panorama*, December 8: 185.

Rossi, Nicola, and Gianni Toniolo. 1992. "Catching Up or Falling Behind? Italy's Economic Growth, 1895–1947." *Economic History Review* 45: 537–63.

Ryan, Michael T. 1981. "Assimilating New Worlds in the Sixteenth and Seventeenth Centuries." *Comparative Studies in Society and History* 3: 519–38.

Sahlins, Marshall. 1992. "Goodbye to Tristes Tropes: Ethnography in the Context of Modern World History." The Ryerson Lecture, University of Chicago, April 29.

Said, Edward W. 1978. *Orientalism.* New York: Random House.

Schwoebel, Robert. 1967. *The Shadow of the Crescent: The Renaissance Image of the Turk (1453–1517).* Nieuwkoop: De Graaf.

Settembrini, Domenico. 1991. *Storia dell'idea antiborghese in Italia, 1860–1989.* Bari: Laterza.

Signorelli, Amalia. 1986. Review of *La nostra Italia. L'Indice* 8:46.

Springborg, Patricia. 1992. *Western Republicanism and the Oriental Prince.* Cambridge: Polity Press.

Tipps, Dean. 1973. "Modernization Theory and the Comparative Study of Societies: A Critical Perspective." *Comparative Studies in Society and History* 15: 199–226.

Tullio-Altan, Carlo. 1986. *La nostra Italia. Arretratezza socioculturale, clientelismo, trasformismo e ribellismo dall'Unità ad oggi.* Milan: Feltrinelli.

Veyne, Paul. 1990. *Bread and Circuses: Historical Sociology and Political Pluralism.* London: Allen Lane.

Vivarelli, Roberto. 1991. "L'anomalia italiana." *La Rivista dei Libri*, November: 13–16.

Wolin, Sheldon. 1985. "Postmodern Society and the Absence of Myth." *Social Research* 52: 217–39.

# Italy, Exile Country[1]

*Antonio Negri*

## Essay

You've asked me to speak about Italy, its identity, and the way an exile relates to it. This is a very abstract problem, touching on some nostalgic repetitions and run-of-the mill feelings an exile might have for his native country. But the problem for an exiled Italian is compounded; it involves an attempt to think of his country, in its entirety, as, in fact, a country made up entirely of exiles. A possible title for my paper, therefore, might be, "Italy, Exile Country." By that I mean that exile is the normal condition of intelligent Italians, and always has been. Exile is the condition for reproducing creative thinking in Italy. Aside from that, all that's left are the academy, the bureaucracy, and the church— or, put another way, the eternal Italian, cause of never-ending exile, past and future.

Both literary history and social history in Italy are continually marked, in fact, by the presence of exile. From Dante to Machiavelli, from Tasso to Leopardi, from Giordano Bruno to Gramsci, from the anti-Trinitarian Socinians[2] in the sixteenth century to the autonomous workers' movements, one always finds that exile is a fundamental element in the constitution of the real identity—the identity of the struggle—of the greatest Italian literature and philosophy. There is not a single episode of any large-scale Italian identity that is not marked by exile. Why? Perhaps it is because Italy is actually a country where all the modern revolutions have taken place and none of them has succeeded. Perhaps it is because the very most admirable aspects of Italian identity are found in all that marks Italian society as a laboratory of utopianism, hope, and rupture, with, therefore, the necessary consequence of exile.

Italy, after all, is the country that invented the liberty of the moderns. Instead of enjoying that liberty, however, it has been enslaved. Italy is the country that invented capitalism, which it has pursued for all the centuries since that invention. When Italy did succeed in adopting it, capitalism came in the form of fascism, or state capitalism. Italy is the country that invented the modern state, yet it has never known a constitutional one. Italy is the country that invented popular counterpower: the Ciompi, Machiavelli . . . the dynamic conception of history as conflict, as tumultuous. Yet even popular counterpower finally developed, in an immense historic irony, as the Mafia. Italy invented the great mechanism of heresy, of utopia, of the utopian struggle. In this, too, everything has always ended tragically. Italy is the only country that has produced all the modern revolutions without having ever enjoyed victory in any of them.

Why? Why does it happen like this in Italy? Why, in this country where generosity, righteous anger, dedication, and hope are so strong, does there also exist the utmost cynicism, the utmost envy, the utmost repression? Why, in this country's identity formations, are these two forces always joined? I don't know. If I want to embark on the difficult search for an answer, however, I probably have to start with a fundamental, and actually anti-Italian, paradox: in Italy, the dialectic of the master and slave has never existed. The master has been too cruel and too strong, while the slave has been too generous and too strong. On the one hand, therefore, we have the disillusioned, ferocious, and cynical power of the master; on the other, hope and an ever-renewed capacity for rebellion. There is no dialectic; the master and the servant do not nourish each other. There is no mediation, no conciliation.

Look at the terrain of social struggle. Perhaps no country other than Italy has seen a third of its population leave in the space of fifty years. From the moment of the unification of Italy in 1870 until 1920, when fascism closed the door on Italian emigration, a third of the population left, a third of the population that had been defeated in the struggle to gain land, to improve its lot, to pursue that little bit of happiness that represents one of the great founding tenets of democracy. This third of the population, these ten million out of the thirty million inhabitants that Italy had at that time—and they were really the salt of the earth—left for America, for Australia, for Europe. The process started up once again after the Second World War. During the sixties and seventies, when I was traveling around Europe visiting Italian workers in Paris, in the north of France, and at Wolfsburg in Germany, I came into contact with large groups of people who had fled yet who continued to maintain a sense of communal strength.

Back then, this communal identity was in fact an identity imparted by exodus, one that never ends but is a constant struggle, constantly beginning anew. When it reaches the international level, this struggle brings with it a content of hope and revolution that is always in search of new homelands. When they are lived within this configuration of Italian identity—the one that ranges from Dante to Machiavelli to poor southern emigrants to the workers who circulate through the immense machinery of European and world industry—exodus, emigration, and exile become a yearning for liberation and renewal that continually perpetuates itself.

Italian identity is, therefore, at the very least, a very big problem. For me personally, this problem is resolved in the sense that I find myself on one side of the question, that of the other Italy, the Italy of exiles, the Italy that is part of this long story of refusal and exodus. When I look back at the history of Italy as I have lived it, I find nothing that convinces me that to have situated myself here in this second Italy, in this radical, fundamental break, is mistaken. In fact, in all my experience I find nothing but a constant affirmation of the continuity of this ambiguous relation of rupture with my country.

In my early childhood, I found myself face to face with fascism. Then, I found myself facing the ferocious restoration of a harsh capitalist system. This, moreover, occurred after a civil war, after the defeat of the enemy in the civil war, and after the defeat *of* the civil war itself and of all it had represented: communism in Italy, this vast movement that had, in fact, been a movement of hope. Then I lived yet again the reconstruction of dualism, the reconstruction of a generation that refused power, and still once again the restoration of order—the restoration of the melancholic ennui of Italian conformism, of a line of power that is always hypocritical, always dependent, and always totally connected to a deep falsehood.

What can you say when exile comes as a consequence of this deep feeling that lies at the base of your cultural identity, of the only true identity you can have? When exile comes, it's almost a natural consequence, a moment you've expected. It's an expected moment when you look back toward Italy, just to make sure, just to invent a reason for what has happened, to set in place, once again and correctly, the duplicity of your identity, the refusal by one part of the other part. It's the recognition that the other part keeps on getting worse.

What is Italy for me today, seen from France? It's a country of thieves and mafiosi. It's a country with a corrupt, dead political class that looks just like the rococo political class of the eighteenth century, the one Leopardi saw was empty and dead inside. It's a country without a center because, in fact, it has two centers, two souls. Here in France, for example, I'm always hearing a kind of put-down, or simple observation maybe, that French people make about Italy: "You are a country without a state!"

It's not true! Italy is a country with *two* states, with *two* realities. It's a country where, quite rightly, each historic phase becomes the laboratory for its alternative. This is Italy's real identity: on one hand, an eternal Catholic stasis, a cynicism equaled only by boredom or the mild climate, and, on the other, an always overflowing hope, a capacity for building experiences for others, for being, from this point of view, stateless, as they say in France, or internationalists, as Italians say. It is the capacity to search constantly for a new homeland that will go beyond both Italy and any other homeland, God willing, a homeland that will exist within the capacity of one consciousness to communicate with another, of one soul to get along with another.

So now you could say, "But you're fooling yourself, you're living in a utopia you think is reality. You think that utopia really is this possibility of substituting identity. Identity is stronger than this possibility of yours, stronger than your tendency to shift the discussion beyond the conditions of your own identity." No, no, no, it's not that at all. This other identity I recognize myself in, the one that goes from the fact that I'm Italian to the fact that I'm European and internationalist, is something damnably and deeply real. This other Italy is something much more real than the Italy of the poets and the navigators. The exiles' Italy is more real.

When I was a boy, I lived, as it happened, a schizophrenic, double life, where I usually divided my days between the workers' demonstrations at Porto Marghera and the university. At six in the morning, I was in front of the factories; at ten, I was at the university. The clash between these two realities was something I worked out each day in terms of two different kinds of people: there was the real utopia of these people who wanted freedom, and then there was the reality of these other people who still wore the wigs and rouge of another century. On the one hand, there was simple truth, and, on the other, the affected, poetic repetition of power. In this situation, the picture of the real was getting reversed because the only true reality was the reality of 6, 7, 8 A.M. It was the reality of work, the reality of the producers, of these people who have never been recognized in Italian identity as such. These are the people who actually build the only reality there is. If there's any suspicion of unreality, if there's any suspicion that it's all a dream, if there's any suspicion of emptiness, it's all on the other side, in the university life I was living, for example.

Take today. Italian political life is made up of thieves and mafiosi. What's the makeup of Italian cultural life? Their correspondents: weak thought and semiology, in the forms brought to you by Vattimo and Eco. It's nothing more than a kind of renewal of Crocian historicism in more banal, stupid, empty forms: the exaltation of emptiness as continuity. This emptiness is one in which continuity and the hermeneutics of continuity rightly take the place of the innovative contents of history, of the real, of all that constitutes ontological reality and the true affirmation of the real.

What is my identity? Certainly not an association with Vattimo or Eco. It is, instead, an association with this reality of exile, of struggle, this reality of movement. You see, only for exiles is there no memory. Memory is on the side of the others. We are a generation without memory. Being without memory, however, even the memory of an identity, means the opposite of being empty. In fact, it means being, existing. It means bringing something irresistible into your actions and into the solidity of what you are. This, then, is the true identity of the exile, the true alternative that lives in this "little Italy."

Think of Italian neorealism, for example. The other evening I saw *The Bicycle Thief* again. It's clearly the story of a defeat. But it shows a formidable dialectic of the protagonist and the child, of the defeated worker, that is, and the child who cries and laughs and, in crying and laughing, manages actually to constitute knowledge, basal knowledge, real knowledge. This is the basal, real knowledge that great Italian poetry, from Dante to Leopardi and beyond, and great Italian thought, from Machiavelli to Gramsci, has managed to express. This is perhaps a unique accomplishment among the literatures of the world, but it is an accomplishment made by the literature of the other Italy, the literature that really goes beyond the sickly, asthmatic identity of the Catholic church and everlasting power, of endless historic guelfism, of the Italy of the bosses, the Italy of the corrupt, the Italy of thieves.

## Autobiographical Fragment: Paris, August 15, 1992

You ask me for a curriculum vitae. Here it is, briefly (but you can have a look at my *Pipe-line* [Turin: Einaudi, 1983]), or else, from another angle, what Yann Moulier Boutang writes in his Introduction to my *The Politics of Subversion* [Cambridge: Polity Press, 1989]. Anyway, here it is.

From 1933 to 1948 I was a studious little boy who saw the war pass devastatingly over his family—a family of antifascists and communists—had we won? They used to say so, but fascism was still there, all over, and monstrous, as always. I am indifferent politically.

From 1948 to 1958. The years of my theoretical apprenticeship: high school, university, degree, and university teaching. I start to work on German historicism, particularly that of Dilthey; from Dilthey I move on to the young Hegel and to the origins of juridical formalism (closely linked topics). I translate Hegel into Italian, and then, remaining in the Hegelian frame, I spend a lot of time on Lukács (*Geschichte und Klassenbewußtsein*). I travel a lot, I study in Germany and France; I'm a perfect little altar boy. In 1954 I take a long trip to Israel: I come back communist.

The years 1958 to 1968 are years of experimenting. My life, or rather, the life of a young university professor (tenured since 1963), is a militancy laboratory. My theoretical work is on Marx. I read him well for the first time during these years. I address theoretical topics linked to the Marxist definition of "work" and his critique of the state. I take part in working out "Italian workerism" (I'm a member of the editorial board of *Quaderni rossi* [red notebooks], *Classe operaia* [the working class], *Contropiano* [counterplan]). I have heavy conflicts with the official worker's movement organizations.

From 1968 to 1979 I'm a political activist, even though I continue to be a university professor (in Padua, Milan, Paris, Berlin, etc.). I'm a member of the organizing committees of Potere Operaio (workers' power) and then Autonomia (autonomy). I serve as editor of the journals of these organizations. I take part in workers' and other social struggles during those years. My theoretical work is essentially to define the passage from the modern (Descartes, Hegel) to the postmodern in the economic sciences (the critique of Keynesianism) and in the sciences of law and the state (the state-form). I write a series of Marxist pamphlets about these matters that I still hold as good, in fact excellent, examples of political literature (especially *Dominion and Sabotage*). These are exceptional years, and they allow me to live a life in which my sense of social transformation and my personal happiness are melded.

In 1979, I am arrested, under the charge of being the head of subversion in Italy with the idea that the social movements of Autonomy and the Red Brigades are conflated; also under the charge of having committed seventeen murders, among which that of Aldo Moro. I spend four and a half years in the special prisons of the "historic compromise." A hard but beautiful time. Since I obviously can't do any politics, I study: these are years of metaphysics. And also of self-criticism.

In order to see communism triumph, it was clear that one had to avoid all capitalist homologation. The critique of socialism, not only actual socialism but any possible socialism (the reorganization of the workings of the law of value), was pressed forward so radically as to identify in any socialist proposal nothing more than a subordinated figure of capitalist slavery. Communism as ontological desire, therefore. *Marx Beyond Marx* and *The Savage Anomaly: The Power of Spinoza's Metaphysics and Politics*—these are the two books in which I present this new political project in metaphysical form.

In 1983, I am elected deputy from Milan, Naples, and Rome. After three months of freedom, parliamentary immunity is taken from me by an infamous, manipulated vote of parliament (a five-vote difference: three hundred against me, 296 in my favor; the ten Radical Party [the party that had nominated Negri] deputies don't participate, having been threatened by the P2 (the masonic lodge whose membership was a roster of the most powerful men in the government, military, industrial and financial sectors and which was the object of an enormous scandal). The only thing I could do was emigrate. While the Italian tribunals condemn me to thirty years in prison, the French government accepts me as its guest.

From 1984 until today, I have rebuilt my life in France. Initially, I worked on poetic themes: Leopardi and Job. Then, driven by the necessity of earning a living, I mostly spent my time doing sociological studies that documented the social figures (in a labor context) of the postmodern. Actually, for various reasons philosophy has always been a hobby for me: altar boy or militant, political activist or prisoner, exile or sociologist, my profession has never been that of the philosopher.

What luck! Now I live by doing sociological investigations, I teach political science at the University of Paris VIII, I direct a prestigious weekly seminar in Rue Descartes, and I belong to the editorial board of *Futur Antérieur*.

My wish is to start playing revolution again.

Of course I'm joking.

I forgot: I've just published a large work on constituent power, done in these last few years. A recent variation on the themes of power, autonomy, communism.

Translated by L. Scott Eagleburger and Beverly Allen

## Notes

1. Antonio Negri is a political philosopher who played a major role in political events on the Italian peninsula during the 1960s and 1970s. A professor and an activist in the workers' movement, Negri wrote a series of Marxist pamphlets during the 1970s that include essays on the passage from the modern (Descartes and Hegel) to the postmodern in the economic sciences (a critique of Keynesianism) and in the sciences of law and the state (a critique of the state-form). Negri's theoretical leadership, coupled with his public activism, made him one of the outstanding figures in the new left movement known as Autonomy during the 1970s. Under the assumption that Autonomy and the clandestine political violence of the Red Brigades were contiguous, the Italian state arrested Negri, along with dozens of other leading intellectuals, in 1979. The charges against Negri were much more severe than those against the others; Negri was charged, among other things, with having committed seventeen murders, including that of Aldo Moro. Under the Italian juridical system, Negri spent four and a half years in prison awaiting trial. While imprisoned, he elaborated a new political project, which appears in *Marx Beyond Marx* and *The Savage Anomaly: The Power of Spinoza's Metaphysics and Politics*. Also while in prison, Negri, who had been made a candidate by the Radical Party, was elected to the Italian parliament as deputy from Milan, Naples, and Rome. As such, he was entitled to parliamentary immunity and therefore was released from prison. When the parliament voted to deprive him of this immunity, Negri emigrated to France.

In Italy, Negri has been condemned in absentia to thirty years in prison; in France, he holds a position as professor of the Theory of the State at the University of Paris VIII, directs a prestigious weekly seminar in Rue Descartes, and serves on the editorial board of the journal *Futur Antérieur* (future past). Negri's work since he has been living in Paris deepens his analysis of the state-form and includes the major studies *Lenta ginestra* (the slow broomhedge; a reference to the work of the nineteenth-century poet Leopardi, and its inherent political theory), *Il potere costituente* (constituent power), and *Spinoza sovversivo* (Spinoza as subversive). [In the summer of 1997, Negri returned to

Italy, whereupon he was arrested and imprisoned to await further trial or possible amnesty.—*Ed.*]

The texts that follow are, first, a transcription of Negri's presentation at the "Designing Italy: 'Italy' in Europe, Africa, Asia, and the Americas" conference at Syracuse University from which most of the other articles in this book grew. He made his presentation by videotape as any move beyond French borders would deprive him of French political asylum and render him liable to arrest, repatriation, imprisonment, and trial. The second text is an autobiographical fragment he sent us.

2. A heretical unitarian movement associated in Italy with Lelio Socini (1525–62) and particularly his nephew Fausto (1539–1604).—*Trans.*

# They're Not Children Anymore: The Novelization of "Italians" and "Terrorism"

*Beverly Allen*

Its author was a mature youth, a man in whom the signs of aging still fought against the tenacious signs of adolescence.

From "(Prolegomenon to) a Possible Short Story"
by PAOLO LAPPONI, ANDREA LEONI, and VALERIO MORUCCI,
currently serving prison sentences from
twenty-three years to life for "terrorism" in Italy

## From the Inside Out

When I hear the word "culture," I reach for my gun.
GERMAN FIELD MARSHAL GOERING,
as quoted in Castellaneta's *Ombre*

Few events since World War II have conjured for the rest of the world the image of Italy as a nation more than the era of "terrorism."[1] From within literal Italy, however, the *anni di piombo*, or "years of lead," as inhabitants of the peninsula called the period from Milan's Piazza Fontana bombing in 1969 to 1983 or so,[2] were a kind of workshop in cultural constitutions of identity in general and mark a stage in the undoing of fixed national identity in particular. By looking from the inside out, by hearkening to the peninsular representations of Italy during that recent period of national crisis, I follow a remarkable course of events: the remaking not only of the "terrorists" but also of "Italians" by means of literary texts that provided sometimes gut-wrenching challenges to historical fact.

In spite of the fact, for example, that much of the early violence was perpetrated by clandestine fascist[3] groups in collusion with the Italian

52

secret service, homegrown "terrorism" on the Italic peninsula, when seen from the outside, came to stand for pervasive and cancerous radical left violence within the Italian nation-state. On the inside, however, in the context of peninsular Italian life, that is, it was quite another matter. Political differences among the perpetrators were clearly recognized and in fact became highly codified. Initially, the peninsular crisis was more social than political. How could Italians, especially the privileged children of the bourgeoisie, be so ungrateful as to tear at the social fiber with their bombs and kneecappings? The perpetrators, who were, in fact, such "children," were making a terrifying difference in the quality of peninsular life by instilling a fear that in very few years became generalized.[4]

Cultural productions provided the means for effecting numerous ideological operations that would variously interrogate, challenge, mourn, or support the clandestine political violence of the New Order, the Red Brigades, and other "terrorist" groups. One in particular took on the historically contradictory task of differentiating the perpetrators from the dominant class: the novel. The novel's generic architecture, historically primed to constitute national identity and draw the lineaments of the bourgeoisie, reconstituted and redrew that identity and those lineaments throughout the "years of lead." Finally, it had effectively redefined the "terrorists" and established a difference *within* that opened the way for arrests, prosecutions, manipulation of informants, and an abrogation of civil rights unheard of in literal geopolitical Italy since Mussolini and state fascism.

Cultural artifacts of many sorts show how Italy imagined itself during the hot years from the early 1970s to the mid-1980s. The films *Devil in the Flesh* by Mario Bellocchio and *Three Brothers* by the Taviani Brothers are but two that viewers worldwide would recognize. Among theater activists whose productions represented contemporary clandestine political violence, Dario Fo's name stands out. Traditional literary genres other than the novel also engaged in representing this violence. Short stories such as "Piccoli equivoci senza importanza" (Little misunderstandings of no consequence), which established Antonio Tabucchi as a nationally significant writer, or "La prova del fuoco" (Trial by fire) by Carlo Castellaneta are but two examples, and the poem "Il nome di Maria Fresu" (Maria Fresu's name) by Andrea Zanzotto is yet another.

But none of these cultural productions shows so clearly an effort to keep the dominant class intact, whether this meant redefining who the "terrorists" were or even, in fact, who was Italian, than the novel. To claim that the novel could do this, to argue, that is, that the novel could actually reconstitute the body politic so that the "terrorists" who had come from its privileged ranks would become excluded, alien, viral units, we must accept the novel as a genre especially burdened with the social constitution of national identity. We must also take into account the resilient power of genre.

## The Bearable Resilience of Genre

The novel is the art-form of virile maturity.
                    GEORG LUKÁCS

God knows, there are ominous structures of authority
taking form in the contemporary world.
                    KENNETH BURKE

I begin from the premise that social texts and linguistic texts always co-implicate one another, albeit in messy, noncongruent, and ambiguous ways. Here, of course, the social text is clandestine political violence on the Italian peninsula during the "years of lead," and the linguistic texts are novels in Italian that represent that violence.[5] When I speak of co-implication, however, I in no way intend to reduce the terrifying and atrocious physical violence that was called "terrorism" in Italy to a purely discursive status. On the contrary, by articulating the mutual and overlapping social and literary texts of that violence, I want to draw attention to the osmosis that exists between them as I articulate the social effects of genre.

I accept the notion of genre as a historically and therefore aesthetically determined practice with specific ideological markers.[6] For some genres, these markers, identifiable in the social tasks the genre rose to perform at its historical outset, are vestigial. This is the case, for example, with the short story, which has its beginnings in medieval saints' lives. It no longer fulfills or seeks to fulfill its initial task of providing exemplars of proper Christian behavior, but it retains nonetheless such formal characteristics of its medieval practice as the eloquence of the anecdote and a relative absence of character development. For other genres, such as the lyric, the ideological markers carried at the outset are entirely effaced and thus impossible to discern, leaving a formal palimpsest that can "take" all sorts of ideological valences.[7]

The novel, on the other hand, because it is so recent a cultural formation, still carries the weight of its originary markers and thus is a prime example of the material operations of language or of the effects of imaginative literature on a social group. It is a kind of cognitive architecture a writer enters when that writer writes a "novel." Architecture implies space, limits, inside and outside, rooms, doors, shelter, and so forth. With these givens, someone may design and build a dwelling, an office building, a religious shrine, a women's shelter, a public swimming pool, a firehouse, whatever. In all these variants, the preliminary notions of architecture inhere, just as do the preliminary notions of "novel" for all "novels" that are written. Genre, then, is like architecture; it is an ideology of form, to follow Jameson, in which individual novels appear as ideologemes (Jameson 1981, 61).[8]

At least part of the novel's historic task has been to provide the new dominant classes in eighteenth- and nineteenth-century Europe a guide to their own social and subjective constitutions. In particular, national identity as a characteristic of the new bourgeois class inheres in the novelistic genre. Critical thinkers concur regarding the simultaneous appearance of the novel in Western Europe and the rise of the Western European nation-state (Lukács, Bakhtin, Watt). The novel is in fact impossible to imagine prior to the Western European nation-state because it depends on and simultaneously helps to constitute social categories that did not exist until the nation-state was itself an economic, cognitive, and sociopolitical possibility. These categories include the association of the nation with a generally nonmonarchical, generally somehow democratic, always virtually or actually bureaucratic state, and with subjectivities that correspond to the existential possibilities or imperatives of such a social organization.

Historically new categories of social organization and dominant discourse in eighteenth-century Europe therefore necessitate an instrument that interpellates individuals in newly appropriate ways. The novel performs this task by instructing the new social subjects—the male and female adult members of the new dominant and relatively literate class—in their own ontology by representing them as the necessary atomic units of the new political entity; that is, the novel depicts the kind of individual necessary as a subject in the modern Western European nation-state.

Such depiction is due neither to the expressive causality Althusser sees in Hegelian concepts of history nor to a simple homological mirroring of a separate social Real.[9] By itself, in fact, it *constitutes* a new social reality, particularly when one takes into consideration the temporal and individual conditions of the reading experience the novel demands—long-term silent engagement with a widely-distributed reproduced text—conditions that themselves produce, at least for the period of book acquisition and reading, or "consumption," the individual the state depends on.[10] The individual thus produced is autonomous and "free." He, and she, has the historically new attribute of a *psychology*, an internal secular dialogue where power relations between duty and desire are negotiated on a daily basis and create a lifelong narrative. Moreover, he, and she, takes on a sense of self based on a similar external dynamic of identification with the authority of the nation-state. These characteristics braid together to enlist him, and her, in, among other things, the ferocious new network of mortal obligation called patriotism.

## Italy's First Children

"I've learned," he was saying, "not to get into trouble . . ."
The peasant protagonist, Renzo,
in MANZONI's *The Betrothed*

A particularly telling instance of the generic genre function, or genre imperative, of the novel is Alessandro Manzoni's *I promessi sposi* (The betrothed), which directly participates in such social and political projects as the constitution of national and subjective identity, nationalism, and the formation of "consciousness." The peculiar status of this novel as a fictional constitution of the Italian nation-state lies partly in its representation of a liberal Catholic social creed, where the individual overcomes local allegiances, even economic or class ones, in the name of the larger (European) model of the nation-state. He accomplishes this by means of an internalized moral code that projects final solutions to social dilemmas into the realm of Christian revelation—a code I would call Christian-democratic.

Manzoni's novel is also emblematic in another more directly material way. When its author spent twenty years rewriting in Florentine the Lombard dialect of the original 1821 version, he was selecting and imposing a national language on the peninsular bourgeoisie that was concurrently (and clandestinely) engaged in ousting all occupying forces and founding an independent nation-state. No reader could fail to recognize the sociopolitical significance of this *risorgimento* of Florentine in the mouths of Lombard peasants in the 1840 edition, where Manzoni's "realistic" characters converse in a language their real counterparts would not easily have understood.

Nor did one of the novel's more illustrious twentieth-century readers fail to recognize the paternalistic attitude of the author toward his "popular," or peasant, characters. In his well-known prison essay, "Manzoni and His Humble Characters," Antonio Gramsci carefully remarks that the peasants in *The Betrothed* are often teased and shown to be superficial by the narrative, whereas the *signori* are allowed to have "inner lives" (Gramsci 1991, 89). Gramsci notes this aspect of Manzoni's novel as part of his thesis that "Italian literature" has no "national-popular" aspect. I would note, instead, that this aspect of the novel has lasting implications for representations of Italy. The peasant characters of Manzoni's fictional constitution of the nascent unified Italian nation-state are symbolically appropriate as signifiers of national unification because the nature of their work puts them in contact with the earth and thus the "land," and by extension the nation-state, of Italy. Simultaneously, however, their trusting, childlike personalities, undeveloped psychologically, are entirely dependent on more "adult" characters—a cardinal, say, or a feudal lord, or an aged man who has experienced radical religious conversion— none of whom are peasants. "Italy" in Manzoni's novel is to be made from the childlike *popolo*, but someone, some other kind of "Italian," will have to take charge of it until it reaches maturity. "Italy," therefore, is generationally double: childlike in the simplicity and faith of its *popolo* but also endowed with historic tutelary "fathers."

Manzoni's novel is a limit case of the social phenomenon of the genre in nineteenth-century Europe. In it, constantly implicit national identity takes precedence over, exists simultaneously to, or competes with other possible communal identities the subject may have, such as religious or regional ones. Furthermore, the historically new subject of the novel, whether peasant or lord, has a kinship network defined within traditional patriarchal notions of the family but that extends metaphorically to include other individuals defined as fraternal similars within the nation-state context. The sense of familiarity, then, that lies at the kinship-metaphor origins of the nation-state community, may of course exclude "its" deviant daughters and sons, whether these be grown-up, oversexed "terrorists" or even the entire proletariat.

## The State of the Novel

Nations do not make states and nationalisms but the other way
around.                                           E. J. HOBSBAWM

. . . all literature must be read as a symbolic meditation on the
destiny of community.               FREDRIC JAMESON

In several very general ways, then, the historical onset of the novel
provides a constitutive vision of the "personal" side of the institution-
alized nation-state. Most significantly, it replaces the premodern
monarchist equation of political semiotics, in which the king's actual
body is, as both signifier and signified, the state, with a modern democratic one in which everybody's body signifies the state. Modern institutions ordain national identity; the novel offers individual subscrip-
tions to it.

Novels written since the eighteenth century may differ wildly from
the paradigmatic model of Manzoni. They may, in fact, provide utterly oppositional models of individual and social constitution. The
practically limitless ideologemes that the notion "novel" contains,
however, bear nonetheless the skeleton of structural causality, which,
when historicized, claims a role as social actant precisely because of
its initial generic task. Those of us who are novel readers in novel-
producing cultures recognize when a novel is oppositional *because* we
recognize that novels produce social forms. As a genre, then, the novel
bears its resilience well. It is a structural vehicle even for ideologemes
intent on undermining its originary constitutive task precisely because
none can undo its continuing constitutive power.

Once again, I want to avoid any suggestion that the novel as a genre
passively reflects social realities existing outside it. Such metaphoric
topography is a static hindrance to any understanding of the ideological social operations of any cultural production. Therefore, a philo-
logically motivated notion of invention, *inventio*, "bringing in," or
even *transventio*, "bringing across," comes closer to suggesting the
way the novel works socially. By acting on the cognitive and behavioral patterns of individuals, and by coming from an individual who is
acted upon by any number of elements in the social, the novel *inter-
acts* with other sociocultural formations and *transacts* with them the
sustaining or undoing of the status quo. Such an understanding is a
prerequisite for the comprehension of the role the novel played in

national unification and independence movements in Europe in the eighteenth and nineteenth centuries and the ways it contributed consequentially to a reconstitution of national identity in Italy during the more recent "years of lead."

## The State of Italy

"How is such barbarity possible in the late twentieth century?" This
is a false question.                                    JEAN BAUDRILLARD

The mostly clandestine political violence perpetrated during the late 1960s, the 1970s, and the early 1980s in literal Italy was performed by people on the left and on the right and took its aim at both specific individual victims and indeterminate groups of victims (Bocca 1981; Della Porta and Pasquino 1983; Ferrarotti 1979; Galleni 1981; Pansa 1980). On the left, it grew out of two major phenomena: first, the roiling frustration many young leftists felt with the Italian Communist Party's move away from revolutionary commitment and toward participation in the parliamentary government (the *compromesso storico*, or historic compromise); and second, out of a certain Catholicism of many of those same young Communists who saw in the figure of Christ a model of anticapitalist renunciation and revolutionary democracy.[11] The violence and clandestinity adopted by these people was fueled by the *strage dello stato*, the undeclared state policy of collusion with fascist groups in order to foment civil unrest and eventually justify the impostion of a military government, an eventuality that has not yet come to pass (Bocca 1981, 15; Galli 1986, 10–11; Negri 1985, 316; Sanguinetti 1982).

On the fascist right, "terrorism" grew out of both a clandestine collusion with the state and an enduring conviction that only fascism could promote civil order in the face of the unrest fomented by movements for social change—the youth movement and feminism, in particular—of the late 1960s.[12] The fascist collusion with the state secret service predates the formation of clandestine groups on the left by several years, having begun in the early or mid-1960s, whence it grew as the *strage della tensione* (strategy of tension) intended to result in civil disorder (the *strage dello stato*) (Bale 1989; Borraccetti 1986; Corsini and Novati 1985).

Significantly, the early clandestine groups on the left, in particular the Red Brigades, were peopled primarily with students, most of them from the privileged ranks of the bourgeoisie, and secondarily with worker activists who had previously devoted their efforts to public militancy against both bosses and the traditional contexts of the labor unions (Bocca 1981; Galli 1986, 12). This was the era of Antonio Negri's influential theorization of the self-valorization and collective action of the proletariat, according to which a universal refusal to work followed by a demand for pay for no work would place capitalist laws of value into crisis and thus provide a material base for radical democratic social change.[13]

The clandestine political violence of the *anni di piombo*, on the other hand, occurred in urban and exurban industrial areas throughout the Italian peninsula, but mostly from Rome northward, lasting from the late 1960s until 1988 or so, depending on what one counts as "terrorism." In all, it created about four hundred victims, including those who were kneecapped, kidnapped, raped, and murdered either individually or in indiscriminate bombings (Galleni 1981). It had a massive effect, felt mostly in the late 1970s and early 1980s, on the Italian economy and resulted in the emigration of members of the monied classes and a tremendous decline in tourism.

The most well known events of the "years of lead" include, as I mentioned earlier, the 1969 fascist bombing of the Bank of Agriculture in Milan, known as "the Valpreda affair" after the anarchist first accused as perpetrator (Bale 1989; Borraccetti 1986; Corsini and Novati 1985). The kidnapping and murder of Aldo Moro, Italy's leading Christian Democrat, by members of the Red Brigades in March 1978 gained global media attention and shook the political establishment, particularly after the publication of Moro's unanswered pleas to his fellow Christian Democrats (Wagner-Pacifici 1986). A third landmark event was the fascist bombing of the train station in Bologna in 1980, which caused eighty-five deaths and two hundred injuries (Borraccetti 1986) and lowered considerably the level of public tolerance for such violence.

## The Membranous Body Politic

The meaning of the distinction between legitimate and illegitimate violence is not immediately obvious.

WALTER BENJAMIN, "Critique of Violence"

It should be understood by now why we consider synecdoche to be the basic process of representation.

KENNETH BURKE, *The Philosophy of Literary Form*

We had to arrest you because terrorism was becoming a literary
genre.

CANADIAN PRIME MINISTER PIERRE TRUDEAU,
to Daniel Latouche, leading Quebecois separatist and former
"screaming sign painter," at a Montreal dinner party.

During the "years of lead," several constitutions of the Italian body
politic and the power of the state were renegotiated, all of them seep-
ing across lines of distinction and oozing together in attempts at coag-
ulation. Situating fixed bodies becomes ever more difficult, therefore,
except for the literal ones left dead, maimed, or imprisoned. The figurative body politic, subject to constant reconstitutions and undoings
determined by violent acts and discursive practices, shows up as a
membranous entity, adjusting here and there, feeling uncomfortable in
its (libidinous?) osmoses if earlier it had been accustomed to the corset
of clear state powers and clear oppositions.

Juridical discourse took a nostalgic turn. Laws instituted during
Mussolini's fascism and punishing with double sentences any criminal
acts proven seditious were reinstated, thus recasting the mode of Italian jurisprudence in ways still being felt today.[14] Demographically, the
literal geopolitical state of Italy lost some of its wealthiest subjects to
emigration.[15] Cultural productions, the novel in particular, rewrote
the makeup of the dominant class and even of the category of people
who could claim Italian identity. I would conclude this detailed preface of my discussion of the body of imaginative literature that accomplished this with several considerations of how the body politic was
reconstituted by means of a particular *spectacular* aspect of the social
text: the "terrorist" acts themselves.

The clandestine political violence covered by the term begs for
*rhetorical* analysis because "terrorism" is the most literary of violent
political acts; that is, its efficacy depends entirely on its capacity to *get
its message across.* "Terrorism" always functions rhetorically. It lends
itself, therefore, to modes of textual analysis that go far toward clari-
fying how, when, and whether the intended message of any particular event is communicated. Thinking in terms of the textual nature
of "terrorism" suggests that I may view novelistic representations
of clandestine political violence not only as referential operations
but also as intertextual ones, as a kind of writing, that is, that incor-
porates, signals, implies, acknowledges, underwrites, and overwrites

*another* kind of writing being done somewhere other than the page, everywhere, in fact—the social text.

One of the questions that arises, then, in any consideration of the social semiotics of Italy's "years of lead" is how such apparently opposed political locations as fascist and radical left ideologies depended on apparently similar acts of clandestine political violence. An answer to this question arises from a rhetorical study of the signifying properties of the acts themselves (Allen 1987a).

Put exceedingly briefly, the "terrorist" acts created meaning via the trope of synecdoche, where each victim functioned, in the "message," as a part of a whole, where the whole was a class or a political ideology. For example, say that a Communist magistrate is kneecapped as he drinks his morning coffee in a Roman *caffè*. This event *means* that the Red Brigades vehemently disapprove of what the Communist magistrate *represents*, the Communist Party and the judicial system. Other Communists and other magistrates, and especially other Communist magistrates, are threatened by association, by synecdochal association, in fact, since the actual victim stands as a part to the whole of the social body he or she represents.[16]

With their bombings, the fascists also got the message across that if people gathered arbitrarily in a public place were killed by a bomb, all other people were at risk. Thus the entire body politic, in relation to which the group arbitrarily gathered was a part, was threatened. And this was, in fact, the widest aim of fascist "terrorism" during those years: to spread a sense of social disorder that could eventually be used to justify the imposition of a military government (Borraccetti 1986, 42–70; Corsini and Novati 1985, 220–29).[17] It was not initially successful, nor did the kneecappings of individuals initially promote widespread fear in the body politic (Galli 1986, 309).

The synecdochal trope characterized both left and fascist "terrorism," therefore, and eventually allowed for a problematization of their distinction. The mark of difference appeared not in the shared figurative mode of their rhetoric, the synecdocal principle per se, but rather in their variant deployment of what in the terms of textual analysis I would call their signature. The signature, or proprietary stylistic mark, of left "terrorism" was the kneecapping of a single specific victim; that of the fascists, the bombing with numerous nonspecific victims. The consensual reading of these signatures quickly became so wide as to allow counterfeiting, where one "side" would engage in a signature act consensually attributed to the other "side" in order to discredit the other "side" as being exceedingly brutal.

As time went on and instances of these kinds of clandestine political violence proliferated, the events took on ever wider meanings. This affected the semiosis of fascist bombings hardly at all, since their general aim was to spread national panic. On the left, however, the synecdoche began to function all too widely: more people began to feel threatened than simply the ones intended by the perpetrators. For example, in repetitions of the kneecapping of the Communist magistrate, say, not only Communist magistrates, or Communists, or magistrates, felt threatened, but so did anyone who had his or her coffee in a Roman *caffè* each morning. Public opinion, which had contained a measure of tolerance toward the perpetrators if not toward their actions, switched to a mode of intolerance and eventually much more generalized outrage.

## The Body of Literature: The Prodigal Son

A novel without men, or where the men are too childish or too exhausted to survive . . .
    CESARE GARBOLI, from the introduction to *Caro Michele*

You're no one's father. Nothing. Zero.
    Wkhy, in RENATO CURCIO's *WKHY*

Although the clandestine political violence of the "years of lead" came from quite different and generally opposed locations on the political spectrum, and although it was subject at all locations to the processes of meaning production I have just glossed, the kind of "terrorism" that produced the most romance was the "terrorism" of the left. I mean "romance" quite literally: most of the Italian novels, or *romanzi*, treating contemporary clandestine political violence concentrate on representations of leftist perpetrators and their adventures in underground living. In spite of an occasional novel concentrating on the *eversione di destra*, or fascist "terrorism" (*Occidente*, for example, by Ferdinando Camon), and in spite of the occasional fascist character thrown into novels such as Castellaneta's in order to maintain the novel's perennial generic contract with codes of literary realism, it is the leftist "terrorists" who are the preferred novelistic protagonists of the "years of lead."[18]

Whether representing the fascist or the leftist perpetrators, the body of literature constituted during Italian "terrorism" exists, it is urgently important to remember, within and as part of a material context of changing social relations. The materiality of relations outside the novelistic system of socially constitutive representations bleeds back and forth over the boundaries that distinguish it from the novels, which have their own material relationality to their writers, publishers, distributors, and readers. The images these novels present take on constitutive, material reality in the cognition and subjective identity of the readers.

The geopolitical borders of literal Italy during the "years of lead" took on various characteristics determined by political considerations. For example, the state indirectly but effectively exiled Antonio Negri. It *actually* exiled many others on both "sides" with pardons, clean passports, and tickets to Switzerland if they were *pentiti*, or with long prison terms if they were not. The borders of the body politic proliferated. Some coincided with the map of Italy; some were the streets of Paris; some were the walls of Rebibbia and other "special prisons" (Peci 1983).[19]

With these materialities and interchanges of the social and the literary and the political in mind, I read two representative novels as emblems of the social operation the novel in general effected during the "years of lead." The arc that goes from the first of the novels under consideration here to the second is the trajectory taken by the novel in general in its representations of those who engage in clandestine political violence. Initially, the novel as a genre casts the perpetrators as prodigal children, offspring of the ruling class, certainly part of the body politic, certainly Italian, and thus reassuringly recuperable. By processes of gradual demonization and delegitimation, however, the novel during the "years of lead" comes to represent these same perpetrators as abnormal, deviant, a disease invading the body politic rather than members of it. By insistent implication, in fact, the novel genre in particular eventually hints that the perpetrators are *not even Italian*.

The first of these novels is Natalia Ginzburg's *Caro Michele* (dear Michael), published in 1973. This is an epistolary novel in which a bourgeois Italian family lives out the central drama of the parents' divorce. Michael's "terrorist" activities are a marginal mystery, and the relative unimportance of these to the plot implies that, whatever he has done, he is still a part of the family. Much of this is accomplished by allusion, as in the following letter:

December 8, 1970
Dear Michele,
Mission accomplished regarding the little object you forgot in your stove. I've thrown this little object into the Tiber, since it was, as you said, rusty. But I did not go to see the girl in Via Prefetti. I haven't had time. My baby has a cold. Besides, you told me that I should bring money to this girl, but I don't have any money right now. Our father was buried three days ago. I'll write more as soon as I can.
Angelica (Ginzburg 1973, 47)

Thus writes Michael's sister from Rome in response to his letter asking her to retrieve his automatic rifle from its hiding place in the stove in his old apartment and dispose of it. The father's death mentioned here identifies Angelica and Michele, for whatever else they may also be, as children. In Ginzburg's novel, this is precisely what the "terrorist" is above all else: a child, specifically a prodigal son, the scion of a bourgeois family whose personal crises far overshadow the clandestine political violence creeping across the Italic peninsula.

An insistent theme of paternity—traditional, threatened, assumed, ambivalent, or otherwise—further contributes to the picture of Michele as a child. The novel associates paternity, not surprisingly in a patriarchal bourgeois family, with inheritance. Michele's paternity of a former girlfriend's baby is in doubt; therefore lines of heredity are threatened. Ginzburg presents Michele as his father's own favorite child and his only male one. Michele is thus emphatically his father's heir, all the more so because he has entered his father's profession: both are artists, painters, in fact. Nonetheless, Michele abdicates his normal filial role. For example, not only does Michele refuse to return home for the family ritual of his father's funeral—a ritual that would render visible his traditional family role and thus reinstate him in it—but he also refuses to accept the medieval tower bequeathed to him in his father's will. In both these instances, then, Ginzburg's narrative shows that traditional bourgeois continuities are gravely threatened by the "terrorist" boy, Michele. On the one hand, it jumbles the possibility of Michele's own paternity—he is *probably* not the father of his former girlfriend's baby; he is *certainly* not the father of the children of the woman he marries, eventually, in England—and thus undermines his variant appearances as some sort of a father. On the other hand, it paints Michele as a wayward son.

His attempts to abdicate his role as child, however, are in vain, for the other characters never grant Michele full adult status, not even those who suspect he has fathered a child out of wedlock and across class lines and thus acceded to biological if not social parenthood. Suspicions concerning Michele's sexuality further impede his entrance into adulthood via paternity. If, in fact, Michele is bisexual or homosexual, he becomes ever less likely a father, according to the narrative logic, and thus is kept even more a child himself.

The principal positioning of the "terrorist" as a child is reinforced throughout the novel by the way his mother thinks of him. In spite of his apparently adult independence (he has, after all, gone off to live in England and gotten married), she will not cease her mewing complaints about his filial inconsistencies. She refuses to see him as *anything but* a child.[20]

Maternal egocentrism and denial of Michele's political commitment further ground the "terrorist" Michele in his Roman bourgeois context. He is, over and over again, his mother's as well as his father's child, his sisters' brother, and nobody's father: a son, a sibling, and a "failed" father, implicitly too young to bear any responsibility. He is never an adult. He is the child now missing from the family, a condition the other family members see as temporary, one surely to be resolved by his return.

Michele's status as a prodigal son is determined mostly by his out-of-place location, however. His residence in England shows that he has left both family and country, and it implies a congruence between the institutions of the bourgeois Roman family and the Italian nation-state. Although the narrative constantly reinforces Michele's filial status, and therefore his position as heir to the property and values of his father (and by extension the bourgeois family and the nation-state), it also implicitly reinforces Michele's national identity. Michele is Italian *in spite of and because of* his excursion to England. The possibility of his recuperation in both the normative category of family heir and that of *Italian* is rendered explicit by this distance; it disappears only with his murder at the hands of fascists in the foreign land. Ginzburg's novel tells its readers, finally, that even children can die and leave nothing reassuring to dominant discourse in place.

In Ginzburg's exemplary novel, then, I read the "terrorist" in 1973 as a son of the bourgeoisie, a good, if errant, Italian, who should and most likely will return to the peninsula and be recuperated by the national institutions—class and family—where he belongs.

In fact, many of the so-called historic members of such clandestine political groups on the left as the Red Brigades *were* privileged university students from bourgeois families whose Catholic values had grown radical and whose patience with the Italian Communist Party had run out.[21] By taking Ginzburg's novel as symptomatic, I get a filtered picture of the actual relative tolerance felt by much of the dominant class toward the perpetrators of clandestine violence in Italy during the early stages of the "years of lead." Clearly, Michele's class and family identities matter more in Ginzburg's novel than do his politics. Moreover, his class and family identities guarantee his continued *Italianness*, in spite of his current aberrant behavior. The biblical subtext of the prodigal son, plus centuries of historical tolerance on the Italic peninsula for banditry and all sorts of illegal acts against a long series of foreign occupations, give both mother and sister in Ginzburg's book plenty of ready narratives they can lean on in hopes of recuperating the self-exiled child. "Terrorism," in Ginzburg's 1973 book, is still something *Italians* do.

## The Body of Literature: Perverted Adults

The novel is then not so much an organic unity as a symbolic act
that must reunite or harmonize heterogeneous narrative paradigms
which have their own specific and contradictory ideological
meaning.          FREDRIC JAMESON on Manzoni

The symbolic not only exists, it holds power.
          DRUSILLA CORNELL,
          paraphrasing Hélène Cixous

Outside Ginzburg's novel, nine years pass, years that witness the increased clandestine political violence I have described, a violence that bears no aestheticization. After such clamorous events as the kidnapping and murder of the prime minister, Aldo Moro, by the Red Brigades in 1978 and the murderous bombing of the Bologna train station by temporarily anonymous fascists in 1980, even the minimal family-oriented tolerance toward "terrorism" that Ginzburg's novel demonstrates began to disappear. By 1982, practically a decade after Ginzburg's portrayal of the implicitly recuperable young "terrorist"

Michele, Italian readers get a set of radically different novelistic portraits of contemporary "terrorists" in *Ombre* (shadows, shades) by
Carlo Castellaneta. In a double-protagonist plot whose alternations
are marked by switches in narrative voice, Castellaneta presents the
"terrorist" whom a now fear-weary populace and a threatened dominant class see as the source of the menace.

The first protagonist, whose sections of the narrative are all written
in the first-person voice, is a young woman named Marina. Her marginal social identity consists mainly in her status as an unwed mother.
Castellaneta extends this status to one of social pathology, however,
by having Marina abandon her already fatherless child to the care of
its maternal grandparents, thus casting her as that bane of patriarchal
Italian normalcy, the *madre snaturata* (denatured mother). In order
to acquire this status, of course, a woman has actually to be someone's biological or social mother and thus, implicitly, an adult. Unlike
Michele, whose paternal status is gravely undermined and who therefore retains a childlike position throughout Ginzburg's novel, Marina
is a grown-up woman, although she has perverted her normal responsibility as a mother in order to assume illegal responsibility as a
"terrorist."

Marina leaves her child precisely in order to enter a clandestine life
as a member of a network very similar to that of the Red Brigades.
Once she is "underground," however, the narrative figures her, now
known by the nom de guerre "Bruna," as a kind of field of interference
where discourses of "terrorist" political strategy and an ever-ready
female heterosexuality vie for preeminence. As plot would have it, the
sexuality wins out, as Marina/Bruna's sexual relations, both with the
male "terrorist" she is assigned to live with and with one she takes a
liking to, play a greater role in her figuration than does her notable
strategic talent.

*Ombre*'s narrative in fact filters Marina/Bruna's political commitment through a gauze of gender subjugation and sexiness that her
comrades effectively use to gag her with whenever she would strate-
gize. This occurs most markedly during scenes of sexual intercourse
where, for example, the reader has privileged access to Marina/Bruna's
internal monologue: Marina/Bruna is at least as aware of her thoughts
about how to kidnap a politician as she is of the sensations that lead
to the "explosion" that shortly silences all her thoughts in bed (Castellaneta 1982, 151–52; also 99–100). Castellaneta's narrative thus fig-

ures the leftist protagonist's politics in a hazy prurience that has the reader participate voyeuristically in the moment when orgasm apparently transcends politics.

In *Ombre*, therefore, Marina/Bruna may be at times an addled and at times a prescient "terrorist," but she is first and foremost a sexy woman, one capable of orgasm and reproduction: in all cases, an adult. Her stepwise motion is this: she leaves her maternal role, already marginalized, in order to follow her political commitment; she "leaves" her political commitment in order to follow her sexuality.[22] She is the grown-up who has perverted her normal role and is paying for it by the loneliness of her internal exile and the gender oppression of her comrades. Even her abandonment of her parents, who are left holding her son, does nothing to threaten her status as adult, for, unlike Michele's, it is a successful, total abandonment; once she has left her parents, she never contacts them again; she certainly never writes them a letter.

Castellaneta's novel contains a second protagonist, a middle-aged male urban professional who is also a high-ranking fascist "terrorist." This man, who remains unnamed[23] and whose sections of the novel are narrated in the third-person voice, enjoys an enthusiasm for Piazza Fontana-style bombings akin to Marina/Bruna's enthusiasm for high-risk kidnappings. He and Marina/Bruna, in fact, are figured as counterparts in a plot strategy that implicitly reduces the intricacies of the "years of lead" to a simple binary. "Terrorist" murders committed by or because of the machinations of each of these characters appear in a kind of rational tabulation of narrative line and are not represented as lurid. This symmetrical or parallel structure breaks down when the fascist commits a *sex-related* murder; he then appears far more fundamentally evil according to the values the narrative sets up than does the addled, sexy Marina/Bruna. The fascist protagonist's social marginalization derives initially from his international arms dealings and his collusion with shady military figures; his "perverse" sexuality is configured not as that of a *madre snaturata* and a loose woman, as is Marina/Bruna's, but rather as that of an anti-Semitic voyeur and, finally, a sex murderer. The bombing he has organized necessitates his departure from Italy; the sex murder he has committed clinches his alienation from the Italian body politic.

This unnamed male character, whose cover is that he is the editor and publisher of an internationally oriented journal, is a married man whose family life is left vague almost to the point of nonexistence. He is figured in no familial or kinship role other than that implied by the shadowy appearances of a character implicitly his wife who asks at dinner, for example, when his next trip will be. What the narrative does make clear, and glaringly so, is his obsession with the memory of a sadistic sexual relation he had with a working-class Jewish woman called Nora while she was still a schoolgirl. Just as he does with the Marina/Bruna character, Castellaneta confounds seditious strategizing and unbridled libido in this no-name fascist. The difference between the two is that, unlike Marina/Bruna, this character experiences his sexuality only nostalgically, through vividly imaged memories that always seem to crowd in just as he is reaching the thrilling apex of a line of thought about, say, the next bombing (Castellaneta 1982, 76–77).

Castellaneta's strategy for marginalizing these "terrorists" from the normative social body while simultaneously granting them adulthood is to have recourse to sexual perversion. Marina/Bruna, in addition to being sexually charged and a "denatured mother," is also smarter than her male counterparts—another big minus. Lacking the "normal" feminine attribute of tenderness, she does not know how to separate political strategy from lovemaking. She will soon come to realize that the radical stud the movement has her shacked up with expects her to do the dishes but not to have ideas; she will then gravitate toward the feminist movement in place of the "terrorist" one, the novel implies. She will have an opportunity to choose a more ladylike way for engaging in antisocial behavior. For the time being, however, in the chronotopes and for the duration of *Ombre* the novel, her distracted sexual availability and the narrator's repeated insistence on it cast her outside the virginal models appropriated by traditional dominant discourse in Italy for its women *and for its nation-state* when the nation-state is shown in a state of health (Allen 1992a).

By the same token but under a different banner, the fascist male protagonist, who can barely stand the excitement as he waits for the bomb to go off in Bologna, as he peers from behind a door at his secretary making love to an office boy, and as he heads to an apartment in Venice to kill his adolescent former girlfriend, is never shown in a direct sexual partnership with anyone. He is, even more clearly than Castellaneta's young woman "terrorist," the overt pervert in the cast. His activity, whether voyeurism, onanism, or sex murder, labels him an outsider to the community of normalcy shared by Castellaneta's narrator and implied reader.

The othering effected in *Ombre*, then, by means of associating the "terrorist" protagonists with sexual behavior cast as abnormal, holds wider implications than that of their sexual marginalization alone. Given the historic ideological and social task of the novel as a genre in Western European nation-states, this othering reveals itself as a metaphor for expulsion from the Italian body politic itself. By their deviation from norms of sexual and gender propriety and from the bourgeois institutions that apparently demand such normalcy, much more than by their participation in violence and clandestinity (which have honorable histories in peninsular Italy), the "terrorists" *implicitly* render suspect their own national identity. In so doing, they relinquish their subjective location within the body politic they are attacking both with their so-called perversions and with the lead of their bullets and bombs. Not only are they not children anymore, they are also not Italians. The novel thus preserves the nation-state by implicitly, metaphorically, analogically, and tropically constituting it as that which does not include the deviance of "liberated" women, voyeuristic male murderers, and, quite secondarily, the clandestine political violence called "terrorism."

In its narrative swoop of plot, character development, and voice, and through its networks of referentiality and implicit, exclusive communities, Castellaneta's novel, along with many others like it,[24] effects this excision. In so doing, it protects the image of the Italian body politic as a body attacked from the outside, steadfastly fighting off foreign infection, rather than as one whose own parts are suddenly acting up. The story-line braidings of *Ombre* and so many other novels of Italian "terrorism" delegitimate in a metonymic domino effect whatever claim to civil responsibility and oppositional discourse the "terrorists" had earlier enjoyed, even a minimal "identity" as parties to what many actual perpetrators continue to claim was in fact a civil war.

The parallel plots of Castellaneta's novel both entail "terrorist" killings. But closure in *Ombre* inscribes two quite unparallel "endings": Marina/Bruna is arrested, along with her lover and most of their comrades, while the fascist steps onto a plane bound for South America via New York City. However diverse their fates, and whatever else they may be, both of Castellaneta's 1982 "terrorist" protagonists are clearly not children anymore. Unlike Ginzburg's earlier novel, Castellaneta's, written during one of the hottest of those leaden years, does not infantilize its "terrorists." He allows them a passage into adulthood, where they may be considered *responsible for their actions*. This passage to adulthood, however, also entails the "terrorists'" alienation from the bourgeois Italian family and from the "family" of bourgeois Italy: as grown-ups, they are irrecuperable. Since their implicit banning is effected by means of their association with "abnormal" modes of sexuality, moreover, it is not their *politics*, a social discourse ostensibly arrived at through the exercise of reason, that exiles them from a dominant "norm" (such a ticket out of the country, so to speak, would be a tricky business in so politicized a place as literal Italy). Instead, it is their sexuality, something figured as most intimate, innate, and essential. This shift in semiotic locus from the body politic to the body itself is the key to the novel's ideological operation.

## New "Them's," the Same Old "Us's"

What else but the solidarity of an imaginary "us" against a symbolic
"them" would have launched Argentina and Britain into a crazy
war for some South Atlantic bog and rough pasture?
        E. J. HOBSBAWM, *Nations and Nationalism since 1780*

And naturally I didn't say anything, I only waved to him while the
police barge took them away, and I followed along the jetty with
slow, halting steps, trying not to step on the cracks, like when I was
a child and used to have this little ritual of mapping onto the side-
walk's squares my childish decoding of a world still without meter
or measure.
        ANTONIO TABUCCHI, "Little Misunderstandings of No Importance"

What has happened in the social text during the decade between the two novels? Is the shift from Ginzburg's prodigal son child "terrorist" to Castellaneta's supposedly perverse adult ones merely due to the subjective ideological or psychological visions of two politically dissimilar authors? Or do their various constructions within the modern European cognitive architecture called the novel signal something beyond variant authorial subjectivities and ideologies?

Obviously, I have argued for the second interpretation. The novels published in literal Italy during the early "years of lead" (Ginzburg's, for example) set the represented "terrorists" in a community that also included the implied readers. The perpetrators of the violence, that is, belonged to the same group as the readers of the novels. In fact, as we have seen, Ginzburg's novel writes the "terrorist" Michele smack dab into a family romance of the Roman bourgeoisie and keeps any other possible "identity" context for the young prodigal at bay. Most important, this early familiarity between "terrorist" and reader includes the shared national identity, "Italian."

The early novelistic representations, and many representations found in short stories throughout the "years of lead," insist on this similarity as a significant element of the tragedy of Italian "terrorism."[25] In the early representations, "terrorism" is all the more tragic, that is, for being "Italian," for pitting "Italians" against each other in fratricidal combat echoing the civil war aspects of both the Risorgimento, according to Gramsci, and the Resistance. It is a plot line where Romulus and Remus are revisited as moderns, and the she-wolf still suckles them both.

By the early 1980s, however, the Italian body politic had suffered the closest thing to the Kennedy assassination in the United States that it had felt since the war. The Moro affair, including the refusal of Moro's own Christian Democratic Party to answer his captive pleas for the minimal cooperation that might have resulted in his release, had severely strained even the unwilling paternalistic tolerance that I discern in Ginzburg's novel and in much other contemporary discourse. In addition, the government itself had been racked with internal scandal, some of it related to governmental collusion with the Mafia and with fascist groups in the context of clandestine Masonic organizations, some of it related to the Vatican's own banking scandals, and much of it related to revelations of the *strage dello stato*. From the point of view of the dominant class, relative stability could be maintained only by locating the cause of all this malaise in something *other than* the state. The "terrorists," then, who had certainly contributed to the unrest of those years, were cast as its originators.

Such casting was carried out, precisely, in the novel—historically the most appropriate location for portraits of those who legitimately belong to the body politic and those who do not. With the historical congruence of the novel and the modern Western European nation-state in mind, therefore, I read the novels of Italian "terrorism" as ongoing reconstitutions, along the lines of Manzoni's model, of the nation-state, now apparently under siege. In fact, by 1982, with the publication of Castellaneta's novel, I am facing a textuality in which the implicit reader's community *no longer includes* the novel's "terrorist" characters. This refigured community prompts me to draw the following conclusion: from the point of view of the father of the bourgeois Italian family, a guarantor of the state, so to speak, the novelistic exile to abnormalcy and thus implicit non-Italianness of both radical left and fascist "terrorists" constitutes a heterogeneity of equivalence. The "terrorists" are now adults, as he is. Therefore, he is no longer responsible for them. In addition, they exemplify the marginal pathologies that clarify the centered norm, which is his. They are resident aliens, not *really* Italian. They thus begin to resemble both the postcolonial subjects immigrating to Italian cities and clichés of Middle Eastern "terrorists" operating on a global scale (see Graziella Parati in this volume; Bocca 1981; Pasquino 1984, 95–117).

Once again, I want to insist on the materiality of relations *outside* this novelistic system of representation just as I want to insist on the materiality of relations *within* it and *between* it and the social text. The social-historical-geopolitical Italian state literally exiled only the *pentiti* and, indirectly, Antonio Negri; it *actually* exiled many others, on both "sides," with long prison terms, recently themselves put into question by much dominant discourse as it returns, perhaps, to the trope of the prodigal child.

The alienation of the perpetrators of clandestine political violence from the community implied by the materiality of the novel that a mere decade earlier had included them as its children is an exercise in identity subversion performed by a deft, if heavy, hand. The problem is: how can a discourse exclude "terrorists" from the body politic *so that the cause of civic trouble may be located outside that body* when, in actuality, the "terrorists" are still Italians? The novel cannot realistically claim they are foreigners. It must, instead, institute operations of othering and demonization that show them as internal strangers, as resident aliens, and therefore *not quite* Italian because *not quite* the same as the implied reader's "us." This alienation, as I have said earlier, makes no distinction on the basis of the political ideology of the perpetrators except for the fact that there are more instances of it being done to the "terrorists" on the left than to the fascists.

The litero-social operation performed by the novel further shows that a textual cultural production can have an inherent class identity just as it can have an inherent national identity. Moreover, the novel's operation shows that these can prove mutually protective and endure long past the initial historical moment of the genre's ideological task.

Antonio Negri summed up one of the greatest lessons of the culture and the political violence of Italy's "years of lead" when he said that "with our awareness of the present we need to live a critique of the future" (Negri 1987, 10). As cultures renegotiate nationalisms, as social groups form that contradict national identity on a global scale, as people in many places move from the bullets and typesettings of nation-states toward something else, and as ever vaster numbers of people simply move, become refugees, resident aliens, denizens where there used to be citizens (Agamben 1993), I take several lessons from the Italian novels of the "years of lead." Most important, the Italian novel of "terrorism" demonstrates the socially constitutive power of cultural production. Further, it shows that such power often has a class ideology. Negri's own insistence on the contemporary significance of the changed and changing proletariat comes to mind here, for it reinforces from a critical perspective the same image of "terrorists" that the novels, *even including Ginzburg's early one,* employ: whereas the exile of the bourgeois "terrorist" characters is first literary and later, in specific instances, historical, the exile of the proletariat from this social text of terror is first historical and then, in specific instances, literary. Proletarian characters rarely appear in novels of Italian "terrorism." They are outside it almost entirely, exiled—*but as adults*—to the short story, where all their eloquence is anecdotal. But that, quite literally, is another story.

## Notes

1. I have found no satisfactory definition of "terrorism." In fact, my studies have convinced me that the term is most generally used as an indication of forms of violence not acceptable to the user of the term. "Terrorism" is therefore a cipher word that indicates more about the person using it than about the events to which it refers. Because it is such, and so as not to claim any agency myself for the infinitely varying ideological stances indicated by its use, I place it in quotation marks. It is not my word.

2. This epochology derives from a consensus that the bombing in Milan's Piazza Fontana in 1969 (at first attributed to anarchists and only years later to the fascists who, in collusion with the Italian secret service, had actually been responsible for it) marks the beginning of the *anni di piombo.* Those who seek historical causality for this event and the strategy from which it resulted (called the "state massacre," or *strage dello stato*) reach back to the near coup by the military in 1964 (this interpretation was held by Aldo Moro and elaborated by him during his own imprisonment by the Red Brigades [Corsini and Novati 1985, 22off.; Borraccetti 1986, 42ff.]). Consensus on

when the "years of lead" ended is harder to ascertain. Books dealing with this tend to identify the end of the era as the year previous to their own publication. The political scientist Giorgio Galli places it in 1982 because by then the paramilitary forces of the government had been strengthened to a degree that in his opinion would prevent further incidents. I situate it in 1983 because that was when a "terrorist" incident occurred that could no longer clearly be interpreted as such. When an economics professor who had spoken against graduated taxes was shot and killed outside his office at the University of Rome that year, there were no longer any valid interpretative strategies left, and no one could say who had done the deed or why. Without an interpretative key, the point of the event was moot, and what once might have been "terrorism" now revealed itself as only a crime. See della Porta and Pasquino (1983), Galleni (1981), and Galli (1986).

3. I use "fascist" rather than the more common "neofascist" because "neofascist" generally tends to indicate fascist ideology and activity since the end of World War II. Like "neorealist," it contains the metaphor of derivation and reworking. I choose, instead, the term "fascist" without the prefix, indicating thereby the continuity of an ideology within peninsular Italian culture without suggesting that this particular ideology died and then, a generation or two later, was resuscitated by fresh new persons. My own studies do not find any postwar death of fascism, only its temporary political defeat.

4. Some of the activists in the student movement at the University of Trent who later either founded or joined clandestine groups on the left and who identified themselves with what they perceived to be the interests of the proletariat were for the most part privileged university students from the dominant class, what in the United States might be called the middle and upper-middle class. Studies identifying the class provenance of fascist perpetrators are scant, though the main figures of the 1960s and early 1970s would seem in general to come from the same class as did those on the clandestine left. The class makeup, at least of groups on the left, changed over time, so that the second generation of perpetrators was drawn from more marginalized social classes, in particular disaffected working-class youth. See della Porta and Pasquino (1983, 19–38).

5. By "social text," I emphasize the fact that events produce meanings. See Jameson (1981, 35), for a helpful clarification of history as an absent cause and not a text.

6. See, in particular, the "Basic Concepts" section of Williams (1977).

7. Lyric representations in Italian of the clandestine political violence of the "years of lead" in fact demonstrate so wide a gamut of authorial and/or textual ideologies that they provide a telling example of the genre's relative lack of structural causality, a lack that may be expected given the lengthy history of the lyric.

8. Oppositional productions may of course be staged within a given genre, even one as ideologically determined as the novel. Novels in Italian that, with varying degrees of success, present nondominant discourses related to the "years of lead" in literal Italy include Nanni Balestrini's La violenza illustrata (1976) and Gli invisibili (1987), Andrea De Carlo's Uccelli da gabbia e da voliera (1982), and Renato Curcio's WKHY (1984).

9. I refer the reader to Jameson's discussion of Althusser in "On Interpretation" (Jameson 1981), especially pages 23–43.

10. The theoretical models for this social operation I find most helpful include the habitus posited by Bourdieu (though it fails to account for the ways in which cultural production can be used as resistance and subversion and thus appears to me to be too rigid), Althusser's notion of structural causality as articulated in Reading Capital (and glossed by Jameson [1981]), Jameson's own notion of the political unconscious (1981), Kenneth Burke's notion of internalization, the material nature of discourse as described

by Laclau and Mouffe (1985), and the enduring stratified notion of interpretation dating from medieval exegesis according to which imaginative texts accede to transtextual significance.

11. See, for instance, Bocca on *catocomunismo* (Bocca 1981, 1) and Ricci in Curcio and Rostagno (1980).

12. In the autumn of 1993, Italian newspapers were filled with coverage of the appeals trials then being conducted in connection with the Bologna train station bombing of August 2, 1980. In their defense, the fascists Francesca Mambro and Valerio Fioravanti, a married couple serving life sentences for a long series of murders and robberies conducted in the name of fascist (also called "black") "terrorism," claimed that they had been unjustly accused as perpetrators of this massacre by members of the secret service who wanted the investigation to be directed away from the service itself ("Noi, intrappolati dai servizi" [we were trapped by the secret services], in *La Repubblica*, Sunday, October 10/Monday, October 11, 1993, 6).

13. See note 1 to Antonio Negri in this volume.

14. The reapplication of the fascist laws strengthened the powers of the state apparatus, in particular those of the carabinieri, the national police force, which was then in a position to investigate, arrest, and prosecute powerful mafiosi with greater success than before.

15. Consumers of California wines may have noticed some improvements in the vintages produced in the Napa Valley during the 1980s. Such improvements may be due in part at least to graftings brought to California by wealthy Italian winegrowers who were seeking capital investments outside Italy. For a discussion of the mid-1970s economic crisis in literal Italy, see Ginsborg (1990, 351–54).

16. See Peci (1983, 49), for example.

17. See Ferrarotti (1979), who reads an increase in rapes of women in Rome during the mid-1970s as implicitly a fascist attack on the state. This is yet another instance in which the female body is symbolically congruent with the body politic or the state itself, a theme reaching back at least to the widely troped story of Lucrezia in Italian culture (Allen 1987, 1996).

18. This romantic fascination with the radical, antistate criminal is due, I believe, to several culturally specific factors, including the traditional legendary status of bandit-heroes on the Italian peninsula, the general mistrust of the state in literal Italy, long the site of foreign oppression, the association of post-1960s fascism with the state, and a kind of clichéd association of leftist politics, when these are perceived as being against the state, with old-fashioned anarchy, antistate by definition. For a discussion of the history and political status of banditry in Italy, see Hobsbawm (1969).

19. The notorious arrests of leftist intellectuals on April 7, 1979, and their subsequent "preventive" imprisonments and eventual trials, which went on for years and ended in many cases with exoneration, is a limit case of the politically motivated actions taken by the state. See Negri (1979, 1985), Ottaviano (1993, vol. 3), *Metropoli* (1981), Allen (spring 1987), Agamben (1990), Virno (1990).

20. This is particularly evident, for example, in her letter of December 12, 1970, where her complaints about her son might qualify her, given a radically different social context, for a maternal role in a Woody Allen film.

21. See note 4.

22. Another instance of this occurs later in the narrative, when Marina/Bruna and her lover, who is also living clandestinely, bend some of the group's regulations in order to spend time together. I personally find it difficult to avoid imposing a kind of hopeful story ending that would occur sometime long after *Ombre*'s plots end; that is, I would

have Marina/Bruna following her nascent feminist intuitions, which are sprinkled throughout the narration and consist mostly in a sporadic awareness of her own gender subjugation by her male comrades, and going off to join a consciousness-raising group, thus participating in the early stages of the peninsular feminisms active during the "years of lead." This hypothetical reading is not entirely unfounded. Shades of feminism *as a substitute for terrorism* are implied not only in *Ombre* but also in other, transnational, novels about "terrorism," Doris Lessing's *The Good Terrorist*, for example.

23. His namelessness, which would enable him to be called *l'innominato* in Italian, brings Manzoni's novel to mind once again. Readers familiar with Manzoni's novel might find it easy, as I do, to conflate the strongest obstacle to unification in that novel with the fascist character in Castellaneta's work. A major difference, however, is that Manzoni overcomes the impediment to unification imposed by the Innominato by having that character experience a remarkable conversion to Christianity. In Castellaneta's novel, the fascist simply experiences a well-organized, international change of venue.

24. See notes 8 and 25.

25. In order to follow the constitutive litero-social operation I trace here, see works cited by Camon (1975), Castellaneta (1984), Curcio (1984), and Lapponi et al (1983). See also Nanni Balestrini, *La violenza illustrata* (Turin: Einaudi, 1976), *Gli invisibili* (Milan: Bompiani, 1987), and *Vogliamo Tutto* (Milan: Mondadori, 1988); Gianni Cocconi, *Champagne Molotov* (Milan: Editrice Italia letteraria, 1987); Piero Del Giudice, *Le nude cose: lettere dallo "speciale"* (Milan: Spirali, 1983); Paola De Luca, "Giovedì," in Rosaria Guacci and Bruna Miorelli, eds., *Racconta 2* (Milan: La Tartaruga, 1993); Melo Freni, *Le passioni di Petra* (Florence: Valecchi, 1985); Alberto Magnaghi, *Un'idea di libertà* (Rome: manifestolibri, 1985); Giuliano Naria, *I giardini di Atrebil* (Rome: manifestolibri, 1985).

# Works Cited

Agamben, Giorgio. 1990. *La comunità che viene*. Turin: Einaudi. Trans. Michael Hardt, *The Coming Community*, Minneapolis: University of Minnesota Press, 1993.
———. 1993. "Noi rifugiati." *Luogo comune*. Year 3, no. 4 (June): 1–5.
Allen, Beverly. 1987a. "The Telos, Trope and Topos of Italian Terrorism." *Substance* (fall): 37–43.
———. 1987b. "A Terrorism Book Report." *Journal: A Contemporary Art Magazine* (spring): 8–14.
———. 1989. "Terrorism, Feminism, Sadism: The Clichéing of Experience in the Brand-Name Novel." *Art & Text* (winter–summer in Northern Hemisphere): 75–79.
———. 1992a. "One Nation by Terror: Italian National Identity since the *compromesso storico*." *Italica* 69:2: 161–76.
———. 1992b. "Qualche appunto sulla crisi dell'*identità* nazionale in letteratura." *Le voci della poesia: Quaderni di cultura letteraria* 1: 70–73.
———. 1996. *Rape Warfare: The Hidden Genocide in Bosnia-Herzegovina and Croatia*. Minneapolis: University of Minnesota Press.
Althusser, Louis, and Étienne Balibar. 1970. *Reading Capital*. Trans. Ben Brewster. New York: Pantheon.
Bakhtin, Mikhail. 1979. *Estetica e romanzo*. Turin: Einaudi.
Bale, Jeffrey M. 1989. "Right-wing Terrorists and the Extraparliamentary Left in Post–World War 2 Europe: Collusion or Manipulation?" *Lobster* 18 (October): 2–18.

Baudrillard, Jean. 1993. *The Transparency of Evil: Essays on Extreme Phenomena.* Trans. James Benedict. London and New York: Verso.

Benjamin, Walter. 1978. "Critique of Violence." *Reflections.* New York and London: Harcourt Brace Jovanovich. 277–300.

Bocca, Giorgio. 1981. *Il terrorismo italiano 1970–1980.* Milan: Rizzoli.

Borraccetti, Vittorio. 1986. *Eversione di destra, terrorismo, stragi: i fatti e l'intervento giudiziario.* Milan: Franco Angeli.

Bourdieu, Pierre. 1977. *Outline of a Theory of Practice.* Cambridge: Cambridge University Press.

Burke, Kenneth. 1973. *The Philosophy of Literary Form.* Berkeley, Los Angeles, and London: University of California Press.

Camon, Ferdinando. 1975. *Occidente.* Milan: Garzanti.

Castellaneta, Carlo. 1982. *Ombre.* Milan: Mondadori.

———. 1984. *Da un capo all'altro della città.* Milan: Rizzoli.

Cornell, Drusilla. 1991. *Beyond Accommodation: Ethical Feminism, Deconstruction, and the Law.* New York and London: Routledge.

Corsini, Paolo, and Laura Novati, eds. 1985. *L'eversione nera: Cronache di un decennio (1974–1984).* Milan: Franco Angeli.

Curcio, Renato. 1984. *WKHY.* Rome: Fatamorgana.

Curcio, Renato, and Mauro Rostagno. 1980. *Fuori dai denti.* Milan: Gammalibri.

della Porta, Donatella, and Gianfranco Pasquino, eds. 1983. *Terrorismo e violenza politica.* Bologna: Il Mulino.

Ferrarotti, Franco. 1979. *Alle radici della violenza.* Milan: Rizzoli.

Galleni, Mauro, ed. 1981. *Rapporto sul terrorismo: le stragi, gli agguati, i sequestri, le sigle 1969–1980.* Milan: Rizzoli.

Galli, Giorgio. 1986. *Storia del partito armato 1968–1982.* Milan: Rizzoli.

Ginsborg, Paul. 1990. *A History of Contemporary Italy: Society and Politics 1943–1988.* London: Penguin.

Ginzburg, Natalia. 1973. *Caro Michele.* Milan: Mondadori.

Gramsci, Antonio. 1991. *Letteratura e vita nazionale.* Rome: Editori Riuniti.

Hobsbawm, E. J. 1969. *Bandits.* New York: Delacorte.

———. 1990. *Nations and Nationalism since 1780: Programme, Myth, Reality.* Cambridge: Cambridge University Press.

Jameson, Fredric. 1981. *The Political Unconscious: Narrative as a Socially Symbolic Act.* Ithaca, N.Y.: Cornell University Press.

Laclau, Ernesto, and Chantal Mouffe. 1985. *Hegemony and Socialist Strategy: Towards a Radical Democratic Politics.* London and New York: Verso.

Lapponi, Paolo, Andrea Leoni, and Valerio Morucci. 1983. *L'idea fissa.* Rome: Lerici.

Lessing, Doris. 1986. *The Good Terrorist.* New York: Vintage Books.

Lukács, Georg. 1971. *Theory of the Novel: A Historico-Philosophical Essay on the Forms of Great Epic Literature.* Cambridge: MIT Press.

Manzoni, Alessandro. 1954. *I promessi sposi.* Milan: Mondadori.

*Metropoli.* 1981. No. 6 (September).

Negri, Antonio. 1979. *Marx oltre Marx.* Milan: Feltrinelli.

———. 1985. *Italie Rouge et Noir: Journal Février 1983–Novembre 1983.* Paris: Hachette.

———. 1987. *Lenta ginestra: saggio sull'ontologia di Giacomo Leopardi.* Milan: SugarCo.

Ottaviano, Franco. 1993. *La rivoluzione nel labirinto: sinistra e sinistrismo dal 1956 agli anni ottanta.* Soveria Mannelli/Messina: Rubbettino.

Pansa, Giampaolo. 1980. *Storie italiane di violenza e terrorismo*. Bari: Laterza.

Pasquino, Gianfranco, ed. 1984. *La prova delle armi*. Bologna: Il Mulino.

Peci, Patrizio. 1983. *Io l'infame*. Milan: Mondadori.

Sanguinetti, Gianfranco. 1982. *On Terrorism and the State: The Theory and Practice of Terrorism Divulged for the First Time*. London: Aldgate Press.

Tabucchi, Antonio. 1985. *Piccoli equivoci senza importanza*. Milan: Feltrinelli.

Virno, Paolo, ed. 1990. *Sentimenti dell'al di quà*. Rome: Theoria. Rev. and trans. as *Radical Thought in Italy: A Potential Politics*, ed. Paolo Virno and Michael Hardt. Minneapolis: University of Minnesota Press, 1996.

Wagner-Pacifici, Robin. 1986. *Terrorism as Social Drama*. Chicago: University of Chicago Press.

Watt, Ian. 1957. *The Rise of the Novel: Studies in Defoe, Richardson and Fielding*. Berkeley and Los Angeles: University of California Press.

Williams, Raymond. 1977. *Marxism and Literature*. Oxford and New York: Oxford University Press.

Zanzotto, Andrea. 1986. *Idioma*. Milan: Mondadori.

# "Italy" in Italy: Old Metaphors and New Racisms in the 1990s

*David Ward*

The title of a recent book, *Milano-Palermo: La nuova Resistenza* (Milan-Palermo, the new resistance), by Nando Dalla Chiesa, a leading exponent of one of Italy's youngest and fastest-growing political movements, La Rete (the network), illustrates succinctly the main argument of the present essay: namely, that fascism and resistance, in the form of tropes, remain crucial events in the Italian collective memory even for members of Dalla Chiesa's generation, who were born well after the end of World War II and received their political education in the 1960s and 1970s.[1] The essay will explore how fascism and resistance, along with the Risorgimento, are Italy's privileged tropes in the light of which today's political events are understood. The essay will also examine how such tropes have assumed a form of agency that influences, but also limits, how those events are acted on.

The title of Dalla Chiesa's book places Italian civil society's responses to the twin crises, represented by Milan (the widespread political corruption exposed by Judge Antonio Di Pietro and the "Mani pulite" [clean hands] operation) and Palermo (organized crime, especially in the wake of the murders in 1992 of judges Giovanni Falcone and Paolo Borsellino), on a continuum with the Resistance movement. The title suggests that Italian civil society's response to these two emergencies is analogous to the Resistance movement's response to fascism from the spring of 1943 to the spring/summer of 1945. As Dalla Chiesa has found a powerful historical precedent for his own movement's activities in the antifascist Resistance movement, so fifty years ago Partisans cast around for a precedent against which they could measure and name their own heroic actions. Many of them found this reference point in the Risorgimento, the movement that led to the unification of Italy as a single state in the second half of the nineteenth century. The Resistance movement, then, was tacked onto the Risorgimento as a "secondo Risorgimento." But antifascist Partisans were not alone in seizing on the Risorgimento trope, which, in fact, crossed ideological lines in surprising ways. The mantle of the true heir to the Risorgimento experience, for example, was contested by political movements that were at the ideological antipodes from one another. In the 1920s, for example, even Italian fascists had figured themselves as heirs to the Risorgimento legacy.

We find clear evidence of the centrality of the trope in the way that both fascism and the Resistance laid claims on the Risorgimento hero Giuseppe Garibaldi. While Communist-led Resistance groups named their armed bands after the hero of two worlds, twenty years earlier, as a film like *Il grido d'acquila* (The eagle's cry) shows, fascist thugs had also been quick to appropriate the Garibaldian legacy and put themselves forward as the continuation of the historical narrative he had initiated.[2] The hero of two worlds, then, became the hero of two ideologies.[3]

If both the Italian Resistance and fascist traditions attempted to establish a sense of continuity between Italy's Risorgimento past and their respective visions of a new Italy, the presence on the political scene in the late 1980s and 1990s of a new protagonist—the "Lega lombarda" (Lombard League)—would seem to constitute a discontinuity between the Risorgimento past and Italy's future. Certainly, the Lombard League, whose main manifesto promise is to create a tripartite federal Italy divided into semiautonomous republics, has no interest in establishing itself as the continuation of Garibaldi's narrative. This is not to say, however, that the League does not see itself as heir to a prior tradition. We get an idea of the kind of legacy the League seeks to buy into if we take note of a number of tendencies: first, the League's militants often dress up in crusader-like costumes on the occasion of political demonstrations; second, the League idolizes the figure of Alberto da Giussano, a mythical Milanese soldier who in 1176 led the Lombard communes in the battle of Legnano against Frederick I—Barbarossa;[4] and third, the League stages its important political manifestations at Pontida where Di Giussano brought together the representatives of the independent Lombard communes to fight the battle of Legnano. Clearly, the League is attempting to estab-

lish itself as the heir to a Lombard-based tradition of political autonomy and aggressive self-defense against a perceived foe.

If the Resistance is the privileged trope for civil society's response to
emergencies, by the same token fascism has become the privileged
trope for describing the perceived dangers present in developments in
contemporary Italian society. Matching the calls for a new Resistance,
which have come from many quarters, including the ex-Partisan Oscar
Luigi Scalfaro, the president of the republic, whose own election owed
much to the need to disinter Resistance ideals in difficult times, there
have been warnings that a new fascism is on the horizon.

The meteoric rise of the League, for example, has often been likened
to the rise of fascism, despite evidence that would argue for caution.[5]
Unlike Mussolini's Fascist Party, for example, the League is not a national force. It proposes a tripartite, semiautonomous federalist Italy
as a means of wrenching power and financial clout from the Roman
bureaucracy that, in the eyes of its supporters, damages the wealth
and well-being of the northern provinces. And whereas fascism was
an antidemocratic, violent movement, the League has always played
by the rules of parliamentary democracy, if only because they work in
its favor. Nor does the League use or advocate the use of violence.

By far the most elaborate attempt to draw analogies between the
two periods belongs to the weekly magazine *L'Espresso*. In the November 1, 1992, edition, under the title "Vediamo se Bossi è un altro
Mussolini" (Let's see if Bossi [the leader of the Lombard League] is
another Mussolini), Piero Ottone, a well-respected journalist not
given to gratuitous sensationalism, draws an elaborate map of equivalencies between the early 1920s and the early 1990s. In particular, he
establishes analogies between the politicians of then and now: the former king, Vittorio Emanuele III, is Scalfaro; Umberto Bossi is Benito
Mussolini; Giuliano Amato, the former prime minister, is Luigi Facta,
Mussolini's immediate liberal predecessor; another former prime
minister, Giulio Andreotti, is Giovanni Giolitti; Bettino Craxi is the
fascist Roberto Farinacci; Alberto Ronchey, the minister for cultural
affairs, is Benedetto Croce; Mino Martinazzoli, secretary of the Christian Democratic Party is Don Luigi Sturzo; Gianfranco Miglio, the
League's theoretician, is Gabriele D'Annunzio; Achille Occhetto, leader
of the Democratic Party of the Left, is Filippo Turati, the Socialist
Party leader of the 1920s.

Similarly, the "Mani pulite" anticorruption campaign has been depicted as a new Resistance against a new fascism. At the beginning of March 1993, to commemorate the fiftieth anniversary of the strikes in Turin, which for many heralded the beginning of the Resistance movement, "Raitre," the once Communist Party-controlled TV channel, now in the hands of the Democratic Party of the Left, drew an explicit parallel between the catalyzing effect of those strikes on the Italian people in 1943 and the work of Di Pietro in 1993. If the 1943 strikes paved the way for the Resistance to fascism, the news report implied, then "Mani pulite" was paving the way for Resistance against the new fascism.

And in the spring of 1993, in Prime Minister Giuliano Amato's resignation speech, fascism was once again used to figure Italy's present crisis. Amato's speech to the parliament on April 21, 1993, suggested that the failure of Italy's First Republic, founded after the end of World War II out of the embers of the Resistance movement, lay in its continuities with the earlier fascist regime. In particular, Amato underlined how one of the distinguishing marks of Italian fascism, the Fascist Party's occupation of the state, had been carried on into the postfascist era by the political parties' continued tendency to "place" their men and women in positions of power and influence. The only difference, continued Amato, was that whereas under fascism one party had dominated the state, in the postfascist era that same dominance had been exercised by several parties from across the political spectrum.[6]

To the best of my knowledge, Amato did not intend to suggest that postfascist Italy, despite its continuities with fascism, was antidemocratic, or was a regime. The reaction to Amato's remark was, however, violent in the extreme. Two fathers of postfascist Italian democracy, Norberto Bobbio and the former Communist trade-union leader Luciano Lama, went on record as saying that Amato had offended Italy's postfascist First Republic.[7] It must be remembered that Amato's remark was made in the context of a highly charged speech delivered in the Italian parliament, and not an academic environment. Had the remark been made in a classroom or in a scholarly article, Amato, who is a university professor, may well have been able to explain more fully the terms of the parallel he sought to draw between fascist and postfascist Italy. As it stood, however, the remark, and the responses it solicited, act as a reminder that references to fascism continue to irritate an exposed nerve that Italian culture has not yet been able to close. If any lesson can be drawn from this episode, it is that caution needs to be exercised when using fascism as an analogy to describe Italy's present ills. This is not because postfascist Italian society shares no continuities with the way fascist Italy was structured. I doubt whether even the most avid supporters of the Italy born of the Resistance movement would deny that some important continuities with the structures of the fascist regime persist. But what the reaction to Amato's speech pinpointed most accurately is the intrinsic sensitivity still attached to the term "fascist" in today's Italian political discourse. Even though Amato did not suggest that Italian society was anything less than a fully functioning democracy, both Lama and Bobbio found it easy to rebut his argument by listing the democratic credentials of Italy's postfascist First Republic. But this was hardly the point that Amato had wanted to raise.

The heavy-handed way the analogy with fascism was handled by Amato and in the earlier *L'Espresso* example does allow us, however, to focus on the limits connected to seeking equivalencies between past and present events: when we bring present events into a continuum with past ones, the former lose their uniqueness and become faded replicas of the latter. This can have damaging and even tragic effects.[8] In an article titled "Se la storia fa la faccia feroce" (If history pulls a ferocious face), published in *La Stampa* on December 14, 1992, Gianni Vattimo draws attention to how our responses to contemporary violence may be blighted by the limits of processes similar to the ones I have sketched out here. There is a general feeling, he writes, that the episodes of violence that have marked the contemporary world are not central to the West's course of history and are destined ultimately to disappear: the violence in the ex-Yugoslavia, for example, is a residue of a barbaric past that other Western countries have left behind; the fundamentalist violence of some parts of the Islamic world will disappear as the process of secularization makes greater headway; and the Naziskin violence of the ex-German Democratic Republic, Roman proletarian ghetto, and elsewhere in Europe is an example of an inevitable by-product of contemporary society that will be eliminated as material well-being increases in the underprivileged sectors of society out of which that violence is presumed to come.

This kind of analysis of present-day events, argues Vattimo, comes from a deeply rooted Western belief in the progressive, emancipatory nature of history. The danger he perceives in such a view is that it tends to "perform" events, figuring them according to the prior dictates of a gradually unfolding, progressive narrative. The result is an understanding of violence as something that is marginal to the course of history and that has the effect of leaving us defenseless and ill prepared for any "unexpected change in the style of history," slow to understand and respond to a situation where violence may not be marginal, but the order of the day, and require responses that treat it as such.

Turning now to the second part of the essay, I would like to suggest that the major limits in using fascism and Resistance as, respectively, metaphors of and response to crisis, can be seen in the shortcomings of Italian, but also European, civil and political societies' reaction to recent outbreaks of racist violence and intolerance. I would like to suggest that some of the limits of the antiracist movements in Europe derive from the limits already inherent in the antifascist movements of the 1920s, 1930s, and 1940s. Put as briefly as possible, as I see it, the major limits of mainstream European antifascism are, first, the lack of introspective analysis in its characterization of fascism as a phenomenon external to those societies that had experienced fascism, either as a regime or as a movement; and second, the proposal of a non- or antifascist society based predominantly on a vision of the future that is elaborated at the expense of a revision of the past. Postfascist responses to Europe's fascist past, with few but notable exceptions like the Partito d'azione (Action Party) in Italy, are characterized by a general lack of introspection.[9] In Italy and France, the possibility that the fascist regimes and movements that governed all or part of both countries may have had internal causes was, in the immediate postfascist period, only considered superficially even by many of the most convinced antifascists. Neither the Marxist contention that fascism could be put down to the decadence of the bourgeoisie nor, in a specifically Italian context, Benedetto Croce's characterizations of fascism as an imported disease or barbarian invasion did anything to encourage reflection on where and how the history of liberty, either in its liberal or Marxist versions, might have run into a blind alley.[10]

Croce restated on many occasions his conviction that fascism was alien to Italians and Italian culture. He supports this view with reference to the lack of Nazi-style anti-Semitism in Italy, the many attempts to hide Italian Jews when the racial laws came into effect in the late 1930s, and the good treatment afforded Austrian prisoners during

World War II.[11] Although there can be no doubting the historical truth of these episodes and the bravery of those Italian citizens who risked their own lives to protect Italian Jews, to elevate their experience to the level of an interpretative key with which to unlock the entirety of the Italian fascist experience, as Croce did, does little to encourage a more introspective and potentially painful self-analysis that may reveal deeper complicities with fascism.

The conviction that Italian fascism has no real roots in Italian society and is but a pale shadow of Nazi-fascism is at the base of the question asked by Paolo Flores d'Arcais in his article "Macchia nera" (Black stain), written in October 1992 for the weekly satirical magazine *Cuore* (Heart)—"Settimanale di Resistenza Umana" (Weekly of human resistance).[12] On the occasion of a demonstration organized by the extreme right-wing Movimento Sociale Italiano (Italian Social Movement), which saw fifty thousand neofascists march through the streets of Rome and on to Piazza Venezia, and noting the general indifference with which the march had been greeted by press and public opinion, Flores d'Arcais asks what the reaction would have been had fifty thousand German neofascists marched through Berlin and on to the Brandenburg Gate.

On the other hand, the assumed benign nature of Italian fascism has been exploited by astute politicians for their own purposes. The cartoonist Giorgio Forattini often depicted Bettino Craxi, the former leader of the Italian Socialist Party, as a Mussolini figure, dressed in a black shirt and knee-length boots, adopting Mussolini-like body language. To the best of my knowledge, Craxi made no serious attempt to protest against these cartoons or block their publication, whereas on other occasions he was quick to defend any attack made on the integrity of his public image. In fact, the only time he threatened to take legal action against Forattini was when he stopped depicting him as a Mussolini figure and drew him as a member of the "Banda Bassotti," in other words as a thief. The Mussolini analogy did nothing to damage Craxi's political reputation and future, and even did a great deal to enhance it. He was a canny enough politician to realize that he could make political ground out of the analogy with Mussolini by using it to promote himself as the "decisionista" (decision maker), "l'uomo con le palle" (the man with balls), the man able and willing to make the quick, sharp decisions that the quagmire of Italian postwar politics had lacked. At the same time, he realized that the analogy with Mussolini, understood as a threat to Italian democratic life, would neither stick by branding Craxi as a danger, nor jeopardize his party in electoral terms (see figures 1 and 2).

As the intellectuals and militants gathered around the Action Party argued in the immediate postwar years, though no one paid much attention, the conviction that fascism was a parenthesis in the otherwise unsullied course of Italian history was the major shortcoming and mistake of antifascist strategies. It was this conviction that allowed the Action Party's purge proposals to be diluted and prefascist Italy to be proposed as a model on which to base postfascist Italy.[13] It also played an important role in preventing Italy from being refounded along the new, less Italian, lines that the Action Party militants had in mind. These shortcomings, which are part of a tradition of European reluctance to submit the bases of its own wealth, power, and success to scrutiny, which the antifascist movements took on board, have also had a negative impact on the way both government policies and antiracist groups have attempted to meet the new antifascist challenge against European racism.

Summed up in the expression "Fortress Europe," government and European Community immigration policies are a striking example of the refusal to recognize the racism that is latent within European societies. It was only after serious outbursts of racist violence in several countries that European governments began to tighten up their immigration laws and restrict the rights of immigrants or asylum seekers to cross their borders and establish residence. The implicit effect of this policy was to see the cause of the violence not in the European racists, neo-Nazis, and thugs, but in the immigrants themselves. From victims of racist violence, immigrants found themselves figured as its cause.

As to the antiracist movements, a similar process can be seen in what has been called "anti-razzismo psicho-analitico" (psychoanalytic antiracism) and "antirazzismo facile" (easy antiracism).[14] While the former tends to exorcise the racist and transform racism into a question of sickness, madness, or ignorance, the latter—in the manner of Benetton clothes, Mulino Bianco cookies, Barilla pasta, and Philadelphia cheese advertising campaigns[15]—tends to see the antiracist struggle as a twenty-four-hour multicultural party and completely ignores the inequities of power, command, privilege, and language that, at the very least, problematize even the most well-meaning attempts to es-

Fig 1. February 1987. The daily newspaper *Repubblica* introduces a new prize competition called *Portfolio*. Balloon: (Craxi): "How I like this newspaper now that it has *Portfolio*!" By kind permission of Giorgio Forattini.

Fig. 2. November 1989. At a meeting of the Central Committee, Achille Occhetto [the then leader of the Italian Communist Party] proposes that the party change its name. Balloon: (Craxi, leading Occhetto by the hand): "Listen to what your daddy says: I'll take you to Registry office if you want to change your name!" By kind permission of Giorgio Forattini.

tablish democratic dialogue between citizens from the developed and the developing worlds.

Such a mode of conducting the struggle against racism overlooks how the strategies of the politically organized racist groups have changed. Racist arguments against immigration no longer bear on the question of the biological inferiority of the immigrant, for that is now untenable in scientific terms. Rather, racist strategies bear now not so much on the fear of difference, but the fear of equality. For racist groups, the threat now posed by the immigrant is to the integrity of the host country's culture, which they fear risks being diluted by the bearers of other, antithetical cultures.[16] A glance at some of the graffiti in Rome's peripheral quarters attests to this shift in strategy: "Un unico popolo, un'unica cultura" (A single people, a single culture); "A ogni popolo la propria storia, a ogni popolo la propria cultura" (To each people its own history, to each people its own culture); "Immigration, cimitero dei popoli" (Immigration, graveyard of the peoples); or, referring to Aaron Winter, a black Dutch soccer player bought by Lazio, who was thought to be Jewish (but was not): "Per la purezza della Lazio" (For the purity of Lazio), which in Italian echoes "Per la purezza della razza" (For the purity of the race).

In this battle against the perceived threat of a foreign invasion, organized racist groups, in calling for a "Resistenza europea" (European resistance)—another piece of Roman graffiti—attempt to place themselves on a line of continuity with the Resistance struggle against the Nazi, the foreign invader of the country's supposed geographical and cultural integrity, to give their own movement a sense of continuity with a heroic past. These racist groups have been able to locate themselves into the continuum of an antifascist tradition not because they are not fascists, but because they have been able to exploit that aspect of the Resistance that antifascism chose to privilege: namely, the Resistance not so much as a class or civil war (although it was also that), but as a national war of liberation fought by Italy against a foreign invader.[17] The analogy that the "Resistenza europea" slogan seeks to draw is that the same threat posed in the 1940s by an invasion of Nazi culture to the integrity of Italy is now posed by immigrant culture. It is also in such terms that the racism of the Lombard League is best described. Theirs is an attempt to replace Italy's political boundaries, redraw them along cultural lines to protect the integrity of their "northern" culture and figure both non-Italian and southern Italian immigrants as threats to that integrity.

To be sure, there is a great deal of opportunism in the racist right's attempts to create for itself a patriotic dignity that it otherwise would not have, and there is every reason to sympathize with those Partisans who quite understandably hit the roof when they see how their ideals have been hijacked. On the other hand, the very fact that organized racist groups have been able to suggest the analogy is a sign of the limits in the way the Resistance movement chose to characterize itself. The Resistance, in fact, was unable to elaborate an idea of the antifascist struggle that was not largely synonymous with a national struggle against a foreign enemy who posed threats to the nation's integrity.

Let me conclude with some brief remarks on what I see as recent attempts to promote a more introspective, self-critical culture on the basis of which more effective antiracist strategies can be elaborated. It goes without saying that this groundwork is being done on a daily basis by those groups and individuals whose antiracism takes the form of ensuring that the members of the immigrant community receive welfare, enjoy social rights, and have decent living conditions. It is in the cultural field of what is known vaguely as the "sinistra sommersa" (underground left), that part of the left that does not fit neatly into any one of the traditional left-wing political formations, that there are signs of a more self-critical approach. The work of Michele Serra, for example, the former editor of the satirical weekly magazine *Cuore*, is aimed at the construction of a less complacent, more self-critical notion of Italian identity.[18]

In an article written for *L'Unità*, Serra proposes that a "substantive antifascism" must be based on a deep revision of the "customs and culture of every Italian citizen."[19] Serra's article was provoked by the insult *pederasta* (faggot) shouted at Giorgio La Malfa, then a member of parliament, representing the Republican Party, by Lombard League supporters during a political demonstration. It is at the level of basic culture or *costume* that Serra locates the most urgent need for a reform of the Italian self. In a similar direction, I would also like to draw attention to a recent book by Franco Berardi, better known in political circles as Bifo, a former leader of the "creative wing" of the Bologna student movement of the late 1970s. He has recently published a pamphlet titled *Come si cura il Nazi* (How to cure the Nazi). Beyond the ingenuousness of some of the pamphlet's actual proposals, the most interesting aspect of this initiative is it that it touches on the same question of *costume* that Serra raises. Berardi's "cure" for the Nazi takes him on an excursion through authors like Gilles Deleuze and Félix Guattari and into areas of sexual politics, poetry, nationalism, race, and nonviolence. Drawing analogies between neo-Nazi aggression and the phallic aggression of their sexual politics, Berardi argues for the "ethics of touching," the sexuality based on kisses and caresses, rather than on penetration, that has figured in Elizabeth Badinter's recent work.[20] In a country where in recent times introspective reflection on *costume* has been limited, to say the least, Berardi's pamphlet marks a significant step in a new direction.

The cartoons drawn by Altan are also part of this general project. There is no sense at all in these cartoons, many of which feature people in the form of talking turds, that people are victims of circumstance, or that it is destiny that decides futures. Altan's cartoons signal a revision in self-image that sees Italians less as victims and more as architects of their own destiny. If the world is in a mess, it is because we are in a mess.

Altan's cartoons illustrate the change in self-image that has been forced on Italians, along with other Europeans, by the numerous outbreaks of racial violence and intolerance. The picture of Italian innocence, victims of the world, to which many of Croce's early postwar statements contributed, had put down strong enough roots to produce the widely held belief that Italy and Italians were immune from the rampant racism of other Western countries such as Great Britain, France, Germany, and the United States. The arrival of the first immigrant workers in Italy, and with it the many episodes of racial intolerance, have caused a radical rethinking of that self-image.

Another cartoon, this time not by Altan, but published in an October 1991 issue of *Cuore*, shows a bemused Italian being pursued by a German neo-Nazi while pursuing a black immigrant (see figure 3).

The cartoon refers to two episodes of racial intolerance that took place within a few days of each other, one in Frankfurt, Germany, where a group of Italians were attacked and beaten up by Naziskins, the other in Italy, where a group of Italians attacked and beat up immigrant workers. So, who is the Italian here in this cartoon? Victim of the neo-Nazi, as Italians have so often been figured and have figured themselves, or victimizer of the black immigrant? The cartoon captures the dilemma that not only the Italian but also the European self-

Fig. 3. "*RACISM IN GERMANY: BEWILDERMENT AMONG ITALIANS.*" Balloon:
"I don't know if I'm running after the black man or running away from the German!" (*Cuore*,
October 1991) By kind permission of *Cuore*.

image is experiencing: between an old and flattering self-image, the
product of a long humanistic tradition, the present viability of which
new social realities have questioned; and a new self-image that has not
yet been fully elaborated. I make no prediction as to the course such a
new self-image might take. If, however, that process of development is
not to be a repetition of past experience, it will have to be informed by
a new set of tropes. Let me suggest one, which comes from the European Resistance struggle, as a paradigm of the kind of self-critical, introspective culture that twentieth-century Europe has generally lacked.
I am thinking of the late Willi Brandt, who not only changed his
nationality from German to Norwegian to fight the Resistance war
against his former country, but also, as chancellor of the Federal Republic, publicly assumed responsibility and apologized for Germany's
treatment of the Jews.

## Notes

1. Nando Dalla Chiesa, *Milano-Palermo: La nuova Resistenza* (Milan: Baldini and
Castoldi, 1993).
2. See Giampiero Brunetta, *Storia del cinema italiano: 1895–1945* (Rome: Editori
Riuniti, 1979), 234–35; Claudio Pavone, "Le idee della Resistenza: Antifascisti e fascisti
di fronte alla tradizione del Risorgimento," *Passato e presente* 7 (January–February,
1959): 850–915; and Pierre Sorlin, *The Film in History* (Totowa, N.J.: Barnes and
Noble, 1980), 116–40.
3. Even after the Resistance struggle, the Risorgimento trope retains strong powers
of suggestion and legitimation. In the more recent mid-eighties, Bettino Craxi, then secretary of the Italian Socialist Party, made a pilgrimage to a variety of Garibaldian sites.
He made very explicit and highly visible efforts to establish analogies between what he
as prime minister was doing for Italian prestige in the world and what Garibaldi had
done a century or more before him.

4. In a recent television debate, the historian Arrigo Petacco has claimed that no Alberto da Giussano fought in the battle of Legnano. The figure, he continued, was invented a couple of centuries later by the Milan nobility. The source of the legend around Alberto da Giussano comes not from the battle, but from the poem "A parlamento" (At the parliament) by Giosu Carducci in which he erroneously writes that the Milan forces were led by such a figure.

5. After an incident when Lombard League militants insulted Giorgio La Malfa, the then leader of the small Republican Party, there was some debate in the Italian press as to whether or not these were acts of *squadrismo*, the tactics adopted by the violent thugs who terrorized fascism's political opponents in the early days of the regime. Most historians warned caution. See "Ma gli squadristi sono un'altra storia" (But fascist thugs are something different) by Loredana Bartoletti, in *La Repubblica*, July 9, 1992, for the reactions of historians like Giuseppe Galasso, Nicola Tranfaglia, Gaetano Arfè, Giuseppe Tamburrano, Gabriele De Rosa, and Lucio Villari.

6. Speaking of the political message of the April 1993 referendum vote, which introduced a "first past the post" electoral system for Italy's Senate in place of proportional representation, Amato's speech, as reported in the press, contained these lines: "The picture is clear. People want change and have indicated a path that is political, but above all institutional. This represents a genuine change of regime, which, after seventy years, will kill off the party-state model that fascism brought to Italy and that the [post-fascist] Republic inherited, but succeeded only in transforming from a single-party state to a plural-party state" (from "Con l'onore delle armi . . ." [With full military honors], unsigned leading article, *La Repubblica*, April 22, 1993). Amato's remarks were drawn from Luciano Canfora's book *La grande slavina* (The great avalanche) (Venice: Marsilio, 1993).

7. See "Amato offende la storia" (Amato offends history), interview with Luciano Lama by Pier Luigi Battista, and Norberto Bobbio, "Presidente, non faccia confusione" (President, you're confused), both in *La Stampa*, April 23, 1993. See also the speech by Giorgio Napolitano, the then president of the Italian Chamber of Deputies, reported in *La Stampa*, April 26, 1993, under the title "Napolitano: nessuna continuità fascismo-Repubblica" (Napolitano: no continuity with fascism).

8. As James E. Young has argued in his *Writing and Rewriting the Holocaust: Narrative and the Consequences of Interpretation* (Bloomington: Indiana University Press, 1988), Holocaust victims came to understand the events in Europe between the mid-1930s and the mid-1940s through the various names that had been given to those events: sho'ah; churban; and Holocaust, which only gained currency in the late 1950s. Both the terms sho'ah and churban draw on and contain in their etymons a specific tradition that may have led victims, Young and others have argued, to understand the Holocaust as the continuation of a traditional anti-Semitism that was certainly violent, painful, and terrible but, as had been the case in the past, ultimately survivable. As a result, they may have been ill prepared to face the unprecedented nature of the annihilation.

9. For the role of the Action Party in the immediate postwar years, see David Ward, *Antifascisms: Cultural Politics in Italy, 1943–46. Benedetto Croce and the Liberals, Carlo Levi and the "Actionists"* (Madison, N.J., and London: Fairleigh Dickinson University Press, 1996).

10. This is a reaction that is by no means confined to Italy and France, or those countries or parts of countries that had experienced full-blown fascist regimes. Up until recent work in the archives, it was current opinion in Great Britain that there had been no collaboration between the inhabitants of the Channel Islands—Jersey and Guernsey—and the Nazi forces that occupied them for part of World War II. The release of documents in the last few months, however, has revealed a pattern of collaboration, includ-

ing the supplying to the Nazi occupiers of the names and addresses of British and non-British Jews resident on the islands, that has shaken this conviction. The conviction itself seems to be based on nothing other than the deeply rooted belief that no British citizen, by virtue of simply being British, could possibly have collaborated with an enemy so antithetical to their values as the Nazi. So firmly held was this conviction, it seems, that even in the face of evidence of large-scale collaboration in other European countries occupied by the Nazis, only recently have serious attempts been made to go back to archives and documents and reread those years.

11. See Benedetto Croce, "I diritti dell'Italia nella vita internazionale solennemente affermati dall'alta parola di Benedetto Croce: Discorso fraternamente italiano" (Italy's rights in international life are solemnly stated in the lofty words of Benedetto Croce), *Il Risorgimento italiano* (Italian Risorgimento), September 22, 1944. Also in *Pagine politiche: Luglio–Dicembre 1944* (Political pages: July–December 1944) (Bari: Laterza, 1944), 97–116.

12. Paolo Flores d'Arcais, "Macchia nera," *Cuore*, October 26, 1992.

13. For details of Italy's postfascist purge, see Roy Palmer Domenico, *Italian Fascists on Trial: 1943–1948* (Chapel Hill: University of North Carolina Press, 1991).

14. See Giuliano Campano and Giuseppe Faso, "Intolleranza di fine secolo" (Fin-de-siècle intolerance), *La rivista dei libri* 3:2 (February 1993): 20–21.

15. One of the recent trends in Italy has been the presence of young, adopted Far Eastern girls in commercials. *Cuore* has a regular column in which texts of such advertisements are transcribed. Here is the text of the dialogue between Kaori, a Philippine girl, and her foster mother taken from a Philadelphia cheese advertisement:

> HOUSEWIFE (P): Kaori, will you give me a hand? My cousin Filippo is coming to lunch and he's a big eater (*una buona forchetta*).
> KAORI (K): Salmon, green beans, mushrooms, Piladelphia! [Kaori cannot pronounce the "ph" sound.]
> P: Ah! Ah! Ah! Green beans, mushrooms, and Philadelphia!
> [The dish is ready and at lunchtime they serve it.]
> P: Kaori made this for Filippo!
> K: Pi-lip-po buo-na por-chet-ta! [Kaori pronounces *forchetta* to sound like the Italian word for little pig.]
> FILIPPO: *Porchetta?*
> P: *Forchetta!!!* Kaori, you're inimitable (*sei unica*).
> K: Pi-la-del-pia *unico!*

16. See Pierre-André Taguieff, "Antirazzisti, vi sbagliate" (Antiracists, you're making mistakes), *L'Espresso*, April 19, 1992.

17. For the Resistance as Italian civil war, see Claudio Pavone, *Una guerra civile: Saggio storico sulla moralità nella Resistenza* (Turin: Bollati Boringhieri, 1991).

18. In particular see Michele Serra, "Dopoguerra senza pace" (The after-war period without peace), *Cuore* 3:108 (February 22, 1993), and "Ce lo meritiamo" (We deserve it), *Cuore* 3:113 (February 29, 1993).

19. Michele Serra, "Che tempo fa" (Weather report), *L'Unità*, March 13, 1993.

20. Franco Berardi, *Come si cura il Nazi* (Rome: Castelvecchi, 1993).

## Works Cited

Bartoletti, Loredana. 1992. "Ma gli squadristi sono un'altra storia." *La Repubblica*, July 9.

Battista, Pier Luigi. 1993. "Amato offende la storia." Interview with Luciano Lama, *La Stampa*, April 23.

Berardi, Franco. 1993. *Come si cura il Nazi*. Rome: Castelvecchi.

Bobbio, Norberto. 1993. "Presidente, non faccia confusione." *La Stampa*, April 23.

Brunetta, Giampiero. 1979. *Storia del cinema italiano: 1895–1945*. Rome: Editori Riuniti.

Cafagna, Luciano. 1993. *La grande slavina*. Venice: Marsilio.

Campano, Giuliano, and Giuseppe Faso. 1993. "Intolleranza di fine secolo." *La rivista dei libri* 3:2 February: 20–21.

Croce, Benedetto. 1944. "I diritti dell'Italia nella vita internazionale solennamente affermati dall'alta parola di Benedetto Croce: un discorso fraternamente italiano." *Il Risorgimento italiano*, September 22. Also in Benedetto Croce, *Pagine politiche: Luglio–Dicembre 1944* (Bari: Laterza, 1944), 97–116.

Dalla Chiesa, Nando. 1993. *Milano-Palermo: La nuova Resistenza*. Milan: Baldini and Castoldi.

Domenico, Roy Palmer. 1991. *Italian Fascists on Trial: 1943–1948*. Chapel Hill: University of North Carolina Press.

Flores d'Arcais, Paolo. 1992. "Macchia nera." *Cuore*, October 26.

Ottone, Piero. 1992. "Vediamo se Bossi è un altro Mussolini." *L'Espresso*, November 1.

Pavone, Claudio. 1959. "Le idee della Resistenza: Antifascisti e fascisti di fronte alla tradizione del Risorgimento." *Passato e presente* 7 (January–February), 850–915.

———. 1991. *Una guerra civile: Saggio storico sulla moralità nella Resistenza*. Turin: Bollati Boringhieri.

Serra, Michele. 1993a. "Ce lo meritiamo." *Cuore* 3:113 (March 29).

———. 1993b. "Che tempo fa." *L'Unità*, March 13.

———. 1993c. "Dopoguerra senza pace." *Cuore* 3:108 (February 22).

Sorlin, Pierre. 1980. *The Film in History*. Totowa, N.J.: Barnes and Noble.

Taguieff, Pierre-André. 1992. "Antirazzisti, vi sbagliate." *L'Espresso*, April 19.

Vattimo, Gianni. 1992. "Se la storia fa la faccia feroce." *La Stampa*, December 14.

Ward, David. 1996. *Antifascisms: Cultural Politics in Italy, 1943–46. Benedetto Croce and the Liberals, Carlo Levi and the "Actionists."* Madison, N.J., and London: Fairleigh Dickinson University Press.

Young, James E. 1988. *Writing and Rewriting the Holocaust: Narrative and the Consequences of Interpretation*. Bloomington: Indiana University Press.

# Part II

Impositions, Race, and Colonization

# Italy: Cultural Identity and Spatial Opportunism from a Postcolonial Perspective

*Mohamed Aden*

I have always envied writers who can condense in an elegant, offhand sketch the character, profile, values—in fact the entire identity—of a given people. Yet even the very term "people" implies an intrinsic variety and reality so complex that, as a term, it is in itself reductive. I view a people as I view a floral arrangement: magnificent in its ensemble, stunning and seductive to look at. But as soon as you turn a critical eye on it, the different species that make it up, the veins of the foliage, the wilted parts of the petals, the dying stems, or the fervid colors, you realize that its beauty is not uniform, that in order to appreciate its detail or make it attractive, you need great imagination, great patience, perhaps even great love. Likewise, defining a people, coagulating it in a single container—whether you demythologize its cultural background by insisting on some of the contradictions or accidents along its historic route (even if these have at times been glaring) or whether you choose particular sets of current events and ignore the rivulets and dribbles of others—becomes an incredibly difficult task. This is particularly so if you have drawn from that people nourishment and vigor as well as suffering and incomprehension!

The observations and general considerations that follow are those of a man who has lived with Italians as a colonized person, as an administered person under the protection and control of the United Nations, as a student guest—and as a place, himself, of encounter-confrontation, both in Africa and in Italy. My judgment, severe or ambivalent at times, perhaps depends as well on my personal vicissitudes or on what I know as the common feelings of the colonized peoples.

101

This judgment takes comfort, nonetheless, in the research of sufficiently objective scholars, including no few Italians.

Those of my readers who have had the opportunity to visit Rome have probably read the inscription on the wall of the monument erected by Mussolini in the Esposizione Universale di Roma; it proclaims Italians a people "of poets, of navigators, of inventors, of emigrants," and so forth. But the Italians we Africans have known would have merited some very different terms of description.

Although a great deal has been written about the different costumes in which Italy has presented itself on the African scene, such writing has amounted to very little. It has been produced ever since the precolonial era by Italian and other European explorers, ethnographers, and hagiographers of the African regions Italy would later occupy. And many others have continued to do so since then. One need only think of the monumental work on the Italian presence in Africa commissioned by an Italian foreign minister and prepared by a well-endowed commission directed by the former governor of Somalia, Francesco Saverio Caroselli, two-thirds of whose members were, like Caroselli, of unquestionable colonial stripe.[1] Thus was demonstrated the real significance and veracity of the lapidary saying that "history is written by the conquerors." In fact, one can say that those gentlemen rewrote their "own" history in a self-justifying and thereby partial and shameless manner. On the other hand, very little has been written about this fairly well "marginalized" history because the populations on the other side of the barricade were unprepared for such an appointment with the thread of history. Their memory of the facts was growing weak; time and the spiral of new facts and priorities that came with the goal of independence and the struggles necessary to obtain it were obliterating memory. In the meantime, these populations' real archives were literally disappearing in tombs. My generation, which lived a part of this history, prefers to divide the distinct identities of the Italian presence on our continent into three different phases:

1. the phase of colonization, with all its consequences;
2. the phase of the Trusteeship;
3. the phase of cooperation (and reparation?).

## The Colonizer and the Colonized

The Italian, stereotyped as picturesque, jovial, accessible, macho, funloving, a good (but not too diligent) worker, quite simply human, yet also a notable contributor to the abundant blend of culture and technology the West is so proud of, suddenly discovered within himself the calling of the colonizer.[2] The "common Italian," down-to-earth, self-deprecating, irreverent, and individualistic to the point of anarchy, the Italian of a hundred souls and a thousand resources, was tricked. This new cultural task turned out to be one that reduced him to a role that was not his own. Fascism manipulated and exalted him to such a degree that he almost believed (he who hardly ever believed deeply in anything or anyone!) that he had to take on a civilizing mission. It is not easy to understand whether this was inspired by an awkward imitation of the other European "powers," by the externalization of a hidden desire for "dominion" in the sense of usurpation and submission (*faccetta nera*, etc.),[3] or even by the outburst of an expansionist will inherited from his Roman ancestors. In any case, Italy threw itself into the conquest of its own place in the sun. One of its first experiences, the unexpected defeat in the battle of Adwa, made it change its mind a little, but no more than a little. Finally, after a long and varied series of events, it earned the title of colonizer! Since I am writing not the history of Italian colonization, however, but of only one of its particular aspects, the pertinent questions are: Who was the "conquering" Italian? And what was the final result of this vigorous adventure?

Even here any answer risks being partial and certainly not exhaustive. What we can note immediately, however, in the stereotype that I will call "Mario the African," is, precisely, an incredible mutation. Generally modest in origin, a peasant or an apprentice to some trade that he thinks has no future, this recruit for colonial duty in Africa finds at his feet immense territories to do with what he will. Having barely crossed the borders of his national space, he rids himself of that modicum of culture that even Gentili tried to tame him with.[4] The Risorgimento values, the eternal themes of freedom and justice shouted to the four winds and reclaimed by his own compatriots barely thirty or forty years earlier, the effervescent contents of Humanism, Illuminism, and a Liberalism still in formation in Italy are all swept away and replaced by the position papers of Minculpop.[5] Even social rules, ways of dressing (has anyone seen the colonial helmet, so useless in the Somali heat? Had the African sun perhaps become less harsh?), modes of behavior, of moving, of engaging in social relations, of "doing" and "being," are changing under Mussolini's insistent rhetoric and policies and becoming instrumental to a particular end: creating a new fascist civilization blacker than the blacks it has conquered. Grandpa's old

Bible, with its outdated teachings about loving one's neighbor or turning the other cheek, is shelved in a dark corner and forgotten except in moments of psychic desolation or just before a pitched battle. A Gobineau no one had read or understood yet, along with the racist articles of an Interlendi in his magazine, *La Razza*, dictate the code of behavior for the peninsular dominant class and for all others it dominates, including the colonials.[6] The central element of this code, as one can easily guess, is the defense of the "white" race from any possible contamination by inferior and undesirable elements. These inputs from above give "Mario the African" an unhoped-for opportunity. This is his chance not so much to abide by the rules that have been inculcated in him, but rather to effect his own liberation from the cultural yoke of the metropolis. In Africa, all is permitted to him.

"Mario the African" finally feels freed from the restraints of the urban bourgeois mentality. He himself becomes the master of his own destiny and of a morality he himself chooses. All he does or says acquires on its own the force of law. Even before he knows Somali places or meets Somali people, he devalues and takes over everything he finds—men and women, cultures, material goods. In this context, abuse has no meaning; it does not exist in his vocabulary. But there are no limits to the way he uses people and things. The first battles are traumatic, especially in Libya, Somalia, and later Ethiopia. The cost of each conquest is exorbitant, particularly in human terms. One need think only of the operation that the official bulletins hypocritically named "the pacification of Cyrenaica," which was nothing more than a deliberate and systematic act of genocide. The transformation of that area into a concentration camp resulted in more than a hundred thousand dead according to the Libyans, more than sixty thousand according to the historian Del Boca (1984).[7] This does not even begin to include the number of victims who fell during the resistance led by Omar Al-Mukhtar, its brutal suppression, and all that followed.[8]

In the case of Somalia, the occupation crept along, but the battles left embers that in some places have not yet been snuffed out. I remember an anecdote told in the Mudug (central Somalia) after an Italian captain from the contingent that had conquered the region slapped a local elder in the face. The elder's reaction was to burst into laughter. When the captain asked him why he showed such arrogance, it seems the elder replied, "Men like me you either convince or kill; you never just slap us!"

With Italian colonization, in fact, the stereotypical Italian, known for his sociable and pacifist tendencies, begins to practice all the iniquities associated with any colonizer worthy of the name: from forced labor to concentration camps (Danane, for example, or those set up in Ethiopia), from segregation to attempts at genocide.[9] As soon as he steps onto those colonial lands, "Mario the African" fails to see the Other. He believes, as even a man of Hegel's stature did, that here there is not nor has there ever been any human being, any lived history, any reality prior to his presence. And when he devastates lands or massacres peoples, this is nothing but a banal episode of Italy's recuperation of her ancient empire, the Roman one. As the poet Adriano Grande, a first-rate Blackshirt, says in reference to the defeat of the Ethiopian resistance:

> But it is right to pity you: death
> gives you no peace, no release
> from the dark phantasms that propelled you
> to war. There in the savage road
> you lie contorted, much more ferocious
> than these hateless weapons of ours, weapons
> anxious to excavate the earth, not the flesh, and beyond:
> You already stare into the oblivion of times
> without history, with the vultures
> and hyenas that, at nightfall,
> will banquet on your clenched fists.
>
> (Del Boca 1992, 103ff.)

This disdain for the values of the Other, who remains nothing more than a savage to tame or to defeat, is offset by the imminent risk of not being able to finish the mission or to enjoy its fruits:

> Indoor tasks
> —and less happy ones—will soon call me back
> to my people.
> Here, now, they provision me with memories.
>
> (Del Boca 1992, 103)

The adversary's response is almost always defensive. For example, I cite a few lines of a great poet who led the resistance for more than twenty years, Seyid M. Abdille Hassan (in free translation):

> Even if they attack us
> with ships and millions of men,
> Even if you scream out in frustrated rage

or in decay blessed
by your fortune-tellers,
Even if all my life
no one takes pity on me,
don't ever let it pass through your head
that I've become a slave.
                    (Abdille Hassan 1974, 179–80)

In order to reduce these lands and their people to silence, one of the quadrumvirate, De Vecchi di Val Cismon, who had perhaps become a burden in Rome, is invited to the colonies.[10] In Somalia he attempts the first direct conquest of the territories that until then had been under a treaty of protection with Italy. He also introduces racist laws and laws against miscegenation so punitive that many Italians today can hardly believe they ever existed. This is only because the dominant image of Italian colonization in present-day Italy is that it was a bit like a meeting between friendly peoples between whom deep ties of affection and common cultural growth would be born, ties absolutely unlike those inhuman ones created between other colonizers and their colonized. I can understand this simple negation, this refusal on the part of many Italians today to recognize Italy's recent inglorious past. I am baffled, however, when I read the answers of well-known writers and journalists, even those who lived the adventure of Italian colonization, and especially the colonization of Ethiopia, firsthand, such as Indro Montanelli.[11] Responding to a reader, Montanelli asserts, "Let's not demonize colonialism," because both "racism and anti-racism are made in bed!" (La Stampa, September 28, 1992). This is to say that if some Italian went to bed with a native (and the mestizos born—and abandoned—in the Horn are living testimonies that this occurred), then it is not true that he was racist!

The incredible thing is that the famous journalist does not even consider the total lack of an inverse relation and how utterly common it was for all the colonizers and all the racists to exploit the native women. South Africa is the undeniable proof of this; its unrecognized "colored," or mestizos, have become the third power in the country. Above all, it is impossible to understand how anyone could maintain that racism did not exist in Italy's colonies, when it raged, with legislation passed by the colonizing Italian, in Italy's own cities!

In the context of the colonial conquests, the "Italian woman," in her various manifestations, always had a lesser role than that of the men. In the colonies, she always arrived late—after the battles, after the victories. She may have been seeking to live a new kind of serial, an exotic saga. She steered clear of daily politics. She was attended and revered by a multitude of servants, but she remained absolutely invisible to other Africans. By contrast, the "African woman," in spite of the severity of Italian racial laws that prohibited sexual relations between the races, was the object of all sorts of violence and sexual adventuring on the part of the male Italian colonist. The spite in which he held her, as well as her mute resistance, did nothing to discourage the ignorant conqueror.

In order to describe more fully the colonizing Italian's behavior and to legitimate his "distinction" among the other colonizers, it is still necessary to study his actions and measure them against common objective parameters. For example, I have often heard Italians speak of the cultural gifts that Italy is supposed to have regaled on the colonized peoples. But through what channels and by means of what instruments is this contribution of cultural growth supposed to have occurred? One gift of the acts of colonial administration, for example, is the 1938 Decree of the Duke of Aosta, which states that "natives and assimilated peoples" are banned from school beyond the third grade. One thing is certain: after the departure in 1950 of the decade-long British military administration of Somalia, more Somalis could speak and teach English than could speak Italian after eighty years of colonization. Colonialism automatically froze even the growth of "indigenous" culture, suffocating it within its own borders. Given no exchange, collaboration, or interaction with experiences and knowledges other than its own, any culture, however singular, becomes "custom," is changed into folklore, and heads for rapid regression. In this respect, the Italians gave Somalis nothing. Moreover, they impeded any other cultural connection the Somalis might have made, even with the Islamic cultures that were geographically contiguous.

We may take other elements into consideration. For example, the Italians are known for their talent in vast projects of civil engineering, communications, and land reclamation. Even here, however, Italy gains no honor from a simple comparison between the capitals of its colonies and those of other countries. Serious comparisons cannot be made between Mogadishu and Nairobi or Kinshasa, or between Asmara and Abidjan, or between Addis Ababa and Dakar or Lagos. One might say that the Somali cities were and still are located in the poorest areas of the continent and therefore one could not get more out of them or put more into them. Personally, I am not convinced by this simplistic assertion.

Nonetheless, if I admit, but do not concede, that this is the case, then the question arises why Italy would ever have embarked on such a high-risk, low-return enterprise. Italy had no need of intermediate posts from which to defend overseas empires in the Near or Far East, nor did it have global strategies to work out. Why, then, drag thousands of poor southern or Friulian peasants to Ethiopia, or as many Piedmontese in the train of De Vecchi in Somalia? Was it only to demonstrate a vigorous, D'Annunzian, fascist virility? However I look at it, and even allowing for every possible mitigating circumstance, I can only conclude that Italian colonialism was the result of improvisations often left in the hands of unscrupulous or even criminal men like General Graziani and that it helped neither the colonized nor, it seems, the colonizer, in any way whatsoever.[12] This is why, in the absence of a serious debate about Italian colonialism and how it was managed by its protagonists, we are a bit stumped by the genuine surprise of a great many of today's Italians when they hear tell of the enormity of the crimes committed in their name and of the vile rogues and puffed-up puppets who represented them and filled their heads with the great civilizing work accomplished in those far-off countries. These Italians' attitudes are not so much the result of a process of repression as a conscious refusal to recognize themselves in the actions and misdeeds of their representatives. The perception many Italians have of themselves (as good, polite, agreeable, even altruistic) and of the values they, formally at least, claim (such as justice, democracy, and tolerance) do not permit them to accept the weighty reality of the suffering caused by "their" colonization. Thus they refuse all arguments contrary to their innocuous false vision so their sleep will not be troubled. Thus they can enjoy the spectacle of the massacres, foreign to them, perpetrated by the other colonizers, who nonetheless have had the courage now and then to dissect their own cumbersome colonial heritage. I hope that such a moment has arrived even for democratic Italy!

## The Challenge of the Italian Trusteeship in Somalia

The strangest thing in Italian political life is this: as soon as the terrible vicissitudes of the Second World War were over and the country had begun to consider itself filled with the profoundly democratic values of the Resistance, Italy was already wheeling and dealing to get itself assigned as the administrative power in its former colonies. Of these colonies, Libya, thanks in part to a prodigious effort by the Arab countries, quickly obtained its independence (1952) during the reign of the Sanusy.[13] Eritrea, perhaps out of a false sense of moral debt to Emperor Haile Selassie (the cynicism of political arithmetic: you sacrifice an entire people in order to satisfy the imperialist aims of one man!), became federated with and later simply annexed to Ethiopia.

Somalia was left. Its independence movement, known as the League of Young Somalis, which had already been active at the beginning of the Second World War, was opposed to any return of Italy as an administrative power. The League wanted something impossible: a joint administration of the four powers that were members of the United Nations Security Council (Great Britain, France, the United States, and the Soviet Union). England wanted something improbable: seeing as how most Somali "peoples" were, at that time, under English military rule, England wanted the political control of Somalia's future to be entrusted to it. The rivalry between the two superpowers, which was already well established, could not allow the English to control the two outlets to the Red Sea. This same rivalry automatically excluded any presence of the two superpowers, and thus they maintained a hands-off policy.

At this point, the Italian option was left. But whatever induced Italy to agree to become politically and diplomatically active in "retaking" control of one of its own colonies at so difficult and delicate a moment in its own democratic and civil reconstruction remains a mystery. All the same, nothing prevents me from making a few plausible hypotheses. Perhaps the determining element of that choice was something so unthinkable that it might be true. At that time, the Italian foreign ministry, directed by Count Sforza, was supposed to have hired almost all the personnel of the former Ministry of the Colonies.[14] These people certainly still wanted their place in the sun, and they were able to constitute a not inefficacious pressure group outside of as well as within the ministry, one capable, perhaps, of influencing Italian choices in this matter. The fact remains that, when the Italians finally went into Somalia as Trustees, they presented themselves as a movement for a much-desired Somali independence. They were brazen, armed far beyond what was necessary, and unwilling to engage in dialogue with anyone. They wanted to do it their way, and only with the Somalis they liked. The other Somalis called these people the "pro-Italians."

The leaders of the other side, the Somali front for independence, gave the new administrators reason to smirk since many of them had previously been those same administrators' "boys," their native third-class nurses, their porters, and so on. Conflict was inevitable (at least for the Somalis), and it did occur. The Italians' reasons for creating sacrificial victims of this new "contact" that was supposed to signal a new phase of collaboration cannot be rationally explained. I can only guess that they were at least in part the result of a "clash" rather than an "encounter" between two cultures that for historical reasons mutually despised each other and between two visions of political practice that were hard to reconcile.

It was several years, in fact, before people calmed down and admitted that the early Trusteeship (almost half the length of the mandate, which was ten years) had fallen short of its economic and political goals, thus confirming the pessimistic report of the United Nations representatives (from Colombia, the Philippines, and Egypt) who were there at the time.

At this point, a postwar version of "Mario the African," revised by the government in Rome, shook off many of his prejudices, changed his behavior toward the independence movement, and thrust Somalia up onto the banks of independence. But he left two indelible and contrasting signs, signs that still leave many questions unresolved. The first of these signs is the incredible effort on the part of a large portion of the Somali population to become literate and to acculturate, whether in Arabic or in Italian. This was no longer marginalization, therefore, but a kind of capillary immersion in Italian culture and the possibility of going "beyond," even all the way to metropolitan universities. The other sign is found in the Italian "political" will to keep the Somalis in their respective clan enclosures. All the attempts of the Somali Youth League (SYL) to overcome its members' clan loyalty in favor of a wider identity were hampered by the deliberate desire of the AFIS (Amministrazione Fiduciaria Italiana in Somalia [Italian Trusteeship in Somalia]) to keep them there in order to thwart the development of a functional nation-state. The daily politics of the Commissioners and Residents in the country's interior, the reevaluation of the roles of the "Cabila" leaders, the pernicious practice of attributing unregistered votes equaling the number of members supposed to be in his clan to each clan leader during political and administrative elections—all this left as its heritage a society that no longer "culturally" lived its clan values but where, in anything concerning politics, everyone found it necessary to be arithmetically aligned with his or her own clan.[15] What is happening today in Somalia is, at least in part, traceable to the time bomb set back then.

## Cooperation

It is hard to believe that, between two countries where all the assets are on one side and all the deficits are on the other, there can be genuine cooperation. This being the case, let us ban hypocrisy and self-congratulation and try instead to use terms appropriate to the circumstances. Help? Assistance? Charity? No. These terms do not do justice to the operation that during the sixties passed for neocolonialism according to Nkrumah, aid to underdeveloped countries according to others, and aid for development and cooperation according to still others.[16]

The substance of the question is this: the countries that had recently emerged from colonial rule would not have been able to make a go of it on their own either in political terms (something that perhaps should never be said officially) or in economic terms (something that gets shouted menacingly to the four winds). Therefore, it was necessary to aid them. Strangely, the aid from the developed countries generally passed through their respective former metropolises. Put another way, charity began with the European country's own former colonies. Just as the criteria of colonization had been more or less the same for all colonizers, so the criteria of the cooperation phase were also similar. All the same, Italian cooperation undeniably presents several peculiarities that merit emphasis.

First of all, there is the personalized character of concession: a sometimes vague request from the underdeveloped partner is met by the "aimed" assignment of a plan's administration to some individual or structure with distinct political connections. Whereas in other countries, such as Germany or France, structures (corporations or ministries) are founded to meet specific needs, in Italy a department of the Ministry of Foreign Affairs directly administers such management. Cooperation does not occur, therefore, as a function of the "dimensions" and the developmental dynamic of the partner. Instead, it has its own distributive logic, one internal to the metropolitan power. Here is an emblematic example: in March of 1985, Italy appropriated 1,900 billion lire (approximately $160 million) for development and famine control, thanks to the Radical Party campaign whose slogan was, "Let's save three million people" (Arconti 1987).[17] As usual, heated discussion ensued. The undersecretary of foreign affairs, Francesco Forti, a Socialist who had been named high commissioner for special antifamine projects, declared solemnly, "We shall furnish water, food, and medicine, but also seed and agricultural machinery—anything, in fact, that can help our Third World brothers." In the end, he opted instead for huge projects: Tana Beles in Ethiopia (an enormous irrigation project involving the relocation of hundreds of thousands of peasants forcibly uprooted from their places of origin) and, in Somalia, the rebuilding of fertilizer factories that stand like cathedrals in the desert.

It is legitimate, therefore, to speak not of cooperation for development but of "operation" development in the most business-oriented sense of the term. Just as in the history of the ongoing corruption scandals in Italy, so here the connivance between the corporations that built these projects, their obvious party affiliations in Italy, and the politicians and businessmen in Somalia—as well as their respective middlemen—was evident.[18] Naturally, not all the "operations" were so patently off course. Some of them led, in fact, to unexpected results in spite of their cost or the way they were carried out—the aid given to the national university, for example, or the construction of small mooring docks, or even the controversial Garowe-Basaso road. Even with this sort of "operational" collusion, not all Italians knew about or approved of this kind of aid and the way it was managed. In fact, it was other Italians, and not Somalis or Ethiopians, who denounced the arbitrariness and simplemindedness with which Italian aid for development was conducted. It is surely thanks to the Italian Radical Party that the terrible management of Italian aid finally got exposed, in great detail, both in parliament and in the mass media. *Dagli aiuti mi guardi Iddio* (God save me from aid) is the colorful title of the book in which two Radical Party deputies denounced the failed Italian politics of development (Del Boca 1993, 29). Their conclusion definitively condemns not "Mario the Italian" but the ruling class, which used this aid for its parties' profit or for personal gain to the extent that such aid was "beyond all regulations" and was "conditioned by all sorts of special interests" (ibid., 30). But such a stance justifies the Italians who, in this as in other sectors we have discussed, do not recognize themselves in the action of their government or in the transformism of their party.

Italians in general have grown up a lot since the sixties, when I was a student in Italy. They have become culturally and economically wealthy. Their European and Atlantic values have become the shell in which they imprison their universalistic yearnings and the vitality of their ideals. In spite of this, only in Italy could there exist leftist parties with left-attributed programs and ideals and so numerous a following as to be most unusual in the general alignment of the new world order. Or a transnational, nonviolent party aimed at the realization of common ideals of its members' different countries.[19] People like Father Ennio Pintacuda, the well-known anti-Mafia Jesuit from Palermo, understand that the collusion between the Masonic powers and the Mafia must be undone, that the hidden agreements between the state and criminal interests must be revealed, that the kind of corruption now coming to the surface is more than a simple moral problem. It is strangling democracy, reducing it to mere formality. It is the opposite of the kind of substantial democracy necessary to protect and promote those social subjects who are least empowered.

The historical strength of Italians as a nation lies in their ability to fight for their own demands without ever wounding others too deeply. It is because of this that they have been able to keep their own state in continual crisis without ever overthrowing it. Although superpoliticized, they almost always vote for the same party and therefore shun change. They have great entrepreneurs who nonetheless almost always prefer not to overstep the bounds of familiar territory. They are rich but always find a way to chalk up losses to the public treasury and gains to their own. Their relation with others is sincerely cordial, even if in actual situations (immigrations, transmigrations, new international relations, etc.) it is veiled with a thin patina of xenophobia that in other circumstances borders on racism.[20] But I doubt that most Italians fully realize this. All in all, and in spite of their multiple contradictions (or perhaps because of these!), the Italians who have been stereotyped as uniquely extroverted and open to the world seem to me to remain incurable narcissists who paradoxically often refuse to look at themselves in the mirror.

Translated by Beverly Allen

# Notes

1. I am referring to a work consisting of more than thirty volumes that was commissioned in 1952 by the Italian Ministry of Foreign Affairs. The compilation of this work was entrusted to a "Committee for the Documentation of the Work of Italy in Africa," presided over by the former governor of Somalia, Francesco Saverio Caroselli. Like him, fourteen of the twenty-five members of this committee were former governors or other high functionaries in the colonies, and, with the exception of Mario Toscano, they were all "Africanists of undoubtable colonial convictions" (Del Boca 1992, 115).

2. For related considerations on the production of stereotypes, see Karen Pinkus and Pasquale Verdicchio in this volume.—*Ed.*

3. "Faccetta nera" (little black face) is the title of an Italian song written about African women during Italian fascist imperialism. [See Karen Pinkus in this volume.—*Ed.*]

4. Giovanni Gentili (Castelvetrano, 1875–Florence, 1944) was an Italian philosopher who, taking his distance from Benedetto Croce, introduced the notion of "actualism" in the historic process. The fascist state, which he embraced as a new Italian Risorgimento, entrusted him with scholastic reform, and for several years Gentili served as minister of education under Mussolini. He was killed by partisans in 1944.

5. Mussolini's Ministero per la Cultura Popolare (ministry of popular culture).

6. Joseph Arthur Gobineau (Ville d'Avray, 1816–Turin, 1882) was ambassador of France to several countries. During the years 1853 to 1855, he wrote his major work, *Essay on the Inequality of the Human Races*, which inspired all the European racist currents of the late nineteenth century. Interlendi was for many years the director of the Roman journal *La Razza* (The race), where all the fascist rubbish about that subject was elaborated.

7. Cyrenaica is the first region of Libya to have been occupied by the Italians.

8. Omar Al-Mukhtar (1862–Soluch, 1931). A member of the Sinusi religious sect, Al-Mukhtar was leader of the Libyan resistance in Cyrenaica for many years. Wounded in battle, he was captured by the Italians and, by special order of Graziani (see note 12), was hanged at the venerable age of seventy-five in front of a concentration camp containing twenty thousand people. A film about his life made in 1979 by the Syro-American director Mustapha Akkad was censored in Italy for being "harmful to the honor of the army," in the words of minister R. Costa (Del Boca 1992, 112, 125).

9. Danane, a concentration camp located about thirty kilometers from Mogadishu, was where Somali and Ethiopian subversives were held (Del Boca 1992, 41).

10. The quadrumvirate was the four fascist leaders who planned and led the march on Rome of October 1922: Michele Bianchi, Emilio de Bono, Cesare M. De Vecchi, and Italo Balbo. They later became Mussolini's lieutenants, fulfilling diverse functions.

11. Indro Montanelli (Fucecchio-Florence, 1909; now lives in Milan), a rightist journalist and polemical writer (*L'Italia dei secoli bui* [Italy of the dark ages], *L'Italia dei secoli d'oro* [Italy of the golden ages], *La storia di Roma* [The history of Rome]), took part, as a soldier, in the conquest of Ethiopia. A decade ago, he founded the well-known Milan daily *Il Giornale*, financed by Fininvest, Berlusconi's industrial group. Because of disagreements with its owner, Berlusconi, Montanelli left the newspaper in 1994 and, at eighty-five years of age, set out to direct a new newspaper called *La Voce*.

12. Rodolfo Graziani (Filettino, 1882–Rome, 1952), a general in the Italian army, led the pitiless conquest of Libya and Ethiopia at various times during his career. For his criminal acts in those countries he was condemned as a war criminal to nineteen years in prison, but he served only five. He wrote several essays in his own defense, and several of his texts are quoted by historians such as Del Boca.

13. The Sanusy (Es Sinussi) were the royal family in Tripolitania, and later in all of

Libya. Deposed by the Italian colonization, they were reinstated right after independence in 1952 and fell only with Gadhafi's coup d'état in 1969 (Del Boca 1992; Various authors 1993; Evans-Pritchard 1948).

14. After having served in various other diplomatic functions, Count Carlo Sforza (Montigoso, 1872–Rome, 1952) was named minister of foreign affairs in the De Gasperi government (1947–51). As such, he oversaw the entire initial phase of the Italian Trusteeship in Somalia (AFIS [Amministrazione Fiduciaria Italiania in Somalia]).

15. "Commissioners" and "Residents" were the titles of the Italian governors of Somalia's regions and of its districts, respectively. "Cabila" is a term of Arabic origin (*al-qabila*) that Somalis use to indicate their subdivision in clans.

16. For the terminology and the concepts of cooperation, see any of the works of Kwame Nkrumah from the period of his exile in Guinea-Conakry, after 1966. See also Davidson (1971, chapters 6 and 7) and Arnaud et al. (1989).

17. Laura Arconti is a member of the Radical Party and secretary of the "Life and Disarmament" Association in Rome.

18. By "current corruption scandals in Italy" I mean the well-known *tangentopoli* scandals that continue to upset Italy's political and managerial spheres.

19. The writer is referring to the Radical Party in general and to its transnational organization in particular, the Transnational Radical Party.—*Trans.*

20. Recent beatings of *extracommunitari*, or immigrants who come from countries outside the European Community, in Rome and Ostia, for example, would seem to indicate a worsening of the situation that Aden describes. *Extracommunitario* has become, in fact, a euphemism for "African," as it is never used in Italy to describe other non-Europeans—U.S. expatriates in Tuscany, for example.—*Trans.*

## Works Cited

Abdille Hassan, Seyid M. 1974. *Diiwaanka Gabayadii Sayid Maxamed Cabdille Xassan.* Ed. Sheikh Jama Omar Isse. Mogadishu: Somali National Academy.

Arconti, Laura. 1987. "Il Fondo Aiuti Italiani e la sopravvivenza." Pamphlet. Rome: Associazione Vita e Disarmo.

Arnaud, G., et al. 1989. *Rapporto sul terzo mondo.* Rome: Edizioni Associate.

Crispi, F. 1914. *La prima guerra d'Africa.* Milan: Fratelli Treves.

Davidson, B. 1971. *Which Way Africa? The Search for a New Society.* 3d ed. Harmondsworth, England: Penguin.

Del Boca, A. 1979. *La conquista dell'Impero.* Bari: Laterza.

———. 1984. *Gli italiani in Africa Orientale.* Bari: Laterza.

———. 1992. *L'Africa nella coscienza degli italiani.* Bari: Laterza.

———. 1993. *Una sconfitta dell'intelligenza: Italia e Somalia.* Bari: Laterza.

Evans-Pritchard, E. E. 1948. *The Sanusy of Cyrenaica.* Oxford: Oxford University Press.

Galasso, Giuseppe, ed. 1961. *Antologia degli scritti politici di Mazzini.* Bologna: Il Mulino.

Garocci, G. 1961. *Giolitti e l'età giolittiana.* Turin: Einaudi.

Hirsch, B., and M. Perret. 1989. *Éthiopie, Année 30.* Paris: L'Harmattan.

Nkrumah, Kwame. 1963. *Africa Must Unite.* New York: Praeger.

———. 1981. *Ghana: The Autobiography of Kwame Nkrumah.* New York: International Publishers.

Pisani, E. 1988. *Pour l'Afrique.* Paris: Odile Jacob.

Various authors. 1993. *Dizionario di storia.* Milan: Mondadori.

# African Americans and the Italo-Ethiopian War

*Ayele Bekerie*

The 1935 Italian invasion of Ethiopia is an example of the praxis of hegemonic Eurocentrism, which is designed to shape the world in the image of Europe. Italy, like her European counterparts, rushed belatedly to impose its hegemonic will against a people who were solidly centered in their own culture and history. This aggression was indeed contrary to the cultural coexistence and exchanges that prevailed among the Ethiopian people and the people of Rome at the time of the Aksumite period, particularly from the fourth to the seventh centuries of the common era. Moreover, the Ethiopian sense of identity and history—the ability to successfully defend her independence from foreign aggression—has become a symbol of hope and freedom throughout the African world. Italy's brutal attempt to wipe out this symbol ultimately became a powerful catalyst in the struggle against colonialism and oppression.

Mussolini's fascist design against Ethiopia thus became an instrument for voicing the essence and right of Africanness. The brutal Italian invasion galvanized the Ethiopians to reject their false and short-lived sense of Ethio-European solidarity and relocate themselves in Africa. The dynamics of the Italian aggression and the responses of the African world can be perceived by examining the roles played by African Americans at the time of the invasion.

African Americans of all classes, regions, genders, and beliefs expressed their opposition to and outrage over the 1935 Italian invasion of Ethiopia in various forms and various means. The invasion aroused African Americans—from intellectuals to the common person in the street—more than any other Pan-African–oriented historical events or movements had done.[1] It fired the imagination of African Americans and brought to the surface the organic link to their ancestral land and people. The purpose of this study is to examine the cultural responses of the African Americans, particularly Harlemites, to the invasion.

Ethiopia's long-sustained independence, unique and old Christian tradition, along with the references to Ethiopia in the Bible and ancient classic literatures, made it a powerful symbol for African people throughout the world. The common aspiration for freedom linked colonized and oppressed Africans to Ethiopia as a sacred symbol and place of African power, sovereignty, and independence. Virginia Lee Jacobs, in her book *Roots of Ras Tafari*, outlines Ethiopia's symbolic significance as follows:

1. Ethiopia is a symbol for Africa's struggle for independence from European colonialism;
2. Ethiopia is the shrine enclosing the last sacred spark of African political freedom;
3. Ethiopia is the impregnable rock of African resistance against white invasions; and
4. Ethiopia is a living symbol, an incarnation of African independence.[2]

Furthermore, when Italy attempted to claim its share of Africa in 1896 by invading Ethiopia, a share agreed upon at the infamous Berlin Conference of 1884–86, where the Europeans legitimized their "scramble for Africa,"[3] it was decisively repulsed. At the Battle of Adwa, the Ethiopian army led by Emperor Menelik and Empress Taytu defeated the Italian army. This victory was significant from the Pan-African point of view. Like the Haitian victory over Napoléon's army in 1803, it became a source of hope and pride throughout the African world. Ethiopia's ability to keep and defend its independence and sovereignty made it the focal point for Pan-African ideas and movements, such as the Ethiopianism religious movements in South Africa and Nigeria.[4]

African Americans, for the most part, interpreted the 1935 Italo-Ethiopian War as a race war. They looked at the Italian aggressors as white aggressors against black Ethiopians whom they considered their blood relatives.[5] In Roy Ottley's view, "The Italian assault on Ethiopia, at long last, was some sort of tangible idealism—certainly a legitimate issue—around which the Black nationalist could rally, and, indeed,

rally a great section of the Black population. . . . Almost immediately
it put the nationalist organizations on sound agitational footing and
increased their memberships considerably."[6]

African Americans also rationalized their support of Ethiopia vis-
à-vis the Italian American support of Italy. *The Crisis*, the official
journal of the National Association for the Advancement of Colored
People, in its column "From the Press," reasoned as follows:

> Is the invasion of Ethiopia by Italy the concern of 13 million Colored
> Americans? It most certainly ought to be because there are nearly 5 mil-
> lion Americans of Italian extraction in the United States. Most of whom
> read Italian newspapers and belong to Italian organizations. Of this
> number, 1,790,429 are not citizens, but their influence in spreading vi-
> cious Fascist propaganda is great because they associate with and circu-
> late among white citizens. Millions vote and some high officials of Ital-
> ian descent are open supporters of Mussolini's murder tactics. There is
> nothing we can do about Fascism in Italy, but there is a great deal we
> can do about Fascism in America. We can vote against it and all candi-
> dates who endorse it. We can fight for the return of these alien propa-
> gandists to their native lands. And we can stop spending our money
> with those who support this Negrophobic viewpoint. To do less would
> be cowardly negligence.[7]

The African Americans' responses to the war encouraged political,
cultural, and economic nationalism within their communities across
the land. F. Ernest Work associated the defense of Ethiopia with the
preservation of African (black) culture: "Should Mussolini succeed in
forcing an Italian protectorate upon the last independent bit of Africa,
the black man's culture will disappear from the earth under a veneer
of European imposition."[8] Bernard Magubane, a prominent Pan-
Africanist historian, using his analytical skill and foresight, further
explored the African Americans' support of Ethiopia. According to
Magubane, the existence of the kingdom of Ethiopia in normal times
could not be said to have meant much to the ordinary man in the
street, but the threat to its existence posed by a white nation brought
about certain definite reactions among black people everywhere.[9]
Magubane found that the "threat to its existence" was a threat to the
hopes and aspirations of the African people. African Americans demonstrated a "most inspired and concerted agitation for African freedom and independence, and raised African consciousness to a point
where it became a force in the world."[10] In essence, the new level of
African consciousness became a powerful force in the struggle to de-

colonize Africa and to undertake a revolutionary social movement in the United States.

The Italo-Ethiopian War generated a wide range of responses from African Americans. From intellectuals to barbers, from journalists to religious leaders, from athletes to artists, from Harlem to Chicago—the whole gamut of African American life and sensitivities was revealed to the world. Mussolini had ignited a fire, but he had no control over its consequences. Harlem was the center of activities against the Italian invasion of Ethiopia. Because Harlem in the 1920s and 1930s was regarded as "the nerve center of advancing black America, the fountainhead of mass movements, and the progressive vitality of African American life,"[11] it was natural for Harlem to assume the leading role in organizing responses against the invasion.

## The Intellectual and Literary Response

The intellectual and literary responses of African Americans to the war were prolific and rich in creative power. Poems, cartoons, essays, prose, editorials, letters to the editor, journal papers, church sermons, and lectures concerning the war were written and delivered by African Americans such as Romare Bearden, W. E. B. Du Bois, Marcus Garvey, Claude McKay, and Langston Hughes. Hughes, who is perhaps the best known of modern African American writers and was frequently introduced to audiences as "the poet laureate of Harlem," blended nationalism with class analysis to express his opposition to Italian aggression in Ethiopia. The war era was a period of heightened African consciousness and solidarity. Pan-Africanism and African nationalism prospered under the stimulation of this new "race consciousness and racial solidarity."[12] Indeed, the invasion of Ethiopia had deepened the sense of outrage among African intellectuals all over the world.

Carter G. Woodson, the brilliant African American historian, urged African Americans to provide assistance to Ethiopians, "for in spite of an infusion of Semitic blood they are Negroes."[13] W. E. B. Du Bois, one of the world's intellectual giants, predicted increased racial antagonism throughout the world as a result of Italian oppression.[14] In one of his insightful essays, Du Bois wrote:

> The probabilities are that Italy, by sheer weight of armament and with the complaisance of Europe, will subdue Ethiopia. If this happens it will

be a costly victory, both for Italy and the white world. There will be not only the cost in debt and death, but the whole colored world—India, China and Japan, Africa in Africa and in America—all that vast mass of men who have felt the oppression and insults, the slavery and exploitation of white folk, will say: "I told you so! There is no faith in them even toward each other. They do not believe in Christianity and they will never voluntarily recognize the essential equality of human beings or surrender the idea of dominating the majority of men for their own selfish ends."[15]

More recently, E. U. Essien-Udom, a nationalist theoretician, linked black nationalism with Ethiopia when he argued: "the oppressed would find psychological gratification by linking themselves with the omnipotent or with the sacred. Regardless of the Ethiopian claims, for the African world, Ethiopia is the free land of black people ruled by a black ruler."[16] Clearly, these African American intellectuals were aware of the "racial fog" that veiled Ethiopia. Nonetheless, they made distinctions between the historical relevance of Ethiopia as compared to the "non-African" perceptions of its leaders.

Paul Robeson, the great African American actor, placing particular emphasis on the Italo-Ethiopian conflict, connected the role of the artist with the necessity of his full participation in the problems of all oppressed peoples:

The American Blacks have been yearning for freedom from an oppression which has pre-dated fascism. It dates most clearly perhaps from the fascist invasion of Ethiopia in 1935. Since then, the parallel between his own interests and those of oppressed peoples abroad has been impressed upon him daily as he struggles against the forces which bar him from full citizenship, from full participation in American life.[17]

Robeson saw correctly that the impact of the Italian aggression would undermine freedom and weaken the ability of African Americans to participate fully in American society. Therefore, the African American interest in the war was also linked to the need for self-preservation.

Dr. Willis N. Huggins, the first black history teacher in the public school system of New York, was one of the most dedicated friends of Ethiopia. Huggins founded the Harlem History Club, which became an important center for publicizing the Italian aggression and propagating Pan-Africanism. Kwame Nkrumah (the first prime minister of Ghana), John Henrik Clarke (the eminent African and African American historian), Yosef ben Jochannan (Egyptologist), Arthur Schomburg (the founder of the Schomburg Library), and other prominent African Americans learned their initial lessons in African history through the club. John Henrik Clarke considered Huggins his "mentor."[18] As an executive secretary of the International Council of Friends of Ethiopia, Huggins lobbied vigorously in the League of Nations at Geneva for support to Ethiopia. He regularly corresponded with the exiled Emperor Haile Selassie and his ministers in England, France, and the United States. Through his devotion and dedication, Huggins earned the trust of Ethiopian leaders and officials.

As a committed Pan-Africanist, Huggins recognized the significance of Ethiopia's independence in the context of racial pride. In his letter to Joseph C. Arenol, secretary to the League of Nations, he declared: "Blacks are bound by racial kinship to the ancient and illustrious Ethiopian people."[19] Moreover, he argued that "the planned destruction of Ethiopia is not only a heinous crime, but it will increase the hollow mockery of the profession of Christianity, thus bringing more and deeper disgrace to Christian principles."[20] Furthermore: "The neglect of Christian principles perhaps was an indication of the much stronger ideological appeal of white supremacy. Racial solidarity took precedence over Christian brotherhood, international law, treaties of friendship, and all other established international norms."[21]

The Italo-Ethiopian War was analyzed and understood not only in the context of African nationalism or Pan-Africanism, but also in the context of international issues. As African American intellectuals became ever more conscious of Africa, their persistent and consistent sympathy and support seem to have triggered the Ethiopians to reflect on questions of their "racial identity."

The Ethiopians' ambiguity regarding their "racial identity" was a threat to the unity of African Americans and Ethiopians. In his book *The Real Facts about Ethiopia*, J. A. Rogers dealt with the issue under the title "Of What Race Are the Ethiopians?"[22] His assessment was mixed. Although he attempted to establish the "Negroid" foundation of Ethiopians ("every Ethiopian this writer has ever seen would be a Negro and nearer to the 'pure' type than the average Afro-American"), he asserted that "Ethiopians have never drawn a color line against white peoples."[23] Rogers's reporting, however, helped to dispel the "rumors that the Ethiopians were not Negroes [that] nearly ended the unity of Black men in the United States with those in Africa."[24]

Huggins, after a trip to London to visit the chief Ethiopian representative, to check the "racial classification" of the Ethiopians, also reported that "the Emperor is very conscious of the fact that he is today the only black sovereign in the world, and he considers himself as the natural leader of the Negro race. He is fond of repeating the phrase that 'Ethiopia is the trustee for the future of the black races.'"[25]

Certainly, this was a clear indication of the "re-Africanization" process of Ethiopia. At best, however, Haile Selassie was a peripheral supporter of the Pan-African movement. Although his role may not have been entirely negative, nonetheless he cooperated only partially with Nkrumah's visionary drive to establish a United States of Africa.[26]

"Every time a Mussolini takes advantage of the race, I shudder, I weep, and I hang my head in shame," lamented Marcus Garvey.[27] Garvey was one of the most ardent campaigners for the Ethiopian cause. He led the largest black nationalist mass—based in Harlem—in the history of the African world. The organization he founded, the Universal Negro Improvement Association, was revived as a result of the war, and became active in the campaign against the Italian aggression in Ethiopia. Garvey was in England at the time of the war. He was expelled from the United States in the late twenties for alleged mail fraud.

From England, Garvey put his journal, *The Blackman*, to work for the Ethiopian cause. He did not hesitate to criticize the weaknesses of the Ethiopian leaders and *The Blackman* was a powerful Pan-Africanist journal, as Robert Hill recognized:

> *The Blackman* is an indispensable source of information, especially as it contains the only extant transcripts of [Garvey's] last major addresses, which were the speeches he delivered in Canada and the West Indies while on tour there. . . . In addition to regular editorials on current events, particularly running commentaries on the renewal of European imperialism and militarism, *The Blackman* also carried Garvey's perennial messages to his "Fellowmen of the Negro Race."[28]

Through the journal, Garvey campaigned vigorously against the Italian aggression. He denounced Mussolini and called on the African people "to march in line."[29] He urged them to "tell people everywhere . . . that the Ethiopian's God appears to deal with all affairs."[30] He envisioned the reemergence of a glorious Africa. In one of the many editorials he wrote regarding the Italian aggression, Garvey linked the Italian invasion of Ethiopia with imperialism. Italy's intent, according to Garvey, was "for economic and colonial expansion."[31] Therefore, he directed his intellectual energy to bringing unity among African people. Garvey also noted the contradiction in Mussolini's notion of "white supremacy": "In the South of Europe, Mussolini, who claims to be a white man, although the Italian race cannot be really called purely a white race, is preparing to devour a set of people in far off Ethiopia."[32]

Garvey also wrote numerous poems; many of them conveyed antifascist messages. Here is an excerpt from one of his poems, "The Beast of Rome":

> Down from the Seven Hills of Rome
> Came brutes in human form
> They left their cursed, sinful home
> Our Motherland to storm:
> Yes, led by Mussolini's own son,
> They passed the Old Canal,
> And when their war was just begun
> They fought like cannibal.
>
> The Rome of sin and human hate
> Has plagued the world before,
> But God will serve their awful hate
> On Ethiopia's shore.
> Their guns and gas may threaten all
> As hymns they sing at home,
> But ere Adowa's final fall
> The fight shall pass from Rome.[33]

Garvey was perhaps the most passionate and most articulate campaigner for the cause of Ethiopia, which he used to reignite Pan-African solidarity among African people throughout the world. His love and dedication to "the race," perhaps, has no match.

Another intellectual giant in the campaign against Italian aggression was Kwame Nkrumah. Upon his first arrival in Europe on his way to pursue a university education in the United States, he was met by the news of the Italian invasion of Ethiopia. In his autobiography, Nkrumah wrote:

> But just as I was feeling particularly depressed about the future, I heard an excited newspaper boy shouting unintelligible as he grabbed a bundle of the latest editions from a motor van, and on the placard I read: "Mussolini Invades Ethiopia." That was all I needed. At that moment it

was almost as if the whole of London had suddenly declared war on me personally. . . . My nationalism surged to the fore; I was ready and willing to go through hell itself, if need be, in order to achieve my objective.[34]

The "lessons" Nkrumah learned were most important lessons, for he transformed himself into an outstanding African leader and statesperson. He immersed himself in Pan-African causes. He worked with W. E. B. Du Bois, George Padmore (a Trinidadian and a vigorous advocate of Pan-Africanism, author of *PanAfricanism or Communism?* and an adviser to the newly independent state of Ghana), C. L. R. James (a socialist and the author of *Black Jacobins*),[35] John Henrik Clarke, Nnamidi Azikiwe (a Nigerian nationalist and the first prime minister of Nigeria), Jomo Kenyatta (the first prime minister/president of Kenya), and many other outstanding Pan-African intellectuals and leaders. His writings on Pan-Africanism are very thorough with a deep theoretical base; his contributions to the Pan-African and the nonaligned movements make him one of the great world leaders of our time.

The radicalization of African American and African intellectuals, as Kwame Toure (one of the leaders of the Black Power movement in the United States) argues, was accompanied by dynamic mass movements and an extraordinary unification of African political awareness. This radicalization culminated in the liberation of millions of Africans in Africa and the Caribbean. Kwame Toure further connected the campaign and struggle for decolonization with the invasion. Self-determination and independence were tasks taken up for solution by African nationalists and their African American supporters. In other words, the nationalists stopped petitioning the European powers to improve the conditions of their colonial subjects; they demanded total decolonization and independence.

As John Henrik Clarke put it, the war period represented the "renaissance of African consciousness and nationalism."[36] African American intellectuals began to chart a new agenda for freedom and self-determination of all African people. Their antiwar campaign was followed by the 1945 Pan-African Conference at Manchester, England, where resolutions were passed demanding independence and self-determination for colonized people of Africa and the Caribbean. The Italian invasion of Ethiopia led indirectly, but by a logical chain reaction, to the formulation at Manchester in 1945 of a Pan-African program of action against European rule in Africa.

## The African American Press

As a source of information about the war, the African American press was an important vehicle shaping public opinion, and increased its circulation during this period. The African American press responded to Italian aggression by (1) supporting Ethiopia's diplomatic position at Geneva and dismissing the Italian claim as fascist fabrication; (2) lobbying and urging the League of Nations to protect and defend Ethiopia; (3) condemning the Vatican for its ambivalent stand; (4) criticizing American neutrality; (5) advising African Americans to assist Ethiopia for moral and racial reasons; and (6) promoting Pan-African solidarity and activity.[37] As William R. Scott noted, "in keeping with its long held tradition of championing black causes, when the Italo-Ethiopian War erupted in 1935, it was the Black Press which played a major, if not the dominant, role in developing Afro-American sympathy for Ethiopia."[38] The press promoted the general cause of Pan-Africanism in America, and its coverage of the war was considered "an example of racial pride, patriotism, strong Pan-African sentiment, and clear immersion in international affairs."[39] Moreover, according to Marcus Garvey, the press became an instrument of a literacy campaign: "It is rather encouraging to learn that for the last few months, reading among the Negroes has jumped to a high mark of more than 2000%. This is due to interest in the Italo-Abyssinian war."[40] John Henrik Clarke identified the press as an instrument to mobilize the African American people to the cause of Ethiopia. According to Clarke, the two leading African American reporters of the war were J. A. Rogers and Dr. Willis N. Huggins.[41]

While Rogers went to Ethiopia as a war correspondent for the *Pittsburgh Courier*, Huggins went to Geneva to report on the League of Nations meetings concerning the war for the *Chicago Defender*. Clarke summarized the contributions of these two reporters as follows:

> In the collective talent of J. A. Rogers and Dr. Huggins the Afro-American Press was fortunate enough to have two keen observers who could see through the subterfuge and partners of European powers and their frantic schemes to keep their African colonies. Both Rogers and Huggins saw behind the headlines and foretold the future repercussions of Ethio-

pia's betrayal. Their reports were a highwater mark in Black American journalism.[42]

Other prominent reporters included W. E. B. Du Bois, Roy Ottley, Melaku Bayen, James Weldon Johnson, Dr. C. B. Powell, and George L. Schuyler. The leading newspapers of the period were the *Pittsburgh Courier*, the *Chicago Defender*, *Amsterdam News*, the *Baltimore Afro-American*, *New York Age*, the *Ethiopian Voice*, *Negro Liberator*, and *Cleveland Gazette*.

J. A. Rogers was the only African American reporter who reported directly from Ethiopia. Owing to his work, the *Pittsburgh Courier* became "the most important and largest-selling Negro newspaper in the United States and Rogers the most widely read pamphleteer in Black America."[43] In addition to his reports on the war, he wrote about the culture, history, and people of Ethiopia.[44]

African American journals like *The Crisis*, *Opportunity*, the *Journal of Negro History*, *Phylon*, *The Blackman*, and *The African: A Journal of African Affairs* published articles that encouraged African Americans "to see their problems in broad, international perspective."[45] The journals also sought to keep alive the strong African American interest in the fate of Ethiopia throughout the Italian invasion and occupation period. These journals were antifascist, anticolonialist, and strongly nationalist.

The need to promote and sustain African American self-sufficiency and autonomy was the underlying theme. George L. Schuyler, publisher of the *Pittsburgh Courier*, articulated the nationalist view in the following manner: "There are several other groups attempting to raise money to help Ethiopia. All of them are headed by white people, many with ulterior motives, or who are professional Negrophile busybodies and self-appointed shepherds of the Negro races, . . . who believe nothing can be done by or for Negroes unless a white man is directing it."[46]

## Organizational Response

From the time the first newsboys began to shout through the streets of Harlem that Italian airplanes had destroyed Ethiopian towns, the anger of resident Negroes mounted hour by hour. Outside the entrance to Italian fruit stores and vegetable markets in Harlem, chalk inscriptions appeared, reading: "Italians, Keep Out." Street-corner demagogues shouted to their listeners that "Africa is the Black man's home."[47]

Since the "Back to Africa" movement led by Marcus Garvey in the 1920s, the Italo-Ethiopian War ignited the most widespread and diversified mass movements and organizations among African people throughout the world. New cultural, political, social, and economic organizations were established and the old ones revived with a new vitality and an unparalleled determination. These organizations clearly articulated, defended, and demanded justice, freedom, and independence for the oppressed and colonized people of Africa, the Americas, and the Caribbean. The center of mass movements and organizations was Harlem. As William R. Scott observed, "Even though pro-Ethiopian organizations emerged in each geographical section of the country with substantial Black populations, including the deep South . . . , the focal point of pro-Ethiopian activity was in the Black urban North, particularly Harlem."[48]

The most important and one of the oldest organizations of the Pan-African movement and antiwar campaign was the Harlem History Club, which trained some of the great leaders of the African world, such as Kwame Nkrumah, Arthur A. Schomburg, Willis N. Huggins, Hubert Harrison, and John G. Jackson. Indeed, most of the mass organizations that emerged during the war were founded and/or led by "graduates" of the Harlem History Club.[49]

Another important organization formed in Harlem to assist Ethiopia against Italy was the Ethiopian World Federation, formed on August 25, 1937, by Dr. Melaku E. Bayen, a nephew of Emperor Haile Selassie. Melaku was sent to the United States as a special envoy to solicit aid from people of African descent for Ethiopia during the war. This semireligious and nationalistic organization established a weekly organ called the *Voice of Ethiopia*. The *Voice*'s message eventually became a guiding ideology to the Ras Tafari movement that had been formed in 1932.

As a powerful cultural movement with worldwide influence, the Rasta movement today represents a synthesis of Ethiopia's symbolic value and the struggle for freedom and racial pride. Reggae music was born out of the Rasta movement and has become the creative expression of oppressed African people. The music is rooted in Ethiopian spiritualism, and singers such as Bob Marley identify the late Emperor Haile Selassie as a messiah figure.

The Ethiopian World Federation had a Pan-African platform and agenda. It is interesting to note that this Pan-African organization was led by an Ethiopian. Melaku studied and lived in the United States. He also married an African American and resided in Harlem. His commitment to the Ethiopian cause and Pan-African principles was outstanding.[50] He strove hard to bring Ethiopia back into the African world until his untimely death in 1940 at the age of forty. The seeds for the "re-Africanization" of Ethiopia were sown by great Ethiopians like Melaku.

The Italo-Ethiopian War also contributed to the emergence of a movement based on coalition principles. According to Mark Naison, the Communists, white peace movements, and various African American organizations worked together in support of Ethiopia.[51] Although Congressman Adam Clayton Powell Jr. was an advocate of a coalition movement, the Garveyites were against interracial activities and resisted all attempts to work with white groups. The brutality of the Italian aggression against Ethiopians, however, made the coalition movement short-lived. In general, African Americans interpreted the war as a "race war," and therefore they wanted their own nationalist organizations.

Various factors contributed to the perception that the war was based on skin pigmentation: some Italian Americans openly supported Mussolini; the Soviet Union continued to sell oil to Italy; and the United States maintained a policy of "neutrality" that effectively blocked Ethiopia from getting military aid.[52]

## Religious Response

Ethiopia shall stretch out her hands unto God.
PSALMS 68:31

As Christians, many African Americans are familiar with this biblical verse that mentions Ethiopia, the land of free black people. According to Clarence G. Contee, "Ancient peoples and African Nationalists from all areas have used the oft-quoted Psalm . . . as a prophecy of the coming greatness of Africa."[53]

Mussolini, in the eyes of African Americans, committed a sinful act by invading a Christian country. Beyond its colonial ambition, Italy's decision to invade Ethiopia may have its root cause in the nearly one thousand years of rivalry between the Ethiopian Orthodox Church and the Roman Catholic Church. The Ethiopian church, together with the Alexandrian and Greek churches, split from the Roman church at the Council of Chalcedon in 451 A.D. The split was the result of a doctrinal disagreement regarding the nature of God: the Ethiopians adhered to the position of a one-natured God (Monophysitism), whereas the Roman church insisted on the dual nature of God.

In *The Terrible Twos*, Ishmael Reed tied the Italian invasion of Ethiopia to the Vatican's desire to weaken Ethiopian Orthodox Christianity, which was considered a hindrance to the spread of Catholicism in the region.[54] The pope did not even condemn the war; in fact, Italian soldiers were accompanied to the battlefields by Catholic priests. As Reed put it, "The Emperor had his problems with Rome [the seat of the Catholic church]."[55]

According to William R. Scott, African Americans were surprised by the apparent collaboration between the Vatican and Mussolini in the invasion of Ethiopia. He further stated that African Americans "did not abandon their Christian faith; however, their theology became more militant and nationalistic."[56] Willis N. Huggins raised the following two points at the League of Nations in 1935: "The Fascist destruction of Ethiopia would (*a*) increase the guilt of modern Christian nations who, yesterday, raped Africa and carried millions of her children to be enslaved in the Americas, and (*b*) increase the hollow mockery of the professions of Christianity, thus bringing more and deeper disgrace to Christian principles."[57] Huggins associated the neglect of Christian principles to the "much stronger ideological appeal of white supremacy."[58] In other words, racial solidarity took precedence over Christian brotherhood and sisterhood.

Many African American churches denounced the Italian invasion and exposed the Vatican collaboration. Religious nationalism deepened among these churches. Even though one may not find a direct link between the war and the rise of Islam among African Americans, the Nation of Islam also rooted itself in the fallow of deep resentments and disillusionments following the war. Significantly, Congressman Adam Clayton Powell Jr. transformed the Abyssinian Baptist Church in Harlem into one of the major centers of antifascist activity. It was assumed by African American religious leaders that Ethiopia, as one of the oldest Christian countries, with a highly developed culture and language, would not be easy prey to "civilization agents" of Europe. These leaders also thought that the universal brotherhood and sisterhood among Christians of all denominations would take precedence over race distinctions. Nevertheless, Mussolini subordinated logic, history, reason, and common sense to fascist glory and attempted to crush Christian Ethiopia. A clear indication of the Italians' intent to destroy the roots of Ethiopian civilization was the removal, transportation, and erection of the largest Aksum stele—one of the most significant symbols of ancient Ethiopian civilization. There is a strong movement both in Ethiopia and abroad to return the Aksum stele to Ethiopia.

The depth and magnitude of African Americans' outrage against the Italian invasion and their passionate support of Ethiopia could be seen from their reaction to the "Louis-Carnera Bout." When Joe Louis knocked down Primo Carnera of Italy in an international heavyweight bout, Harlemites had their "biggest celebration."[59] It was as if they had knocked down the fascist pseudonation of white supremacy, and they felt that Joe Louis had avenged the defeat the Ethiopians had suffered at the hands of the Italians. As Loften Mitchell put it, "The Brown Bomber, appearing in the darkness when Italy invaded Ethiopia and the Scottsboro Boys faced lynching, became a Black hero the history books could not ignore."[60]

On the streets of Harlem, the celebrants were seen carrying "a yellow, white [sic], and green banner, described as the flag of Abyssinia."[61] The function of the Ethiopian flag as a significant cultural artifact among African Americans of Harlem is evoked by Ralph Ellison in *Invisible Man* as the narrator identifies the "little Ethiopian flag" among the many objects thrown out on the street of Harlem when an old couple lost their apartment lease.[62]

The Ethiopian flag has tricolors of green, yellow, and red. When one looks at the colors of the flags of independent African countries, or the costumes of African people during the annual Carnival in Brooklyn, Detroit, Miami, Toronto, London, Port of Spain, Trinidad and Tobago, the most common and popular tricolors are green (land and productivity), yellow (hope), and red (blood shed in struggle and victory). Perhaps it is not merely coincidental that more than twenty African and Caribbean countries have these colors in their flags. These tricolors are usually found in homes of African people with decorative and revered symbolic values in miniflags, belts, caps, hats, wall hangings, and other artifacts. The national images of these countries and millions of African people throughout the world are linked with the national image of Ethiopia. Ethiopia's green, yellow, and red flag symbolizes the whole African world's quest for dignified identity, freedom, and political power.

## Notes

1. Pan-African movements are movements that pursue and advance the social, cultural, political, and economic interests of Africans, African Americans, Afro-Caribbeans, and the rest of diasporic Africans throughout the world.

2. Virginia Lee Jacobs, *Roots of Ras Tafari* (San Diego: Slawson Communications, 1985), 68.

3. Ali A. Mazrui and Michael Tidy, *Nationalism and New States in Africa* (London: Heineman, 1986); see also Kwame Nkrumah, *Africa Must Unite* (New York: International Publishers, 1970), 6.

4. Bernard Magubane, *The Ties That Bind: African-American Consciousness of Africa* (Trenton, N.J.: Africa World Press, 1987), 163–65.

5. Roy Ottley, *New World A-Coming* (New York: Literary Classics, 1943), 111–12.

6. Ibid., 105.

7. "From the Press," *The Crisis* 43:10 (October 1936): 307.

8. F. Ernest Work, "Italo-Ethiopian Relations," *Journal of Negro History* 20:4 (October 1935): 447.

9. Magubane, *The Ties That Bind*, 160.

10. Ibid.

11. Ottley, *New World A-Coming*, 1.

12. Ali A. Mazrui and Michael Tidy, *Nationalism and New States in Africa from about 1935 to the Present* (London: Heineman, 1986), xii.

13. Cited in William R. Scott, "Black Nationalism and the Italo-Ethiopian Conflict, 1934–1936," *Journal of Negro History* 63:2 (April 1978): 122.

14. W. E. B. DuBois, "Inter-Racial Implications of the Ethiopian Crisis: A Negro View," *Foreign Affairs* 14:1 (October 1935): 88–92.

15. Ibid., 83.

16. E. U. Essien-Udom, *Black Nationalism: A Search for an Identity in America* (New York: Dell, 1965), 20.

17. Philip S. Foner, ed., *Paul Robeson Speaks: Writings, Speeches, Interviews 1918–1974* (New York: Brunner and Mazel, 1978), 147.

18. Interview with John Henrik Clarke, April 12, 1988, Ithaca, New York. See also Gil Noble, "A Profile on Dr. Ben," *Like It Is*, WABC-TV (air date March 8, 1987), 12.

19. Willis N. Huggins and John G. Jackson, *An Introduction to African Civilizations with Main Currents in Ethiopian History* (New York: Negro University Press, 1973), 91.

20. Ibid., 92.

21. Ibid.

22. J. A. Rogers, *The Real Facts about Ethiopia* (1936; reprint Baltimore: Black Classic Press, 1982), 3–8.

23. Ibid.

24. Ottley, *New World A-Coming*, 4.

25. Ibid., 112.

26. See Kwame Nkrumah, *Ghana: The Autobiography of Kwame Nkrumah* (New York: International Publishers, 1981).

27. Marcus Garvey, "Unpreparedness a Crime: The Negro Is Guilty," *The Blackman* 1:12 (late March 1936): 8.

28. Robert Hill, in Marcus Garvey, *The Blackman* (New York: Kraus-Thomson, 1975), 19.

29. *The Blackman* 1:2 (January 1934): 16.

30. Ibid.

31. *The Blackman* 1:8 (late July 1935): 17.

32. *The Blackman* 1:9 (August–September 1935): 3.

33. *The Blackman* 1:10 (late October 1935): 7.

34. Nkrumah, *Ghana: The Autobiography of Kwame Nkrumah*, 27.

35. C. L. R. James's article "Abyssinia and the Imperialists" has been published in *The C. L. R. James Reader*, ed. Anna Grimshaw (Oxford: Blackwell, 1992). James considered that the Italo-Ethiopian conflict, "though unfortunate for Abyssinia, has been of immense benefit to the race as a whole" (66).

36. Interview with John Henrik Clarke, April 12, 1988.

37. Scott, "Black Nationalism and the Italo-Ethiopian Conflict," 120.

38. Ibid., 288.

39. Ibid., 120.

40. *The Blackman* 1:11 (late December 1935): 11.

41. John Henrik Clarke, "Kwame Nkrumah: His Years in America," *Black Scholar* 6:2 (October 1974): 9–16.

42. Ibid., 9.

43. Ottley, *New World A-Coming*, 102.

44. See Rogers, *The Real Facts about Ethiopia*.

45. Wayne F. Cooper, *Claude McKay: Rebel Sojourner in the Harlem Renaissance: A Biography* (Baton Rouge: Louisiana State University Press, 1987), 327–28.

46. George L. Schuyler, "Views and Reviews," *Pittsburgh Courier*, December 7, 1935, 10.

47. *New York Herald Tribune*, October 4, 1935, in Allon Schoener, ed., *Harlem on My Mind: Cultural Capital of Black America 1900–1968* (New York: Random House, 1968), 140.

48. Scott, "Black Nationalism and the Italo-Ethiopian Conflict," 123.

49. Interview with John Henrik Clarke, who was also a member of the club, April 12, 1988, Ithaca, New York.

50. The most detailed account of the Ethiopian World Federation and its leader Dr. Melaku E. Bayen was given by William R. Scott in his excellent work "A Study of Afro-American and Ethiopian Relations: 1896–1941" (Ph.D. diss., Princeton University, 1971).

51. Mark Naison, *Communism in Harlem during the Depression* (Urbana: University of Illinois Press, 1983), 196.

52. See Brice Harris Jr., *The United States and the Italo-Ethiopian Crisis* (Stanford, Calif.: Stanford University Press, 1964).

53. Clarence G. Conte, "Ethiopia and the Pan-African Movement before 1945," *Black World* 21:4 (February 1972): 42.

54. The collaboration between the Holy See and the fascist state in Ethiopia was also reported by the *Telegraph* of London. The report was published by Garvey's journal, *The Blackman*, 2:2 (July–August 1936): 15.

55. Ishmael Reed, *The Terrible Twos* (New York: Atheneum, 1988), 45–46.

56. Scott, "Black Nationalism and the Italo-Ethiopian Conflict," 121–22.

57. Ottley, *New World A-Coming*, 109.

58. Huggins and Jackson, *An Introduction to African Civilizations*, 92.

59. Loften Mitchell, "Harlem Reconsidered—Memoirs of My Native Land," *Freedomways* 4:4 (1964): 475.

60. Ibid.

61. *New York Herald Tribune*, June 23, 1935, quoted in Schoener, ed., *Harlem on My Mind*, 139–40. The colors of the Ethiopian flag are green, yellow, and *red*.

62. Ralph Ellison, *Invisible Man* (1952; reprint New York: Vintage Books, 1990), 271.

# Shades of Black in Advertising and Popular Culture

*Karen Pinkus*

## Blackness in an Italian Context

During the course of research into the iconography of blackness from fascist Italy, it became apparent to me that many of the representational issues I was confronting remained both unresolved and troubling.[1] What had begun as a particular historical and taxonomic investigation inevitably spilled into the present, and into sociological, political thought beyond my own defined area of expertise. I felt then that although I could not write an account of race relations in postcolonial, postmodern Italy, I could still reflect on questions of blackness based on the images I had seen and had attempted to contextualize from the 1930s. I could begin with the most obvious observation one can make on the subject: for a white American, blackness may indeed pose a complex series of associations, but it does *not* primarily signal a *national* other, as it must for an Italian. The generation of Italians now in their twenties is probably the first to have seen black bodies circulating in urban and suburban areas, but even today in certain regions, blackness always elicits a gaze; a black body is *black* before it is anything else (gendered, clothed, still or in motion, old or young, African or Western, and so on).

Nevertheless, this distinction between a nation-state and a nation-race should not be taken as an effacement of another fundamental reality existing in both Italy and the United States: the universal subjectivity of whiteness with regard to blackness. As film critic Richard Dyer has noted, "white" is taken in representational practices as so "normal" as to be devoid of any meaning at all, whereas "black" has

134

always signified "other," "difference," and has therefore been endowed with more specific meanings within particular historical or geopolitical limitations.[2] White is neutral, black is marked or charged in various ways. The question of a representation of "whiteness" from a "black" subjectivity can only be acknowledged here, but in any case, it is not one raised in the context of Italian cultural studies for obvious reasons. In Italy, the meanings of blackness center around broader questions of national identity and the (fascist) colonial legacy, even where these questions may seem to be effaced, literally "whitened," in everyday consciousness.

In his famous essay *On Laughter*, the philosopher Henri Bergson asked the question: "Why does a negro make us laugh?"[3] His response is that *we* laugh because the black face strikes *the eye* as "unwashed," or "daubed over with ink or soot." Only within the presumption of the universal subjectivity of white can black be this discoloration. Clearly, the impulse behind the joke is "harmless," and related to an "innocuous" tradition of caricature and comedy. Yet the same kind of ad hominem logic underlies the culture of advertising in Italy, which began as a visual language shared between a group of bourgeois gentlemen in the industrialized urban centers of the north, around the turn of the century. And although the industry of advertising has substantially expanded, in terms both of available media and targets, the originary moment of comic exaggeration that saw signs of difference exchanged for the pleasure of consumption still remains in place at the level of nostalgia and mass cultural "history."

## Black Style

Beginning in the early part of the twentieth century, blackness was used in Italy to sell a variety of products in the so-called open market. In a significant way, the black body was part of the fascist regime's program to create a classless consumer—one who would identify his or her needs with a national economy rather than with a class-affiliated commodity culture. The introduction of race as a category into popular imagery helped solidify this mythical block of consumers: in this sense, the advertising industry collaborated with explicit goals of the regime. Simultaneously, in the context of *propaganda*, the regime manipulated blackness, first to attract Italian soldiers to Africa, and then, after the conquest of the empire, to repel them. Again, although this hidden history is repressed in current advertising, I would argue that it persistently emerges in certain representational contradictions.

In particular, I regard the nuances involved in the *styles* of blackness, the abstraction and reduction of the black body to a pure volumetric-geometric type, as highly significant. In periodicals such as *La difesa della razza* dedicated to the cultivation of a racial consciousness, the Italian public found photographs of every nature of corporeal manipulation: ear and lip disks, bound feet, hints at unspeakable genital deformation. In fact, the word "deformation" becomes a key term in the fascist educational campaigns, associated with blackness, but also, very concretely with the *entartete Kunst* (and specifically *art nègre*) copied from German publications. Deformation is thus a racist term, but also an aesthetic one. Picasso is the artist of deformation, par excellence, and it would be impossible to separate a popular conception of Cubism from the discourse of the racist scientists.

The bold graphics of the 1920s and 1930s, stemming from Futurism and other international art movements, transformed blackness into a set of recognizable features: large lips, pendant jewelry, wide-open mouths, ingenuous stares, large rounded breasts for women; for men, short-cropped hair and apelike cheeks. Finally, the color black itself became utterly irrelevant.

In the many transformations of Italian Futurism, the geometricizing current represented by Depero, Balla, and then by the "second wave" in Milan and Turin emerges as a major style in advertising. Specifically, the Futurist aesthetic of pure tone and geometry becomes integrated with a particular fantasy about the smooth black body. The logical relation between smoothness and desire does not present itself at first glance, because the German and Italian racial propagandists condemned *all* representations of blackness as *art nègre*, conflating a specific term whose greatest relevance was to Analytic Cubism, with a generic one without regard for stylistic or formalist criteria.

Depero, who exemplified the smoothness of the body stocking in various portraits of black men and women, belied this misidentification of the black body with *art nègre* in a short piece called "Josephine Backer [*sic*] on the Champs-Élysées and Experimental Theater at Montmartre." He describes a stage show with sets featuring the classic emblematic or decorative attributes of blackness: palm trees, cactus, coconuts, and bananas. These attributes alone—regardless of the style in which they were depicted or the elements of the accompanying performance—were enough to label the event as "black." After characterizing the scenographic elements, Depero comments, "I don't love *art nègre*, but the savage virginity, the barbaric sincerity, and jazz music do overcome me and I am rather amused by them. Magistrally deafening harmonies and syncopated melodies, gurgling, murmurs, and tremors transport you in a raucous atmosphere of exotic life, and undoubtedly communicate new emotions of an unexplored life."[4] Swept away by Josephine in Paris, Depero first "blackens" the whole affair (she is black before she is anything; the music is black before it could have any possible relation to the atonal experiments of the Futurist art of noise, for example), and then associates it with the only term he knows for a black aesthetic: *art nègre*. But what is more interesting about the comment, coming from the pen of a rather wide-eyed provincial Italian craftsman who runs a studio in a small Dolomite town near the Austrian border with his beloved wife Rosetta, is Depero's absolute insistence on the untried sexuality of the spectacle. Not that he denies that this smiling Negress stands for sex—that would be impossible given the cultural saturation of the black female as fixed icon—but he applies his own peculiar form of aesthetic colonialism to the vision before him. Josephine Baker, this smooth figure in a body stocking, is a virginal continent to be discovered, a new life for the provincial, exactly the model of Africa diffused in the popular press and by the pioneers and soldiers who were drawn there, long before the rise of fascism. Disregarding the very questions of aesthetic style that might seem to most preoccupy the Futurist imagination obsessed with manifestos and clarifications of its own uniqueness, originality, or national affiliation, Depero's major impulse as a viewer is to assert his own power over blackness, and to appropriate it for his own pleasure. Yet when he himself goes to represent the black body, he moves away from the actual primitivist aesthetics of *art nègre* and makes the black body into a multicolored, smooth picture.[5] Finally, then, the Negroid lips, creamy white eyes, and pickaninny features of Depero's "cartoon" advertising have little to do with "primitivism" in the aesthetics of *art nègre*, Fauvism, Expressionism, or other movements termed "degenerate"—*entartete*—by the Nazis, modeled on interpretations of African sculpture and tribal artifacts.

## The Colonial Moment

It seems to me important to posit an acute moment in the history of blackness in Italy at the height of the Ethiopian campaign in the late

1930s. This is not the place to recount the history of that campaign.[6] Instead, I am interested in the cultural creation of a "colonial consciousness or will," as Alessandro Lessona, the colonial minister, put it earlier in the decade.[7] Lessona's speech, part of the mobilization effort inspired by a perceived threat to Ethiopia's divisive, tribal feudalism by Haile Selassie's constitutionalism, implied that, fundamentally, the Italian public was disinterested, or at best that blackness had no particular geographical or temporal referent for Italy. Where blackness was equated with "the Islands" for France during the nineteenth century, and was thus inevitably linked with institutional slavery and all the cultural anxiety this might arouse in a liberal state, the case of Italy is one of an apparently retarded nation taking over the last piece of unclaimed Africa, at the last minute; the *arte d'arrangiarsi* translated to international politics.[8] The regime staged a well-documented campaign in its effort to stimulate this famous "consciousness," and the sanctions imposed by the League of Nations in 1935 only helped its coherence. But advertising of the so-called disinterested free market also collaborated in endowing blackness with various meanings.

The primary thrust of the regime's *propaganda* effort was to move the troops "down there" (*laggiù*, a spatial pointer used to refer to Africa that might also be a euphemism for the female genitalia), and one incentive was an erotic figuration of the black female body, especially the Somali, the "smooth" *faccetta nera* who really became abject after the introduction of the racial laws in 1938 (figure 1). In the context of both propaganda and advertising, blackness is split with a gender division. The female is the "civilizing force," and it is through her that Italy will gain access to the darkest forces of barbarism. She will soften the warriors and help transform children into docile manual laborers. But, of course, there are problems with this history, not the least of which is the putative separation of sexuality from the charged war machine of fascist imperialism.[9]

Yet this myth of a positive encounter between white male and black female persists. In a recent piece by Luciano De Crescenzo in *La Repubblica*, the author expresses nostalgia for his first erection, inspired by a pinup photo snapped by a cousin in Ethiopia and passed around among the adolescents back home. The photo depicted a young girl who was "actually a bit ugly, but her breasts were exposed, and this was enough." Of course, we are reminded, the photo was take long before the advent of magazines like *Playboy* or vulgar television

Fig. 1. "Faccetta nera" chocolates. (Salce Collection, 12077)

shows that would allow a young man to view white women (ultimately, the real object of desire) in their "natural" states. As in the self-ironizing variety program in Italy (one thinks of De Crescenzo's friend Renzo Arbore, for example, with his Brazilian "Cacao" girls), access to the female body emerges from a multilayered cultural discourse as the ultimate leveler, and finds consensus among the widest possible audience. Both men and women in fascist Italy consent to the "healthy" encounter of black female and white male. But does De Crescenzo mean to imply that the race card is only played in his early erotic fantasies because of a mere coincidence of availability? Can we really take seriously the notion that the act of beholding a frayed photograph of full-frontal female nudity is only a question of constituting male sexuality and has nothing to do with the conquest of an African nation, or that De Crescenzo's erection has nothing to do with the huge national erection that followed the declaration of the empire?

Describing his visit to the Triennale d'Oltremare, a large regime-sponsored exposition dedicated to bringing Africa closer to provincial, bourgeois Italy, De Crescenzo remarks that the jiggling breasts of a belly dancer "created in us a healthy democratic and antiracist consciousness that has stayed with us to this day."[10] If a white male finds his sexuality through a black woman, naked and available like no Italian, what has this to do with war, with toxic gasses, with aerial bombardments, mass executions, the sacking of villages? While one hand grips the photograph, what the other hand is doing is only natural, as natural as the black natives fighting one other with predictable periodicity. De Crescenzo's attempt to redeem male sexuality is masked by his nostalgia for a popular song, "Faccetta nera," sung by soldiers and supposedly "constructed" for them by the regime propaganda machine:

> If from the highlands you glance down toward the sea,
> little black woman, you slave among slaves,
> you will see, as if a dream, so many ships
> and a tricolored flag will wave for you.

> Black face, beautiful Abyssinian,
> wait and hope, for Italy is drawing near;
> and when we are together with you,
> we will give you another law and another king.

> Our law is the slavery of love
> but freedom to live and think,

we Blackshirts will vindicate
the fallen heroes, and we will liberate you.[11]

The real importance of "Faccetta nera" for my purposes is not the mention of Blackshirts as conquerors and redeemers but the sexual slavery implied in the "liberation" of the black female from the black male. His absence from the song is the most significant aspect of its meaning, and, coincidentally, he is also absent from De Crescenzo's reminiscence. In fact, the occasion for De Crescenzo's short article is the recent revival of this song by a number of neofascist youth groups. In response to public outrage, De Crescenzo suggests that although the youth themselves are odious, one must not "blame the little ditty" ("Sono solo canzonette"). Like the pickaninny in America, the song is part of cultural history, and it must remain as a witness to certain "past" values, even if it reminds us of unpleasant events. De Crescenzo can only make this point, he can only refer to "Faccetta nera" as long as the culture believes this song to be, precisely, a *historical* artifact. Yet for a generation of men that now passes itself off as "dead," blackness was fundamental to the formation of their self-identity. It is hard to imagine a more conflicted and contradictory piece of opinion writing than this article on "Faccetta nera," and it reveals a gaping omission, namely, the complicity of the entire culture in this construction of "healthy male sexuality" as essentially fascistic.

During the 1930s, Italian women not only tolerated representations of the black female, they winked at her encounters with white males. In adventurers' prose descriptions, as in the advertising, the Somali stands as a figure for (illicit) sexuality, for submission, and if her iconographic counterpart, a white male, is missing from the representation in question, his presence is both presumed and necessary for constructing a full reading of the scene.[12] He is the viewer, eclipsed from the stage of representation, but essential to the completion of that representation itself. In other words, the image of the black female obeys the rules of a male gaze as the only dominant visual mode, precisely because, on an empirical level, it is the male who has access to the means of reproducing images in the context of the colonial encounter.

Within this encounter, the black female equals sex, quite clearly, but there is something more to be said about the specific fantasy of the smooth Negress. Of all the African women encountered by the Italians on their many misadventures "down there," it was almost universally agreed that the Somalis were the most desirable, in a sense because their beauty was *believed* to be only an exaggeration of whiteness, and not a "degenerate" opposite of it. In other words, the Somali female was invested with the same aesthetic values promoted by the Futurists under the mistaken label of *art nègre*. Although the Somali female does not, in fact, lack the physical attributes branded by racist science as "degenerate," the Italian public inscribed her body with a mythology of smooth sensuality. What is important is precisely what she is *not*, namely, a "Hottentot Venus" type, "pathologically" endowed with steatopygia, or a protruding buttocks.[13] Her putative lack of body hair removes her one degree from the "unevolved" figure of the ape, the model by which black physiognomy in general was understood after Lombroso's nineteenth-century criminal anthropology.

De Crescenzo's cousin and his compatriots in Italian colonialist adventure grew up with an older discourse that tied the black "deformity" of the buttocks to a deformity of the genitalia, and thus linked black sexuality in general with disease. Clearly, the black female desired by the fascist represents only a more extreme version of the classic European whore. The fantasy Somali beauty was legendary in Italy, thanks to a propaganda campaign consisting of firsthand, intimate accounts like the following:

> The [Somali female] body is enclosed in an elastic girdle. . . . You no longer think of the rigid armaments of the bones or of curtain rods or of the volume and wriggle of the muscles. . . . The tiny, steep breasts are planted nicely apart, at the top of the thorax; and as for their stomachs, completely flat. The waist is highly flexible; the hips are solid but swivel nicely; the lower back is perfectly hollowed; the legs are long and rather subtle and gracefully loose, flowing from tiny knees; the ankles are dry, strengthened with pure metal from the long walks they take following the caravans.[14]

"Smoothness" is the key term, and nowhere is there ever any mention of the buttocks, so central to the nineteenth-century vocabulary of blackness. In fact, the white woman seems to have everything to envy the black. Whites, too, aspire to silkiness, and that is why the stocking has had such an important place in bourgeois female dress. A women's magazine of the 1930s explains:

> We must remember that we live in an age in which black beauty has upset white beauty, to which we had attributed supremacy: blacks have silky skin, not only on their legs, but on their entire body, like a sweater.

Just look at Josephine Baker! She is nude, but her nudity is dressed. And since Europeans cannot transform themselves into Antilleans or Senegalese, they invented stockings and they show them with pride. . . . Oh, competition![15]

Essentially, the stocking is the single motif of sexuality that the white women allows herself, and it represents the bourgeois aesthetic that proclaims that a covered body is more sensuous than an uncovered one. Bourgeois fashion or the definition of what is seductive always works along a hierarchical scale; it always implies competition. If the black body can transform itself into a body stocking, this is also to say that it can sexualize itself entirely, from top to bottom.

Finally, then, the black satisfies the taboo of virginity, for she prepares the man to enter into sexuality with the white. Freud's troubling 1917 essay on this subject presupposes a society much like that of bourgeois, fascist Italy, that is, a *modern* one in which modern neurotics act out the archaic affect of the horror of rupturing the hymen.[16] As is well known, "The Taboo of Virginity" is one of several texts in which Freud links the neurotic with the so-called primitive, precisely the (mythologized, idealized) figure who is represented in advertising of the black body. The intrinsicalness of monogamy to capitalism comes into conflict with archaic hostility felt by the female toward the male, a hostility that is, however, worked out through ritual defloration or some version of the *ius primae noctae* within *primitive* societies. Freud is forced to admit that, in modern life, second marriages often work better (and let us not forget that Freud was himself the product of a second marriage), because this "archaic reaction exhausts itself on the first husband."[17] Second marriages, for the *woman*, then, but what about the man? Obviously, the possibility that all women might seek to marry twice is a social conflict and would lead to anarchy, but rather than carry this to its logical conclusion, Freud says that most women manage somehow to keep their hostility in check. It seems that where this essay falls apart and leaves a gaping hole in the logic of exchange is where the dynamic of the "positive" sexuality of the black female emerges. She substitutes for the white woman in her self-sacrifice to the male, and she subsumes the cultural anger that Freud leaves "up in the air," while leaving the white woman with her hymen intact. The product she sells, aside from a particular brand name, is also a product called "the white woman," something so desirable for the *modern* world that she is worth having in exchange for one's consumer capital, at any cost.

But if they constructed a desirable "white" Somali female, the fascists only displaced their disgust onto the black male. More specifically, the abjection of the male is a direct result of this revision of female sexuality in the context of "a healthy consciousness." The male becomes a terrifying, feminized figure with earrings and lipstick. Not only is his sexuality incomprehensible (the dark continent), but he is also castrated and impotent, reduced to his mere apelike physiognomy. In order to understand advertising, we must forget the idea that blackness was merely exploited as propaganda to mobilize troops, and see it as a larger code into which the Italian public could project its own fantasies, whether negative or positive. All sorts of cultural taboos of the Italian bourgeoisie were invested in blackness: masturbation, incest, polygamy, excessive sexuality. Given the status of blackness (and especially the black male) as a garbage dump, it seems odd that advertisers who wanted to make a positive association for their product would choose blackness as a site for representation.

In point of fact, however, blackness was used during the 1930s to sell a wide variety of products, some from a strictly European context (heavy machinery, gasoline, film), others strictly "colonialist" in flavor (bananas, chocolate, coffee), still others related to the enterprise of colonization itself (trucks, tents, raincoats). Many of the advertisements for the second category of goods—the fruits of colonization— go far beyond a proximity of the product with blackness; they make an utter identification. A banana grows as a tassel from the fez of a Somali black head. A black head is formed by, its very shape defined by, the bananas that surround it, constituting nothing less than the entire ethos from which blackness emerges. "I am coffee," is the utterance offered by a black head in a popular advertisement, and on closer inspection, we find that this head, peering over the edge of a white china cup, is actually an enlarged coffee bean (figure 2). There is no longer any distance between blackness and the products that its very subjection may yield for an Italian public on the brink of being-consciousness-of-blackness. Gino Boccasile exploits this, brilliantly, in his iconic conflation of the product and the laborer. But if this representational trick is done outside of the context of official, racial information, it actually represents a very significant moment in the history of cultural persuasion in Italy, the selling of racial identity along with

Fig. 2. "I am coffee." Gino Boccasile's coffee bean-head. (Salce Collection, 3096)

the brand name of a product as two inseparable events in the development of the modern consumer. Boccasile's Caffé Bricco ad is a joke that, like Freud's *Witz*, functions as a pact between two men (the producer and the consumer), at the expense of a third (the black bean head). The ad successfully interpellates the Italian public as a national-racial consumer.[18]

## Imperial Relations

Most of these images—from *faccetta nera* to the impish Moor—belong to the period of intense cultural "consciousness"-raising before the Ethiopian conquest. Yet we can already witness the translation of an atrocious war into high-bourgeois style in Boccasile's 1936 advertisement for Ramazzotti aperitif (figure 3). A white woman in the foreground in a stylized version of colonialist khaki and safari helmet stares off into the sun. In the background stands a female "Moor" figure holding a serving tray. The putative link between the product (an extremely well-known bitter, here advertised as particularly thirst-quenching when mixed with club soda) and the scene of power relations seems to be anything but necessary. Ramazzotti had been sold in an extremely varied series of ad campaigns, and connected with assorted images. The only fixed element in its advertising history is the foregrounding of the bottle itself, whose label is unchanged to this day. The decision to sell the product through the juxtaposition of a haughty sun-drenched white body with a servile Moor amounts to this: the victory in Ethiopia was the most significant event for a whole generation of Italians who had come of age during fascism, and very simply, the equation of leisure time—the woman is enjoying a vacation in the sun, the drink is a late-afternoon luxury—with the pleasure of colonial domination now seems almost inevitable.

Of course the scene is pure fantasy: this woman will never find herself in Africa any more than the smiling Negress in top hat will find herself in Italy, first serving aperitifs in an open-air café, putting on a pressed uniform for the first time, but then working her way up from bartender to petit bourgeois comfort, sincerely intent on bettering herself and assimilating into the middle class. The foregrounding of the bottle of seltzer water is ironic, since the spritz action of the tap is associated in some advertising with maleness itself, with the kind of primitive power of micturition that put out the fires in psychoanalytic

Fig. 3. Boccasile's transvestite drama. (Salce Collection, 03097)

legend. The transvestite drama not only reconfirms gender roles (because femininity is only displaced for a moment, and in a highly theatrical way), it draws racial boundaries as sharp as the silhouettes of the graphic forms themselves. It is because the two figures are so utterly separated in reality that Boccasile can permit himself this fantasy proximity in an advertisement that sells "class" and "style" as inextricable from whiteness.

## Black Residues

Ultimately, Boccasile's serving Moor is also a fantasy that displaces a *class* reality, namely, the subordination of southern Italians (called blacks or Moroccans in slang, even to the present), to northerners. The regime may have managed to temporarily suspend the southern question by pointing its magic wand elsewhere and casting a spell of national, racial identity over Italy, but it was inevitable that the wounds would be reopened. With the loss of the colonialist euphoria, reconstructionists had to deal with the havoc wreaked on the Italian countryside by the regime and its lack of any coherent policy. During the boom years following World War II, it was the southern Italian "black" who would come north and serve the powerful elite.[19] In its fascination with the black body in all of the various incarnations I have discussed, the regime managed to move the gaze of the public "down there"—beyond the failed land-reclamation programs in Sicily, beyond the impoverished feudalistic villages of Calabria—to Africa. But the southern question is by no means resolved at the time of the present writing, and the Northern Leagues, currently gaining power on a platform of separatism, racism, and antigovernment-sponsored aid programs for the south, have helped bring the gaze back to Italy itself.

The question is, what has happened to blackness, in the meantime? Would an image such as Boccasile's staged power play still work in the context of the open market, or is it inevitably linked with the *historical* moment of colonization?

The answer is far from obvious. If these reduced, servile bodies of the 1930s now strike the eye as kitsch or provoke a slight sense of embarrassment, it is because they have been replaced with more European black bodies in mass culture. Bodies dressed up in Benetton, in youthful Bata sneakers, or even in high fashion.[20] The only traces left of Africa are the colorful ribbons or vaguely "tribal" jewelry that are, in any case, assimilated into the fashion vocabulary of the West. Blackness has been co-opted by a new youth-oriented target for which "being in fashion" also means having some relation (but is it a truly serious one?) with issues of world peace, the environment, and multiculturalism (figure 4).[21]

This is the thrust of the "United Colors of Benetton" campaign with its obsessive insistence on the "one of every color" variety. Ironically, of course, this multicoloration of the advertisements is really a reference to the mix-and-match stock of colors available for the consumer of clothing. Benetton works by offering a limited number of patterns or shapes, but a large array of dyes in a given season. The eye is attracted to the stacked sweaters in a store window, and items are displayed so as to persuade the consumer to buy an ensemble, a series of shaded layers or a bright clash of scarf over vest, and so on. In this context, blackness is only one of a whole series of colors, but this proposed all-inclusiveness only masks the single most significant binary of colored/white, empowered/subordinated, on which the real economics of the international clothing and textile industries are based. The positive, youthful association of the Benetton name with a new world order of global unity is also another way of forgetting the colonialist legacy, and then, by association, the very mechanisms of power forged under the regime that may still persist at some level in Italy today.

This is not the place to discuss current forms of racism in Italy. Just as the market, marching toward maturity in the 1930s, helped in the process of arousing a "colonial interest or will," so the current market helps erase the traces of this passionate moment in Italian public consensus. Perhaps, finally, the strongest factor linking the earlier graphic forms with more current mass cultural ones is precisely the black/white distinction as a mechanism for displacing a disturbing discourse about class in Italy itself. Boccasile's serving Moor and haughty woman in safari garb hardly make sense today, or at best they have achieved the status of kitsch, inasmuch as their bodies are posed as part of a theatrical piece whose very narrative structure resounds with "nostalgia" and a sense of "otherness" or "pastness," and yet which also conveys a vague sense of pleasure along with this particular and rather distasteful historical referent.

Fig. 4. "Antiracism" Moschino Jeans advertisement.

## Whitening Blackness

When David Bowie wed Iman Abdulmajid in Florence, the couple gave an exclusive story to the Italian magazine *Moda*. Wrapped in a white bandage-gown, the "Somali princess" was a picture of slim, Western, high fashion. The question of why the couple had chosen to be married in Italy produced a series of aesthetic clichés. Iman responded: "The Italians know how to have fun. Italian was my first foreign language. . . . Somalia was an Italian colony and so I was raised among Italians. . . . For beauty, for art, for the Italians themselves, and for the wonderful cappuccino. Florence has all of this to offer."[22] In an eighteenth-century palace, the event was staged for photographers, a drama of white against black that emerges from the magazine essay as if the linkage of the two superstars were just the next in a series of "fashion statements." This year, the sharp contrast of black and white is in! Bowie has shed his glam sparkling suits and sequins of the 1970s, his androgynous Day-Glo wigs of the 1980s, for the sophisticated elegance of a Thierry Mugler tuxedo: the return of a (repressed) classic. Black and white are cyclical, bound to reappear with a certain regularity. As the wedding couple walk down the runway/aisle, they pose for a journalistic service on the new season's colors, and, having chosen "beautiful Italy" for this fashion show, they only emphasize the merely aesthetic nature of this union. The magazine and its photographers are complicitous in this reduction of a complex love affair to "black and white," but they cannot be blamed for doing so. If they had reported on the wedding with color blinders on, they would have been guilty of ignoring the essence of this cultural moment.

Iman, quite apart from her own efforts and intentions, is a cultural construction, an image of Africa that appeals to the Western eye, photographed in African "styles" in various villages for a photo essay in *La Repubblica*. In the accompanying piece the reader learns that she was not satisfied with her natural breasts, and decided to Westernize her body with plastic surgery, "in order to be able to wear more décolleté fashions." And yet the essence of the photo essay is to display Iman in her natural habitat, like a nature documentary shot on location. Iman is represented in an ethos that is theoretically uncontaminated by "fashion." And finally, what are breasts but fatty tissue, superdeveloped in the overdeveloped nations of the West where diets are rich in fat? But Iman has no need of weight reduction, in the myth. "She doesn't like exotic vacations or visits to spas. Whenever she has time she flies to her Africa."[23] The contradictions in this single essay, or in the larger cultural imagination, are based on many of the same questions about blackness raised by the advertisements of the 1930s. To be fair, however, Iman herself has been a very important contributor to the relief efforts in Somalia. In particular, she appeared on talk shows and lobbied the Bush administration in an effort to arouse international consciousness of the famine long before the parades of starving babies on nightly news broadcasts. Iman's humanitarianism has been reported in the press, along with "human interest" information focusing on her modeling career, her marriage, and her social life. Ironically, then, her ties to a mythical Africa have opened up a passage for Western "interest" or "consciousness" (to repeat the fascist phrases) in a "real" Africa.

The body of Iman, coveted by one of the supreme icons of "fashion"—for my generation Bowie signifies this above all—should be read in the contemporaneous context of the daily parade of starving Somali bodies in the media.[24] What should be the role of Italy in the provision of humanitarian aid to its former colony whose very divisiveness not only accounts for the current famine, but forms part of the mythology of "tribal brutality" and feudal production that shaped the colonial impulse itself?[25] Haile Selassie's efforts at a constitution and the stirring of nationhood in Ethiopia were the essential factors that motivated the invasion in the 1930s. Now, as Italy digs into its deficit-ridden pockets, the questions of patronage and nationalism have become all the more vexing. The rhetoric linking Italy with Africa is vague, and incidentally, de-fascitized, nostalgic, on both sides. Like Iman's summation of what Italy represents, current discourse tries to circumscribe issues of political domination and subjugation while implying some sort of indistinct natural connection between the two geographical areas. The interim foreign minister of Somalia articulated this blurred sense of affinity: "I am turning to the nation and the government of Italy: we Somalis are linked to Italy. We have been faithful to you for generations. Now, help us. . . . You know very well where Somalia is located. Make sure your aid reaches the ports of our territory."[26] This statement was accompanied by horrendous images of babies, held up for the camera like the *faccetta nera* of fascist conquest. The slippage between the "smooth" fantasy of the Somali female and the body of a Somali baby with its inflated stomach and twiglike legs reveals a set of fundamental contradictions that first surfaced during the Imperial Moment but persist, with ever-greater complexity, into the present.

## Notes

1. For questions of blackness in fascist Italy, see my "Selling the Black Body: Advertising and the African Campaigns," in *Bodily Regimes: Italian Advertising under Fascism* (Minneapolis: University of Minnesota Press, 1995); also Angelo Del Boca, *Gli italiani in Africa Orientale*, 3 vols. (Bari: Laterza, 1976), especially vol. 2, *La conquista dell'impero*; Luigi Goglia, *Storia fotografica dell'impero fascista 1935–1941* (Bari: Laterza, 1985); Adolfo Mignemi, ed., *Fotografia/immagine coordinata per un impero. Etiopia 1935–1936* (Turin: Forma, 1984); Luigi Preti, *I miti dell'impero e della razza nell'Italia degli anni '30* (Rome: Opere Nuove, 1965); Rolando Quadri, *Diritto coloniale* (Padua: Cedam, 1953); Giorgio Rochat, *Militari e politici nella preparazione della campagna d'Etiopia. Studio e documenti 1932–1936* (Milan: Franco Angeli, 1971); Alberto Sbacchi, *Ethiopia under Mussolini* (London: Zed Books, 1985); Emanuela Trevisan Semi, *Allo specchio dei falasci: Ebrei e etnologi durante il colonialismo fascista* (Florence: Editrice La Giuntina, 1987).

2. Richard Dyer, "White," *Screen* 20:4 (fall 1988): 44–64.

3. Henri Bergson, *On Laughter* (New York: Doubleday, 1956), 86. For Bergson's possible relation with Cubism and the black body of "degenerate art," see Mark Antliff, *Inventing Bergson: Cultural Politics and the Parisian Avant-Garde* (Princeton, N.J.: Princeton University Press, 1993).

4. Fortunato Depero, *Fortunato Depero nelle opere e nella vita* (Trent: Legione Trentina, 1940), 271–72.

5. Futurist, "cartoonish" blackness has much in common with those caricatures of servility, the American pickaninnies. The pickaninny is now an object of intense collectionism in America, its kitsch value coexisting with a more serious-minded interest for scholars of black and white encounters. The objects themselves—salt-and-pepper shakers, letter openers, figurines, printed matter, ashtrays—are kept in glass cases in vintage or antique stores; they still bear an aura of ambivalence, danger. One just has to go through the experience of seeking them out, fingering them, asking prices, deciding the value of a particular piece (I'll throw in this cute shit-eating grinner—now how much would you pay?) to realize the intensely uncomfortable problematic aroused by black kitsch Americana. Does a little black boy lose its value if sold separately from the white plantation owner running behind him with a whip? Is he worth less than a larger and more robust "mammy" figurine? These sorts of questions are ultimately decided by the market, and probably not resolved openly in the banter between antique dealer and collector. Why are these feelings of discomfort not aroused (or at least not in the same way) by the purchase of a framed antique watercolor of a Negro emerging from a field of cotton? Where does the danger of blackness lie, if not in style itself? The most embarrassing question of all, it turns out, concerns the techniques, the styles, the brush strokes, the color adjustment, the lens filters, the f-stop-adjustment-for-Negro-skin-calculation-factor, that yield representations of blackness (by and for a white audience). In other words, it is precisely at the level of style that a jolting and disturbing temporal disjunction between "then" and "now" emerges. It is the same disjunction that allows for the pickaninny to be classified as both "an antique" and kitsch—qualities that cannot be presumed to be inherent in the object during its "primary" phase.

6. For discussions of the Italian presence in Africa from African and African American perspectives, see the contributions of Aden and Bekerie in this volume.

7. Lessona is quoted in Renzo De Felice, *Mussolini il duce. Gli anni di consenso, 1929–1936* (Turin: Einaudi, 1974), 604.

8. For France's "spatialization" of blackness with the islands, see: Léon Hoffman, *Le nègre romantique* (Paris: Payot, 1973), 148.

9. This kind of history without libido no longer seems possible since Klaus Theweliet's monumental *Male Fantasies*, vol. 1, *Male Bodies: Psychoanalyzing the White Terror*, trans. Stephen Conway; vol. 2, *Women, Floods, Bodies, History*, trans. Erica Carter and Chris Turner (Minneapolis: University of Minnesota Press, 1987; 1989).

10. Luciano De Crescenzo, "Faccetta nera," *Il Venerdi di Repubblica*, August 21, 1992, 21.

11. Quoted in Del Boca, *Gli italiani in Africa Orientale*, vol. 2, 287. Another version of the song was circulated after the conquest:

Black face, get away from me,
   I want a white woman, made like me.
   I am also a soldier and I go to war
   to defend all good things
   but in my heart I carry my bride
   because black face is not for me.
   I love the national product
   she is like a madonna who protects me from evil.
Translations of both versions are mine.

12. For stereotypes of the black female body, see Sander Gilman, "The Hottentot and the Prostitute: Towards an Iconography of Female Sexuality," in *Difference and Pathology: Stereotypes of Sexuality, Race, and Madness* (Ithaca, N.Y.: Cornell University Press, 1985). For a reading of black female bodies that is acutely aware of the "missing" white male, see Christian Maurel, *L'exotisme colonial* (Paris: Laffont, 1980), and Malek Alloula, *The Colonial Harem*, trans. Myrna Godzich and Wlad Godzich (Minneapolis: University of Minnesota Press, 1986).

13. Let me stress, however, that this "smoothness" is indeed a fantasy because Somali women do not, in fact, correspond with the body descriptions given in the media; they do not lack the buttocks of other African women.

14. Quoted in Del Boca, *Gli italiani in Africa Orientale*, vol. 2, 90.

15. From an article in *Lei*, February 1, 1935, 19.

16. Sigmund Freud, "The Taboo of Virginity," *Standard Edition of the Complete Psychological Works*, ed. and trans. James Strachey (London: Hogarth Press, 1953), vol. 11.

17. For the effect of Freud's father and the "second marriage" topos on various aspects of psychoanalysis, see Marie Balmary, *Psychoanalyzing Psychoanalysis: Freud and the Hidden Fault of the Father*, trans. Ned Lukacher (Baltimore: Johns Hopkins University Press, 1982).

18. "Interpellation" is a term taken from Althusser to describe a process whereby individuals come to feel themselves "hailed" as a group. Advertising often functions in this way, but the identification of the group as a national-racial one in Italy is new under fascism. For the general mechanisms of interpellation as a form of "false consciousness" in advertising, see Judith Williamson, *Decoding Advertisements* (London: Marion Boyars, 1978), 47.

19. On the southern Italian in relation to racial identity, see Pasquale Verdicchio in this volume.—*Ed.*

20. For an interesting discussion of Benetton's role in the politics of multiculturalism, see Vernon Silver, "All Cash Is Not Created Equal," *New York Times*, February 7, 1993, "Style," 3.

21. Interestingly, although the color black obviously makes its periodic appearance in fashion, when Italian postpunk youths of the mid-1980s began to wear black clothing and makeup, they were termed *i dark* by the media, appropriating the English word as if to defer even further the question of blackness as a cultural sign. Even these "cultural others," the *dark* who looked to London for their visual vocabulary, did not take up the issue of race. For more on this, see Gianfranco Manfredi, "Arrivano i dark: canti che ti passa," *Panorama*, December 15, 1985: 168–70.

22. "Nozze calde: nera su bianco," *Moda* (photos by Giovanni Cozzi) (July 1992): 12–25.

23. Francesca Alliata Bronner, "La favola di Iman," *Il Venerdi di Repubblica*, June 19, 1992, 64.

24. For David Bowie as the antidote to hippie "political correctness," see the important book by Jon Savage, *England's Dreaming: Sex Pistols and Punk Rock* (London: Faber and Faber, 1991).

25. The stirrings of nationalism in Ethiopia and the growing movement to form a constitution were very important moments in the mobilization of Italian consensus. In a famous memo of 1934, Mussolini summed up the new fascist policy in the wake of such changes: "The problem of Italian-Abyssinian relations has changed lately: from a diplomatic problem to a problem of force; a 'historical' problem that we must resolve with the only means available for the resolution of such problems: with the use of arms. Taking previous events into account, we must draw the only logical conclusion: time is against us. The more we delay in liquidating the problem, the more difficult will be the task and the greater the sacrifices. . . . Once we have agreed on this war, our objective can only be the destruction of the Abyssinian armed forces and the total conquest of Ethiopia. The empire cannot be made otherwise" (quoted in *Storia d'Italia. Dall'unità a oggi* [Turin: Einaudi, 1975], vol. 4, Part II, 2242–43).

26. Paolo Filo Della Torre, "Italiani aiutateci," *La Repubblica*, August 21, 1992, 12.

# Is *Aida* an Orientalist Opera?

*Paul Robinson*

Among the more remarkable events of recent intellectual history is that Edward Said, famous avant-garde literary critic and passionate advocate for the Palestinian cause, has begun to write about music. Moreover, not just about any kind of music, but about classical music in the elite (and canonical) European tradition—the symphonies of Beethoven, the operas of Wagner, the chamber music of Schubert and Brahms. Several years ago, Said took over the music column in the *Nation* magazine, and more recently he has published a book, *Musical Elaborations*, based on a series of invited lectures at the University of California at Irvine.

Most of Said's musical writings have been innocent of the theoretical and ideological concerns that distinguish his literary criticism and his politics. He comes across as a knowledgeable music lover, with a special devotion to the great German composers of the long nineteenth century (from Mozart to Strauss). As it turns out, Said is himself a pianist, who enjoys playing chamber music with friends. I have for some time suspected that music offers him a kind of asylum, a realm of unguarded pleasure, where he can lay aside the heavy burdens of his scholarly and political callings. In the world of pure sound, to which no representative meaning can be attached, he is liberated from the need to be ever watchful for orientalist subtexts or anti-Arab prejudices.

But not always. Instrumental music may be largely without denotative significance, but opera is another matter. Opera weds music to language and hence to literature—and often to politics as well. Thus, not surprisingly, when he has turned his attention to opera, Said has sometimes found himself on more familiar intellectual terrain (where, if I am right in my speculation, music no longer provides the wanted asylum). A case in point is his review of John Adams's opera, *The Death of Klinghoffer*, which treats the Achille Lauro incident. In general, Adams's opera got rather frosty notices from the musical press. Said, however, greeted it with enthusiasm in the *Nation*, in part, one suspects, because of the opera's sympathetic treatment of the Palestinians. An earlier example—and the one I wish to devote my attention to in this essay—is an article Said wrote in 1987 for *Grand Street* on Giuseppe Verdi's opera *Aida*. Entitled "The Imperial Spectacle," the article can fairly be described as an effort to interpret *Aida* as a product of Europe's developing imperialist culture in the nineteenth century.[1] (With only slight modification, the article has been incorporated into Said's book *Culture and Imperialism* [Alfred A. Knopf, 1993], 111–32.) In other words, it aims to understand this most famous of all Italian operas in terms of Said's theory of orientalism—the theory that the whole of Europe's culture is deeply inscribed with invidious representations of the non-European Other.

Said's contention that *Aida* is implicated in Europe's imperial order is in some respects unexceptionable. He draws attention, for example, to the circumstances of the opera's composition. Verdi was commissioned to write the opera by the viceroy (or khedive) of Egypt, Ismail, who wanted an opera by one of Europe's foremost composers for his new opera house in Cairo, which itself had been built in connection with the opening of the Suez Canal in 1869. (Had Verdi refused him, the viceroy was prepared to turn to Wagner or Gounod.) Put crudely, Verdi's opera was to form part of the cultural superstructure of the European presence in Egypt, a presence reaching back to the Napoleonic invasions at the end of the eighteenth century, and which, by the time of *Aida*'s premiere in 1871, had transformed Egypt into a semicolony. Indeed, the opera, as Said rightly says, was intended as "an imperial *article de luxe*" (103), purchased to entertain the European population of Cairo, whose real purpose was to administer Egypt as a piece of Europe's overseas empire. With a certain symbolic appropriateness, the new opera house—modeled on the neoclassical opera houses that sprang up throughout Europe in the nineteenth century—was located on the north-south axis dividing the Eastern Muslim portion of the city from the Western European portion. Naturally, its portals faced westward. On this imperial site, Verdi's brilliant operatic display was first seen and heard.

At the same time, Aida is of course an opera about ancient Egypt, and, as such, it was intended by Ismail to serve as a significant piece of nationalistic propaganda. Verdi seems to have cared nothing for this objective, and, as far as anyone has been able to tell, he never expressed an opinion about modern Egypt, although he was often told that his opera would do much to advance its cultural consciousness. A substantial part of Said's argument depends on his drawing attention to the origins of the opera's story in the richly elaborated traditions of French orientalist scholarship. *Aida* is in fact based on a scenario written by the great French Egyptologist Auguste Mariette, a scenario that Mariette urged on Verdi through the offices of their mutual acquaintance, Camille du Locle, the director of the Opéra-Comique in Paris. Said views Mariette as driven by the ideological desire to "stage" (89) Egypt for European cultural consumption. His scenario constructs an Egypt that is a locus of satisfactorily grand European origins but, more important, an Egypt that has been orientalized—rendered exotic—so that it can find its appropriately subordinate place in Europe's imperial imagination. Said makes the ingenious speculation that the settings and costumes Mariette proposed for the opera were directly inspired by the idealized reconstructions of ancient Egypt contained in the anthropological volumes of Napoléon's *Description de l'Égypte*, perhaps the first great document to package Egypt for Europe's imperial consumption. In this fashion, the famous scenes in the opera—the Royal Palace in Memphis, the Temple of Vulcan, the Gate of Thebes—are transformed into tableaux vivants from the pages of Napoléon's *Description*. Of course, any discussion that confines itself to the circumstances of the opera's commission or the origin of its libretto and mise-en-scène, although illuminating, does not really get us to the heart of the matter. *Aida* is an orientalist opera only if the drama Verdi actually constructed—under those circumstances and out of those materials—embodies the ideological project Said ascribes to it. Above all, it is an orientalist opera only if its ideological agenda is significantly embodied in its music; for, as Joseph Kerman has shown, in opera the composer is the dramatist. Things that can be identified solely in the text and that do not find expression in the music for all practical purposes cease to exist. As we all know, a good deal of what is uttered in opera is incomprehensible, and not merely because it is usually uttered in a language we cannot understand. If *Aida* is an orientalist opera, then, it will have to be because of its music.

An immediate embarrassment confronts Said's theory about *Aida*: although the opera does indeed represent an imperialist situation, it is an imperialist situation in which Egypt itself plays the role of aggressor. Verdi's Egypt is an imperial power seeking to subdue its African neighbor, Ethiopia. Indeed, the opera is set against the background of Egypt's war of conquest against Ethiopia (as well as the guerrilla response of the Ethiopians), and its conventional romantic plot turns on a conflict between desire and patriotism in which a young Egyptian general, Radames, finds himself in love with an Ethiopian slave, Aida, the captured daughter of the king of Ethiopia. In terms of Said's orientalist metaphor, white Egypt ought properly to be equated with imperial Europe, while black Ethiopia stands unambiguously in the role of the imperialized non-European Other. Furthermore, Verdi's sympathies in the opera are wholeheartedly on the Ethiopian side. Egypt is represented as an authoritarian theocracy, tyrannized by its intolerant priesthood—a clerical elite headed by the High Priest (and basso profundo) Ramfis, who is the opera's heavy—while Ethiopia ("conquered and tormented," in the words of its wily and heroic leader Amonasro) is repeatedly celebrated as a country of vernal beauty and natural rectitude. In his correspondence, Verdi referred to Egypt as "a land that once possessed a grandeur and a civilization that I could never bring myself to admire."[2] Under these circumstances, Said's contention that *Aida* serves to "stage" Egypt for European imperial consumption begins to look rather dubious. A more natural reading would be to see the opera as an anti-imperialist work, in which the exploitative relation between Europe and its empire has been translated into one between expansionist Egyptians and colonized Ethiopians. Revealingly, when fascist producers staged *Aida* in Mussolini's Italy, they often presented a blackshirted Radames subduing Amonasro's Ethiopian hordes, and Amonasro himself became an obvious stand-in for Emperor Haile Selassie, engaged in a bloody anticolonialist war against contemporary Italy.

The antithesis between militaristic Egypt and suffering Ethiopia is not, moreover, merely the dramatic backdrop of *Aida*. It is also deeply embedded in the music Verdi composed to represent the two nations. Egypt is characterized by music that is regular, diatonic, and brassy—music that can be described, I think, as distinctly European, in that it finds Verdi relying on the most traditional harmonic, melodic, and rhythmic means to conjure up an impression of power, authority, and military might. Two prominent musical episodes illustrate this association of Egypt with an aggressively traditional European idiom. The first is the "battle hymn" "Su! del Nilo," sung by the King and the High Priest and then by the assembled Egyptians in act 1 as they prepare to send their army into combat with the Ethiopians. The piece is four square, closed, and classical, its harmonies familiar, and its accompaniment emphatic. Significantly, Verdi himself feared that the tune smacked of the "Marseillaise," which puts it firmly on the European side of the imperialist divide. A second example is the "victory hymn" "Gloria all'Egitto," which the Egyptians sing after they come back from thoroughly defeating (indeed enslaving) the Ethiopians. Musically, it is constructed of the same sort of stuff as "Su! del Nilo," only it is even noisier and, appropriately, more triumphalist. Viceroy Ismail was so pleased with this tune that he wanted to adopt it as the Egyptian national anthem, in spite of the fact that it is much too short. One final feature of Verdi's musical treatment of the Egyptians needs to be noted: he typically sets the music of the Ramfis and the Egyptian priests in the form of a canon—that is to say, a fugue—thereby linking them musically with one of the oldest, most traditional, and most European of musical procedures, associated above all with the religious music of Johann Sebastian Bach.

Unlike the Egyptians, the Ethiopians are given no collective musical expression in the opera. Rather their concerns find voice in the two principal Ethiopian characters, the captured king, Amonasro, and his daughter, Aida. Much of the time, to be sure, Aida and Amonasro sing in an idiom that is not markedly different from the high European style that Verdi uses for all his major characters in the opera. But on a number of significant occasions, Aida in particular is allowed to speak of her native land—whose luxurious beauty she contrasts with the aridity of Egypt—and on these occasions Verdi sets her utterances to music that is the polar opposite of the sort of music he writes for his massed Egyptians. Instead of four square diatonic marching tunes, he writes music distinguished by its sinuous irregularity, its long legato lines, its close intervals, its chromatic harmonies, and its subdued woodwind orchestration, in which the reedy tones of the oboe play an especially prominent part. At such moments, Aida's music verges on the exotic. Perhaps the most famous example is her apostrophe to the virgin forests of Ethiopia, as she seeks to persuade her lover to flee with her back to her native land. It conjures up a world of alien loveliness—the world, I would suggest, of the non-European Other.

Having constructed this antithesis between imperial, Europeanized Egypt and oppressed, orientalized Ethiopia, I should not leave the impression that there is no basis in the opera's music for Edward Said's claim that *Aida* presents, as he puts it, "an Orientalized Egypt"(92). On the contrary, a not inconsiderable amount of music associated with the Egyptians in the opera is written in the peculiar "oriental" style devised by nineteenth-century European composers—particularly French composers—to treat exotic subjects. This oriental music can be characterized in terms of a number of almost clichéd melodic, harmonic, and timbral devices, which I need not describe here and which bear no necessary relation to the actual musical practices of non-European cultures. It is the sort of music that we associate with snake charmers. These conventions were universally recognized at the time (and can still be recognized today) as denoting the strange, the exotic, in a word, the "oriental." They make their significant historical debut in Meyerbeer's opera *L'Africaine*, which took Europe by storm in the 1860s and made a strong impression on Verdi. They can also be heard in a number of other operas that are roughly contemporaneous with *Aida*, notably *Carmen*, *Le Roi de Lahore*, and above all *Samson et Dalila*. We need, then, to consider Verdi's deployment of these exotic or oriental conventions in *Aida* in order to assess Said's claim that the opera presents "an Orientalized Egypt."

Verdi confines his oriental music in the opera to two functions, both of them ceremonial: he uses it for liturgical exercises and for ballets. None of the principal Egyptian characters (the young general Radames, the Egyptian king, his daughter—the spurned other woman—Amneris, and the High Priest Ramfis) expresses himself or herself, as it were, orientally. Rather, all their singing is in Verdi's standard high European mode, as is all the choral and march music he writes for the assembled Egyptian masses. (In purely quantitative terms, the oriental idiom occurs in no more than a tenth of the opera's music.) Nonetheless, the oriental style can be heard in three important liturgical episodes—first, in the great Consecration Scene in the Temple of Vulcan, where Radames performs the ritual preparations for the coming battle with the Ethiopians; second, at the beginning of the so-called Nile Scene (act 3), which opens with priests and priestesses chanting in the temple of Isis; and, finally, in the last scene of the opera, the Tomb Scene, where, sealed in a vault below the Temple of Vulcan, Aida and Radames sing their final duet—"O terra, addio"—as the priestesses above are again heard intoning the liturgical chant that we know from the earlier Consecration Scene. A related—albeit livelier—exotic musical language is used by Verdi for the opera's three ballets: the dance of the priestesses in the Consecration Scene, the dance of the Little Moorish Slaves in Amneris's apartments, and the seven-part grand ballet in the middle of the famous Triumphal Scene of act 2. In sum, there are three liturgical scenes and three ballets for which Verdi composes "oriental" music.

Several considerations, however, undermine any ready or unqualified association of this exotic liturgical and ballet music with the Egyptians. These considerations account for our tendency to hear this music as somehow belonging to a different sonic realm form than that normally inhabited by the Egyptians. In some cases the dissociation occurs because the performers in a particular liturgical episode or ballet are either themselves non-Egyptians or are connected with non-Egyptian paraphernalia. Thus, most obviously, the Little Moorish Slaves who entertain Amneris are of course captives—like the Ethiopians, they are the victims of Egyptian imperialism—so the exotic character of their dance music hardly serves to create what Said calls "an Orientalized Egypt." If anything, it has just the opposite effect. Likewise, the dancers in the Triumphal Scene ballet, although presumably Egyptian, "perform their steps around the idols and trophies taken from the conquered Ethiopians,"[3] so that the exotic music of the ballet comes to be associated in our minds less with Egypt than with Ethiopia. Interestingly, in the famous Berlin production of *Aida* by Wieland Wagner (which I saw in the early 1960s), the whole Triumphal Scene takes the form, as Said accurately records, of a "parade of Ethiopian prisoners carrying totems, masks, ritual objects as elements of an ethnographic exhibition presented directly to the audience" (96–97), which was part of Wieland's effort to transfer the "setting of the work from the Egypt of the Pharaohs to the darker Africa of a prehistoric age" (97).

Furthermore, one needs to note that all of the opera's exotic music, in both its liturgical episodes and its ballets, is associated with women—to the point that the antithesis between exotic and nonexotic music in *Aida* comes to seem a code as much for gender difference as for ethnic difference. Thus the distinctly exotic chant in the Consecration Scene is sung by a priestess, to which the answers of the temple priests are set in the familiar diatonic harmonies of the high European style. The succeeding ballet for the priestesses—written in the oriental manner— is, of course, danced exclusively by women. Likewise, the great ballet of the Triumphal Scene, despite its vigorously masculine music, calls exclusively for ballerinas. Even the dance of the Little Moorish Slaves— already, one would presume, sufficiently feminized by being so described—is also, Verdi says, to be performed by ballerinas. The only oriental music in the opera actually assigned to men is that for the priests in the temple of Isis at the beginning of act 3 (the Nile Scene), and, significantly, their chant again has a feminine association: the priests sing to "Isis, mother and bride of Osiris." One should perhaps note here that all of the archaeological evidence available to Verdi when he composed the opera indicated that the ancient Egyptians had no priestesses, only priests, but Verdi asked Mariette if it might be possible to invent the priestesses, and Mariette—no stickler for authenticity—was only too happy to oblige Verdi with as many priestesses as his heart desired.

Finally, on every occasion when Verdi introduces exotic music into *Aida*, he immediately answers it with music of impeccably occidental credentials. Moreover, these occidental responses are always set in the mouth of some unambiguously Egyptian character, either one of the principals (such as Amneris or Ramfis) or the masses chorus of Egyptian citizens and soldiers. It is as if Verdi were unconsciously seeking to inhibit any association of the Egyptians with the oriental—which also explains why, ethnically speaking, *Aida*'s exotic music seems to occupy a kind of no-man's-land. I want to cite here just one instance of this dialectic of exotic thesis and occidental antithesis, namely, its first occurrence in the opera. This is the chant of the priestess in the Temple of Vulcan at the start of the Consecration Scene. The invisible soprano's wailing incantation "in an invented Phrygian mode,"[4] set above distant harps and supported by female choristers, has many of the musical earmarks of the oriental style, including a repeated grace note on the sharpened tonic, diminished thirds, augmented seconds, and a curling arabesque, all of which, in the words of the Verdi scholar Julian Budden, "color the music with a sense of strange Eastern ritual."[5] But the priestess's melody is immediately answered by a litany of the priests, which is composed in the deeply ingratiating harmonies of the high European idiom. I suppose one might say that it is an instance of "East meets West," except, of course, that all of the singers are Egyptians. Significantly, I think, the orientalizing singer (the priestess) is female, while the occidentalizing ones (the priests) are male.

The same sort of juxtaposition, in which the exotic East is trumped by the conventional West, occurs in each instance where Verdi momentarily introduces oriental musical effects. Thus the exotic dance of the priestesses in the Consecration Scene is immediately followed by Ramfis's emphatically diatonic invocation to the gods, a foursquare arpeggiated tune with the vocal line firmly supported by pulsating trombones, and the entire Consecration Scene ends with Ramfis and Radames trumpeting the priestess's apotheosis of "immenso Ftha" in euphonious thirds, sung at the top of their lungs (and very near the top of their registers as well). Likewise, the dance of the Little Moorish Slaves is immediately followed (and, as it were, ideologically canceled) by the familiar Western harmonies of Amneris's servants and by Amneris's own sumptuously diatonic invocation of love. The orientalist extravaganza of the Triumphal Scene ballet—the most sustained stretch of exotic music in the opera—is followed immediately by a repetition of the pompously Westernized victory hymn, "Gloria all'Egitto." Finally, the exotic chant to the goddess Isis at the beginning of the Nile Scene—like the dance of the priestesses in the Consecration Scene of act I—gives way to a thoroughly Western and warmly ingratiating arioso for Ramfis, inviting Amneris into the temple. Repeatedly, the music of the Occident seems to negate that of the putative Orient.

I do not want to deny that some of this oriental music, as it were, rubs off on Egypt, thus giving substance to Said's contention that Aida has the effect of creating "an Orientalized Egypt," one alluding subliminally to the incorporation of nineteenth-century Egypt into the European empire. Under closer examination, however, it is not precisely Egypt that is orientalized by Verdi's exotic music but rather Egypt's imperial victims (the Moors and the Ethiopians), and, among the Egyptians themselves, state functionaries and entertainers, almost all of whom turn out to be women (and thus, presumably, not fullfledged members of Egyptian society). So the ideological import of Verdi's exotic musical gestures in the opera is more complicated than Said allows, and in some respects at least it seems to be exactly opposite from the construction he insists on.

If we ask what is the source in Verdi's imagination of the ideological universe on display in *Aida*, I would suggest that we look not to Europe's burgeoning oriental expansion of the late nineteenth century but to the politics of the Italian Risorgimento in the 1840s. *Aida* is in fact the last of the operas in which the imprint of Verdi's deep commitment to the Risorgimento can still be detected. It is heir to the tradition of operas like *Attila*, *I Lombardi*, and, above all, *Nabucco*. *Nabucco* was Verdi's first great success, and in it the political repression of Italy by the Austrians is metaphorically represented by the subjugation of the ancient Hebrews under the Babylonians. Its famous chorus of liberation, "Va, pensiero," became one of the battle cries of Risorgimento patriots, who identified Verdi's operas with their aspiration of national unification. In Verdi's imagination, Italy was always a colonized country, the victim of Hapsburg imperialism. In writing *Aida*, I would contend, he associated Ethiopia with Italy, just as he associated Egypt with Hapsburg Austria. Likewise, Ramfis and the Egyptian priesthood are products of Verdi's Risorgimento anticlericalism; they are equated in his mind with the Hapsburg Catholic hierarchy and the reactionary politics of the Roman papacy. The ideological heart of *Aida*, so to speak, lies in the magnificent outburst of Amonasro in his duet with Aida, where he calls on her to remember her people "conquered and tormented" (*vinto, straziato*). Verdi sets Amonasro's plea on one of those great arching phrases of which he was the supreme master, carrying the voice upward in an arc of passion to a sustained high note, and then bringing it back down to rest in the sonic territory from which it began. It is my favorite phrase in the opera—a wonderful opportunity for the high baritone—and it identifies Amonasro and the Ethiopians with all those conquered and divided nations that people Verdi's Risorgimento operas of the 1840s and that stand for his own "conquered and tormented" Italy.

In sum, one can make much more sense of the politics of *Aida* if one regards it first and foremost as an Italian opera, rather than an orientalist opera, and if one sees it as the final installment in the tradition of Verdi's political operas reaching back to the 1840s. This perspective also accounts for the opera's profound musical conservatism. In spite of its sophistication and refinement, *Aida* is still a traditional numbers opera, whose musical language looks backward to *Rigoletto* and *Traviata* rather than forward to *Otello* and *Falstaff*, just as its politics look back to the Risorgimento rather than forward to the fully realized European imperium.

# Notes

1. Edward W. Said, "The Imperial Spectacle," *Grand Street* 6 (winter 1987). All references to this work will be given in the text.

2. Letter to Camille du Locle, February 19, 1868; quoted by Julian Budden, *The Operas of Verdi*, vol. 3 (New York: Oxford University Press, 1981), 161.

3. Ibid., 226.

4. Ibid., 212.

5. Ibid., 211.

# Part III

Immigrations

# Strangers in Paradise: Foreigners and Shadows in Italian Literature

*Graziella Parati*

Since the early eighties, Italy has lost its status as a monocultural and monoracial country and has become a place of immigration from Africa, Eastern Europe, and Asia.[1] The new multicultural Italy is far from being a peaceful cultural melting pot of the nineties: Italians have often responded with racism and violence to the changes taking place in their country. Such a response suddenly became visible in the summer of 1989 with the murder of Jerry Masslo in Villa Literno. In his native South Africa, Jerry Masslo had been a political activist and had lost his father and one of his sons in the fight against apartheid. After coming from South Africa as a political refugee, Jerry Essan Masslo joined the crowds of immigrants who worked in the tomato fields in southern Italy, where he was killed by four local *teppisti* (hooligans).[2] It is a frightening paradox that it is in Italy and not in South Africa that Jerry Masslo found his death. Masslo was aware of the reality that it is impossible to "leave South Africa" behind. In an interview with the journalist Massimo Ghirardelli that took place one year before Masslo's death, he revealed that "No black man, no African man forgets what racism is, and I have found it here: it is unacceptable."[3] Jerry Masslo's funeral became a political event and a public demonstration of the desire of many Italians to fight against growing racial tension. Such demonstrations did not stop the frequent episodes of racist intolerance that took place in 1990 and marked the beginning of the increasingly inefficient handling of the problems in the new multicultural Italy.

Since then, other immigrants have begun to write their life stories and have created the first group of immigration writings, which, I

have no doubt, will be followed by other works. This article will analyze the texts of the African writers, and their creation of a hybrid
identity and their appropriation of the Italophone literary space. I will
explore the concept of alterity mirrored in African writers' texts written in Italian and the construction of otherness in hybrid literary contexts in which the collaboration between an Italian author and an
African writer has created representations of the transition from an
apparently mono- to a multicultural sense of the Italian nation.

In the new multicultural Italy, the minister Claudio Martelli proposed the creation of immigration laws that became later known as
*sanatoria*. Martelli's proposal was opposed by two right-wing parties:
the Partito Repubblicano and the Movimento Sociale Italiano. However, it was later approved. *Sanatoria* is a revealing term; it implies the
need to *sanare* (to heal), to restore the health of the diseased body of
a country exposed to foreign entities that become the illness to be
fought. This terminology borrowed from the rhetoric of illness and
adopted in the discussion on the *emergenza immigrazione* (immigration emergency) is based on the assumption that becoming a country
of immigration involves the contamination of its (almost) monocultural past and present. The *sanatoria* is intended as a remedy that
can neutralize the contamination. It is a word that lends itself to a
wide range of racist discourses on "foreigners," the *extracomunitari*,
and the "others." In their book, *I razzismi reali* (Real racisms)(1992),
Laura Balbo and Luigi Manconi elaborate the possibility of creating a
new multiracial Italy not as a utopian nonracist country but as a *paese
poco-razzista* (a less racist country).[4] Unlike France, Italy does not
have a party that defines itself entirely as xenophobic. Undoubtedly,
the Movimento Sociale Italiano and the Lega del Nord can be considered racist parties, but racism is not the core of their political agenda.
The law's translation into practice is directly responsible for the public
identity of most of the immigrants now living in Italy. Law number
39, dated February 28, 1990, was created to regularize the position of
the illegal immigrants that had entered Italy before December 1989.
About 220,000 immigrants took advantage of the *legge Martelli*
(Martelli law) and contributed to restore the "health" of the country.
Far fom being successful, such a law applied to the people already
present in Italy but did not create an efficient plan to solve future immigration to Italy.

## Redesigning the Face of Italy

The ongoing discussions on immigration and integration in Italy have recently been enriched by the voices of the immigrants who have begun to textualize their experiences. Autobiographical narratives are numerous and refer to public events that influenced the immigrants' lives, such as Jerry Masslo's murder and the creation of the *legge Martelli.* Authors such as Salah Methnani, Saidou Moussa Ba, Pap Khouma, Mohamed Bouchane, and Moshen Melliti, who create their own public history and private stories, appropriate and rewrite the accounts that Italian newspapers have constructed about the immigrants.[5]

In a 1991 issue of the magazine *Panorama* (March 24, 1991), Claudio Martelli stated that "Underneath it all, there is a preference for the white immigrant rather than for the darker one" (52). We can understand Martelli's statement by paying attention to the neologisms invented to define the immigrants' identities. While Eastern Europeans, Africans, and Asians are all defined as *extracomunitari* or paradoxically *cittadini extracomunitari*, the "white" immigrants have been spared the humiliation of being called *vu' lavà* or *vu' cumprà*. *Vu' cumprà* is a derogatory term used by Italians for all the street salesmen from Africa. It mocks the way these street vendors mispronounce *vuole* or *vuoi comprare* (do you want to buy?). Consequently, the same term has been used in variants such as *vu' lavà* (do you want to wash?) that add to the stereotype of the stupid immigrant who is unwashed (i.e., uncivilized).[6] It is by appropriating the very language through which Italians discriminate against the immigrants that some African authors have attempted to destroy the stereotypes about immigrants from the Third World. Naming these new writers in Italian has been and still is the problematic center of this essay. The temporary solution is to define them as African-Italian authors, since their texts construct African identities within an Italian national and linguistic context.[7]

The narratives written in Italian by immigrants are inevitably influenced by the writers' exposure to French colonialist culture, as most Africans who write in Italian come from Senegal, Morocco, and Tunisia. Such a background is inscribed in their texts, but does not become an explicit subject of works that are written in Italian. Their books recount specific life experiences as outsiders in a country that is culturally different from France and cannot parallel the French cultural influence in Africa. There is a discrepancy between the colonizing culture that dominated part of these new Italian-African writers' lives and the literary language into which their lives are being transcribed. These hybrid literary creations are based on the accumulation and relative assimilation of different Western cultural traditions filtered through non-Western languages and traditions.

In approaching these different levels of cultural intertextuality, I realize that the absence of African criticism on the texts that I analyze may lead me to assume an ethnocentric stance.[8] I am attempting to compensate for the lack of an African critical perspective by including oral testimonies from interviews with various authors who somehow can direct and influence my critical approach to their own texts.[9] I do not presume to understand the African cultural background in the books that I will discuss, but, with critical humility, I will venture a few hypotheses on the important role that African-Italian literary creations play in changing contemporary Italian literature.

What I plan to theorize here is the need to create a context for Italophone literature in which multinational and multiracial voices can become part of the discussion of the Italian cultural tradition. Such a space must not become a ghetto where literary voices are associated with specific racial and national identities. The risk is that one would reach a simplistic essentializing that could define Italophone voices as part of a new margin with connotations of inferiority. In recent and not so recent years, some Italian authors have created narratives (Giulio Angioni, Erminia Dell'Oro, Marco Lodoli, Maria Pace Ottieri, etc.) that complement the voices of Methnani, Ba, Khouma, or Bouchane. In the novels by Italian writers, the African immigrants become protagonists of narratives that do not attempt to create homogenizing representations of immigrant identities. This essay, therefore, cannot supply permanent solutions but a preliminary and revisable approach to "other" men's and women's narratives.[10]

## African-Italian Narratives

Many of the texts written by immigrants are written in collaboration with an Italian writer. Both Alessandro Micheletti and Saidou Moussa Ba appear as authors of *La promessa di Hamadi* (Hamadi's promise) (1991). Ba describes the writing of the text as coauthoring: some notes were written by him in French and were used to develop the plot of the novel that was written in Italian in a close collaboration between authors. Mohamed Bouchane's *Chiamatemi Alì* (Call me Alì) (1990) was originally a diary written in French and Arabic by Bouchane himself. While taking classes to learn Italian, Bouchane wrote a composition in Italian that was inspired by his own personal writings. Carla De Girolamo, Bouchane's Italian teacher, suggested that his diary could be published and met weekly with Bouchane to transform his bilingual French/Arabic work into an Italian text. Pap Khouma's *Io venditore di elefanti* (I, an elephant salesman) (1990) was created with Oreste Pivetta, who also wrote the introduction to the autobiographical text, when Khouma was still learning Italian through a grammar book bought in France. "My experience," writes Khouma, "has been obviously followed by many other immigrants like me, people who know as their official language the language of the colonizers, French, English, Spanish, or Portuguese."[11] The language learned in order to become "normal people" (13) allows Khouma to leave the colonizers' language behind and acquire a literary voice mediated through the experience of an Italian journalist.

In his book *Decolonising the Mind*, Ngugi Wa Thiong'o asserts that adopting a new language involves a separation from the past "toward other worlds."[12] He refers to the colonizers' languages imposed over the African native languages, so that acquiring an education has meant abandoning an African past to embrace the superiority of Western knowledge. As language is intended as both a "means of communication and a carrier of culture" (13), such a separation becomes a mutilation, an exile from a community. "Language as culture," adds Ngugi, "is the collective memory bank of a people's experience in history" (15). This evident separation from the original language appears in the Italian texts written by Africans in Italy. However, the context is somewhat different from the one described by Ngugi, as the center of the discussion is migration, and the inevitable coming together of different languages and cultural contexts in a process of geographical and cultural translations.[13] In *The Post-Colonial Critic*, Gayatri Spivak states that "the diasporic cultures are quite different from the culture that they came from originally."[14] Most African-Italian writers come from already multicultural backgrounds and therefore hybrid diasporic cultures. Most of them have had to learn French, since most of these writers come from former French colonies. Embracing Italian means to create another "collective memory bank" that aims to construct other "people's experience in history." The emphasis is not so much on one history, but on plural interpretations of many histories and, in this case, on a specific community and a specific history of immigrants and immigrations to Italy. Italian has become the language shared by many groups of immigrants from Africa, Asia, and Eastern Europe, groups that do not share a common original language. The narratives created in Italian by immigrants themselves define their present history, the history of migrations, and address a larger reading public. However, in creating such a history, some African-Italian writers have avoided inscribing the story of their lives in the countries from which they emigrated. Mohamed Bouchane's narrative starts with his arrival in Italy. When asked in the interview, he refused to talk about his life in Morocco. For most of these authors, talking about life in Italy means to describe their involuntary exile, which involves a forced separation from their country. Their silence about the past expresses the attempt to focus on the present. The discourse on difference and separation that African-Italian writers create in their autobiographical texts also defines the immigrants' "difference" from both the culture left behind and their "otherness" in the new land.

Being an Italophone writer is the result of acts of mediation through various cultural and linguistic planes. These planes are appropriated by African writers in order to create multicultural narratives that allow them to become visible in the Italian literary world. Cultural and linguistic *métissage* is based on the attempt to intertwine traditionally diverse cultures and literatures in order to create a hybrid entity that destroys the separation between the dominant Western literary tradition and the non-Western tradition of, very often, the colonized. In the case of African-Italian texts, the final literary creations are based on several "acts of *métissage*." Defining *métissage* as an act, rather than a condition, describes the deliberate creation of a space in between cultures and traditions that African-Italian writers appropriate and modify. In this hybrid context, the French tradition and language become intermediate passages that lead to the acquisition of a third (sometimes a fourth) culture and language. The colonizer's language and literature are therefore displaced from their usual privileged position in order to become secondary to the appropriation and personalization of another culture.

The African-Italian acts of *métissage* are further problematized by the active intervention of an Italian writer within the immigrant writer's text. It is, in this case, the Italian author who appropriates the African cultural background and the Francophone experience of the African author. Therefore, Saidou Moussa Ba, Pap Khouma, Salah Methnani, Mohamed Bouchane, Moshen Melliti, and Nassera Chohra become the mediators who allow their Italian collaborators to learn about the Francophone culture of the former colonies. The result is that the Western eyes of the Italian authors approach the French colonial cultures through the non-Western eyes of the African-Italian writers.[15]

Far from becoming "normal people," as Khouma stated, these African-Italian writers become, within Italian literature, the "narrow door" that opens the European/Italian literary tradition to non-Western traditions. These African-Italian authors create an "*international dimension both within the margin of the nation-space and in the boundaries *in-between* nations and peoples.*"[16] Ironically, Italians have named the immigrant as *extracomunitari*, attaching to such a term negative connotations, and, therefore, they openly reveal a limited Eurocentric approach to reality. I am not attempting to theorize a utopian creation of a world literature, but, in order to draw our attention to them, I privilege those writings that are part of the new developments in Italian culture and that expand both the boundaries of Italian literary tradition and the definition of Italian culture.[17]

Most of the texts mentioned earlier were born from notes in other languages, but created in final publishable form in Italian. I would first like to consider the case of Moshen Melliti's *Pantanella. Canto lungo la strada* (Pantanella: a song along the road) (1992). Melliti arrived in Italy from Tunisia in 1989 and after working with a group of volunteers at the Pantanella, an abandoned pasta factory where a large number of immigrants had found shelter, wrote a book in Arabic. The novel describes the experiences of a group of illegal immigrants who lived in precarious conditions at the Pantanella. The book was translated into Italian by Monica Ruocco and was published exclusively in Italian. This text was created in Italy, and its content is directly related to an Italian situation, but its form, the language, belongs to a completely "different" literary tradition, which required the mediation of a translator. Melliti's work further expands the limits of *italophonie* and the concepts of "difference" and marginality. First written in Arabic and then translated into Italian, Melliti's text, therefore, is now part of Italian literary and cultural tradition.

Similarly, but originating from a different context, Tahar Ben Jelloun's work in Italian expands the boundaries of Italian literature. In order to approach Tahar Ben Jelloun's book, *Dove lo stato non c'è. Racconti Italiani* (Where the state does not exist: Italian tales) (1991), I need to negate the previous assumptions based on the separation between *francophonie* and *italophonie*. Ben Jelloun, a well-known Moroccan author who usually writes in French, published *Dove lo stato non c'è* in collaboration with Egi Volterrani. It is a collection of short stories written in Italian that add to the already multiple definitions of the flexible boundaries of the Italophone space. Immigrants are the protagonists of only one of the short stories in Ben Jelloun's book. "Villa Literno" describes the lives of Africans in the south of Italy and their relationships with the local people. The main character in the story is an old man, Antonio, who is initially afraid of what people call *l'invasione nera* (the black invasion)(29). He soon realizes that the "invasion" is not made of threatening shadows: "The shadows are not ghosts anymore. The shadows are men who lean their cheeks on the humid ground and sleep without dreaming. They do not even have enough strength to dream" (33). The other stories deal with centuries-old problems in southern Italy, and in particular with the Mafia. By displacing the readers' attention from the consequences of immigration to the never-solved problems in the south, Ben Jelloun claims that the diaspora is not the cause of the southern Italian socioeconomic and political problems. In fact, in "Villa Literno," Antonio tells the story of Jerry Masslo's murder to the strangers who want to listen and describes the "black problem" as the screen behind which it is easy to hide the "real" problems of the poor south.[18] Ben Jelloun's contribution leads to a discussion of the hybrid context of Italophone studies and the changes in the French cultural influences on Italian literature through the centuries. The literary connections between French and Italian literature weave together the works of those who have been considered major writers in both languages. French has also been for centuries the "right" foreign language to learn in Italian schools. However, the new link between Francophone and Italophone realms is a connection between what have been considered "marginal" voices and literary texts. Ben Jelloun's intervention in Italophone literature creates a space of hybridity and *métissage* in which separations can be overcome through a process of translation from one mixed plane to another. Translation is the key word in attempting to define Italophone literature and immigrants' narratives. "To transfer" and "to translate" come from the same Latin root and, together in this context, they define the dual act of geographical and cultural "translation," which is the opposite of separatism.

Ben Jelloun's Italian work, inscribed within his previous Francophone literary production, is complemented by Nassera Chohra's French-Algerian-Italian writings. Nassera Chohra and her Muslim Algerian family live in Marseilles, where she was educated within the French school system. Her autobiographical text *Volevo diventare bianca* (I wanted to become white) (1993) was written in Italian, as Chohra now resides near Rome and has adopted Italy as her homeland.[19] In a recent interview, Chohra rejected the idea of "models" by adamantly refusing to reveal her readings and favorite authors. This proclaimed independence from "sources" is accompanied by the revelation that she read other North African women's narratives only a posteriori, after finishing her own autobiographical act. Her book, she states, was conceived during a difficult pregnancy when she started thinking about her own mixed identity and about the connotations attached to being nonwhite. Therefore, she said, the book was intended to prevent her child from being as ashamed of his black mother as Chohra had been of her own mother.

Chohra's text may be read as a dialogue between her identity as a French-Algerian woman and her role as a French-Algerian-Italian woman-writer-wife and mother. She narrates her life in Marseilles, her childhood desire to become white (by literally bleaching her skin), and her experiences in the French capital, where she wanted to become an actress. Only the final chapter in Chohra's text is dedicated to her experience in Italy, and it was solicited by Alessandra Atti di Sarro, the editor. This chapter does not tell an immigration story and, therefore, offers an alternative to the stereotypical assumption that any "black" person traveling in Italy is an immigrant. The trip to Italy is Chohra's exploration of a country as a tourist before deciding to turn it into her new home.

The "plural" national and personal identities of each individual author defeat any attempt to create an essentializing definition of "what an immigrant writer is." Even the texts that have been literary models to the African-Italian writers come from both Western and non-Western traditions. For instance, Mohamed Bouchane stated that Mohamed Choukri, a Francophone Moroccan writer, was present in his mind while he was transforming his diary into a book. Salah Methnani's literary models are authors as different as the American writer on Morocco Paul Bowles and Tahar Ben Jelloun. Pap Khouma told me in an interview that he had been inspired by Günter Wallraff's *Ganz Unten* (1985), which he had read in the Italian and French translations. Translated into Italian with the title *Faccia da turco* (Turkish face)(1986), Wallraff's book tells the story of his transformation into a Turkish immigrant and his undercover life among immigrants.[20] Khouma's autobiographical story of a Senegalese man in Italy is, therefore, inspired by the narrative of a German journalist who disguises himself as a Turkish man and then writes his personal experiences in German, which Khouma reads in the Italian translation. This synthesis that destroys the separation among different cultural and linguistic models is representative of the attempt to destroy a hierarchical structure of influences and create a context in which writers become the "translators of the dissemination of texts and discourses across cultures."[21]

The notion of dissemination intended as fragmentation and appropriation of both the original and the "other" cultures is the center of Saidou Moussa Ba's literary work. Saidou Moussa Ba published *La promessa di Hamadi* (Hamadi's promise) in 1991. This text, which draws from the author's personal experience in Italy, is created as a novel and not as an autobiography. Ba tells the story of two Senegalese brothers, Hamadi and Semba. Hamadi decides to emigrate to Italy and leaves his wife behind. Semba dreams that his brother is in trouble and leaves for Italy in order to help him. In an interview, Ba revealed that his aim was to inscribe part of the tradition from which he came into the Italian story that he wanted to construct. The book begins with a chant written according to the tradition of the narratives transmitted by the griot, who preserved the history of Senegal as oral tradition and who used to recite the history of the important families at public functions and celebrations. The story thus constructed aims to bridge separate cultures in the description of two brothers, two illegal immigrants in Italy, who live the experiences shared by many other Senegalese immigrants in Italy.[22] Hamadi, the older brother, is the narrator of the story; he appears as the protagonist in the narrative only at its beginning and at its end. The close relationship between the brothers, who, after having been separated, communicate through enigmatic dreams, leads Semba, the younger brother, on a trip from Senegal to Italy that becomes a rite of passage. His search for Hamadi is a quest to construct his identity in a different and hostile culture, which he first rejects and then strives to understand. According to the laws of animism, dead people remain with the living and continue a life after death with the people they love. Ba translates this belief into the narrative and creates a narrator, Hamadi, who is dead. It is a dead man who tells the story of his brother's journey and creates a link between past and present, between Senegal and Italy. Before leaving his country and searching for his brother, Semba asks a woman, Maali, to predict his future. "Hamadi," says the old woman, "will hide on the lowest level, but you will climb to the highest point, you will see him there and you will talk for a long time. But it is a road that you have to travel alone. I cannot tell you more" (18). The woman's prediction is filtered from African culture to an Italian context when Semba finally finds his brother. They meet on the highest peak within an urban context, the top of the Duomo in Milan.

On this highest point, in this marginal space that still belongs to the city but is a separate world in itself, Hamadi shows his brother his worldview:

> In this society we should behave like chameleons. Yes, change color, be at the same time a bit African, a bit European, a bit Asian. . . . We should be ready to open doors, to accept others and to learn from them, to exchange the best that we have for the best that others have to offer. . . . When two nations, like two people, meet, they can give each other the best or the worst of themselves. Here it is, we and white people at at this point: each one of us must choose which direction to follow. (136–37)

Hamadi illustrates here the concept of racial and cultural *métissage* as an interweaving of traces that links Western and non-Western cultures and destroys the idea of multiculturalism based on separatism and a dichotomized portrayal of racial difference. The "act of *métissage*" is therefore characterized by the lack of unity, of "one" nationality and of one racial identity. The male subjectivities that Saidou Moussa Ba creates are defined by fluid ego boundaries that partake of both their native cultures and the new Western world.

## Gendered Selves

The Italian-Ethiopian writer Maria Viarengo (her father is Italian and her mother is Oromo) asserts, in her yet unpublished autobiography, her right "to be two," both Maria and Abebù, the name given to her by her Ethiopian mother. Her autobiography, written in Italian, is scattered with words and sentences in her native language. Maria Viarengo told me in an interview that she was disconcerted when *Linea d'ombra* published part of her autobiographical text, translating her title from Oromo into Italian.[23] "Scirscir 'ndemna" became "Andiamo a spasso?" (Shall we go for a walk?). This is the literal translation, and yet it is not the same, because the translation creates a separation from both the maternal language and the images it evokes. The translation also strengthens the link with the paternal and destroys the message inherent in the choice of the mother's tongue. This external intervention in order to make the text more understandable for Italian readers defines the limits inherent in arbitrary literary translations that privilege Italian readers but violate original texts.[24]

In the transnational space of Italophone literature, Maria Viarengo occupies a privileged position. In her autobiographical text, she tells her story as daughter of the only white man, the rich man, in an Ethiopian village. Born in 1949 in the ex-colony, Maria Viarengo is the only woman writer who recounts her experience as daughter both of an Italian man and of a native woman. Being the daughter of an Italian has, for instance, saved her from the destiny of her Oromo girlfriends who had to go through the ceremony of infibulation.[25] Her bilingual education is based on the supremacy of Italian over Oromo. In fact, she was sent to another ex-Italian colony, Eritrea, to be educated in Italian. The father's culture is therefore privileged to the extent that she has learned not only Italian but also the paternal regional dialect, Piedmontese. In her published autobiographical text, Viarengo constructs her hybrid identity in Italian, Oromo, and Piedmontese. However, the "Italian identity" acquired while in Africa loses its initial connotations when displaced into her father's land. At the age of twenty, Viarengo moves to Italy, where she is surprised to find a country different from the one where she had previously spent holidays moving from one hotel to the other "thanks to father's money" ("Andiamo a spasso?" 74). In fact, her feelings of being equally Italian and Oromo are not mirrored in the way Italians perceive her:

> I have heard people call me anfez, klls, meticcia, mulatta, caffelatte, half-cast, ciuculatin, colored, armush.
> I learned the art of looking like somebody else, I always looked like whomever others wanted me to be.
> I have been Indian, Arab, Latin American, Sicilian. (74)

To be able to modify oneself in order to become acceptable to the society in which one lives means to model one's identity on the preconceived theories of Africans in Italian society. Married to an Italian man, Maria Viarengo had to bear the humiliation of being treated by people as the caretaker of the white children (her own children) with whom she went strolling. Therefore, the privileged multiple identities she previously acquired were suffocated by superimposed roles aimed at creating an essentializing definition of her hybrid self.

Maria Viarengo has also contributed, by writing two chapters, to *Uguali e diversi: Il mondo culturale, le reti di rapporti, i lavori degli immigrati non europei a Torino* (Equal and different: the cultural world, the network of relations, the occupations of non-European immigrants in Turin) (1991).[26] This is the first published research on the lives and problems of immigrants that relies on the collaboration of a group of immigrants. Of the twenty-four collaborators, only six are Italian. This successful project is different from others in which the authors' discourse on alterity is limited and limiting, as is the case with Renato Curcio's *Shish Mahal* (1991).[27] *Shish Mahal* is an accurate description of the occupation and later the forced evacuation of the Pantanella in Rome. Curcio's introduction is dominated by a narrating first person explaining the social and political motivations that led to the decision to write the book. However, in a text that strongly criticizes the terms Italians use for immigrants, Curcio uses the word "shadows" (52) to refer to the immigrant women about whom he writes in his work on immigration: "Words: shadows. Where are and how do the wives, the daughters, the girlfriends of the guests at Shish Mahal live? Nobody wonders about that even if, some time ago, Joussef Salman revealed in an interview, "Our women? We keep them outside, living in *pensioni* in and around Rome. We pay with enormous sacrifices" (52).

This is a revealing dichotomy: the men at the Shish Mahal are represented as "good" providers. Women are shadows kept at the margins of the struggle. Curico's choice of the term "shadows" needs to be questioned. It appears that Curcio is creating a dichotomized portrayal between light and darkness that traps us into a very limiting discourse on gender and gendered identities. I have to agree, however, that immigrant women's voices are barely surfacing today in Italy. Apart from Maria Viarengo's privileged position and Nassera Chohra's autobiography, immigrant women are less visible than are immigrant men. Very often, their roles in this new country enclose them in domestic spheres where their lives are completely regulated by the families for whom they work. These families carefully measure the free time allowed for *collaboratrici domestiche* (domestic collaborators).

Amelia Crisantino, a sociologist who lives and works in Sicily, interviewed and wrote about the women who immigrated to Palermo. In *Ho trovato l'Occidente: Storie di donne immigrate a Palermo* (I discovered the West: stories of women immigrants in Palermo) (1992), Crisantino discovers the complex, almost hierarchical, social structure that regulates the relationships among ethnic groups.[28] During her search for possible interviewees, Crisantino meets with resistance, as clearly reflected in this woman's words: "White people always want to know things, they think they understand. In my country it is bad manners to ask a person about his or her life. If you write a book, then will you give us the money that you earn? I mean, what is your job, how much do you earn?" (174).

This interviewee refuses to be read as a text and attempts to change her role from interviewee to interviewer and to transform Crisantino into the text to be explored. Crisantino's book has limitations; it filters women's words through the narration of her search for their life stories. Consequently, the narrator in the text becomes the protagonist, and the women interviewed sometimes become objects in the narrative. By contrast, *La terra in faccia: Gli immigrati raccontano* (Dirt in your face: immigrants narrate) (1991), edited by Giuliano Carlini, the role of the interviewer remains secondary.[29]

On March 4, 1990, the Comune di Milano and the Coordinamento donne 8 marzo organized a conference and published the proceedings in a volume titled *Le mille e una donna. Donne migranti: incontri di culture* (A thousand and one women: migrating women: the intersection of cultures) (1990).[30] In this collection, the speech of a Moroccan woman, Majuba Agig, is transcribed as she attempts to draw a parallel between old and new forms of immigration. She states that "we do not take more than those who arrived twenty years ago, the *meridionali* [southern Italians]; we are the brothers of the *meridionali*" (58). Majuba Agig attempts to create a larger discourse on immigration that connects the new movement from the south to the north to previous internal and external migrations in Italian history. The emphasis is, in fact, on a revision of the concept of Italian history by redefining its margins. Many immigrants expect Italy to react differently than other European countries, with less racist attitudes, that is, toward immigrants from Africa. Saidou Moussa Ba told me that when he came to Italy he thought that Italians would be sensitive to his problems because Italy has its own tradition of emigration to the United States and northern Europe. He has been disillusioned, as very little has come back to Italy about the struggles of, for instance, the Italian Americans.

Italy is the choice of many Africans who cannot accept a move from the colony to the (ex-)"motherland," in most cases France. In *Io, venditore di elefanti* (1990), Pap Khouma describes his initial trip to "Paris, the capital of the empire"(46), where he feels rejected by both the French and the Senegalese who have lived for a long time in Paris. "I cannot stand Paris any longer," he writes. "I feel mistrust and hostility around us. The Senegalese people reject us, as if we were there to steal something" (49). Italy becomes the alternative country where an anti-immigrant tradition is not yet established but where an immigrant nonetheless faces insurmountable discrimination. For many Italians, any immigrant is a *Marocchino*. If immigrants are black they become *Marocchini neri* (103). Pap Khouma's identity is invented in each new encounter with an Italian. He becomes an unknown text that is always misread, as in this exchange with the police:

"Dance some break dance."
"No, we do not do break dance."
"How come, you are black and you don't do any break dancing!"
"We do not dance break dance."
"Then dance an African dance." (79)

Pap Khouma's goal was to stop selling "elephants," the objects from Senegal, and cigarette lighters or cigarettes. He rejected the stereotypical identity of the *vu' cumprà*, the men who sell objects that, according to Italians, represent their culture. This paradoxical act of selling the symbols of one's culture ("My Africa for sale," says Khouma [61]) as translated into "souvenirs" defines the alienation of the immigrant man isolated in a marginal space defined both by the new Western culture and by the symbols, often the stereotypes, of his country of origin. In this tra(n)s-*latio*, in this movement to Italy, the objects to be sold "become," for Italians, the immigrants' native culture. In this *reductio ad unum*, "difference" is tangibly objectified and visible on the market. For many immigrant women, the act of selling "objects" is often translated into the act of selling their bodies. In *Io, venditore di elefanti*, Khouma describes the Senegalese women in Italy: "They, the girls, sold everything, everything. And they justified themselves this way: 'We have to sell in order to live. Like you do with your necklaces.' They charged a lot of money" (37).

In the same text, Pap Khouma approaches the problematic of gender and race and defines the condition of the immigrant as a result of a forced "feminization." Faced by the representatives of the Italian state and order, Khouma says, one has to talk with "downcast eyes," to be obedient and humble (14; 62). This subordinate public role is echoed in the private sphere in which gender-specific activities in the country of origin are completely redefined. "I have always laughed at those young men, " writes Khouma, "who do women's jobs. But we are not in Dakar and I can do nothing but adapt" (73). This adaptation to new roles is felt as a weakness that makes them malleable, vulnerable, and more defenseless. Both Khouma and Methnani describe the aggressive sexual invitation of Italian men who translate the African men's economic-cultural and ethnic difference into a marketable objectification of their "exotic" bodies (Khouma, 92–98; Methnani, 65–67). Geographical displacement creates a new concept of the gendered selves and their roles in relation to the new structure of a given ethnic community.

## Religious Identities

To inscribe his life in the literary space of an autobiographical narrative necessitates for Pap Khouma an active definition of his identity in order to defy stereotypes. The act of writing reflects Khouma's independent declaration of existing as a Senegalese man, different from the others, one individual who must not be lost in the crowd of the black *Marocchini*. Such a declaration of independence, however, is reversed at the end of the book. After stating his difference, Khouma defines his sameness with the other Senegalese immigrants. "This is the life of a Senegalese man," writes Khouma, "the life that I have known for a time that seems very long to me" (143). The "I" thus constructed has fluid boundaries that always allow the protagonist to consider and write his self in relation to a community. Most of the narratives written by African-Italian men contain descriptions of the totally male communities that characterize these early years of immigration. Pap

Khouma defines these small communities as hierarchically organized. They represent the weak link with the African motherland, although that motherland is their economic point of reference (money is not kept in banks but left with the elder) as well as their emotional one. The self and the community are linked less by ethnic identity than by religious practice, as in Mohamed Bouchane's *Chiamatemi Alì* of 1990. Mohamed, the protagonist of this book in diary form, comes from Morocco. According to Mohamed, living in Italy involves a struggle for survival, to find lodging, work, and to learn a new language. Since his padrone calls him "beast" (108) and most of the Italian people he meets cannot pronounce "Mohamed" correctly, he renames himself, refusing the Italian names with which people try to "christen" him. He chooses "Alì" because it is still a name from his country, a name that does not diminish his identity as a Moroccan and, most of all, as a Muslim. Mohamed/Alì's greatest struggle is to remain a devout Muslim, find food he can eat, and defy any attempt to weaken his religious identity. Alcohol, says even Pap Khouma, is a great temptation; people are more willing to treat you to a glass of wine than to offer you food (87).

Mohamed Bouchane is the only author who defines himself through his religious identity. The name of Allah appears as a constant word within Bouchane's Italian narrative and changes the rhythm of the narrative: "I went with Taufik to see the area where, inshallah, we will soon live" (146). The book itself begins with "In the name of Allah Clement and Merciful" (7). During our interview, Bouchane continued to stress the importance of his struggle to remain a devout Muslim in Italy, a country where, he feels, "integration" is more difficult for him than for other immigrants. Bouchane also eleborated on the meaning of integration. The dividing line among immigrants lies, according to Bouchane, in their religious faith. Integration is possible for the Catholic immigrants but impossible for Muslims. Bouchane cannot construct his own familial group as it is impossible for a Muslim man to have a relationship with an Italian woman. He has, in fact, returned to his country and married a Moroccan woman. The possibility of integration through sexuality surfaces in other narratives. Immigrant men desire Italian women, in Khouma's narrative, because "going out" (i.e., becoming visible as a sexual human being) with local women means beginning to belong to the new country (70).

Mohamed meets with much resistance because people either do not attempt to understand him or they try to convert him, as in the case of one of the priests who "help" the immigrants. Once he finds work, it is hard for him to respect his religious holidays and the fasting during Ramadan and, at the same time, keep his job. Mohamed's difficulties are created by the rigidity of the traditionally monoreligious society. Sometimes the Italians' resistance is motivated, however. To require the new immigrants to adapt totally to preestablished rules is as unacceptable as to renounce Italian traditions and indiscriminately accept new rules incompatible with Italian society. This is the case with polygamy. A man, Mohamed Bokri, emigrated from Morocco to Italy. After a few years, he asked for permission to bring his family to Italy. However, his family included two wives. The Italian state first prevented him from reconstructing his familial group; then, after he appealed the judgment, it allowed him to be joined by his family. This decision by an Italian judge has established a precedent for the temporary legalization of polygamy. In order to "respect" new cultures, Italy once more seems to define women's issues as secondary. "How can one reconcile," ask Balbo and Manconi, "the acceptance of the other, of the other's traditions and of the other's forms of relation . . . with the need not to overshadow, even from an ideological point of view, a value the value of the equality between men and women that our society recognizes and normatively regulates?" (78). It is not possible to answer such a question in this context, but it needs to be asked in order not to adopt "easy" antiracist attitudes that proclaim the right of people from other cultures to be accepted and not required to change or adapt to Italian culture. The idea of solely unilateral malleability can be ideologically and theoretically acceptable but impossible to translate into practice. It would be another way to look at the immigrants as a mass without individual faces, an attitude that the immigrants themselves cannot accept.

## Conclusion

For African-Italian authors to become visible, they have had to become texts. Such an act has allowed them to be known, to acquire individual identities, to exist as a partially knowable "others" for the Italian reading public. "This," writes Pap Khouma, referring to his autobiography, "is the life of a Senegalese man, the life that I have known for a time that seems very long to me, a lucky time in the end, because, as people say in my country, if you can tell it, it means that it brought you *fortuna*" (143). To appropriate the new language and to inscribe one's identity within a text that becomes an echo of other people's experience involves the creation of a new *fortuna*, indeed, a new configuration of the future both for the Italian-speaking immigrant writers and for Italian literature.

These authors' tales of their lives in an alien nation and their narration of their selves has been debated within a hybrid critical context that mixes oral narratives with novels, autobiographical texts, and short stories. My deliberate act of "formal *métissage*" is dictated by the need to allow their voices to be heard within my critical approach to Italophone studies and Italophone texts. The discussion of these new interventions in Italian literature needs to be reopened as more texts are being written, texts closely tied to the rapidly changing socioeconomic conditions of immigrants in Italy. In fact, the ongoing process of the creation of nonessentializing concepts of sexual, racial, cultural, and ethnic difference is reflected in the national and narrative contexts that the immigrants have created and will continue to create. What is also needed is a new discussion about the language that Italians are using to talk about the new Italian citizens. In 1993, the outdated and unacceptable term of *gente di colore* (colored people) was still being used; such a term implies the existence of a dichotomy that, however, does not appear in the Italian language. As it would seem useless to create the neologism *gente senza colore* (people without color), we need to use new definitions that do not refer to one's ethnic and racial origin, but to a person's identity as a site of "cultural hybridity."

## Notes

This essay was completed in December 1994.

1. The spectrum of my analysis is rather limited as I refer throughout my essay to the very recent immigrations from Africa and to the literary production written in Italian by African immigrants since 1990. I am aware of the number of people who emigrated from Eritrea to Italy, but my interest is for emigrations that destroy the link between the original country and the colonial motherland. Even within this limited context, I cannot do justice to each author and only present his/her work as an introduction to the concept of Italophone literature. See also Mohamed Aden Sheikh, *Arrivederci a Mogadiscio* (Good-bye to Mogadishu) (Rome: Edizioni Associate, 1991), a narration of Aden Sheikh's life story in Somalia, his education in Italy, his political involvement during Mohamed Siad Barre's government, and his imprisonment once Barre established a rigid dictatorship.

2. I am translating the word *teppista* into the British word "hooligan" because the English word is commonly used in Italian.

3. This interview took place in November 1988 and was broadcast after Masslo's death. The transcription of the interview is now in the *addenda*, edited by Patrizia Restiotto and Alessandro Micheletti, in P. A. Micheletti and Saidou Moussa Ba's *La promessa di Hamadi* (Hamadi's promise) (Novara: De Agostini, 1991), 196.

4. Laura Balbo and Luigi Manconi, *I razzismi reali* (Milan: Feltrinelli, 1992), 26. On immigrants and immigration, see especially Laura Balbo and Luigi Manconi, *I razzismi possibili* (The possible racisms) (Milan: Feltrinelli, 1990); Nino Sergi, ed., *L'immigrazione straniera in Italia* (Foreign immigration to Italy) (Rome: Edizioni Lavoro, 1987); Nino Sergi and Francesco Cherchedi, eds., *L'immigrazione straniera in Italia. Il tempo dell'integrazione* (Foreign immigration to Italy: the time of integration) (Rome: Edizioni Lavoro, 1991); Ugo Melchionda, *L'immigrazione straniera in Italia. Repertorio bibliografico* (Foreign immigration to Italy: bibliographical index) (Rome: Edizioni Lavoro, 1993), which contains the largest bibliography published on immigration to Italy; and Maria Favaro and Mara Tognetti Bordogna, *Donne dal mondo. Strategie migratorie al femminile* (Women from the world: female migratory strategies) (Milan: Guerini, 1991).

5. Mario Fortunato and Salah Methnani, *Immigrato* (Immigrant) (Rome and Naples: Theoria, 1990); Pap Khouma, *Io, venditore di elefanti. Una vita per forza tra Dakar, Parigi e Milano* (I, an elephant salesman: a forced life between Dakar, Paris, and Milan), ed. Oreste Pivetta (Milan: Garzanti, 1990); Mohamed Bouchane, *Chiamatemi Alì* (Call me Alì), ed. Carla De Girolamo and Daniele Miccione) (Milan: Leonardo, 1990); Micheletti and Ba, *La promessa di Hamadi*. The other texts analyzed in my essay will be Nassera Chohra, *Volevo diventare bianca* (I wanted to become white), ed. Alessandra Atti Di Sarro (Rome: E/O, 1993); Tahar Ben Jelloun, *Dove lo Stato non c'è. Racconti Italiani* (Where the state does not exist: Italian tales), ed. Egi Volterrani (Turin: Einaudi, 1991); Moshen Melliti, *Pantanella. Canto lungo la strada* (Pantanella: a song along the road) (Rome: Edizioni Lavoro, 1992); and Edoardo Albinati, *Il polacco lavatore di vetri* (The Polish window washer) (Milan: Longanesi, 1989). All translations are mine. There are as yet no texts written by immigrants from Eastern Europe, but it is indeed just a matter of time. Albinati's text is probably the only Italian novel in which Polish immigrants in Rome are the protagonists.

6. In the end-of-the-book glossary of *La promessa di Hamadi*, the expression *vu' cumprà* is placed in its historical context: "*Vu' cumprà*: The expression appears for the first time in 1925, in a poem by Raffaele Viviano, 'O' Tripolino.' The poem refers to a Neapolitan man who moved to Libya to become a peddler. However, the immigrants, who have not done philological investigations, interpret it as a contamination of the French 'vous' with the Italian 'comperare,' understanding its negative connotation" (157). It is ironic that an expression used to define an Italian peddler in the colony is now used to describe the immigrants who sell their merchandise in the streets in Italy.

7. When I first began to prepare this essay, I intended to approach the African-Italian narratives through critical texts in Francophone literature. I soon realized, in fact, the difficulties in my position as a Western woman reader and critic who must modify both her critical background and her approach to male autobiographical narratives. Francophone critical texts have proven inadequate. Such a problem is underlined by Christopher Miller in "Introduction: Reading through Western Eyes," in *Theories of Africans* (Chicago and London: University of Chicago Press, 1990), 1–30.

8. I am aware of the problematic use of terms such as "Western" or "non-Western." The complex term "non-Western cultures" does not indicate their complete separation

from what is considered Western. I use such a term because, as Charyl Johnson-Odim and Margaret Strobel affirm, "it seems less affirming to refer to people by a negative term denoting something they are not. Still, the terms 'non-Western' and 'Third World' can be useful for particular purposes if we remain aware of their limitations" (Cheryl Johnson-Odim and Margaret Strobel, eds., "Introduction," in *Expanding the Boundaries of Women's History: Essays on Women in the Third World* [Bloomington and Indianapolis: Indiana University Press, 1992], x).

9. The interviews are still unpublished. I interviewed Saidou Moussa Ba on December 26, 1992, Maria Viarengo on December 28, 1992, Pap Khouma on March 17, 1993, Nassera Chohra on June 8, 1993, and Mohamed Bouchane on June 10, 1993.

10. See Giulio Angioni, *Una ignota compagnia* (An unknown company) (Milan: Feltrinelli, 1992); Erminia Dell'Oro, *L'abbandono, una storia eritrea* (The abandonment, an Eritrean story) (Turin: Einaudi, 1991); Marco Lodoli, *I fannulloni* (The loafers) (Turin: Einaudi, 1990); Maria Pace Ottieri, *Amore nero* (Black love) (Milan: Mondadori, 1984).

11. Pap Khouma, "Poi sono diventato insegnante" (Then I became a teacher), *La terra vista dalla luna* (The earth seen from the moon) 62 (July–August 1991): 13.

12. Ngugi Wa Thiong'o, *Decolonising the Mind: The Politics of Language in African Literature* (Portsmouth, N.H.: Heinemann, 1986), 12.

13. Migrations from Africa are dictated mainly by economical reasons and lead back to a discourse on economic colonialism as defined in Ngugi's book. However, in recent migrations, the choice of the country to which one emigrates reveals an active search to find alternatives to the "natural" emigration to the colonial motherland. Italy has become one of the alternatives, often chosen after experimenting with life in France, as in the case of Pap Khouma's story.

14. Gayatri Chakravorty Spivak, *The Post-Colonial Critic: Interviews, Strategies, Dialogues*, ed. Sarah Harasym (New York and London: Routledge, 1990), 64.

15. The discussion of cultural and literary *métissage* also appears in daily newspapers. On May 21, 1993, *La Stampa* published an interview with Assia Djebar, who was in Italy at the Salone del libro in Turin. Paola Dècina Lombardi, the interviewer, asked: "Michel Serres has located the future of culture in *métissage*. What is your experience of 'interweaving of cultures'?" Assia Djebar answered: "Like me, other Algerian writers are *métissés* in the French language. We went against the mainstream. At the time when there was only one party, because we fought in defense of minorities for a dialogue with 'pieds noirs' writers, we were emarginated. But *métissage* is inscribed in Algeria. The price to pay is a certain isolation. The isolation is balanced by participation in conferences like this one in Turin or by organizations such as the Carrefour Européen de Strasbourg pour la Littérature, of which I am a permanent member" (5). See Françoise Lionnet, "Métissage, Emancipation and Female Textuality in Two Francophone Writers," in *Life/Lines: Theorizing Women's Autobiography*, ed. Bella Brodski and Celeste Schenck (Ithaca, N.Y.: Cornell University Press, 1988), 260–81; and Françoise Lionnet, "Of Mangoes and Maroons: Language, History, and the Multicultural Subject of Michelle Cliff's *Abeng*," in *De/Colonizing the Subject: The Politics of Gender in Women's Autobiography*, ed. Sidonie Smith and Julia Watson (Minneapolis: University of Minnesota Press, 1992), 321–45.

16. Homi K. Bhabha, "Introduction: Narrating the Nation," in Homi K. Bhabha, ed., *Nation and Narration* (New York and London: Routledge, 1990), 4.

17. Not much attention has been given to new immigrant authors in academic environments. Armando Gnisci has published the only book of the literature of immigration in Italy. I would like to thank him for drawing my attention to his books, *Il rovescio del*

*gioco* (The reverse of the game) (Rome: Sovera, 1993) and *Noialtri europei* (We Europeans) (Rome: Bulzoni, 1991), and his article "Verso un nuovo concetto di letteratura nazionale-mondiale" (Toward a new concept of national-world literature), *I quaderni di Gaia* 5–6–7 (1992–93): 135–40.

18. Antonio states: "Here in Villa Literno, racism has no right of citizenship. . . . Before . . . Villa Literno had problems. Nobody worried too much about them. People survived on very little. After the arrival of the Africans, Villa Literno has the same problems, but one believes or lets people believe that the problems are caused by the foreigners. However, it is the state who is the stranger here. It does not even dare to be seen. . . . The state is absent, Rome is absent, the tomato-field owners, who use the African labor force, are absent. They believe that they are not using men but tools, which do not need to eat, to sleep, or take care of their bodily needs" (31).

19. If Chohra has "left France behind," she nonetheless maintains a close connection to the language. In fact, she released the rights to translations of her book in all languages but French; she plans to do the French translation herself.

20. Günter Wallraff, *Faccia da turco: un "infiltrato speciale" nell'inferno degli immigrati* (Turkish face: a special undercover agent in the immigrants' hell) (Salerno: Tullio Pironti, 1986).

21. Homi K. Bhabha, "Dissemination: Time, Narrative, and the Margins of the Modern Nation," in *Nation and Narration*, 293.

22. In our interview, Saidou Moussa Ba said that he has been criticized by other immigrants for "saying too much" about their precarious life and their survival strategies. They perceive his narration of collective experiences as a violation of their world and of their lives.

23. Maria Viarengo, "Andiamo a spasso?" (Shall we go for a walk?), *Linea d'ombra* 54 (November 1990): 74–76.

24. I also asked Ba what disagreements he had had while collaborating with Micheletti. He revealed that Micheletti represented a point of view that identified any white person as a racist. Saidou found this radical approach to a discourse on race and identity unacceptable. The guilt of being white has led some antiracist groups to "do too much," said Ba, "to the point where their voice has replaced the voice of the immigrants and, in the end, prevented them from speaking."

25. Interview, December 28, 1992.

26. Various authors, *Uguali e diversi: Il mondo culturale, le reti di rapporti, i lavori degli immigrati non europei a Torino* (Equal and different: the cultural world, the network of relations, the occupations of non-European immigrants in Turin) (Turin: Rosenberg and Sellier, 1991).

27. Renato Curcio, *Shish Mahal* (Rome: Sensibili alle Foglie, 1991). Renato Curcio, well known in Italy for his political involvement in the seventies as one of the leaders of the terrorist group Brigate Rosse (Red Brigades), founded a publishing company while in prison called Sensibili alle Foglie (sensitive to the leaves).

28. Amalia Crisantino, *Ho trovato l'Occidente: Storie di donne immigrante a Palermo* (I discovered the West: stories of women immigrants in Palermo) (Palermo: La Luna, 1992).

29. Giuliano Carlini, ed., *La terra in faccia. Gli immigrati raccontano* (Dirt in your face: immigrants narrate) (Rome: Ediesse, 1991).

30. Francesco Ciafaloni et al., *Le mille e una donna. Donne migranti: incontri di culture* (A thousand and one woman: migrating women: the intersections of cultures) (Milan: Comune di Milan, 1990).

# The Preclusion of Postcolonial Discourse in Southern Italy

*Pasquale Verdicchio*

The field that has come to be known as postcolonial studies challenges historical fictions that value certain cultural expressions over others. However, it sometimes falls short in its representation of postcolonial groups due to its characterization of postcoloniality almost purely in terms of problematic designations such as white versus nonwhite, or First versus Third World. If postcolonial discourse is to effectively unmask the workings of imperialism, it must be opened up to study colonial possibilities that exist(ed) in less clear-cut situations. First and Third World are not always separable in geographic space and granted racism's unambiguous influence and effects, race is an ambiguous category. The phenomenon of emigration plays a key role in such cases where the historicization of emigration trends can only enlarge the scope of postcolonial studies.

Subaltern groups have generally been contextualized within their immediate national situations. However, the status of certain groups is also related to their previous national history and must therefore be viewed in a light that considers that amplified situation. I am of course referring to immigrant groups whose decontextualization is more often than not tied to the historical construction of their nation of origin. As a case in point, the history of the Italian south is one of colonization, where colonialism was the unspoken agenda when Italy was "united" by Piedmontese forces in the 1860s. As unrecognized postcolonials, southern Italian immigrants to North America, by far the greater part of immigrants from Italy, are among those groups that straddle the borders of nationalism in a continuous identity flux. The exhumation and examination of this position is, I believe, of great importance to the enrichment of postcolonial critiques.

My interest in the subject comes from personal experience and the need to clarify my own position vis-à-vis Italy and my adopted homes, Canada and the United States. As a southern Italian in Italy, I have been made aware of the southerner's status as "other" by more than a few incidents. In Canada, I have participated in many initiatives as a member of a group officially categorized as part of an ethnic minority and perceived as nonwhite.[1] To further complicate matters, in the United States the term "Anglo," which I still utter in Canada to signify the dominant culture, is used as an equivalent for "white" and indiscriminately applied to groups such as Italian Americans. The three situations share a contradiction: while the dominant culture, officially or otherwise, designates southern Italians, Greeks, Portuguese, Turks, Arabs, and so on as "other" or nonwhite, "persons of color" often tend to view these same groups as white.

Initiating this topic in a North American context is not meant to equate it or have it compete with the plight of African Americans, who suffered the insanity of slavery, or with the struggles of any other group, including the often-ignored aboriginal peoples. By being neither "black" nor "white," but described as both by one or the other, the southern Italian experience is an anomaly that may unveil the foolishness and hypocrisy of racial exclusiveness.

The discussion I outline in this essay addresses questions relating to the place of postcolonial discourse in a "European" context, one that from a distance is regarded as stable, culturally unified, and cooperative. Is the colonial/postcolonial terminology only applicable to situations of race difference? If so, can such situations be constructed in order to support an imperialist/colonialist agenda? And, finally, since the group in question is the e/im-migrant southerner, is the emergence of postcolonial discourse in any way dependent on geography, or is it possible outside the place of colonialism?

Antonio Gramsci's work is an aid in responding to such questions. That his writings have proved so useful to cultural workers outside of the immediate situation from which they arose lends insight into the complexity of the Italian situation itself. In his meditations on the southern question (1966) and the role of intellectuals (1977), Gramsci, the Sardinian founder of the Italian Communist Party (PCI), provides approaches to questions of cultural determinacy that continue to be of value. Stuart Hall, in his essay "Gramsci's Relevance for the Study of Race and Ethnicity," considers how Gramsci may provide a departure point for the student of postcolonial situations. Hall rightly corrects Perry Anderson's categorization of Gramsci as just another "Western Marxist" "who, because of [his] preoccupations with more 'advanced' societies, [has] little of relevance to say to the problems . . . between the imperial nations of the capitalist 'centre' and the englobalized, colonized societies of the periphery" (Hall 1986, 8). However, Hall himself is a little quick in thinking of Italy, but also Europe, as a coherent and homogeneous whole, possibly viewing the colonialism within Italian and European borders as less authentic or important than colonialism elsewhere.

> In relation specifically to racism, [Gramsci's] original contribution cannot be simply transferred wholesale from the existing context of his work. Gramsci did not write about race, ethnicity or racism in their contemporary meanings or manifestations. Nor did he analyze in depth the colonial experience or imperialism out of which so many characteristic "racist" experiences and relationships in the modern world have developed. His principal preoccupation was with his native Italy. (Ibid.)

Of course, writing in the early part of the century, Gramsci could not have treated the meanings and manifestations of racism that would appear sixty to seventy years later. Nevertheless, since the relationship between northern and southern Italy had been constructed in terms of "racial" and ethnic differences prior to unification, the context in which Gramsci addressed the southern question was already conditioned by these elements.[2]

## Beginnings: Race, Ethnicity, Geography

The expression "Italy ends at Rome. Naples, Calabria, Sicily, and all the rest are part of Africa," spoken perhaps by a respectable nineteenth-century Grand Tour traveler, is still heard today in Italy, and it encapsulates the whole question of what might constitute the nation. Definitions of southern Italians as "other" are further fed by commonly stated references to Naples as "the doorway to the Orient." Supporting documentation for these beliefs is found in S. De Renzi's nineteenth-century study on the medical topography of the Kingdom of Naples, in which he observes that southerners bear "so little resemblance to the serious and stern inhabitants of the middle and upper regions of

Europe, and [are] so close to the customs of eastern peoples, with which they have in common both the climate and the products of their soil."[3] The cultural distance and exoticism of the south prior to unification are further recalled by anthropologist Ernesto De Martino, who, in order to point out that "one does not have to go far to find the 'other'" (Pasquinelli 1977, 19), recalls that missionaries of the Society of Jesus who went to the south after the Council of Trent referred to the south as the *Indias por acá* (22).

The need to differentiate between the north and the south is closely related to the desire to define a homogeneous population that could constitute for Italy a long-sought national identity. This is what fed the theorists of "race" who took on the "southern question"; adherents to the Lombroso school, Oriani, Niceforo, Sergi, and Ferri among them, based their theories on somatic differences and anthropological definitions (Ganduscio 1970, 112). And, for those who found somatic definitions of race difference unpalatable, Virgilio Titone described race not as a somatic category but as a psychological one. For Titone, the "stratification of customs, fashions, morals, habits, about which a people may have forgotten and that, without their knowing it, are still at work and alive, determine that people's character and racial physiognomy" (in ibid., 111). Such reasoning would have people become victims of their own culture, deemed, of course, inferior to that of the dominant culture. This last type of "racial" differentiation seems to be of the sort that conditions antimulticulturalists and, though examples of somatic differentiation are also quite common, is probably the one at work today in Italy as elsewhere.

The construction of southerners as an "inferior and unmodifiable race" (Ganduscio 1970, 112) served greatly to justify the military interventions that ensured the unification of the peninsula against southern resistance in the mid- to late 1800s. The Risorgimento is recognized as the era in which the Italian national spirit found renewed strength and was reborn. The image of a united Italy during this period, when national zeal was most feverish, is well present and evident in the work of both pre- and postunification literary figures, the most notable being Carlo Pisacane, Ippolito Nievo, Giovanni Pascoli, Mario Rapisardi, and Enrico Corradini.

In *Mezzogiorno tra riforme e rivoluzione*, Pasquale Villani is of the opinion that "during the very period of the Risorgimento (1734–1860) southern society began to take on that physiognomy and that structural character with which it came to form part of the Kingdom of Italy and gave birth to the southern question" (Villani 1973, 4–5). Of course, prior to unification the problems of the south would not have been regarded as of particular interest to a national program. However, given the lack of economic integration of the peasants within the land/agricultural system, the periods of foreign subjugation of the south, most notably at the hands of the French and the Spanish, were most likely the times during which the conditions for the southern question, as inherited and aggravated by the Italian state, developed.

Nevertheless, the notion of a "reemergence" of the Italian national spirit is rather artificial. Aside from its geography, the only other time Italy was unified was under Roman colonization. Following that, with the development of individual city-states, and with foreign domination of many areas of the peninsula, a number of writers wrote idealistically of the concept of a united Italy. Many consider Dante to be the first to have idealized an Italic nation based on the concept of linguistic unity. Ippolito Nievo wrote that Dante was instrumental in

> reconstituting in Italy the concept of a great national and popular poetry, based on the reliquaries of that poetry in *volgo* [the vernacular] that had retained through the tempests of the centuries its faith and its nature. This new poetry no longer lay slave and enclosed in the august circle of an intellect, but rose in freedom, strong and omniscient, to move in the vast sphere of the fortunes of a nation. (Mollia 1970, 6)

Nievo's extension of Dante's intentions, far beyond the confines of the Florentine context that would be his immediate concern, is nothing if not imaginative. As a reading of Dante's *De Vulgari Eloquentia* (book 1, 13) reveals, his view of the other languages and cultures of the peninsula, and especially those of the south, was rather negative. Dante cast Florence as the new Rome that would again unify Italy, an idea that conditioned much of the Risorgimento and in some way persists in the popular and touristic advertising of Florence as the representative city and culture of Italy. The concept of an all-encompassing "Latin civilization" has reemerged from time to time when questions of national legitimacy have been involved and, given recent developments on the Italian political front, it can safely be said that such a concept did not fade with fascism but has in fact contributed to its resurgence.

A determinant role for Dante in Italian nationalism is, therefore, an exaggeration. Aside from the fact that Dante's work is not representative of a popular poetry, it is also not representative of a national literature in the sense of its being "Italian." Dante's writings are merely indicative of a Florentine sense of independence that opposes an aulic vernacular to the sacredness of the dominant Latin language. In his consideration of "imagined communities," Benedict Anderson offers that "nationalism has to be understood by aligning it, not with self-consciously held political ideologies, but with the large cultural systems that preceded it, out of which—as well as against which—it came into being" (Anderson 1983, 19). In these terms, then, a linguistic break such as Dante undertakes is indicative of an attempt to remove and distance the essence of a particular community (Florence) from the larger one with which it is identified (linguistically, Latin). As such, Dante's is to be read as a critique of the hold of Latin over the Florentine culture that he sought to foreground. In other words, he proposes a process not of unification but of differentiation and makes of that a project of Florentine cultural imperialism over adjacent states.

Francesco Petrarca follows suit in a very particular representation of a unified Italy with one of his major compositions, poem CXXVIII of the *Canzoniere*, which begins "Italia mia, benché il parlar sia indarno." This poem expresses distress at a "nation" torn apart and broken, as well as the hope that someday its rent body might find unity.[4] What is rather telling in this composition, however, is a view of Italy that even then was exclusive of its southern regions.

> Oh, my Italy, even though my words are in vain
> for the mortal wounds
> that often I see across your beautiful body
> allow at least for my sighs to hope for
> the Tiber and the Arno
> and the Po, where sad and pained I sit. (Vv. 1–6)[5]

Missing from the composition is any reference whatsoever to the southern portion of the peninsula. This would indicate that the idea of a united Italy rests, at least in Petrarca's view, in the lands that go from Rome to the Alps. It could be argued that there are no major rivers in the south that the poet could have used as points of reference; had he wanted to give an inclusive view of the peninsula, however, there would have been other ways of signifying such an entity.

These two brief examples demonstrate that a certain concept of Italy exclusive of the south found currency long before the Risorgimento and the modern age. This should not seem unusual, since the south had been a territory culturally tied, through earlier colonization and development, to a Mediterranean sphere rather than a European one. What is important to remember is that, as a Mediterranean region, in the drive for unification and establishment of Italy as a European power, the south became identified with other lands to conquer and colonize.

## Constructing a Unified Nation

Ippolito Nievo, a Risorgimento writer caught up in the fervor of unification and obsessed with the installment of a national and popular literature that would reflect the status of Italy as a nation, is directly involved in the fight to unite the peninsula. Having participated in the ousting of the Austrians in the Piedmontese liberation of Lombardy in 1859, and in complete ignorance of what awaits him, he joins Garibaldi and the Mille (thousand) in their May 1860 expedition to annex the south in their "national revolution" (Mollia 1970, 215). Nievo's letters from the south, published under the title *Lettere garibaldine* (Garibaldine letters), offer observations and views of those lands and its peoples and the activity of the nationalist troops there.

Indeed, passages regarding the population in whose "liberation" Nievo was taking an active part are quite judgmental and revealing:

> The Sicilians are all women; . . . God help us if it had been up to them
> to liberate us . . . ! The whole of the revolution was concentrated in the
> bands in the countryside known here as *squadre* and composed mostly
> of emeritus brigands that do war on the government only so as to be
> able to war with the landowners. In fact, we now have to police those
> who yesterday were our allies. (Nievo 1961, 27)

The view of southerners as feminized, inferior, uncivilized, and ineffective is recounted over and over in Nievo's letters to his family and friends. From Naples, he writes to his brother, also stationed in the south, in Gaeta, that the newly installed unification government of the southern provinces under Nigra "diplomatically wastes time, carefully feels around, floats aimlessly while the Pulcinella population continues to be a mystery," and asks his brother further not to judge the south "by those few brigand peasants" (133).

Nievo accused those he terms "brigands" of using the pretext of liberation to do war against the landowners for purely criminal purposes. However, the few bothersome *contadini-briganti* (peasant brigands) soon came to form a new, unforeseen dimension in the national "war of liberation." Garibaldi had unquestionably received great support from these *contadini* in his battles against the Bourbons for the liberation and unification of the south. But these same peasants also entered in conflict with their northern "liberators" when they occupied the *latifondi* (large estate holdings). The peasants' takeover of lands came to represent a direct affront to the attempts at maintaining a bourgeoisie-based power structure. Such a power base negated outright "the agrarian revolution [the peasants had hoped for], but from which both moderates and democrats backed away" (Galasso 1977, 324).[6]

Reaction to peasant initiatives was strong and swift. Only months after they had supposedly liberated the region, Garibaldian forces under the command of Nino Bixio carried out a mass execution of those who had occupied the lands near Bronte (Mangano 1976, 8). The new Italian nation quickly recognized the contestation as more than what a few marauding bands of thieves might represent, and the insurrection was put down with the engagement of a full two-fifths of the national military force, as well as carabinieri and national guardsmen, for a total of 250,000 men. The repression resulted in more than ten thousand dead, both in battle and by executions, and twenty thousand imprisoned or exiled (12).[7]

While the period that goes from 1887 to 1894 was one of economic crisis for the whole of Italy, the contradictions of unification were ever clearer in the south. In his writings on the Risorgimento, under the heading "The Problem of Political Direction in the Formation and Development of the Nation and State of Modern Italy," Gramsci outlines some basic discrepancies that conditioned the opinion of northern Italians regarding the inhabitants of the south:

> The misery of the south was historically inexplicable for the popular masses of the north; they did not understand that unification had not taken place on the basis of equality, but as hegemony of the north over the south in the territorial relationship of city-countryside. In other words, that the north represented an "octopus" that enriched itself at the cost of the south, and that its economic-industrial increment was in direct relationship with the economic and agricultural impoverishment

of the south. The northern person thought instead that, if the south did not progress after its liberation from the Bourbon regime, it meant that the causes for the misery were not external, to be found objectively in economic and political conditions, but rather internal, innate to the southern population. More so because there was a rooted belief of the great natural fecundity of the soil. Only one conclusion was possible, the incapacity, the barbarous state, and the biological inferiority of the population. These already common opinions (Neapolitan "lazzaro-nismo" was an ancient legend) were consolidated and even theorized by the sociologists of positivism (Niceforo, Sergi, Ferri, Orano, etc.), as-suming the power of "scientific truth" in a time of scientific superstition. Therefore, a north-south polemic on race, and the superiority of the north and the inferiority of the south, developed. Meanwhile, in the north, there remained the belief that the south represented a "lead ball" for Italy, and that the modern and industrial northern civilization would have fared better without this "lead ball" dragging it down. (Gramsci 1991, 80–81)

The ambivalence toward the character and intentions of southern-ers facilitated the repression of the *briganti*, as well as of the Sicilian workers' Fasci (1890–94),[8] which culminated in the declaration of a state of siege on January 3, 1894 (Mangano 1976, 28). By under-standing unification as a "failed revolution," one can see that this period might have actualized the revolutionary energy of southerners by bringing northern and southern masses together in their mutual discord with the newly centralized state. But such was not the case.

During this period, Francesco Crispi's government, with its passion for a stable and unified Italy, made a most brilliant development in the context of his imperialist and colonial policies. With the argument that agricultural land was scarce and that overpopulation was the real source of the plight of landless southern peasants, Crispi developed a program of colonization of foreign territories that offered plenty of land for the taking. And, although Italy was economically ill equipped to support a colonial program similar to that of other European pow-ers, it was able to sustain it purely on "the popular passion of peas-ants blindly following the need for land ownership: it was a case of resolving internal politics, postponing its resolution ad infinitum" (Gramsci 1991, 77).

In the final analysis, however, Crispi's imperialist program was but an extension of the Piedmontese expansion into southern Italy. Uni-fication, though not officially sanctioned as such, was nothing if not colonialist in nature. Resistance to it was represented as criminal and was therefore discounted as having no sociopolitical validity. Further, the annexation and repression of southern Italy belongs chronologically to a period of colonial expansion. The year 1890 marks the beginning not only of the campaign against the Sicilian Fasci (1890–94), but also of aggressions against Eritrea. As such, the southern part of the peninsula appears to have served as the staging area in preparation for Italy's imperialist policies abroad.

## The Emigration Alternative

> It's not land that is lacking . . . it is in the conditions of social relationships . . . that the sources and causes of the migratory phenomenon must be found. Only these conditions and these relationships can explain the process of formation of that artificial overpopulation in agriculture that finds in emigration its expression and its release. (Emilio Sereni, in Mangano 1976, 23)

Sereni's comments offer a view of emigration as another phenomenon that emerged from the socioeconomic situation of the colonized south much like brigandage. Like the latter, emigration too has been avoided by Italian historiography and cultural commentators. Emigration is the result of the failure to include southerners in the national program and the repressive conditions heaped upon the south after unification. It could almost be said that emigration was the only successful revolution to have taken place in southern Italy. During the period spanning 1876 to 1976, twenty-five million emigrants left Italy, more than 50 percent of these prior to the First World War (Rosoli 1978, 11).

Given its prominence, emigration as a literary theme is not unconnected to its use as part of a political agenda that sought to redefine it as part of a national/imperialist agenda to populate colonies rather than as the result of the failure of that same agenda as applied to the south.[9] Giovanni Pascoli's "Italy" (1897), a long poem on the subject of emigration, and his oration "La grande proletaria si è mossa" (The great proletarian nation has moved) (1911), along with Enrico Corradini's *La patria lontana* (The distant fatherland) (1910), a novel directly engaging the political debate of the early 1900s on emigration and imperialist expansion, offer important insights into the contradictory policies surrounding the phenomenon of emigration.

"Italy" was written in 1897, during a period of heavy emigration. It is obvious, however, that Pascoli's composition is merely a pretext for yet another sentimental representation of the countryside and its people that is the commonplace of his other poetry. Aside from being told that immigrants work cheaply, in silence, and suffer abuse and name-calling at the hands of foreigners, which is undoubtedly meant to raise a sense of national pride, the reader confronts the problems of emigration only in function of a pitying, paternalistic nation that feels for its people and offers the warmth of familiarity. The emigrants themselves have no voice; they take a backseat to a nationalistic sense of the fatherland that awaits its children, lost in the unfriendly world. Pascoli's romanticized notion of emigration in "Italy" is but a timid instance of what developed into a more aggressive nationalist representation casting emigration in the mold of colonialism, a co-optation supporting the interventionist/imperialist agenda that led Italy into its African campaigns and eventually into the First World War.

Pascoli's "The Great Proletarian Nation" and Corradini's *Distant Fatherland* disguise imperialist interests with a critique of emigration. Both readily subordinate questions pertaining to the validity of a unification that caused the vast movement of peoples, and concerns for those masses excluded from the national project, to the subject of Italy's imperialist interests and its place among European nations.

Both Corradini's *Distant Fatherland* and his 1911 *La guerra lontana* (The distant war) seek to establish a balance between nationhood and imperialism/nationalism by stressing the importance of "social peace within the nation and of imperialist war outside of it" (Tessari 1976, 26). In *Distant Fatherland*, which takes place among Italians in Rio de Janeiro, the drive for imperialist conquest and expansion is well declared and represented by its main protagonist, Piero Buondelmonti.

Beginning with the first few pages of the novel, the concepts of work and nationhood dominate, and strong ties between the two are constituted. All discussions take place, as might be expected, among a privileged class. The emigrant laborers, who do the actual work and are traveling on the deck of the same Brazil-bound ship, do not participate in the discussions. Nevertheless, the laborers are brought into the conversation tangentially by Buondelmonti's assertion that, for Italians abroad to be truly be Italian, "nationalistically speaking, the land on which they work should become Italian" (7). Much of the book outlines the relationships between characters of different ideological viewpoints that come to serve as a sounding board for Buondelmonti's philosophy. The emigrants are marginal and unimportant and merely mentioned as "the world's refuse that moved below on deck," whose bestiality and primitiveness is illustrated by violent episodes involving a Sicilian woman in one and a Neapolitan man in another (16, 19). Yet Corradini's use of emigrants to signify the dispersion of Italy's national strength is central to the imperialist philosophy that needs bodies to enforce it. Emigrants abroad are "alone in their battle!" . . . every one of them was alone within the collective life of the foreign land. . . . "They are so strong! What would have been of them if they had all possessed the strength of their nation?" (53).

The failed attempts of 1894–96 at expanding Italian rule over the Eritrean territories conquered in 1890, supposedly to fulfill the promise of land to its peasants, had precipitated yet another wave of emigration. The failure of colonialism equaled for nationalists such as Buondelmonti the diminishing of the Italian nation.

The outbreak of war at the novel's end offers the possibility of rescuing the tarnished national image. When a ship carrying returning emigrants to aid their country nears the Mediterranean, the hearts of the returnees rise, and Italy's status as an expanding empire is represented in the reference to the Mediterranean as *lago romano* (Roman lake) (254). Buondelmonti speaks to the group, addressing their identity in terms of their status as emigrants. He stresses the need for emigrants to fight and work for their motherland:

> You have given the motherland the example. You are few, but your return is of great significance, because you, my friends, left as emigrants and are returning as warriors. . . . If Italy wins this war, she will regain her spirit and will again take the paths of her Fathers. Then, those who will come after you will not have to do as you did, emigrate to foreign lands, armed only with the labor of your arms and patience. They will be able to emigrate to lands conquered by the motherland. Italy will not only be where Italy is today, but it will be everywhere there are Italians, as today England is everywhere Englishmen are. (254)

Such is the solution offered by Corradini and others of like mind. Not a resolution of the problems that caused emigration, but a paradoxical promise to cancel emigration with emigration itself, a strategy that maintains the myth of the nation intact and retains the privilege and advantage of recalling its marginalized masses for use in its imperialist program.

Pascoli's "The Great Proletarian Nation," an address pronounced to Italian troops on the occasion of Italy's declaration of war against

Turkey in September 1911, continues Corradini's typification of emigration. Already in 1909 the democrat Gaetano Salvemini, asserting the need for imperialist action as a way to rescue Italy from its subordinate status among other European nations had offered the following: "Through past historical evolution, as within the limits of each state there formed a grouping of dominant classes and a grouping of subordinate classes, so in international relations there exist stronger and weaker states: bourgeois states and proletarian states" (Rosa 1965, 99).

It is within Salvemini's definition of the state of states that the expression "proletarian state" first came to prominence; it was to find great success as a nationalist buzz phrase. Pascoli's address in September 1911, at the beginning of a war whose end (October 1912) would see Italy taking possession of Libya and a number of Aegean islands, extends Corradini's sense of nationalism and reclamation of the emigrant masses.

Pascoli expands the artificial causes of emigration and needs for colonialism, including the lack of land and overpopulation, and briefly describes the hardships that emigrants suffer abroad in order to set the ground for the superficial glorification of those same masses within the imperialist program: "Before, she sent her workers elsewhere since there were too many at home and they had to work for little pay. . . . They had become a little like the blacks in America, these conationals of him who discovered that land; and, like the blacks, they were placed outside of the law and humanity and were lynched" (Pascoli 1971b, 557).

Pascoli proudly pronounces that "the great proletarian nation has found a place for them" (91). However, that place is outside its national boundaries, a space that it now reclaims through historical right. The argument that Libya had been part of the Roman Empire is meant to convince emigrants that Libyan soil is by right Italian soil where

> the workers will not be doing poorly paid and unappreciated work for foreigners who also regard them as lowly beings, but, in the highest and strongest sense of the words, will farm their own and their motherland's soil. . . . They will live free and in peace on that land that will be one with their native land . . . for that too is Rome. (Ibid.)

Although the promise of land was indeed seductive, such rhetoric of course overlooks facts such as forced conscription. It is more than certain that those who had not been willing participants in the war for unification were most likely not fully convinced imperialists. In the end, Pascoli's program was no more accepting of the emigrant masses, since what it offered was exclusion from the land of birth.

## Reclaiming an Identity

Extant typifications such as "Africa begins south of Rome," the textual elaborations of difference, of which I have quoted but a small sample, and the historical activity associated with their ideological construction, provide the link between southern Italians and other colonized peoples. The immense drain of human resources through emigration and the unrecognized conditions of colonialism in the south worked to preclude any possibility of a coherent postcolonial discourse within the Italian borders. Yet the potential for that expression was not lost, for it is my contention that Italian immigrant writing, as it has emerged in Canada and the United States, is an expression of that postcolonial condition.

It is usually accepted that the formation of "historical blocs," which might function in opposition to the state apparatus, is "specific to the national context." Anne Showstack Sassoon's discussion of the concept of "historical bloc" (1980)[10] suggests that, although there is an "international conjuncture, a special emphasis is placed on the national dimension as the basic unit to be analyzed" (121). However, it is my contention that the emergence of a "historical bloc" may be forever stalled within a particular national situation, whereas within another it may find paths of expression. Freedom from the national situation that precipitated emigration is a potential stimulus to a group's reconsideration of its historical position and consolidation into a viable discursive presence.[11] Sassoon's "international conjuncture" is, of course, the end to which Marxism aspires, but it provides an insufficient placement for isolated, unrepresented groups whose international internal references may remain unspoken because of unresolved national situations.[12]

The period of conscientization demonstrated by southern Italian immigrant culture taps into what was unattainable within the Italian national context.[13] As such, "historical bloc" formation and postcolonial discourse are corresponding paths that, in the case of southern Italian e/im-migration, could be said to have been hindered at home but have in fact emerged abroad, even if somewhat altered, as the expression of a decontextualized subaltern.

At this point, the fact of emigration brings me back to the questions posed at the beginning of this essay, especially regarding the emergence of postcolonial discourse outside of the place of colonialism. My answer is a definite yes. Examples include Antonio D'Alfonso's poetry collection *Black Tongue* (1983), in which the "black tongue" signifies the marginality of southern immigrants to Canada; Dodici Azpadu's (1983) explanation that "in [her] life and in [her] writing, [she] nourishes appreciation for the neglected and ignored non-white qualities of Sicilian character"; and the work of Rose Romano, especially in the small collection of poems *Vendetta* (1990), who with Azpadu represents the concerns of a sexually diverse (lesbian), gendered subaltern.[14] The work of these authors is indicative of the unanswered questions, among which is the question of race, that still linger in the relationship between southern Italians and both their adopted homes and Italy.

Given the common figuration of colonized lands in the feminine[15] (remember Nievo's "Sicilians are all women"), I would like to address specifically the work of southern Italian American women who explore the "racial" dimension of southern/Sicilian immigrants. It is within their writing that the elements of differentiation that are at the root of the north/south conflict in Italy are best expressed. In fact, it is possibly precisely their status as women within a traditional culture that aids them in linking categories of prejudice, in highlighting their effects, and in providing a strategy for resistance.

In her groundbreaking anthology *The Dream Book: An Anthology of Writings by Italian American Women*, Helen Barolini's introduction addresses social, economic, and political aspects of Italian emigration and tradition that have not afforded women exposure in the field of literature. Barolini's writing often speaks of Italian American women writers in comparison to women writing from other ethnic groups. Her closest comparison seems to be made with black women writers, and she in fact paraphrases Zora Neale Hurston, from "What White Publishers Won't Print," as follows:[16]

> Publishers say they cannot afford to be crusaders. But black writer Zora
> Neale Hurston replied that she refused to be humbled by second place
> in a contest she never designed, and she identified what comes out of
> safe, marketable publishing as candidates for the American Museum of

Unnatural History, that is, a weird collection of stereotypes—non-dimensional figures that can be taken in at a glance, as the expressionless American Indian, the shuffling Negro, the inarticulate Italian, and so on. (Barolini 1987, 44)

This link, which provides testimony to the marginal position of Italians, offsets the forgetfulness that dominates the contemporary psyche of Italian Americans regarding their status in the United States.[17]

The racial positioning of southern Italians in a North American context is problematic, given the slavery paradigm that has fixed a white/black binary system of confrontation. Given such a dichotomy, southern Italian expression risks being silenced once again. Aside from African Americans, the dominant paradigm in the United States has included other groups deemed racially inferior, such as southern Italians, Jews, and Arabs.[18] The question of in-betweenness, of being or not being of color, is what makes the Italian situation, among others, particularly fruitful in undermining the absorptive category of "white."

Among Italian American writers who have taken on the question of this position are Rose Romano, Dodici Azpadu, Mary (Bucci) Bush, and others included in a special issue of *sinister wisdom* (no. 41). Throughout the pages of that issue on Italian American women, it is obvious that the question of racial identity is of extreme importance to southern Italian women. First and foremost, it is all-important that the identification of many of the women is with their southern Italian/Sicilian roots rather than with a more generalized sense of *italianità*.[19] This is, of course, the result of historical conditions, as I have previously outlined. Second, many of the women to whom the question of race is central are lesbian, which may point to unresolved questions of differentiation within that community as well as within the Italian American community. The subject clearly deserves lengthy elaboration. Within the confines of this initial introduction, however, I will only briefly concentrate on the work of Rose Romano and Dodici Azpadu.

The invisibility of southern Italians is a theme central to the writings of Rose Romano. Although her critique is positioned within the lesbian community, it addresses a problematic that concerns southern Italians in general, inside as well as outside the "Italian American" community. In "Coming Out Olive in the Lesbian Community: Big Sister Is Watching You," Romano addresses the question of southern Italian invisibility as propagated by the racial dichotomy model:

I have been censored in the lesbian press and ostracized in the lesbian community because I call myself Olive. Politically correct lesbians have agreed with the division of people into two categories: white and "of color." I look white; therefore I am white. There is no distinction made between different groups within the white community—if I am white, I am assigned wasp [sic] history and culture. . . . I have been told that by calling myself Olive I am evading my "responsibility of guilt." (1–2)[20]

Dodici Azpadu's first novel, *Saturday Night in the Prime of Life*, is an important illustration of the ambiguous character of southern Italian identity and an example of the silencing of that culture. The book's jacket note states that Azpadu seeks "to nourish appreciation for the neglected and ignored non-white qualities of Sicilian character." Almost in opposition to this, the publisher's note observes that "though primarily Neddie and Lindy's story, the context—the trap—is the male-dominated Sicilian culture that affects the women who exist inside and outside of it." The novel itself, however, in which the Sicilian American Neddie and her WASP lover Lindy attempt to maintain a relationship despite familial opposition, stresses Neddie's attachment to Sicilian culture and identifies it as a signifier of racial otherness. In such a case, "the trap" of Sicilian culture appears to be its status in the eyes of non-Sicilians. The negative effects of Sicilian culture and identity reflect the prejudices and misconceptions that Lindy, and especially her parents, may harbor.

When planning a meeting with her parents, Lindy asks herself if "she [had] even mentioned to them that Neddie was Sicilian" (Azpadu 1983, 23). This question foregrounds the reasons for Lindy's parents' opposition to the relationship beyond the fact of Lindy and Neddie being lesbian. Neddie's family is hopelessly bigoted with regard to Neddie's sexuality, but Lindy's family appears to be more preoccupied with Neddie's ethnic identity. Lindy knew "her parents suspected that this person called Neddie was actually a man. . . . If they never met again, she thought, her parents might prefer not to see the obvious in Neddie. . . . But even if they could ignore that, could they also ignore what was obvious in her deeply olive complexion, her wiry hair, her face and hand language?" (23). Lindy too, shares somewhat in her parents' dislike for Sicilians: "[Lindy] knew the Zingaros only from snapshots and stories, and from their effect on Neddie's life and on her own life. . . . [Neddie's mother's] nose, eyes and mouth epitomized an unpleasant racial mixing which only in Neddie did Lindy find attractive. . . . How could she love Sicilian ways in Neddie, yet dislike them in Neddie's family?" (29–30).

Further, it is the uncertainty of her own ability to set aside her prejudiced view of Sicilians that also precipitates much of the imbalance within Lindy's relationship with Neddie: "Aren't there ways to help her keep that blood circulating without relying on family ties; Lindy felt the inadequacy that always discouraged her. Racial comfort was what Concetta could give that she could not. Neddie will consider leaving me" (62).

Neddie's struggle with her family is not about wanting to break away from Sicilian culture; it is about her family's inability to accept her being lesbian. And so, although Lindy is aware of the power of Neddie's identity as a Sicilian, she does not readily accept that Neddie's struggle is a double one, as both lesbian and Sicilian.

It would seem that the publishers of *Saturday Night* felt uneasy in setting Neddie's struggle in the proper context. They chose to present the novel in terms different from the ones set by the author herself. Although Azpadu may be offering a critique of the "male-dominated Sicilian culture," it is also a critique engaging the dynamics of the lesbian relationship in which Neddie's Sicilian identity inscribes her as other.

The immediacy of ethnic/racial realities in the lives of those within the southern Italian sphere who wish to recognize the influence of those realities on life in the United States or Canada, plus the political successes of the northern Lombard League in Italy, with its program of "repatriation" of southerners and other ("extracommunitarian") immigrants, maintain an open space where these issues go unresolved. An analysis of the imbalances within the Italian nation that were a major cause of the emigrant flux from the south, and that therefore altered the social and cultural development of the region and its populations, is missing. What has emerged today, from the League and other similar proponents of regional purity, is a self-defined environment of victimization in which the "illegitimate" south has become the cause for the political and economic troubles suffered by the nation and, most important, by the "legitimate" north.

The south today is not the south of the period of unification. It is a part of the Italian nation that has developed industrially and civically at a slower rate than the rest of Italy. However, as part of a postindustrial society that never had its own industrial developments, the Italian south still bears the scars of the processes begun in 1861. These scars are reminiscent of a colonized land, and are most evident in the state of the economy, the educational system, health care, and other basic institutions in the south. Ironically, emigration turned out to be the south's most successful revolution, since it is only abroad that many southern Italian citizens have found expression and have been able to actualize their identity. I stress again that the wish of southern Italians for cultural recognition is not a desire to represent themselves as victims,[21] nor is it a wish to do the "victim limbo," as David Mura termed it.[22] It is merely a desire to express the difference that is at the root of southern Italians' exclusion from their own land. That same difference played a great role in their marginalization within the societies into which they immigrated. If such a difference is not visible to people like Mura, this is because of the same cultural blindness of which he accuses "whites." Rather than fall into simplistic dichotomies, it would be more useful for critics to consider how Asian Americans, African Americans, Latinos/as, and others may have enabled other (invisible) minorities to find the courage to take their cultures out of mothballs. Southern Italian Americans today are eager to dance not a "victim limbo" but a tarantella to exorcise the long-lasting effects of cultural deferral.

## Notes

1. The Association of Italian Canadian Writers was founded in 1986 in Vancouver. Italians, designated as an "invisible minority" in Canada, are considered to be "nonwhite" by the general population.

2. The works of Alfredo Niceforo are particularly important in positivist constructions of southern Italians as subhuman and racially inferior: *La delinquenza in Sardegna* (Delinquency in Sardinia) (Palermo: Sandron, 1897); *L'Italia barbara contemporanea* (Contemporary barbarian Italy) (Milan-Palermo: Sandron, 1898); *Italiani del Nord e Italiani del Sud* (Northern and southern Italians) (Turin: Bocca, 1901). Although Niceforo's writings are postunification, much of the same disdain for southerners is found in the letters of Cavour during the expeditions to unify the south during the 1860s: *Carteggi Cavour su La liberazione del Mezzogiorno e la formazione del Regno d'Italia* (The letters of Cavour on the liberation of southern Italy and the formation of the Kingdom of Italy) (Bologna: Zanichelli, 1949 [vols. 1 and 2], 1952 [vol. 3], 1954 [vols. 4 and 5]).

3. S. De Renzi, *Osservazioni sulla topografia medica del Regno di Napoli* (Observations on the medical topography of the Kingdom of Naples) (Naples, 1828–30, vol. 2, 43 [Galasso 1982, 174]).

4. Margaret Brose's recent work on the concept of a feminized nation within the

writings of both Petrarca and Ugo Foscolo offers powerful insights into the literary construction of the concept of Italy and *italianità* ("Love Songs from the Tomb: Female Voice in Foscolo's 'Dei sepolcri'"; unpublished manuscript).

5. Francesco Petrarca, *Canzoniere*, critical text and Introduction by Gianfranco Contini, notes by Daniele Ponchiroli, Nuova Universal Einaudi 41 (Turin: Einaudi, 1980), 174; my translation. A note to these lines tells the reader that "the Tiber, the Arno, and the Po, the three most important and known rivers of the peninsula, indicate the whole of Italy."

6. See also Gramsci's "southern question" regarding the unactualized agrarian revolution.

7. With the first parliamentary commission on the south in 1863, Massari offers the opinion that in fact fairer land divisions might have diminished the popular base of the insurgents. However, the report attributes the principal responsibility for the events to "southern ignorance and superstition" (Mangano 1976, 13).

8. The Sicilian workers' nationalist movement that was also active during the latter part of the Second World War, when Sicilian workers again called for the liberation and independence of Sicily as a sovereign nation.

9. "There is no historical example of colonization by population; it has never existed. Emigration and colonization follow the flux of capital invested in various nations and not vice versa" (Gramsci 1991, 43; my translation).

10. I discussed these terms in "Las indias por acá: Desperately Seeking Italy," at "Telemarketing a Cross-Dressed Columbus," conference at the University of California at Irvine, October 1992; "Cultural Tectonics: Southern Italy in the Age of Europe," Philological Association of the Pacific Coast Conference, November 1992; "Bound by Distance: Italian-Canadian Writing as Decontextualized Subaltern," *Voices in Italian Americana* 3:2 (1992).

11. In Gramscian terms, possibility equals freedom. Therefore, even a superficially open environment such as the Canadian "multicultural mosaic" provides sufficient possibility for groups to take up a struggle for self-representation.

12. For example, the study of Italian-Canadian, Chinese-Canadian, or Haitian-Canadian writing as a purely Canadian phenomenon, identified only with the plight of either the Canadian working or immigrant class, would be both incomplete and misleading, as would be a reading that merely reduced their relationships to a static dominant-subordinate dichotomy.

13. "Conscientization" is a term used by Paulo Freire (1988) to refer to a population's "critical self-insertion into reality."

14. My own work demonstrates similar concerns; there, the expression of differentiation is enacted most obviously on the linguistic-syntactic level. See *Nomadic Trajectory* (1990), particularly the pieces "Aridane: Come and Gone" and "Parthenope."

15. Such representations are common in literature, imperialist rhetoric, and political commentary. An exemplary citation from Niceforo reads: "No other people of Italy are as light, fickle, and restless as the Neapolitans; a lightness that is truly womanly. . . . The Neapolitans are, in contrast to the manly populations, such as northern Italians, Germans, and the English, a womanly population" (in Vito Teti, *La razza maledetta: origini del pregiudizio antimeridionale* [Rome: manifestolibri, 1993], 73; my translation).

16. In Zora Neale Hurston, *I Love Myself* (Old Westbury, N.Y.: Feminist Press, 1979), 109.

17. A similar reminder is offered by Spike Lee in the films *Do the Right Thing* (1989) and *Jungle Fever* (1992), which problematize the self-positioning of Italian Americans as "white" while they struggle with their ambiguity within that racial construct. See

also my "If I Was Six Feet Tall, I Would Have Been Italian: Spike Lee's Guineas," *Differentia* 6–7 (spring–autumn 1994): 177–91.

18. See Davis (1991, 13) for a gloss on Madison Grant's *The Taming of the Great Race* (1916).

19. *Italianità* ("Italianness") is a term that expresses an essentialist view of Italian culture and is strongly tied to fascist concepts of national cultural purity.

20. Rose Romano, "Coming Out Olive in the Lesbian Community: Big Sister Is Watching You," unpublished manuscript presented to the American Italian Historical Association Conference, 1989.

21. See ibid., 1.

22. David Mura, "Secrets and Anger?" *Mother Jones* (September–October 1992): 21.

## Works Cited

Alighieri, Dante. 1977. *De vulgari eloquentia*. Milan: Signorelli.

Anderson, Benedict. 1983. *Imagined Communities: Reflections on the Origin and Spread of Nationalism*. New York and London: Verso.

Azpadu, Dodici. 1983. *Saturday Night in the Prime of Life*. Iowa City: Aunt Lute Books.

———. 1984. *Goat Song*. Iowa City: Aunt Lute Books.

Barolini, Helen, ed. 1987. *The Dream Book: An Anthology of Writings by Italian American Women*. New York: Schocken Books.

Corradini, Enrico. 1910. *La patria lontana*. Milan: Treves.

———. 1911. *La guerra lontana*. Milan: Treves.

Davis, F. James. 1991. *Who Is Black? One Nation's Definition*. University Park: Pennsylvania State University Press.

D'Alfonso, Antonio. 1983. *Black Tongue*. Montreal: Guernica.

De Amicis, Edmondo. 1962. *Cuore: Libro per i ragazzi*. Milan: Garzanti.

Freire, Paulo. 1988. *Cultural Action for Freedom*. Cambridge: Harvard Educational Review.

Galasso, Giuseppe. 1977. *Il Mezzogiorno nella storia d'Italia*. Florence: Le Monnier.

———. 1982. *L'altra Europa: Per un'antropologia storica del Mezzogiorno d'Italia*. Milan: Mondadori.

———. 1987. *Storia delle città italiane*. Bari: Laterza.

Ganduscio, Giuseppe. 1970. *Perchè il Sud si ribella*. Ed. Carla Marazza. Palermo: Libri siciliani.

Gramsci, Antonio. 1966. *La questione meridionale*. Rome: Editori Riuniti.

———. 1977. *Gli intellettuali*. Rome: Editori Riuniti.

———. 1987. *Prison Notebooks*. Ed. and trans. Quintin Hoare and Geoffrey N. Smith. New York: International Publishers.

———. 1991. *Il Risorgimento*. Rome: Editori Riuniti.

Hall, Stuart. 1986. "Gramsci's Relevance for the Study of Race and Ethnicity." *Journal of Communication Inquiry* 10: 5–27.

Hurston, Zora Neale. 1979. *I Love Myelf*. Old Westbury, N.Y.: Feminist Press.

Mangano, Attilio. 1976. *Le cause della questione meridionale, I grandi eventi storici e le loro cause*. Milan: Istituto Editoriale Internazionale.

Mollia, Franco. 1970. *Ippolito Nievo*. Florence: La Nuova Italia.

Mura, David. 1992. "Secrets and Anger?" *Mother Jones* (September–October).

Nievo, Ippolito. 1961. *Lettere garibaldine*. Ed. Andreina Ciceri. Turin: Einaudi, Saggi 288.

Pascoli, Giovanni. 1971a. *Poesie*. Vol. I, *Tutte le opere*. 12th ed. Milan: Mondadori.

———. 1971b. *Prose*. Vol. I, *Pensieri di varia umanità*. 4th ed. Milan: Mondadori.

Pasquinelli, Carla, ed. 1977. *Antropologia culturale e questione meridionale: Ernesto De Martino e il dibattito sul mondo popolare subalterno negli anni 1948–1955*. Florence: La Nuova Italia.

Petrarca, Francesco. 1980. *Canzoniere*. Critical text and Introduction by Gianfranco Contini. Notes by Daniele Ponchiroli. Nuova Universal Einaudi 41. Turin: Einaudi.

Romano, Rose. 1990. *Vendetta*. San Francisco: malafemmina press.

———. N.d. "Coming Out Olive in the Lesbian Community: Big Sister Is Watching You." Unpublished manuscript.

Rosa, Asor. 1965. *Scrittori e popolo: Saggio sulla letteratura populista in Italia*. Saggistica 3. Rome: Samonà e Savelli/Libreria internazionale Terzo Mondo.

Rosoli, Gianfausto, ed. 1978. *Un secolo di emigrazione italiana: 1876–1976*. Rome: Centro Studi Emigrazione.

Sassoon, Anne Showstack. 1980. *Gramsci's Politics*. New York: St. Martin's Press.

Sterpa, Egidio. 1973. *La rabbia del sud*. Turin: Società Editrice Internazionale, Collana Le Firme.

Tessari, Roberto, ed. 1976. *Pascoli, D'Annunzio, Fogazzaro e il decadentismo italiano: irrazionalismo e crisi dell'ideologia borghese tra '800 e '900*. Turin: Paravia.

Teti, Vito. 1993. *La razza maledetta: origini del pregiudizio antimeridionale*. Rome: manifestolibri.

Verdicchio, Pasquale. 1990. *Nomadic Trajectory*. Montreal: Guernica.

———. 1992a. "Bound by Distance: Italian Canadian Writing as Decontextualized Subaltern." *Voices in Italian Americana* 3:2.

———. 1992b. "L'Italia in Bocca." *Viceversa*, February–March, Montreal.

———. 1992c. "The Subaltern Written/The Subaltern Writing: Pasolini's 'Gennariello' as Author." *Pacific Coast Philology* 27: 1–2.

———. 1994. "If I Was Six Feet Tall, I Would Have Been Italian: Spike Lee's Guineas." *Differentia: Review of Italian Thought* 6–7 (spring–autumn 1994): 177–91.

Villani, Pasquale. 1973. *Mezzogiorno tra riforme e rivoluzione*. Bari: Laterza.

# Anarquistas, Graças a Deus!
# "Italy" in South America

*Francesca Miller*

Between 1876 and 1925, nine million Italians emigrated to the Western Hemisphere. The majority—51 percent—emigrated to the United States; 25 percent, or more than two million, went to Argentina, and one million three hundred thousand entered Brazil, settling primarily in the southern states of São Paulo, Paraná, Santa Caterina, and Rio Grande do Sul. Although the absolute number of immigrants to South America was less than to the United States, the impact of the Italian migrants on Brazil and Argentina was disproportionately greater because of the much smaller total populations of the two Latin American countries.[1]

The proportionate impact of the Italian immigrants on the local populations in South America may be read in the census records: in 1893, the city of São Paulo recorded that 35 percent of the city's total population—forty-five thousand people—were Italian-born. Thirty-eight years later, in 1920, Italian immigrants comprised 16 percent of the city's population—91,544 of 579,093. What is not visible in the latter statistics is the number of city residents who were the Brazil-born children of the earlier Italian immigrants. It is this story—the story of the immigrant generation and their children—that this essay will explore through the examination of correspondence, memoirs, newspaper and journal accounts, song, poetry, and local histories.

Central questions include, first, a theoretical exploration of the idea of Brazil as *deserto*, or empty space. What happened when the imaginary passive peasant of the Brazilian planters' colonizing projects reached the imaginary Eden of the immigrant family's hopes? What survival strategies did the immigrant devise when the promises of colonization recruiters proved empty? What was the relation of the immigrant generation, and subsequently their children, to the incipient Brazilian nativist movement in the 1890s, and later, the nationalist impulses of the 1920s? Using *Anarquistas, graças a Deus!*, Zelia Gattai's memoir of growing up in an Italian-Brazilian household in São Paulo in the early twentieth century, as a central text, this essay explores ideas about national definition, the politics of identity, and generational change.[2]

The engaging title of Gattai's memoir, *Anarquistas, graças a Deus!* (Anarchists, thank the Lord!), invokes images of the Italian immigrant as political radical and the Italian immigrant as culturally Catholic. The latter were the preferred immigrants and the target of the immigration schemes supported by the wealthy owners of the coffee plantations who sought a cheap, compliant labor force with which to replace the forced workers who had fled the land in the wake of the final abolition of slavery in Brazil in 1888. The former, men and women who sought a new life in a land where they could be free of papism and poverty, came to establish their own colonies. Zelia Gattai's heritage includes the history of political and economic migrants alike: her maternal grandparents left a grindingly poor existence in rural Veneto in 1886 with their five children to take up the offer of free transport in return for their promise to work on a coffee estate; her paternal grandparents came from Florence in 1889 to help build the Colonia Cecilia, the most famous anarchist agricultural colony in nineteenth-century Brazil.

To both groups of immigrants, Brazil was presented as a tabula rasa, a *silva*, or wilderness. The word *deserto* is used repeatedly in the advertisements published by the colonizing agencies, meaning not the hot sands of a Sahara, but that the land was deserted, unpopulated, and especially, uncultivated. Alexander von Humboldt described the New World as a place where "man and his productions almost disappear amidst the stupendous display of wild and gigantic nature." As Mary Louise Pratt describes so eloquently in *Imperial Eyes*, the Humboldtian positing of South America as empty space awaiting the civilizing hand of Europe was adopted and adapted by South American elites in the nineteenth century in an effort to forge a new hierarchy that would preserve their social, cultural, political, and racial predominance.[3]

Between 1885 and 1930, the period of the most intense migration from Italy to South America, both the Argentine and Brazilian elites employed the Humboldtian vision to attract European immigrants "to people the land." In Argentina in 1853, Juan Bautista Alberdi coined the phrase "to govern is to populate": "He bade his country men draw upon the surplus population of Europe, confident that even those . . . ground down by the old tyrannies, would rise to new moral and physical stature in the free air of America."[4] In Brazil, a central concern of the elites was to "whiten" (*branquear*, or bleach) the population, as well as to effect the somewhat antithetical ends of attracting a compliant agricultural labor force and peopling the wilderness with skilled European settlers.

Intriguingly, the depiction of Brazil, and to a lesser extent all of South America, as *deserto* figured large in the vision of Italian nationalists in this same period. Occupation of foreign territories with Italian troops had proved impracticable in Africa, and the new hope for empire was based on the idea of demographic colonization, a Magna Italia. The idea was to give governmental support to Italian settlements that would in time overwhelm and dominate the native population through numerical superiority. The arguments for selecting South America for this venture contained elements of racial Darwinism as well as the Humboldtian vision. Not only did South America seem propitious to the proponents of Italian empire because of "the Latin environment familiar to Italians" but "because of the expected and predicted disappearance of the inferior races of blacks, Indians and mulattoes in the competition for survival."[5] Believing as they did that South America was a wilderness, there was little recognition on the part of the Italian nationalists that nationalism might be as potent a force in the larger Latin American nations in this era as it was in contemporary Europe.

At the time of the arrival of the earliest migrants, Brazil was at least as regional as Italy. If the Italian immigrant typically identified herself or himself by town or region, the native-born Brazilian of the coastal littoral would have identified herself or himself by village or *municipio* (administrative region), or simply by the great house to which he or she was attached. Only the national elites possessed a sense of what might constitute "Brazil."[6] So it is not surprising that, in São Paulo, the way in which the passionate debate surrounding issues of patriotism, national definition, citizenship, and cultural identity was articulated was not so much as to who was or was not a Brazilian as to who could or could not be described as a "paulista," a term already construed to exclude a significant number of native-born but racially undesirable Brazilians.

Zelia Gattai's father, Seu[7] Ernesto, described the *paulista* in sardonic terms as "the authentic rich, with tradition and *fidalguia*."[8] The heritage claimed by the "true paulista" derived from the original Portuguese (male) explorers of the region who had taken indigenous women (always described as the daughter of chief so-and-so) as their wives. This racial heritage was a badge of honor, especially at the remove of some twenty generations, and it did not include Afro-Brazilians or contemporary American Indians. It also served to differentiate the haughty paulista from the newly arrived and much-scorned Portuguese immigrant.[9]

Where did the "Italian"—or, more accurately, Florentine, Venetian, Tuscan, Piedmontese—fit into this? A number of studies argue that the Italian "colonists" were indifferent to "Brazilian politics," but I will suggest in this essay that the sons and daughters of the immigrant generation adopted and attempted to re-create the term "Brazilian" as an inclusive term, a national designation that included them.

Prior to 1906, the great majority—approximately 90 percent—of immigrants who came to Brazil from the Italian peninsula came from the provinces of northern Italy. The tradition of seasonal migration into and out of this region was ancient, and the young men who constituted most of the migrants to the New World were seen as part of this pattern. Whereas their forefathers might have gone north into Europe to harvest crops and work as stonemasons and carpenters in the summer months, returning to their homes in late fall, the new generations went to New York, Buenos Aires, Montevideo. The expectation was that their wages would go into the family coffers, or form a nest egg with which to purchase a farmstead in Italy, and that they would return home. The reversal of seasons in South America seemed especially auspicious: the young men could work the harvest in December, January, and February, and return to Italy for the planting and harvest in that region. In Argentina, to the dismay of the national leaders who wished to attract permanent European settlers, the migrants were known as *golondrinas*, or migrating swallows.[10]

Both Italian and Brazilian statistics indicate that the pattern of migration to and from Brazil differed slightly from that elsewhere in the Western Hemisphere: although young men were the most numerous immigrants there as well, a significant number of immigrants came to

Brazil in family groups, and they came to stay.[11] This was true of Zelia Gattai's grandparents, who emigrated with their children, hoping to make a new life in a "new land." Gattai's family stories illuminate not only the specific experience of her grandparents, but give insight into the broader history of "Italy" in South America in this period.

Gattai's own parents were both young children when their families brought them to Brazil. She tells of asking her maternal grandfather, "Were you an anarchist, Grandfather?" (Here it must be noted that Gattai grew up in a household where the anarchist convictions of her parents seemed as natural to her as did the Catholicism of the Neapolitan family who lived next door.)

He replied, "No, no. We were neither anarchist nor monarchist. Our family were *gente de igreja*, people of the church, all Catholics. Our history is very similar to that of the Gattais, but completely different."

"The same but completely different? How can that be?"[12]

Zelia's maternal grandparents, the *familia* Da Col, were in fact far more representative of the Italian immigrants to Brazil in the nineteenth century than were her anarchist forebears. The Da Cols were agricultural workers who owned no land in rural Veneto and responded to the call for colonists to work the rich coffee fields of Brazil. The hope was that through their labor they would earn money to purchase their own property, and find better lives in "the free land of Brazil," as the brochures advertised.

In 1876 they sailed from Genoa with their five children, a voyage in which the migrants were confined below deck. Seasickness, rotting food, and lack of fresh air and sanitation made the voyage a nightmare. The youngest child, whom the family believed they could safely transport because she was still nursing, died when the mother's own malnutrition caused her milk to dry up. On their arrival at Santos, the port town of the state of São Paulo, the family was immediately transported with other immigrants straight to the interior. At the plantation they were assigned to, Zelia's grandfather observed, "We were treated as slave substitutes; all the things they promised were lies."

Zelia relates that her grandfather would tell her no more of that initial experience. But her uncle, who was nine years old at the time, continued the story. On the first day after their arrival, the males of the family, including the nine-year-old boy and his seven- and five-year-old brothers, were marched to the coffee fields.

Toward noon, the overseer brought out a Brazilian, a Negro, who had been picked up for "trespassing" on the estate lands. He was tied to a tree, and the overseer prepared to beat him.

Horrified, and blind with indignation, the young colonist Eugenio Da Col did not hesitate. He leaped forward and freed the Negro, who ran away. The wrath of the overseer was turned on him.

Eugenio tried to enlist the aid of the other Italian workers, but they stood back silently. He wondered if they couldn't understand his mountain dialect, but no. Who could not understand his words and action? A *católico convicto* (Catholic of conscience), he acted according to the dictates of his heart.[13]

The family was thrown off the *fazenda* that afternoon. They were refused pay for the work they had done in the morning, on the grounds that they owed the *fazenda* for their passage. Weakened from their voyage, left to their own devices in an indifferent land, they set out to walk to the barrio of Bras, adjacent to the city of São Paulo, where they hoped to find friends from their region. They were aided on their way by rides in oxcarts and handouts of food, and in Bras, Eugenio, who was a skilled carpenter, secured a job working for a childhood friend "who was importing wood from Amazonas."

The story of Zelia's paternal grandparents was told to her by her father Ernesto, who was five years old when his family emigrated from Florence to Brazil.

> The voyage of the Gattai family began two years before we set sail on the *Città di Roma* from Genoa. My father had the opportunity to read a little book titled *Il Commune in Riva al Mare*, written by Dr. Giovanni Rossi, who was a scientist, botanist, and musician. In the booklet that fascinated my father, Rossi idealized the foundation of a Colonia Socialista Experimental in a country in Latin America; it did not specify which country—a society without laws, without religion, without private property, where a family would be constituted in the most humane form, assuring women the same civil and political rights as men. . . . In Rossi, Francisco Arnaldo Gattai found someone with dynamism and intelligence, disposed to turn a dream into reality, and he and others of his comrades, who were also disciples of the thinking of Bakunin and Kropotkin, joined in the plans "to create a new road for humanity, which is starving, ragged, wretched, perhaps forgotten by God."[14]

Rossi settled on Brazil as a location for his utopian anarchist experiment subsequent to a meeting with representatives of the Brazilian emperor Pedro II in Milan in 1888. The contract, signed by the emperor in 1889, stated that the land given to the colony was "uncultivated and uninhabited." Posters lauded the project as dedicated to "Fraternity, Love, Justice, Mutual Help, Rational Division of Work, Machines for the Use of All, Equitable Division of Produce, Marriage and Family, Continual Progress, Abundance, Art." Education, intelligence and reason, morality, order, and peace would inform the experiment.[15] Rossi's caveats were few, and were cast in heroic terms: "An adventure only for idealists hardened in the struggle, disposed to realize a great social experiment, who don't fear sacrifice." Having read Rossi's advertisement and booklet, the thirty-year-old Francisco Gattai consulted with his wife, and she agreed that they and their five young children should join the experiment. They left Italy in 1890.

The colonists arrived in Brazil to discover that the Empire of Brazil, founded at independence in 1822, had been overthrown in a revolt carried out by military officers but fomented by forces that wished to replace the "outdated" constitutional monarchy with a republican form of government. When the members of the Colonia Cecilia expedition arrived in Brazil, an interim military government was in place, overseeing the promised transition to a republican form of government. The elderly former emperor Pedro II, with whom Rossi had signed the contract for the land, had gone into exile, and the Italian colonists were left to fend for themselves in a decidedly unsettled political situation. The promised seeds, farming implements, and livestock were not forthcoming, but the regional authorities did honor the contract for the lands, which were located in the southeastern state of Santa Catarina. After a long and hungry trek, during which the Gattai's baby daughter perished, the colonists found that the allocated land was far inland from the fertile coastal plains already held in immense estates by Brazilian landowners. More crucially, the land was far from any depot or railhead through which they could ship and receive goods.

But the two hundred men, women, and children who made up the initial colonizing group had resources and the support of one another. They were committed to the experiment; collectively they possessed many skills, and they had brought tools and seedlings with them. They raised their black-and-red anarchist flag over the Colonia Cecilia, and proceeded to clear the rocky land. Despite hardships, by the end of their first year they could claim some success.

In some ways, it was this initial success that undid the colony. More immigrants were attracted, many of whom did not share the anarchist convictions of the original colonists. Some wanted to claim their own land, violating a primary tenet of the original colonists, who rejected the concept of private property. The records of the first two years of the colony's existence are thick with the minutes of endless meetings, in which the colonists sought to adhere to their commitment to decision by consensus.

Ultimately, it was not internal tensions that destroyed Colonia Cecilia. The local Brazilian Catholic church and neighboring Brazilian landowners were just as hostile to the idea of a prosperous anarchist colony growing among them as any Old World priests and latifundistas might have been. The colonists were bedeviled with thefts and arson. More mouths to feed than was yet feasible forced many of the men to migrate to work on railroad construction elsewhere in southern Brazil. In 1892, two crushing blows felled the experiment. The first came from the Brazilian clergy who owned the land immediately adjoining the colony. The priest had repeatedly denounced the "godless anarchists"; the principle of "free love" was especially repellent to him.[16] Just prior to the harvest, he opened the fence that separated the church properties from the colony and drove his cattle through to destroy the crop. The second blow came from the local government, at the behest of the Brazilian landowners: the male immigrants were threatened with forced conscription.[17] The colonists dispersed; the Gattai family headed for São Paulo.

In the words of Zelia's maternal grandfather, the histories of the two immigrant families, one "Catholics of conscience" and the other "convinced anarchists," were "very different, but the same." Hardship, the deaths of their youngest children, the betrayal of promises, and the almost total absence of lines of official recourse marked each family's initial experience in Brazil, and the Gattais, like the Da Col family before them, fled the *deserto* to find friends and work in São Paulo.

Prior to the arrival of the Italians (and Spanish, Germans, Armenians, Syrians, Lebanese, Polish, Japanese, and Portuguese), São Paulo was a sleepy administrative center for the coffee trade. It was the presence of the immigrants, especially the Italian and Spanish immigrants, that transformed São Paulo into a true city with newspapers, schools, commercial enterprises that served the needs of the rural economy, and a plethora of businesses that quickly emerged to serve the burgeoning urban population.

The immigrants, in effect, created an economic and social stratum that had not previously existed in Brazil: an urban middle and working class. Brazilian historian Eunice Ribeiro Durham, in his book *Assimilação e Mobilidade*, describes the genesis of the new economic sector: "The *fazendas* [coffee estates] were not self-sufficient, and constituted, therefore, a market for the work of artisans as much as for the great houses of commerce. . . . There is a market for furniture, household goods, and a need for skilled labor that can make and repair machines, vehicles, and agricultural implements. These businesses were, from the beginning, dominated by immigrants."[18]

The northern Italian immigrants were in general far more cosmopolitan than the local Brazilians among whom they settled. Many of the Italian men were literate; in the case of Zelia Gattai's grandfathers, each had been attracted to the colonization ventures they joined by reading flyers and booklets advertising the projects. Moreover, the Italian migrants had, perhaps perforce, knowledge of a far wider world than did most poor Brazilians engaged in rural labor. The Italians came from a land in political ferment; for those with socialist and anarchist convictions, in particular, political discourse—and the politics of dissent—informed their worldview.

The society the early immigrants found in Brazil was deeply divided. The great landowners and their commercial and governmental adjuncts dominated an ill-educated, impoverished laboring class whose economic, political, and social disenfranchisement was reinforced by racial demarcation. It was also a society in transition, a transition in which the new immigrants played a crucial, if unanticipated, role.

By the late nineteenth century, concurrent with the arrival of the first great influx of European immigrants, economic and political power had shifted decisively from the slave-dependent sugar plantations of the northeast littoral to central-southeast Brazil, in the triangle bounded by the national capital, Rio de Janeiro, the interior mining center of Minas Gerais, and the state of São Paulo. National politics in the new "Republic of the United States of Brazil," established with the Constitution of 1891, were dominated by the landowning families of São Paulo, a fact underlined with the inauguration of the first civilian president, Prudente de Morais of São Paulo, in 1894. His term marked the beginning of the period known as the "old Republic" (1894–1930).

Although their wealth derived from the land, the landowning families were an urbanized class who maintained great houses in the city of São Paulo and looked to Europe—principally France—for their fashions, high culture, and manners. Their interests were in the perpetuation of the profits of the coffee trade, and they had little interest in or understanding of the growing urban population. For them, immigration was a strategy to gain hands to work the coffee estates. However, their insistence that the business of the national government was to protect the coffee export trade from competition also had the effect of protecting the nascent domestic manufacturing industry from foreign competition. Ribeiro Durham writes: Immigration and concomitant economic-demographic growth greatly broadened the original market. The immigrants produced and consumed . . . the city, born to serve the countryside, came to constitute a major market in itself for goods and services, pharmacies, dry-goods stores, and so on. In this class of small businesses we see a large proportion of Italians."[19]

For the Italian immigrant, the hoped-for goal was independence. In the nineteenth century, the great majority of immigrants, known as *colonos*, or colonists, came as agricultural laborers, but their ultimate goal was economic independence. They planned to work on the coffee and tobacco estates only until they could amass enough money to purchase their own land, if not in Brazil, then at home in Italy.[20] Those who left the land for the urban areas similarly sought work in order to develop a nest egg. In the 1890s, men with skills and the tools of their trade were able to make the rural to urban transition most readily. Even before the arrival of the Italians, a small artisanal class composed mainly of German immigrants was in business in São Paulo. These establishments employed the newly arrived Italians, allowing them an initial adjustment and introduction to the existing economic system and a familiarization with the opportunities available for skilled workers.[21]

The Italian immigrants were involved in every imaginable variety of enterprise. The immigrant populations transformed the Brazilian diet. In her study of Italian immigration in São Paulo, Lucy Maffei Hutter states:

> Small industry throughout the state of São Paulo was, at the beginning of this century, almost entirely in the hands of Italians, who manufactured beer, liquor, and a variety of foodstuffs. The same was true of small commerce. . . . The *colonia Italia* in the urban sector was made up of

operations devoted to a great variety of work, such as carpenter shops, shoemakers, barbers, fruit stands, dry-goods stores, artisans, mechanics, cabdrivers, longshoremen, newsstands, door-to-door salesmen, gilders, bootblacks, and so forth. Another profession that was common among the Italians but later became almost exclusively the monopoly of the Lebanese and Syrians was that of peddler, an occupation entered into by those who did not wish to submit to the regime of the coffee *fazendas* but who did not have sufficient capital to set themselves up in shops.[22]

Women worked alongside their husbands in all of these enterprises, and also as seamstresses, modistes, midwives, and music teachers.

The various strategies of immigrant survival are specifically visible in Zelia Gattai's family memoir. Eugenio Da Col's carpentry skills gave the migrant family their initial income, but it was expected that every family member would work and contribute to the household income and, it was hoped, to the savings that promised a better future. Zelia's mother, Angelina, went to work in the textile factory in Bras at the age of nine.

Had Angelina grown up in rural Veneto, she would likely have attended the Catholic church to which her parents belonged, and whatever learning she acquired would have been by rote. In Brazil, the textile factory formed her world. She learned to read—in Italian—in a workers' club, where she acquired a lifelong love of the writings of Émile Zola and Victor Hugo and a commitment to the precepts of socialism.[23] At the age of fifteen she met Ernesto Gattai at one of the club meetings. The eighteen-year-old Gattai was employed in his father's shop, which repaired bicycles and buggies and all manner of vehicles. Gattai and Angelina were wed within the year. At first they lived with his family, and both continued working. Then Ernesto's passion for all things mechanical led to their first opportunity to change their lives for the better.

Young Ernesto was in love with the automobile. In 1907, so few had yet been imported to Brazil that his application to the mayor of the city of São Paulo for a license as *conductor de carro automóvel* is the eighth listed in the city records. The newspapers published the arrival of each new car, and when Ernesto saw that the Prado family, one of the wealthiest and most socially prominent families of São Paulo, had acquired a luxury sedan, he set off to apply for the position of chauffeur.

He secured the job, and for the next two years, Ernesto and Angelina and their firstborn child, Remo, lived in an apartment over the garage on the grounds of the Prado estate in São Paulo. Expenses were few, the salary good, and the rapidly growing Remo was clothed in hand-me-downs from the Prado's slightly older son. Although they had taken in a young relative of Angelina's, and gave what they could to needier family members, the Gattais saved every penny they could. Zelia relates the conclusion of this chapter in her family's life as follows: "But Ernesto was not born to serve patrons. He was not a man to wear gloves, to spend his time opening the doors of cars, standing immobile as a statue while his patrons got in or out of the automobile, to take orders. He positively was not born to that, putting up with what have you. He had enough, and he left the job."[24]

Ernesto Gattai had already found what wanted for his next enterprise: a small house where his growing family could live, attached to a large (and filthy and ramshackle, according to Zelia's mother) barn that housed old carriages and the donkeys and burros that pulled them. The property was owned by one Rocco Andretta, "an old Italian, from the south of Italy." Rocco was under threat of eviction from the local authorities for the derelict state of his property; the neighborhood was improving, and the donkeys and burros had to go. Gattai contracted with the old man to undertake the renovation of the property in return for free rent. Paint and elbow grease went into the renovation; the bulk of the accumulated savings were put into acquiring the equipment needed to furnish an automobile repair shop.

That her husband would put their savings into such an enterprise was a horror to Angelina Gattai. "Why not invest in land, or a farm, where we can raise food? Or a partnership in a store that has already proved profitable?" It was not apparent in São Paulo in 1910 that the automobile was more than a novelty for the rich, but Ernesto Gattai was not only undeterred but confident of his prospects. The property was at the junction of two of the main streets of the city, and he believed in the future of the automobile.

As is illustrated in the story of the Gattais, two factors were crucial to the immigrants' success in this period: first, the need for their skills in the changing economy; second, there was no existing native-born entrepreneurial class. Thus the newcomers did not have to face entrenched competition in the work they sought out. The avenues of social mobility created by the immigrants developed parallel to, rather than intersecting with, the existent society. Their very presence in the city offered, by example and through regional and kinship networks, an avenue of escape for those who wanted to leave the countryside. In both the city and the rural areas, the immigrants opened up new paths of economic advancement. In the country, especially in southern Brazil, immigrant families bought land and set themselves up as small independent farmers. In the city, the native-born poorer classes were made up of "unskilled workers, domestic help and menial laborers." Moreover, the low status accorded to the native-born poor was reinforced by racial demarcation. Ribeiro Durham writes that the urban poor were "blacks, mulattoes, and failed ex-agricultural colonists."[25]

The degree to which the channels of social mobility created by the immigrants did not intersect with the existent society is well illustrated in the fact that the areas of paid employment that proved resistant to penetration by the newcomers were the liberal professions and the government bureaucracy. *Bachareis*, as those men who held law degrees were known, and national, state, and local government bureaucrats made up the preexisting urban middle classes; they were also the locus of the most virulent patriotism.[26] They defined themselves as "true Brazilians" and were the source of vociferous nativism and anti-immigrant sentiment. They sought identification with the national elites, and feared identification with black(er) "native-born Brazilians." The primary target of their xenophobia was the Portuguese immigrants, but their resistance to "foreign" integration extended to all immigrant groups.[27]

However, the absence of first- and second-generation Italians in the liberal professions should not be wholly attributed to the hostility of the native Brazilian middle class. There is also evidence that the upwardly mobile Italians, who defined success in terms of prosperity, were not interested in bureaucratic jobs. Ribeiro Durham comments that

> scholarship was not seen as an important channel of social ascension among the early Italian population. Literacy was considered a necessity, but for that primary school was sufficient. The work of the sons was considered necessary to family prosperity and those few who showed any interest in studying were generally directed into technical courses like accounting whose usefulness was more immediate. Those Italians in the liberal professions before 1920 had acquired their qualification before immigrating.[28]

The predominance of native-born Brazilians in government bureaucracy was reflected in the indifference and a hostility of the local governments toward the immigrant community, and in the almost complete lack of schools, hospitals, and clinics. Aid for the destitute, widowed, or ill was nonexistent. There were no effective channels through which workers could seek redress of abuses; throughout this period, the response of the Brazilian government to signs of dissension was repression through force.[29] The "social problem" was regarded as a "police matter." In response, the Italian community created its own protective associations, which supported schools and hospitals and raised money to support those in need. Many of the associations were affiliated with their local Catholic parish; others, such as the ones Zelia Gattai's family was associated with, were affiliated with workers' associations.

By the time Zelia Gattai was born in 1916, the fourth of five children, her father's automobile repair business was flourishing. The Gattais' neighborhood was filled with Italian, Spanish, and Portuguese immigrants, and intermarriage among them and with Brazilians was changing the composition of the immigrant barrios. The senior Gattais regularly attended the meetings of the local anarchist and socialist clubs at as Classes Laboriosas (the working classes). Zelia describes the scene: "Seu Ernesto always read the announcements in the newspapers looking for conferences and acts of solidarity, so that he would not miss one. My sisters and the baby, Tito, and I were incorporated into the political-cultural caravan. . . . The Classes Laboriosas was a hall for festivals and congresses, situated in the center of the city."[30] The presence of the neighborhood children transformed these meetings into parties, diversions. The atmosphere was festive, everyone brought their children, a custom—or necessity—for poor people.

Zelia writes that for her the early part of the evenings was the most exciting, because the children were employed to hawk the new issues of newspapers and journals, such as *La Laterna*, an anticlerical journal, or *La Difesa*, a socialist journal, and there were raffles for prizes and books to support the publications and to pay for the rent of the hall. "[My sister] Vera and I were part of the group of vendors. There were two competing groups for sales and artistic participation: that of the Italian girls, and that of the Spanish. We, logically, were part of the first group, despite the fact that we felt ourselves to be wholly Brazilian [*embora nos sentíssemos completamente brasileiras*]. But this is how we were designated."[31]

That Zelia should identify herself as "wholly Brazilian" indicates her generational location in the Da Col–Gattai family. By the time she was participating in the cultural congresses, her family was prospering, and had an established place in the Italian-Brazilian community. Her identification as Brazilian also reflected her schooling: whereas the earlier generation of immigrants and their firstborn children rarely attained more than a rudimentary education, Zelia was not only in school but in a Brazilian school.

Zelia's parents had little education, but valued learning. Zelia describes her father reading *o Estado de São Paulo*, the premier daily newspaper of the city:

> He read correctly, if slowly, word by word. His writing was also slow, but his calligraphy was good, full of personality. He had barely three months of school, sufficient to learn the alphabet. The rest, everything he knew, was the result of the force of will to learn. But as for calculations, he was a colossus. "It is not necessary to have good grammar to add up numbers," he would say after computing a problem considered to be very difficult.

The Gattai family's anarchist principles mandated equal opportunity for females, but for many Italian girls school was considered downright dangerous. Zelia writes of the attitude of a family of Neapolitan neighbors on the topic: "School is not for girls! Girls must learn to take care of a husband and a house! There's none of that in school! Why should a girl learn to read? In order to read notes from lovers!"

She comments further: "The theory of keeping girls illiterate in order to prevent them from corresponding with lovers was not exclusively an idea of the Andrettas. Many other residents in the neighborhood, principally families from southern Italy, also used this as an excuse to keep their daughters out of school."[32]

Zelia's reference to the presence of southern Italian neighbors indicates a change in the composition of the immigrant population from the time her grandparents arrived in Brazil. Immigration from northern Italy peaked in 1897, when the Italian government virtually forbade emigration to Brazil. The horrible tales of the immigrants' experience at the hands of the coffee barons, the indifference of the Brazilian government to the immigrants' plight, and the shocking reports of Italian consular officials and Italian clergy had alerted the Italian government to the terrible difficulties many immigrants were encountering in Brazil. Unable to secure assurance from the Brazilian government that conditions would improve, in 1897 the government of Italy took its case to the World Court at The Hague, which issued a set of decrees regarding international immigration known as "The Italian Protocols." In-migration to Brazil, from all countries, dropped from 174,000 in 1897 to 34,000 in 1903.[33] When immigration to Brazil regained momentum in 1909, one of the notable changes was that the new Italian migrants were from the south: Apulia, Naples, and Sicily. But if the Italians in Brazil distinguished among themselves by region of origin, and by their community affiliations, in the Brazilian community, they were all seen as Italian.

Regions of origin were reflected in the Italian protective associations, workers' organizations, and church parishes.[34] The role of the Italian priest in Brazil in this era offers insight into the growing nativist movement. One of the issues in the coup that brought an end to the old regime was ultramontanism, and patriotic Brazilians were sensitive to the predominance of European clergy in their church. Since independence, the Brazilian government held the right to confirm or reject papal appointments to the country. In the early twentieth century, the Catholic clergy were enjoined to promote identification with Brazil among their congregations. Riolando Azzi describes the practice of one priest of Calabrian origin: "Upon concluding the service, he warmly counseled his compatriots to love their second *patria*, to respect its laws, and to cooperate in creating progress and peace in the present life, besides loving God and serving him as good Christians." Azzi comments, "This did not stop him, however, from simultaneously continuing to be preoccupied with preserving the values of *italianidade*."[35]

There is also evidence of national rivalry among the clergy. Describing the reaction of the Calabrian priest to an encounter with French Capuchin monks in southern Brazil, Azzi quotes the priest: "They ought to go evangelize the Indians, and leave the Italians to the Italians."[36]

Patriotic instruction was inserted into the catechism. Bartolomeu Tiecher recounts learning the following lines: "Commerce and industry form our progress. And, now, where before there was a wilderness [*um deserto*], today we find villages and cities! Viva Brazil! Viva our labor!"[37]

It is significant that the beliefs and credos of the Italian in Brazil were nurtured through associations that were fundamentally transnational. Although the community associations and neighborhood congregations typically exhibited the regional characteristics of their membership, they were part of organizations that were not identified with or confined within particular national boundaries. This is true of international socialism and the anarchist movement of the period, and it is true of the Roman Catholic Church. It is congruent with the concept of a *Magna Italia* community, and it did not necessarily conflict with the adoption of Brazil as a new *patria*. In his book *Poemas de um Imigrante Italiano*, Angelo Guisti writes:

> Forgetting the initial difficulties, the Italian held dear the vision of himself as a Brazilian, because Brazil marked a new hope for a home. It could be said that the first Italians had a domestic vision of Brazil, as *sua patria*, because many of them could have Italy as their homeland, but few could have "their Italy," that is, a piece of Italy itself to plant, till, harvest, and give their own family name.[38]

The Italian immigrants and their children could continue their sense of self as Catholic, or socialist. Their *italianidade* rested in family and their associative communities; their adoption of Brazil as a new home did not in and of itself threaten these associations.

In the 1920s, Brazil was seeking to define what was, and was not, Brazilian; 1922 was the centennial celebration of Brazilian independence. In São Paulo, the event was marked by "The Week of Modern Art." The intellectuals who conceived the week meant it to assert Brazil's cultural independence from Europe. They declared that all of the arts, including architecture, music, and literature as well as the visual arts, required "Brazilianization," conceived of as the use of indigenous, African, and Brazilian themes, colors, and styles of expression.[39] Brazil was seen as the land of the future; Europe, the land of the past. It is within this context that eight-year-old, third-generation, Italian-Brazilian Zelia Gattai proclaimed, "we felt ourselves to be wholly Brazilian."

To what degree did the presence of the immigrant community mandate a construction of a Brazilian nationalism that could include them? Cultural nationalism, like the earlier nativist movement, contained strong components of antiforeign sentiment, but it was also concerned with building loyalty to a national "imagined community,"[40] that would give cohesion to the vast territory and multiple peoples contained within "Brazil."

For their part, Italian-Brazilians expressed their contribution to the building of Brazil in journals, poetry, and song, as this excerpt from the song "La 'Merica," published in a collection of documents from the Italian community in Porto Alegre, Rio Grande do Sul, Brazil, demonstrates:

> From Italy we came, thirty-six days by train and ship
> Till we arrived in America.
> America . . . A beauty more lovely than flowers.
> In America we arrived
> It had neither wheat nor hay
> There we slept in the barren terrain
> Like the wild beasts in the forest.
> America is long and large
> It is formed of mountain and plain
> And with the industry of our Italian arms
> We built farms and cities.[41]

The song echoes the idea of America—Brazil, in this case—as *deserto*, an uninhabited land ripe for cultivation. What the Italian immigrants found was far from the Eden of their dreams, but the strategies they evolved for survival did create a "new world" in Brazil.

## Notes

1. Samuel L. Bailey, "The Italians and Organized Labor in the United States, Argentina, Brazil and the United States, 1880–1914," *Journal of Social History* 3 (winter 1969): 123.

2. Zelia Gattai, *Anarquistas, graças a Deus!* 16th ed. (Rio de Janeiro: Record, 1991).

3. Mary Louise Pratt, *Imperial Eyes: Travel Writing and Transculturation* (London and New York: Oxford University Press, 1992). The Humboldt reference is from Alexander von Humboldt, *Personal Narrative of Travels to the Equinoctial Regions of the New Continent* (1814).

4. Hubert Herring, *A History of Latin America from the Beginnings to the Present*, 3d ed. (New York: Alfred A. Knopf, 1968), 719.

5. Dino Cinel, *The National Integration of Italian Return Migrations 1870–1929* (Cambridge: Cambridge University Press, 1991), 87. Cinel is citing Geralamo Boccardo, *Giornale degli Economisti* (1886).

6. In Brazil, the late nineteenth and early twentieth centuries were, quite literally, an era of national definition: between 1880 and 1910, Brazil extended its borders to incorporate an additional 1.9 million square miles of territory, a process that involved negotiations with Argentina, Uruguay, Paraguay, Bolivia, Peru, Venezuela, and, in the Guianas, the colonial powers of France, Britain, and the Netherlands. The final abolition of slavery in 1888 and the fall of the constitutional monarch in 1889 signaled a definitive shift in the locus of economic and political power away from the slave-dependent sugar plantations of the northeast to the coffee-growing, metropolitan central south.

7. "Seu" is an honorific, literally meaning "he himself," used by Zelia Gattai in affectionate humor to indicate the respect in which her father was head of the household and his own sense of self-importance in his household.

8. Gattai, *Anarquistas*, 10.

9. For discussion of anti-Portuguese sentiment in Brazil, see June Hahner, *Poverty and Politics: The Urban Poor in Brazil 1870–1920* (Albuquerque: University of New Mexico Press, 1986).

10. See James R. Scobie, *Buenos Aires* (New York: Oxford University Press, 1974).

11. Cinel, *The National Integration of Italian Return Migrations*.

12. Gattai, *Anarquistas*, 149.

13. Ibid., 151.

14. Ibid., 150.

15. Jean-Louis Comolli, *"Le Cecilia": une Commune Anarchiste au Brésil en 1890* (dossier d'un film) (Paris: Daniel, 1976).

16. The doctrine of "free love" and female sexuality were often problematic for anarchists. In the aftermath of the demise of the Colonia Cecilia, founder Giovanni Rossi proposed that a new colony be established in the interior state of Mato Grosso. In a confidential letter, Rossi complained that few Italian women accepted the anarchist principle of open marriage and proposed buying Indian girls from tribes in the interior "and initiating them into these principles, free from the corrupting influence of bourgeois society" (letter written November 26, 1896, cited in Eric Gordon, Michael M. Hall, and Hobart A. Spatting Jr., "A Survey of Brazilian and Argentina Materials at the International Instituut voor Sociale Geschiedenis in Amsterdam," *Latin American Research Review* 8 [fall 1973]: 39). How Rossi reconciled his opposition to private property with the idea of buying young women is not explained, and his proposal could be dismissed as one more variation on the male fantasy of sexually initiating young women. But more interesting in terms of the present discussion is the view of the Indian (maiden) as a tabula rasa, "uncorrupted" by the ways of the Old World, a living *deserto*, awaiting the awakening hand of the enlightened anarchist (male). In her body, the Indian girl is Rousseau's pure Nature and Humboldt's undeveloped empty space. It must also be observed that Rossi's view of anarchist women, and not anarchist men, as the source of dissension in the ranks of anarchist circles is consistent with historical patterns of discrimination within the political left throughout the nineteenth and twentieth centuries in Latin America. See Francesca Miller, *Latin American Women and the Search for Social Justice* (Hanover, N.H., and London: University Press of New England, 1991).

17. Comolli, *"Le Cecilia,"* 16.

18. Eunice Ribeiro Durham, *Assimilação e Mobilidade* (São Paulo: University of São Paulo, Instituto de Estudos Brasileiros, n.d.), 45.

19. Ibid.

20. Hahner, *Poverty and Politics*, 233.

21. Ribeiro Durham, *Assimilação e Mobilidade*, 41.

22. Lucy Maffei Hutter, *Imigração Italiana em São Paulo de 1902 a 1914: o processo imigratorio* (São Paulo: Instituto de Estudos Brasileiraos, 1986), 116.

23. Gattai, *Anarquistas*.

24. Ibid., 14.

25. Ribeiro Durham, *Assimilação e Mobilidade*, 45.

26. Ibid.

27. Ibid.

28. Ibid.

29. See Hahner, *Poverty and Politics*.

30. Gattai, *Anarquistas*, 99.

31. Ibid., 104.

32. Ibid.

33. Dino Cinel's statistics in *The National Integration* (p. 107) for the out-migration in this period reinforce the conclusion that the pattern of migration from Italy to Brazil differed from that to Argentina or the United States in that more people came in family groups. The out-migration from the United States was five men to every woman; from Brazil, it was two men to every woman. Cinel also shows that there was only one period when out-migration exceeded in-migration from Brazil: 1905–6, during the coffee crisis. It may also be speculated that the relatively small proportion of return migrants from Brazil reflects the extreme difficulty migrants encountered in commanding any redress for the difficulties they encountered; the loyalties of the local, provincial, and national bureaucrats were firmly tied to the landowning class.

34. In 1906 the Brazilian government instituted the Taubate Convention, a valorization program on coffee production that had the effect of driving up coffee prices. See Rollie E. Poppino, *Brazil* (New York: Oxford University Press, 1970), 152. Flush with success, the government was also eager to encourage further European immigration. See also Jose Maria Bello, *A History of Modern Brazil 1889–1964* (Stanford, Calif.: Stanford University Press, 1962), 199. Animated by extreme optimism, the government of Afonso Pena (1906–9) drew heavily against the administrative department for "Peopling the Land" and installed special services in Europe that the scandalmongers referred to as "Golden Embassies." The response was impressive: nearly a hundred thousand immigrants arrived in Brazil in 1908.

35. Riolando Azzi, *A igreja e os migrantes* (São Paulo: Edições Paulinas, 1987–88), 356.

36. Ibid.

37. Luis A. de Boni, *La 'Merica. Escritos dos primeiros Imigrantes Italianos*, Colegão Centenário da Imigração Italiana no Rio Grande do Sul (Porto Alegre: Escola Superior de Teologia, n.d.), 6.

38. Angelo Guisti, *Poemas de um Imigrante Italiano*, 65.

39. Luciana Lombardi, "The Week of Modern Art in Brazil" (Ph.D. diss., UCLA, 1976, Introduction). Gwen Kirkpatrick, in *The Dissonant Legacy of Modernismo* (Berkeley: University of California Press, 1989), discusses parallel urban modernist movements in Uruguay and Argentina as "representing a fundamental questioning of European cultural hegemony" (4).

40. Benedict Anderson, *Imagined Communities: Reflections on the Origin and Spread of Nationalism* (London and New York: Verso, 1983).

41. De Boni, *La 'Merica*, 6.

# Part IV

# Postmodernity and Global Italy

# Venice, Venice, and L.A.:
# Cultural Repetition and Bodily Difference

*Mary Russo*

The quincentenary commemoration of Christopher Columbus's expedition to the New World might appear in hindsight as the last feeble hurrah for "Italy" as a consolidating term in Italian American cultural relations.[1] The long-awaited celebration of what has sometimes seemed a felicitous intercultural "discovery" became, instead, an occasion of fierce, if bloodless, skirmishes in what lately have been called the "culture wars" in the United States. Contending forces gathered around the issues of cultural influence and identity and around the very definitions of intercultural encounter.[2]

Culture may be seen as enclosed or as flowing, with very different models of cultural identity and cultural interchange attendant upon each metaphor. Recent scholarship in international cultural studies in general and in the reconsiderations of nationalisms in particular has focused intently on the latter model, adopting the language of postmodernism with its emphasis on disjunctures, simultaneity, networks, volatility, and movement. This intellectual trend, however, has prompted only limited resistance to the hierarchy and monumentalization of traditional Italian studies within the academy in the United States that has tended to fixate on a few powerful and canonical figures while ignoring the historical conditions and the national and transnational interactions that give rise to the production and consumption of these authors and texts as cultural commodities. Outside the academy as well, the popular images of Italy, Italian Americans, and Italianicity remain largely unchanged, still reflective of the ideological assimilation of immigrants in the late nineteenth and early twentieth centuries.

Although the quincentenary occasioned some very complex and interesting scholarship and discussion, it tended as well to reestablish, or at least to attempt to reestablish, stable categories of ethnic identity. Take, for example, one of the much-publicized debates within the largest funding agency for the quincentenary, the National Endowment for the Humanities. Lynne Cheney, who was the director of the Endowment at the time, explained the denial of a grant to complete a previously funded project on Columbus's expedition on the grounds that the project represented "European-bashing and Columbus-bashing and would offend Hispanic-Americans and Italian-Americans."[3] That Hispanic Americans would identify with, or in the same way, as Italian Americans in relation to Europeanness or with Columbus, or that putative members of such groups would share the same sense of cultural insult, is not at all clear. Furthermore, one might question which Italian Americans or Hispanic Americans are being interpellated in such a formulation, in relation, for example, to class or gender. What strikes me as most interesting here, however, is not the lack of differentiation in evoking various ethnic identities, but rather the arrangement and utter predictability of the terms of such contests, pushing and pulling as they do between assumption of cultural pride and its antipode, cultural offense. Moving between these stations, ethnic identity politics in the United States too easily becomes an activity of alternately shoring up or breaking down, boosterism or wounding.

Since this essay is, in one sense, a reflection on the hyphenation between Italian and American, one might begin by professing ambivalence in relation to Italian American identity as it is constructed in such statements as Cheney's. A history of immigration, settlement, and continued hardship is hidden beneath the assumption that Italian Americans are, most of all, generic white Europeans (certainly not a constant in treatment of southern Italian immigrants in North America),[4] and therefore "naturally" on the side of Europeanness, likely in other words—in Lynne Cheney's words—to be offended by "Columbus-bashing" or to be thrilled by affirmative quincentenary celebrations.

Historically, Columbus was not discovered by Italian Americans; he was, arguably, discovered for them in a time when calls for decent working conditions, housing, and education were being denied. This attribution, or misattribution, of a certain due pride or offense is not exclusively the purview of cultural conservatives; it would seem, however, that such binarisms have worked to reinforce conservative cultural authority, especially in cases like Cheney's where a certain weak, if not utterly cynical, version of multiculturalism is evoked.

For both political and historical reasons, the cultural influence of Italy and Italians in the United States can no longer be considered apart from the larger history of imperialism and the very complex operations of the new global cultural economy. The multiple trajectories and shifting parameters of "Italy" as a critical case study make it a particularly useful addition as well to those considerations of multiculturalism that focus on mere multiplicity or that reserve discussions of heterogeneity, uneven development, ethnicity, and race for the symbolic and geopolitical locations outside the West. The history of Italian migration to the United States has involved divided loyalties at every turn. Migration was rarely imagined as one-way. Families, regional identities, political affiliations, and class allegiances placed compelling and often contradictory demands on the immigrant to leave and to return to Italy. At the same time, "Italy," or at least "Italianicity," became associated with places, body types, and ethnic notions within the United States.

The focus of this essay is on the repetition and displacement of "Italian American" as a modifier attached to a body and to a city. The examples I have chosen are deliberately eccentric in relation to the usual definitions of Italian American places and people. For one thing, these examples "take place" in southern California rather than New York City or Little Italy. They do not, however, "take place" at the same time or together. My examples, Tina Modotti and Venice, are to be understood as intercultural statements with what Michel Foucault has described as a "repeatable materiality."

As a way of short-handing the theoretical frame of these examples as cultural repetitions, let me refer to a section of Michael Foucault's *Archaeology of Knowledge*, where he describes the "repeatable materiality" of the enunciative function:

> The statement, then, must not be treated as an event that occurred in a particular time and place, and that the most one can do is recall it—and celebrate it from afar off—in an act of memory. But neither is it an ideal form that can be actualized in any body, at any time, in any circumstances, and in any material conditions. Too repeatable to be entirely identifiable with the spatio-temporal coordinates of its birth (it is more than the place and date of its appearance), too bound up with what surrounds it and supports it to be free as a pure form. . . . it is en-

dowed with a certain modifiable *heaviness, a weight relative to the field in which it is placed, a constancy that allows of various uses, a temporal permanence that does not have the inertia of a mere trace or mark, and which does not sleep on its own past.*[5]

Foucault's formulation of repeatable materiality offers a useful model for rethinking the ways in which traditional models of cultural exchange or influence can be modified to take into account the landscapes and horizons that shape and constrain the uses of the various enunciations of culture and cross-culture. Most important, his notion of a relative weightiness associated with the materiality of such statements (of which cities and bodies are only two kinds) belies a certain fashionable postmodern notion of limitless access and flow associated with metaphors of spatialization. In contemporary cultural studies, "bodies are becoming like cities, their temporal coordinates transformed into spatial ones."[6] Bodies and cities, like other statements, are located culturally within a domain or institutional field and constrained by its uses within that field. In another cultural domain, however, a new (and old) statement of that city or body emerges: "the difference of the same."[7] The place of this intercultural or intracultural exchange may be figured as a harbor, a border, a landing strip, a trade zone, or a page of translation. "Italian American" in this essay is meant only to indicate a space of cultural transitivity through which identities are formed differently.

This essay takes up two examples of international and transnational Italian American identity associated with a body and a city. Geographically, both these examples "take place" in southern California. The focus of the essay, however, is on their repetition and displacement as intercultural "statements."

## Displacing Europe: The Body of Tina Modotti

With this frame in mind, I want to interpose the much-reproduced body of a woman who only with the profoundest historical irony and ambivalence could be called Italian American, although the trajectory of her life goes from Italy to California to Mexico, back to Europe, and back again to the Americas and Mexico City: the artist and revolutionary Tina Modotti. Her life story suggests how different "Italian Americanism" must have seemed in the era of internationalism, emergent workers' movements, and early twentieth-century socialism. These international identities had far less to do with a sense of self than a sense of one's position—not a statement of who you are but, as the old labor song asks, a question of "which side are you on?"

Modotti's life recalls the international role of Mexico and Mexico City in the 1920s and 1930s, as well as the lesser-known history of immigration by Italians to California. As a working-class immigrant to California in 1913, Modotti plied her trade as a seamstress and in the textile industry. Moving from San Francisco to Los Angeles, she was taken up by the Hollywood culture industry, and got small roles as the generic dark or Latin woman. The photographer Edward Weston—later her mentor and companion—remarks in his notebooks on their shared amusement at seeing her in these roles. When Weston and Modotti go to a movie in Mexico City, the next stop on her trail of images, they are startled to see Tina herself on the screen: "We had a good laugh over the villainous character she portrayed. . . . our movie directors cannot picture an Italian girl except with a knife in her teeth and blood in her eye."[8] Her Hollywood roles emphasize the interchangeability of actress of the "southern" or Mediterranean type and the close identification of things "south of the border" with Italy in the ethnoscape of California as North American.[9] Carlos Fuentes wrote his play *Orchids in the Moonlight* with this film history of the Latina actress—the Dolores del Rio type—in mind, but set the play in Venice, California, to emphasize the coincidence of these tropes (to emphasize the nonliteralness of ethnicity and identity, he suggested the possibility of casting against type two large blonde women in the parts of the aging Latin actresses).[10]

Edward Weston, on the other hand, in his radical aestheticization of photography, was only too happy to erase all ethnic contents, using the image of Modotti's body to produce his idea of the impersonal and impartial nude. He describes one session with Modotti as his "finest set of nudes," which are "lacking in any human interest which might call attention to a living, palpitating body."[11] In his exquisite photographs, the smooth delineations of her body suggest the abstracted desert spaces of the Southwest.[12]

Diego Rivera, taking his turn, refigures Modotti in his murals as the mythic Earth Mother or as Mexican peasant. Writers, meeting her in this period, referred to her as "an international beauty." Again, another Mexican, the writer Elena Poniatowska, narrativizes as romance this internationalist production of the female Other in her short novel

*Dear Diego*.[13] The scenarios, then, of such a life—a "fragile life," as Pablo Neruda poetically described Modotti's—would seem exemplary of the process whereby a very series of images comes to stand for those very places and the very body that is constantly displaced.[14]

Modotti's own photographs show that she learned much from both Weston and Rivera and from the previous production of images of herself. Her photographs of everyday Mexican life and politics were in her own time overwhelmed by the historical momentum of politics in Mexico and Europe, and by the expanding reputations of the men with whom she associated, including Weston and Rivera, but also Julio Antonio Mella, a founder of the Cuban Communist Party who was assassinated at her side. Arrested and sentenced to deportation for alleged conspiracy, Modotti was issued an Italian visa stamped "valid only for the return trip to Italy." Given her antifascist activities in Mexico, this could mean only imprisonment or death.

Legally a United States citizen, Modotti was offered a new passport, but only on the condition that she return to the United States and not engage in further political activities. Without documents, Modotti boarded a Dutch freighter that stopped along the southern borders of the United States, including New Orleans and Cuba, where she was denied entry. After four weeks, she arrived in Holland only to be met by Italian authorities demanding her extradition. With help from several workers' organizations, she made her way to Berlin and then to Moscow. She gave up photography for reasons that appear to be as aesthetic as political, and devoted herself to political activity in Poland, France, and Spain until 1938, when she returned to Mexico.[15] She died there three years later. Her years of invisibility, when she was no longer a subject or producer of images, and the loss of many of her prints, further dramatized her amazing and, to some, tragic life.

Modotti's trail does not end in Mexico, however. Her photographs have by now circulated back onto the transnational culture markets, setting auction records. When a platinum print from 1925, "Roses, Mexico," sold for $165,000 in April 1991, a trade magazine reported that "what Van Gogh represented to the painting market of the Eighties, Tina Modotti now signifies for the price of photographs in the Nineties."[16] As the article emphasizes, no one is saying that she is the greatest photographer in history, but somehow her name, the scarcity of her prints, and her biography have combined to make her a best-selling commodity. Her work has, in other words, floated to the top of the art exchange so that the obscure name of the third-class passenger to the United States in 1913 returns emblazoned as signifying riches, world-class venues, and jet-set furnishings—a choice bit of what is disdainfully referred to as Eurotrash, a degrading term for the catastrophic cultural leftovers of the twentieth century.

What can such an ignominious term have to do with the noble life and transmuted fortunes of Tina Modotti? Simply this: she cannot be recuperated otherwise. Like the misrecognized, overproduced, scattered, and now greedily hoarded images of her body, historical identities are increasingly mobile. Even saints and revolutionaries turn up in strange places. As much contemporary visual art and performance would indicate, one cultural strategy focuses on the possibilities of layering and rearranging these leftover signs and commodities, "caught" as they are (to quote Homi Bhabha) "in the vicious circuits of surplus value that link First World capital to Third World labor markets."[17]

Indeed, it is something like labor that causes the "heaviness" alluded to by Foucault because these cultural displacements are weighed down with a certain bodily memory, "a weight relative to the field in which it is placed."[18] Any contemporary consideration of interculturalism needs perforce to be attuned to gradients as well as the rapidly changing direction of cultural flows.[19] The mobility that I have tried to suggest is characteristic of both international and transnational bodies and is for these reasons neither free nor arbitrary.

The material repetition of the identity and images of Tina Modotti might be taken as a sign of the enduring legacy of Italian culture in America in a nostalgic history of immigration. It might also be traced historically to the Mediterraneanization of the West Coast in the early part of the twentieth century, and hence, a further imposition of culture as European. What I have tried to show, however, is a more reciprocal process and one that is complicated by a geography of displacement and refiguration.

Interculturalism, as others have argued, can be both a communal possibility and a market projection. Markets and imagined communities (to borrow Benedict Anderson's term for nationalism) are notoriously volatile entities and always involve certain overprojections, incompletions, and leftovers.[20] In the realm of cultural exchange, these "extras" may be thought of as disappointments, ruins, devastations, or cultural misunderstandings, or they may be thought of more expansively as discoveries or markers of a new world (this is only one of the ironic lessons of Christopher Columbus). The detritus of such symbolic convergences—to recycle the term, its Eurotrash—turns up in strange places, and it is always worth questioning what can, or should be, usefully recovered. In fact, the very term—"Eurocentrism"— that has served performatively as an index of or pointer to the historical evidence of cultural imperialism, needs to be reoriented itself at every critical juncture and location because the old adage that "East is East and West is West" simply does not hold. To illustrate this shifting symbolic geography in the temporal space that is the locus of my essay, I refer to a sign in downtown Santa Monica announcing the relocation of a deep-discount department store featuring imported goods. It reads: "Europa [arrow] has moved around the corner."

## Venice, Venice, and L.A.

The mobility that is characteristic of bodies and identities is similarly operative in the transmigration of cities and nations. Arjun Appadurai has identified various dimensions of global cultural flow as the transformation of landscapes into related "ethnoscapes, "technoscapes," "financescapes," and "ideoscapes." These landscapes are "deeply perspectival"; defined, that is, by shifting points of view, languages, histories, and most of all by groups and individuals who wander in and inhabit these places. Following Benedict Anderson's notion of nationhood as an "imagined community," Appadurai understands these places (of the heart, mind, and imagination) as contributing to "imagined worlds" shared by groups and persons dispersed around the globe.[21] These imagined worlds created by the disjunctive relations between ethnic, commercial, media, and ideological dimensions of cultural flow are lived in by real persons and groups. The attachment to places, names, nations, keywords (such as "democracy") is highly compelling for individuals and groups who must travel and locate themselves in these landscapes without center or periphery. Even the touristic desire to arrive at a new destination and find a new perspective is frustrated. How does "Eurocentrism" change its meaning in this new cultural geography?

Typically, the European intellectual has experienced the western United States, particularly southern California and Los Angeles, as a distant center from which to find perspective on Europe. It is also served as a point of arrival—a destiny—for European culture. Jean Baudrillard, in a moment of delirious solipcism, writes, for example: "Dawn in Los Angeles, coming up over the Hollywood hills. You get the distinct feeling that the sun only touched Europe lightly on its way to rising properly here, above this plane geometry where its light is still that brand new light of the edge of the desert."[22]

And later, despondently: "I want to excentre myself, to become eccentric, but I want to do so in a place that is the centre of the world. . . . In reality, you do not, as I had hoped, get any distance on Europe from here. You do not acquire a fresh angle on it. When you turn around, it has quite simply disappeared."[23]

Baudrillard's sublime bewilderment in the landscape of the Far West is but the latest installment of the long narrative of the European intellectuals "orienting" themselves in California.

Mike Davis, in *City of Quartz: Excavating the Future in Los Angeles*, describes the earlier migration of European artists, intellectuals, and exiles, including Adorno, Brecht, Mann, Schoenberg, and Stravinsky, who came to L.A. to find a perspective on the modern world.[24] Many, notably Adorno, went back to Europe with a sharpened critique of modernity. In his opening chapter, "Sunshine or Noir," Davis describes L.A. as playing a double role of utopia and dystopia for European and U.S. intellectuals. He suggests that Marxists and post-Marxists have focused their attention on Los Angeles because Los Angeles has become a stand-in for capitalism in the twentieth century. In Davis's words, it is simultaneously "the archetypical site of massive and unprotesting subordination of industrialized intelligentsias to the programs of capital" and "fertile soil for some of the most acute critiques of late capitalism."[25] Its relation to Europe is similarly contradictory, functioning at once as a peripheral destination West and as an ex-Eurocenter.

As a high-voltage signifier, "L.A." shares much with Venice, Italy. Venice, Italy, like L.A., is symbolically exponential, piling hyperbole upon hyperbole. Henri Lefebvre, in *The Production of Space*, chooses Venice as the exemplary city.[26] In a much-quoted exchange from Calvino's fictive *Invisible Cities*, Kublai Khan asks Marco Polo why he has not mentioned Venice in describing all the cities he knows. Marco smiles: "Every time I describe a city I am saying something about Venice."[27] Nietzsche, in a throwaway line from *Ecce Homo*, writes: "when I say beyond the Alps, I really merely say Venice."[28]

Since both are, in every sense, highly capitalized cities, similar and extravagant claims have been made for Venice and for Los Angeles. The foundational myths of both cities tell of the improbable, even miraculous, rise of these cities from the desert and the sea. Spectacle of spectacles, they are both evoked as ultimate dream machines, super-images, and control screens for all manner of culture games and exhibitions. In historic terms, the relationship between these symbolic superspaces might be stated as follows: L.A. is to posturbanity what Venice was to the urban. Or, L.A. is to late capitalism what Venice was to high capitalism—a crossroads city for the East-West and the North-South axis. Or Venice (as in Thomas Mann's novella *Death in Venice*) is the *stazione termine* for modernist anxieties about the end of Western culture, and L.A. (after Baudrillard) is where the sun sets for postmodernism at the geographical and symbolic extreme West—having gone about as far as it can go. Nonetheless, in anticipation of its postmodernity with respect to L.A., Venice was—long before EuroDisney—identified as the Disneyland of Europe.

The semiotic overproduction of these cities leads to other rather unexpected coincidences or, to return to the early formulation of Foucault, certain material repetitions. Searching for displaced Italianicity, Venice turns up in Venice, California. This beach town, which has alternately been seen as a part of L.A. and its Other, is an interesting example of certain Italian and American connections.

Although a tourist returning from Venice in the nineteenth century might have collected a few tiny gondolas to remember the trip, knock-offs of Venice turn up in all sizes in the twentieth century, many of them in the United States. Umberto Eco, in his touristic writings about the United States, contemplates cultural knockoffs with regard to their distance or proximity to their originals. In *Travels in Hyperreality*, he goes "in search of instances where the American imagination demands the real thing and, to attain it, must fabricate the absolute fake; where the boundaries between game and illusion are blurred, the art museum is contaminated by the freak show."[29]

At the Ringling Museum in Sarasota, Florida (which he fails to mention is about five miles away from the adjacent town, called Venice), Eco describes the complex made up of the circus museum and an impressive painting and sculpture museum, the latter including a Venetian palazzo whose architect, he writes, "deserves (in the sense that Eichmann does) to go down in history" (27). Although he says it is hard to apply a "punishing irony to these pathetic ventures," he does so, while reminding himself and the reader that "sibling-palazzos" of the Ca' d'Zan of Sarasota exist along the Grand Canal of Venice (28–29). The difference is, for Eco, that a real city can redeem the ugly, the artificial, and kitsch, integrating them into a "good urban context" (29). In contemplating Venice and its facsimiles, however, the question becomes: what is, or can be a "good urban context"?

## Venice in L.A.

It is hard to imagine a "good urban context" for Venice in California. Like the "original," the coastal town is constantly changing and recovering old layers of artificiality. Three years ago, when I last visited, there were few canals left, and the ones that were left were being drained and dredged. Only the Grand Canal was intact. Ocean Front Walk was crowded with Venetian regulars, the homeless, refugees from other areas of the L.A. sprawl, and weekend tourists. L.A. is, of course, one of the most racially and class-segmented urban areas in the world. On Venice Beach, however, at certain times, the world can seem more positively heterogeneous and intercultural. The Muscle Beach enclave was featuring its weekly weight-lifting contests, which on this particular Saturday included three young competitors of different races who had Down's syndrome, all madly cheering for each other. Muscle Beach is only one of many sites in Venice devoted to the maintenance, transformation, or masquerade of the body. Tattoos and piercings, purgations, tannings, bleachings, manicures, electrolysis, braidings, and so on are available on a walk-in basis near the beach; more expensive services like liposuction, lifts, and dietary consultations are advertised as "by appointment."

Architecturally, the old St. Mark's Hotel is still a central landmark, not so much because it orients the tourist geographically, but because it does so culturally in relation to new intensities of space and simulation. On one side of the hotel, there is a trompe l'oeil facade of the Venetian arcades, facing a parking lot and a street of half-flourishing businesses; on the other side, there is a fabulous multidimensional mural, with a giant Botticelli on in-line skates, pointed arch windows, and a free-floating skateboard. A tattered, superannuated Venetian citizen lifts the viewer into contemporary hyperspace (figure 1).[30]

Venice, California, was founded in 1904 by a wealthy businessman, Abbott Kinney, who imagined a new Venice in America. Kinney's

Fig. 1

dream was of a cultural Renaissance on the West Coast, with Venice, California, as a magnet for artists, musicians, and intellectuals. He built a system of canals linked to the ocean, colonnades, and bridges in imitation of the Italian originals. He even imported authentic gondolas and native Italian gondoliers to travel the canal. Kinney's dream, however, was not realized and it quickly deteriorated from an Italianate culture park to a precursor of Disneyland for weekenders and a real estate gimmick.

In 1925, Venice was incorporated into the City of Los Angeles, inaugurating a very problematic relationship between the beach town and the metropolis. Horst Schmidt-Brümmer published a collection of photographs and text on Venice's vanishing communities. *Venice, California: An Urban Fantasy*, published in 1973 as part of the resistance to the city council's controversial vote to target Venice for massive urban renewal, put the Venice-L.A. relationship starkly as "Venice versus Los Angeles":

> A crucial difference between Venice and Los Angeles is the pace of everyday life. In Venice, pedestrians determine the tempo; in Los Angeles, the automobile does. . . . In contrast to the automated mobility of Los Angeles, Venice lives on a fluid interchange of human contact. This contact arises from unpredictable encounters and random meetings which create a spatial cohesiveness not found in Los Angeles.[31]

The history of the town in the decades after incorporation makes the opposition seem compelling. First, Venice was opened to the oil companies, and "the oil derricks scattered throughout now transformed the entertainment area into an industrial park."[32] The canals were filled in and made into roads; the beaches were closed and quarantined because of pollution. Only when Venice began to go dry in the early fifties did a residential community begin to reemerge and reestablish itself as the alternative and vanishing "urban fantasy" that Schmidt-Brümmer records and envisions. What he saw in the short history of Venice was a historical allegory of victimization ("Where oil derricks demolished the vision of a new Venice, now the new apartment structures will obliterate the chances for a community").[33] At the same time, his photographic commemoration of the community as counterhegemonic and counter-L.A. suggests the prefigurative politics characteristic of the late sixties and early seventies.

In contrast, a mid-eighties collection of photographs of Venice by

Claudio Edinger focuses on individual eccentricity.[34] His subjects are chosen for their artwork or for their unusual lives. His Venice is "a curious historical spot" and a "high-energy human circus," which he places securely within the Los Angeles sprawl (7). Indeed, his text and photographs merely extend his audience's sense of the L.A. "lifestyle." Although the collection is called *Venice Beach*, his subjects are often shot inside their apartments or condominiums, surrounded with those personal items that define their individuality. Artists and more everyday eccentrics are shown side by side. He photographs Charles Arnoldi, a painter and sculptor who complains that "Venice is like a zoo" and blames political activists for driving a lot of "good people" away in a gallery; across the page, he shows Domenick Covolo, at ninety the town's oldest "double Venetian," in his tiny, marvelously cluttered apartment (162–63). Covolo was born in Venice, Italy, worked as a chef in New York, and was working at the time he was photographed as an advertising model.

Edinger's brief history of Venice continues where Schmidt-Brümmer's leaves off. For Edinger and his collaborator, Charles Lockwood, the fifties and sixties, with successive populations of Beats and "hippies, flower children, and borderline crazies who had done too many drugs," contributed to making Venice "a seaside slum" (17). Contradicting Schmidt-Brümmer's account, the early seventies produced "the first tentative signs of improvement" (17). As the town "acquired a raffish sort of chic," real estate prices soared, and restaurants, antique shops, art galleries, and condominiums went up. "Sleek, affluent-looking people from Beverly Hills or Marina del Rey, who wouldn't have dreamed of setting foot anywhere near Venice a year or two earlier, couldn't find empty parking spaces for their Mercedes or Porsches along Main Street most nights of the week" (19). The author of the book's preface does allow that this atmosphere of upscale carnival is cruel and even dangerous for those who cannot afford it. Since this book was published, the free and easy lifestyle has become even more expensive. What seemed a housing "pinch" for the poor and aged in 1985 in areas like Oakwood has turned into an unprecedented homelessness both massive and chronic. The recession has taken its toll on many small businesses, and Venice (California), like Venice (Italy), is still partly about seediness and decay. Of course, it does not stop there. In the early 1990s, a national fashion and lifestyle magazine featured an article on an L.A. sculptor and movie star's husband ("the L.A.

Bernini") who planned an elaborate studio and gallery with Renaissance Venetian features to be built in Venice, California.

Again, it is at the moment of death and decline that Venice is at its symbolic best. A signifier stretched out and worn to shreds, it nonetheless returns spectacularized anew in facsimiles and simulations. Tony Tanner writes in a literary study of of Venice, Italy: "as it slips or falls out of history, Venice—the place, the name, the dream—seems to lend itself to, to attract a new variety of, appreciations, recuperations and dazzled hallucinations."[35]

What happens to Venice affects us all.
JOHN RUSSELL, writing against the
proposed Expo 2000 theme park in
the lagoons of Venice (*New York
Times*, December 10, 1989)

To emphasize how reciprocal, labyrinthine, and repetitive cultural trajectories can be, I want to conclude with this latest version of Venice, a design for a simulated Venice alongside the original. Expo 2000 was planned as as a gigantic exposition with a synthetic lagoon and artificial islands, situated next to Venice. Other features were to include a fish farm and a floating "Florian" bar. In response to the proposed theme park, John Russell, a critic for the *New York Times*, appealed to the international art market and community to stop this (to him) global atrocity. Russell imagined eventuality as a dystopic future. His attack on the proposed Expo 2000 project was ironically entitled "Imagine Venice as a Floating Disneyland." Russell reported that, "at the entrance to Venice, there were to be clouds of cold-water vapor with color images projected by laser beams." He added that this "high-tech freak show" would have threatened the preservation of Venice itself because an additional 150,000 tourists more than usual would surely flock from the simulated Venice to the real thing, which is already overloaded environmentally, especially with regard to sanitation. The exposition would also have integrated Venice into a larger spectacle, redesigning its position in relation to the lagoon and to the mainland.

Under pressure from the groups inside Italy and from the international cultural interests that sustain Venice, the proposal was withdrawn, but it is interesting to contemplate two Venices side by side, the real Venice of carnivals and museums and the unrealized plan for a simulated "high-tech freak show" of the same name. "Venice," in this two-headed model, certainly defeats the residual vision of a good, originary context that might be revisited and challenges a widespread version of postmodernist cultural as free and unimpeded. To imagine all cultural identities as multiple and weighted with ambivalences and contestations forces a reconsideration of terms like "Italian American."

Venice, California, might be simply traced reductively to the Mediterraneanization of the West Coast in the early part of the twentieth century, and hence seen as a further imposition of culture-as-European. Instead, the reciprocal process of cultural shifts is complicated by a geography of displacement and refiguration. The examples of Tina Modotti and Venice, California, emphasize an eccentric narrative of cultural immigration and cultural difference, neither typically "Italian American"; each suggests, however, a certain intercultural locus of enduring heaviness and inertia that is not yet realized or ready to go away.

## Notes

1. As many contributors to this volume have indicated, there are many different symptoms of the provisional and volatile nature of "Italy" as a signifier of sameness. For instance, the Italian team's ignominious defeat in the 1994 World Cup competition—an event which may or may not have felicitously contributed to the rise and fall of Silvio Berlusconi—did not reverse what I would describe as the productive disintegration of "Italy" as a consolidating term. A friend born in Ethiopia and living in the United States—in very complex ways both African and American (sometimes with, sometimes without the hyphen)—reported that those fighting words "forza Italia" were heard simultaneously in a Philadelphia bar as merely a cheer for an innocent losing team and as a reminder to the Africans present of a vicious colonial imposition.

2. For a discussion of intercultural exchange in relation to women's writing, see my "Oleografia: scrittura al femminile negli Stati Uniti e in Italia," in *Immaginari a confronto: I rapporti culturali tra Italia e Stati Uniti—la percezione della realtà fra stereotipo e mito*, ed. Carlo Chiarenza and William L. Vance (Venice: Marsilio Editori, 1992), 99–112.

3. John Milne, "Politicizing of Humanities Grants Alleged," *Boston Globe*, August 11, 1992, 10.

4. See, for instance, the contribution of Pasquale Verdicchio in this volume.

5. Michel Foucault, *The Archaeology of Knowledge and the Discourse on Language*, trans. A. M. Sheridan Smith (New York: Harper and Row, 1972), 104–5; my emphasis.

6. Celeste Olalquiaga, *Megalopolis: Contemporary Cultural Sensibilities* (Minneapolis: University of Minnesota Press, 1992), 93.

7. Homi K. Bhabha, *The Location of Culture* (New York and London: Routledge,

1994), 22. See also his description of Alan Sekula's photographic project on harbors as a place where material goods appear in bulk at a point of exchange (8).

8. Edward Weston, *The Daybooks of Edward Weston*, vol. 1, *Mexico* (New York: Aperture, 1961), 56.

9. On the concept of ethnoscape, see Arjun Appadurai, "Difference in the Global Economy," in *Theory, Culture, and Society*, vol. 7 (London, Newbury Park, and New Delhi: Sage, 1990), 298.

10. Carlos Fuentes, *Orchids in the Moonlight*, in *Dramacontemporary: Latin America*, ed. Marion Peter Holt and George W. Woodyard (New York: PAJ, 1992), 144–86.

11. Weston, *The Daybooks of Edward Weston*, 136.

12. This well-worn trope of the female body as landscape is drawn from the same imperialist archive as the opening axioms of Jean-François Lyotard's *Pacific Wall* (inspired by his residence in La Jolla). These axioms, dedicated to Marilyn Monroe, describe "the white skin of Western—meaning the most Western of European-descended American women is absolute West. My name for the situation of this skin is California" (Jean-François Lyotard, *Pacific Wall*, trans. Bruce Boone [Venice, Calif.: Lapis Press, 1989], 7).

13. Elena Poniatowska, *Dear Diego*, trans. Katherine Silverman (New York: Pantheon, 1986).

14. See Mildred Constantine, *Tina Modotti: A Fragile Life* (New York and London: Paddington Press, 1975). Constantine's title is taken from a poem written by Pablo Neruda as an elegy to Modotti.

15. The relative importance of these explanations for the sudden twists and turns of her life and work are still contested. For an account that seeks to refocus attention toward her role as an artist and her early modernist aesthetic, see Sarah M. Lowe, "Introduction," in *Tina Modotti: Photographs* (New York: Harry Abrams, 1995), 9–13.

16. Richard B. Woodward, "Tina Modotti: The $165,000 Question," *Art Auction* (November 1991): n.p. The article emphasizes that her "dark, soft beauty and innate sense of drama were landing her parts as a temptress in Hollywood silent films," and, of course, that she and Weston had "a scorching affair."

17. Bhabha, *The Location of Culture*, 20.

18. Foucault, *The Archaeology of Knowledge*, 105.

19. Peter Stallybrass and Allon White, *The Poetics and Politics of Transgression* (Ithaca, N.Y.: Cornell University Press, 1986), 196.

20. See Benedict Anderson, *Imagined Communities: Reflections on the Origin and Spread of Nationalism* (London and New York: Verso, 1983).

21. Appadurai, "Difference in the Global Economy," 296–98.

22. Jean Baudrillard, *America*, trans. Chris Turner (London and New York: Verso, 1988), 52.

23. Ibid., 28–29.

24. Mike Davis, *City of Quartz: Excavating the Future in Los Angeles* (New York: Vintage Books, 1992).

25. Ibid., 18.

26. Henri Lefebvre, *The Production of Space*, trans. Donald Nicholson-Smith (Oxford: Basil Blackwell, 1991), 73.

27. Italo Calvino, *Invisible Cities*, trans. William Weaver (San Diego: Harcourt Brace Jovanovich, 1974), 86.

28. Friedrich Nietzsche, *On the Genealogy of Morals and Ecce Homo*, trans. Walter Kaufmann (New York: Vintage Books, 1969), 251–52.

29. Umberto Eco, *Travels in Hyperreality* (San Diego: Harcourt Brace Jovanovich, 1986), 8.

30. This mural was used in the recent film *L.A. Story* to denote L.A. "spaciness." Venice is depicted as the natural habitat for body cultists and "airheads."

31. Horst Schmidt-Brümmer, *Venice, California: An Urban Fantasy*, trans. Ernst Wasmuth Tubingen (New York: Grossman, 1973), 21.

32. Ibid., 20–21.

33. Ibid., 25.

34. Claudio Edinger, *Venice Beach*, introd. Charles Lockwood (New York: Abbeville Press, 1985).

35. Tony Tanner, *Venice Desired* (Cambridge: Harvard University Press, 1992), 5.

# Decolonizing the Screen: From
# *Ladri di biciclette* to *Ladri di saponette*

*Marguerite R. Waller*

We're tired of trees. They've made us suffer too much.
> GILLES DELEUZE and FELIX GUATTARI,
> *A Thousand Plateaus*

I'm going back to commercials.
You suffer too much in films.
> HEIDI, the model,
> in *Ladri di saponette*

I want to begin by discussing temporality and spatiality, the stuff out of which subjects and their realities are visually figured on film. My film texts are "Italian," whatever we decide this signifier means, and I am interested in the resistance they offer to the effects of an encounter between the "Old World" and the "New World" that reverses the direction, if not the intention, of the colonization process we associate with Columbus. Both Vittorio De Sica's neorealist *Ladri di biciclette* and Maurizio Nichetti's postmodern *Ladri di saponette* investigate how it feels to be "discovered" as a potential source of superprofits by corporate, multinational "Hollywood." These two films also, I will maintain, enable spectators to experience "postcolonial" subjectivities, generated by resistance to what Felix Guattari calls the "molecular" colonization of late capital (Guattari 1980, 235).

## Time

When Benedict Anderson's imagined community model of nation takes as the ground of national community a "homogeneous empty time," it unwittingly privileges a particular construction of the subject and of the nation. Anderson's subject can be characterized by the totalizing gaze that both implies and depends on imagining time as a neutral frame, not involved in the production of the meanings it appears simply to contain. As minority-discourse theorist Homi Bhabha has pointed out, the temporality of Anderson's imagined community thereby camouflages the diacritical relationship between politically produced centers and their provincial or colonial margins, universalizing the view from the center (the "god trick" Donna Haraway calls it), while discrediting the subject positions of a center's many constitutive "others" (Bhabha 1992; Haraway 1991, 193). In his cannily constructed argument, Bhabha, as a postcolonial critic, works from both positions at once. He deconstructs the implied subject of Anderson's model from within the frame of Western epistemology while he protests the limits of that epistemology from his position as one whose hybrid subjectivity it would discredit. In the "contest for political and social authority within the modern world," he argues, Anderson's nationalist subject illegitimately articulates "emerging" or counter-hegemonic cultural identities as ontological negatives—as lack, excess, or ungainly hybrid—only by effacing its own temporal heterogeneity, its secondariness to the temporalities of the rhetorical processes from which it and its essentializing logic derive (Bhabha 1992, 46). Taking a slightly different tack, Arjun Appadurai concurs that "one man's imagined community is another man's political prison," as he counters Anderson's model with a pointedly asynchronous, multiple, disjunct framework of "ethnoscapes, technoscapes, finanscapes, mediascapes, and ideoscapes" within which to conceptualize the (re)production of cultural subjects in the current global cultural economy (Appadurai 1990, 6–7, 11).

## Space

Gilles Deleuze and Felix Guattari complement these considerations of temporality and the subject in their elaboration of notions of space as they support or subvert statist ways of thinking and seeing. Homogeneous space, they contend, works like a three-dimensional grid, "striated by . . . the verticals of gravity, [and] the distribution of matter into parallel layers." That is, it implies and depends on "an independent dimension capable of spreading everywhere, of formalizing all the other dimensions, of striating all of space in all of its directions"

(Deleuze and Guattari 1987, 370).[1] It is, therefore, the space of an image of thought that derives from a society "modeled upon the difference between 'governors and governed'" (368). Against this Euclidian space of centered, "tree" thought, they propose the heterogeneous space of the "rhizome"—a plant structure that is neither root nor stem (the potato, for example). Although quite compatible with various forms of sociality, the organization of rhizome space wards off the formation of the State (capital S). Within its heterogeneous space a nonobjectifiable understanding of multiplicities—nonmetric and acentered—takes shape. The image of thought Deleuze and Guattari associate with this space is antigenealogical; unlike a tree, it does not plot a point or fix an order (7). This space's multiplicities cease to have any relation to the One (8), which means that "any point of a rhizome can be connected to anything other" (7). Rhizome semiotics, for example, assembles "very diverse acts, not only linguistic, but also perceptive, mimetic, gestural, and cognitive. . . . There is no ideal speaker-listener, any more than there is a homogeneous linguistic community" (7). In science, "it is not . . . a question of extracting constants from variables but of placing variables themselves in a state of continuous variation" (369). And, as the opposite of the history that is "written from a sedentary point of view in the name of a Unitary State apparatus," rhizome history is "a heterogeneous assemblage, a flow, with pauses, straggling and forward rushes" (23). The rhizome subject would, then, ontologically resemble the descriptions being circulated with increasing insistence by U.S. gender theorists. Like Donna Haraway's cyborg, Judith Butler's performer, or Emily Hicks's holographic border dweller in its shape-changing, temporal, and relational fluidity, this subject is described as "a stream without beginning or end that undermines its banks and picks up speed in the middle" (25).

From these abbreviated comments on relations among models of space, time, subjectivity, and political organization, I move to the question of how "Italy" might be "designed" in reaction to the visual language dominating its cinemas and, now increasingly, its television screens (Hay 1993). How "nation" might be reimagined (historically, geographically, ethnically, etc.) from within such an Italy is an inseparable correlative question on which the encounter between *Ladri di biciclette* and *Ladri di saponette* in the space/time of late-twentieth-century electronic media provides some unusual perspectives.

## Rita Hayworth as/in a Rhizomatic Space/Time Warp

"You must avoid the wrinkles," says Antonio Ricci's supervisor as he smears paste lavishly over Rita Hayworth's bust. "To do this job you must be very intelligent. You must have the eye and be quick." De Sica, who was known previously and subsequently as a romantic actor and comic director, who twelve years later would play the sublime con man in Rossellini's *Il Generale della Rovere*, here camps it up, parodies, manipulates, disrupts, and displaces what feminist film theory has urged us to see as the "Oedipal" structure of Hollywood narrative and visual pleasures. By "Oedipal" I mean a phallocentric subjectivity that figures sexual and other kinds of difference from itself as castration or lack (without, of course, seeing its own governing status as figurally fabricated). It works very much like the "nationalist" subjectivity with which Bhabha finds himself at odds (de Lauretis 1984, 148; Mulvey 1989, 15). De Sica, like Bhabha, seems to have appreciated thoroughly the relation between this Oedipal subject and the vulnerability of other subjectivities to its imperial dynamic. Historically, *Ladri di biciclette* was, in fact, a response to the flood of Hollywood films with which the U.S. occupation forces, in collaboration with the Italian authorities, were saturating postwar Italy, while more than $1million U.S. were being spent by the CIA to prevent a left coalition from winning the 1948 elections (Dratch and Frankovich 1980; Molyneaux 1988, 3–4). De Sica refused David O. Selznick's offer to finance *Ladri di biciclette* on condition that an American, Cary Grant, play the lead and the story be changed to one in which hard work, good luck, and perseverence lead to Antonio and Maria's happy assimilation into postwar capitalism. Instead, he created a film in which unknown Italian nonactors play the leading roles in an almost nonnarrative film whose story line, André Bazin quipped, "would not deserve two lines in a stray dog column" (Marcus 1986, 58). The "decolonization" of the Italian screen performed by this meticulously worked-out "neorealist superspectacle" (Bondanella 1983, 57–59; Marcus 1986, 56) works not, I propose, as a defiant Oedipal refusal, but as an ironic *perversion* of Hollywood's visual and narrative seductions. This perversion, in keeping with the film's major departures from Hollywood film form, subtly but rigorously implicates the role of several varieties of Oedipal behavior in perpetuating certain identifications—with one's city, nation, or even gender role—that block a more rhizomatic perception of the political and economic relationships manifest in the desperate poverty of the Italian working classes.[2]

*Ladri di biciclette*'s canonization as the epitome of cinematic purity, and the virtual icon of an "Italian national cinema," could, then, be seen as co-optation. As Nichetti's *Ladri di saponette* acknowledges in many registers, De Sica's film, in Italy and abroad, has been recuperated, or, to borrow again from Deleuze and Guattari, "reterritorialized" as an "art film," whose "anti-Oedipal" strategies are rarely read as such, but figure instead as representations of a kind of noble impotence. It is, for example, the last film the uncompromising, unemployed screenwriter sees before he is murdered by the venal Hollywood studio executive in Robert Altman's *The Player*.[3] It is the film *Northern Exposure*'s Dr. Joel Fleischman watches on television while hysterical love-interest Maggie does Anchorage with another man. It is appropriated wholesale by Pee-Wee Herman and director Tim Burton for *Pee-Wee's Big Adventure* in trying to avoid (hetero)sexuality altogether. *Ladri di saponette*'s own little Bruno is media-literate enough to dress himself as the immiserated neorealist child laborer when he wants to ingratiate himself with the blonde *semi-nuda straniera* who has materialized in his family's apartment.

In my brief discussion of the film here, I can focus on only a few instances of what I take to be its anti-Oedipal modus operandi, but they will be enough, I hope, to suggest a model of *italianità*, neither long-suffering nor impotent. I will then turn to Nichetti's brilliantly dangerous supplement *Ladri di saponette*, not only as it updates De Sica's decolonization of the screen to include the tumultuous world of Italian television in the 1980s and the circumstances of an overheated multinational consumer economy, but also as it theoretically and practically addresses the question, raised by the reception of *Ladri di biciclette*, of how to prevent an anti-Oedipal subject from being confused with a castrated subject. How does a rhizomatic *italianità* differ from its statist reification?

The gaze that would assimilate "Italy," as a kind of economic colony, to the striated space and homogeneous empty time of the modern capitalist nation-state is disrupted in *Ladri di biciclette* even before Lamberto Maggiorani's Ricci frustrates any spectatorial desire to identify with the male lead. I speak of the opening credits. In the first of many strategies inviting the spectator to disassemble and displace the homogenizing effects of sync sound filmmaking (Doane 1985,

570–71), the film's lushly sentimental music plays for a few moments over a black screen, separating the gaze of the audience from the gaze of this film's tardy camera (Mulvey 1989, 26). Then, as soon as the first photographic images *do* appear, they are obscured—put under erasure—by the text superimposed on them. Together, text and image suggest, somewhat as philosopher Jacques Derrida does when he uses a word but crosses it out, that the signifiers being used here have a logic different from the more obvious, referential one directly accessible to the eye (Derrida 1972, 6). In splitting the spectator's gaze between looking and reading, the opening shots of the film, I would say, create a dynamic, spatiotemporal visual field that cannot be "seen"; that is, it cannot be mastered in any objectifying or metrical sense, as if from some external vantage point. By implication, spectators are also dynamically de-essentialized. Deprived of the physical, visual field that grounds various arboreal pleasures, we cannot experience the sensation of omniscience, we cannot visually identify with an ego ideal, and we cannot become the voyeurs of fetishized images of women. On the other hand, the spectator becomes well situated to experience the more rhizomatic cognitive pleasures of making connections across this heterogeneous flow of signifiers.

For example, engaged in relation to the unstable image created by the superimposition of this particular text on these particular images, one might connect two different axes of reference usually kept rigorously separate in feature films. The characters and events we see on screen refer not only to Italian working-class experience, but also to the director, cinematographer, technicians, actors, editors, various technologies, and sizable financial investment referred to in the credits. The rhetorical and material dimensions of these moving pictures, in other words, may be as significant as their thematic content, and any of these axes of reference can be read/seen in relation to any of the others—"all the variables themselves in a state of continuous variation" (Deleuze and Guattari 1987, 369). A next move might be to realize that any spectator could see/read any film text in these ways, even or especially the arboreal texts of capital, fabricated in Hollywood, monopolizing Italian screens.

Take the image of Rita Hayworth, for example. Laura Mulvey, without saying it in so many words, has shown that it is the voyeuristic, objectifying, "masculine" gaze that figures and is figured by the uniform, striated space of capitalist society, of which Hollywood has long been a microcosm. The guarantor of that subject's mastery is an image of woman, whose sexuality, as it is figured in this economy, both represents and conceals the threat of castration, the possibility that the sovereign subject and his phallic thought-tree are ontologically a house of cards—or, to borrow Nichetti's grander, postmodernized metaphor, a cathedral of plastic Lego blocks (Mulvey 1989, 20).[4] William Nericcio, theoretician of Latino(a) subjectivity, has recently considered the deconstructive possibilities that the conundrum of the "identity" of one such guarantor—Margarita Carmen Cansino—presents to the marginalized Latino subject enmeshed in an Anglo-centric system of phallic mastery and cultural domination. Considered so "American" that her image graced the hydrogen bomb tested on Bikini Island (as thoroughly depopulated for the occasion as Guanahani became after Columbus), Cansino was, as Nericcio recounts her story, nevertheless, possibly born in Spain, was possibly part Gypsy, and was discovered by a Hollywood agent in a Tijuana nightclub, where she worked as her sexually abusive father's dance partner (Nericcio 1992, 532–34). After two name changes and more than a year of painful electrolysis to raise her "Latin" hairline, Rita Hayworth—double victim of patriarchal violence—emerged to star in Hollywood features such as Charles Vidor's 1946 release *Gilda*, the film alluded to by the poster that Antonio Ricci has been arbitrarily chosen from among the mass of unemployed workers to disseminate.

De Sica's selection of Rita Hayworth to figure the seductions of Hollywood film language thus proves very pointed. In identifying, across the body of Hayworth-Gilda, with an imperial, patriarchal Anglo subjectivity, the hypothetical Italian spectator actually falls into the anomalous position of the historical Cansino-Hayworth herself. The "Italian" spectators' desire to have, or to look like, the epitome of American glamour, the icon of American economic and military supremacy simultaneously affirms and denies the essentialism of national and ethnic (as well as sexual) difference, placing him/her in the position of both colonizer and colonized. Perhaps the most vulnerable and demeaning position on the colonial map, painstakingly described by Frantz Fanon, Albert Memmi, and others, this position has commonly come to be described as analogous in some ways to the position of the "white" woman within modern Western patriarchy, the "woman" for whom Hayworth, ironically, is passing. (Hence the familiar stereotype of the non-Anglo male as macho yet somehow effeminate, sexually threatening yet castrated, the non-Anglo female as doubly disenfranchised.) When this psycho-politico-sexual colonization takes place through the mediation of an ethnically Mediterranean, Gypsy, or mestiza Latina "Rita Hayworth," whose own "American" *figura* is the product of an extreme instance of the same colonization process, a thoroughly antigenealogical cyborgization, or *mise-en-abîme* of the whole identification/objectification machine is engendered. As the pattern can be seen to repeat itself on every level throughout the whole system, what are made tangible are not identities and identifications, but the political intentions they perform.

As an element in this rhizome, the film *Gilda*, whose narrative about a good-bad girl, monopoly capital, class, and foreign policy raises very much the same issues as *Ladri di biciclette*, does not, then, have to be opposed to De Sica's film. Playing with the topological possibilities of imagined cultural space, the Italian film ruins any inside/outside distinction, taking the Hollywood film as both its cultural context and catalyst of its internal plot. Reciprocally, as we have just seen, the image taken from within *Gilda* deconstructs into an allegory of the role Hollywood film has tried to play in the Italian context. The use of Hayworth, then, is precisely not xenophobic, not about Americans versus Italians, but about the seductive disguises—operated through nationalisms and sexualities—assumed by exploitative economic and political relationships (Appadurai 1990, 16; Parker 1992).[5]

Ricci falls out of this symbolic economy when his bicycle, symbol of his paternal authority, patriarchal sexuality, and inclusion in the postwar economy, is stolen—coincidentally as he is trying to take the lumps out of a Hayworth poster he is affixing to a wall (figure 1). I would not argue that every spectator has to be as obsessed as I am with the seemingly inexhaustible intertextual itineraries opened up by Ricci's contact with this poster (though clearly Nichetti travels them passionately), but Ricci's own subsequent itinerary through an unfamiliar, heterogeneous, and labyrinthine Rome and the cinematic rhetoric through which that itinerary is unfolded, do repeatedly transform the means of seduction into the means of connection. The camera has earlier wandered away from Ricci and his superviser to some accordian-playing child beggars being harassed by a middle-class man. Similarly, it pans from Ricci's own bicycle in the pawnshop to the hundreds of bicycles and mountains of linens being pawned by other people and later cuts from Ricci and his friends searching for

Fig. 1. Vittorio De Sica's *Ladri di biciclette* (*The Bicycle Thief*). Antonio Ricci (Lorenzo Maggiorani) is confronted with the image/enigma of Rita Hayworth (aka Margarita Carmen Cansino) in a consequential moment of cinematic intertextuality.

one bicycle to the thousands of bicycles and bicycle parts circulating in the outdoor market. Their search takes Ricci and his son Bruno to a church full of homeless men and to the squalid quarters and impoverished family of the alleged thief. Sooner or later it becomes impossible to imagine the recovery of the bicycle and the reinstatement of Ricci as *attachino* of Hollywood movie posters as a satisfying denouement to this synecdochic journey through the largely unseen Rome of the dislocated and desperate. Readable as one man's or one family's tragedy only within a linear Hollywood plot structure, the ending of *Ladri di biciclette* reads much more polyvalently to the extent that the depravity, the obscene, virtually pornographic reductiveness of the Hollywood paradigm has been exposed. If Antonio has/is "nothing" at the end, if his story appears tragic from within the ideological and metaphysical space of postwar bourgeois culture, nevertheless the painful changes brought about in his self-image, in his position in the family, in the nature of Bruno's allegiance to him, can also be seen as prerequisites to dissolving the glue of patriarchal identification. Only when Antonio can no longer play good guy to someone else's bad guy, breadwinner to a dependent household, and wise paterfamilias to a son who must learn not to require that his father be Cary Grant, can he become part of the rhizome collective from which, at the beginning of the film, he was visually set apart. Only then can he and Bruno walk hand in hand into the crowd, turning their backs to the monocular camera lens, exiting through the vanishing point of the striated space that has grounded and limited their story.

"La gente," whose intonation is all important to the character played by De Sica himself in the music rehearsal scene, cannot necessarily be distinguished lexically from the category by the same name in whose name states are formed, wars are fought, and union leaders, like the one to whom Ricci first appeals, silence their followers. The spectator, like Bruno, who often serves as on-screen stand-in for the spectator, also has to undergo a change in his or her psychological and perceptual habits in order to interact with Ricci other than as a representative, knowable figure with whom we can or cannot identify. There is nothing in particular to know about Antonio Ricci, no mystery about his past (as there is about Vidor's Gilda and Johnny), and we are not positioned vis-à-vis him as global, knowing subjects. If we experience him and ourselves instead as moving intersections of forces and relationships, traversing, as Deleuze and Guattari (1987) put it, a space held by movement rather than a space holding movement (363), we can begin to experience in a sensory way, the texture of an inter-subjectivity (which is also an intrasubjectivity) that is not governed by genealogical, Oedipal narratives. The exhilaration I invariably feel at the end of this film, I attibute at least as much to the film's techno-rhetorical means of giving the spectator a taste of this collective intra/ interrelationship, as to the withering away of Oedipal desire in the relationship between Antonio and Bruno being enacted on-screen.

## The Work of Miscegenation in an Age of Electronic Communication

To the degree that there is Oedipalization, it is due to colonization.
DELEUZE and GUATTARI, *Anti-Oedipus*, 189

De Sica's point of exit is Nichetti's point of entry—literally. If you jux-taposed the ending of *Ladri di biciclette* with the beginning of *Ladri di saponette*, Nichetti's character, "Nichetti," would appear to enter the televisual labyrinth exactly where Antonio and Bruno disappear through the cinema screen's vanishing point. The mise-en-scène of Nichetti's *Ladri di saponette* is the television broadcast of a film, also called *Ladri di saponette*, directed by a young director, also called Maurizio Nichetti, who arrives at a television station to appear with the introducer of his film, a real-life Italian television personality, who unenthusiastically introduces the film and the filmmaker to the televi-sion audience. During the subsequent broadcast, the film is subjected to all the usual abuses of commercial interruption (every eleven min-utes in what filmmakers refer to as "real" time), while it is watched with varying degrees and kinds of spectatorial distraction by a middle-class family into whose living room we are also periodically trans-ported. These different televisual spaces have already begun to intersect in subtle ways when, apparently due to a power outage, a statuesque, blonde actress in a commercial plunges into a blue swimming pool but surfaces in the middle of a river in the black-and-white film, as its hero, Antonio Piermattei (also played by Nichetti) is riding his bicycle along the river on his way home from work. Figures from the black-and-white film subsequently leap the gap into the commercials and into color. The bleak narrative by "Nichetti" about a working-class family that loses everything goes completely awry, and, despite the efforts of its director ("Nichetti"), who plunges into the film-within-the-film to try to get it back on its gloomy track, the story races toward a happy ending in which the Piermattei family members are reunited around a kitchen full of shopping carts piled high with consumer goods.

The late 1980s media context of this brilliant revision/update of *Ladri di biciclette* is frequently alluded to and elaborately thematized along the way. Nichetti is one of a group of filmmakers, including Nanni Moretti and Roberto Benigni, who have set themselves the task of retrieving, resurrecting, and reproducing the specificity of "Italian" film, but without (re)producing the patriarchal nationalism that De Sica's film so subtly associated with U.S. capital's imperializing of the unconscious. In the face of the threatened closure of Cinecittà, the continuing domination of theatrical screens by Hollywood film, and the swamping of the small screen by new, private television networks programmed almost entirely with U.S. series, Nichetti and his cohort are trying to offer Italian spectators images of themselves that reflect (upon) their own local and global subject positions.[6] Nichetti's *Ladri di saponette* seems to acknowledge the congruence between this group's position and the paradoxical position of neorealist film, which was socially and economically marginal, but, nevertheless set itself the task of working out "a national-popular language" that addressed the "tensions, fears, and desires of Italy's rapidly changing social and cultural environment" (Hay 1987, 35). Appropriately, perhaps, in such a coercively Marshall Planned nation, this positioning resulted in a palpably "national" cinema that by no means represented the state and was only sporadically "popular" in the box-office sense. In the 1980s, though, even a modest and/or mediocre new Italian film, not to mention all the old neorealist films, could reach a mass audience (eight million in one evening, according to the young woman who guides "Nichetti" into the labyrinthine studio building) by making its way into the cosmopolitan Babel of Italy's television programming. Among the many imponderables of this accessibility are the facts that television spectatorship is very different from film spectatorship and that, at least until a post–*Ladri di saponette* ruling prohibiting the practice, films on television could be interrupted every eleven minutes by commercials (as Nichetti's black-and-white film-within-the film is). A less obvious change is the reconfiguration of the center/margin relationship within which an earlier generation of filmmakers operated. Television, especially contemporary Italian television, is already a kind of faux rhizome of discontinuous, narrative- and nonnarratively based elements (especially when the channel-hopping spectator is figured into the picture), unified and fascisized by the common goal of selling soap. The challenge to the filmmaker, then, becomes not how to deconstruct centered, patriarchal tree-thought, but how to divert this fundamentally *non*multiple but rhizomatic-seeming flow from coopting every kind of image for the reproduction in every direction of the fetishized economic and political relations of late capital.

Although "Nichetti," the auteur director whose retro-neorealist film is being aired on television, objects strenuously to the properties of this electronic medium, the film that includes him among its spaces, times, and dramatis personae has a more complex take on how the project of offering Italian images to Italian audiences might be related to ads for soap and junk food (Nichetti worked for several years making commercials, whose discipline of telling a story in thirty seconds he says he enjoys) and to the proliferation of non-Italian programming. Both the ads and the incursion of Nordic faces and bodies are synecdochally represented by the tall, blonde, English-speaking model Heidi, whose incongruous presence in the Piermattei apartment becomes one of the film's most polyvalent and effective strategies. In fact, from the moment "Nichetti" arrives at the television studio, the space he operates in makes oppositions like "Italian"/"non-Italian," "film"/"commercial," and even "spectator"/"screen" difficult to sustain. Like an Escher drawing, the camera work and the editing of this overture produce a space in which subjects and objects, agents and acted upon, oscillate in and out of each other's positions. As a result, although everything is visible, not much is "clear." People do not stay put in genres, categories, or communications media. Let me use the film's opening moments to demonstrate in more detail how we are thus dispossessed of our sense of direction and spatial orientation, how both the action and the viewer are "deterritorialized."

While "Clara," and a camera that seems, at first, to represent the point of view of "Nichetti," careen down the studio's checkerboard hallways, the edits frustrate any spectatorial attempt to rationalize the geography of the production facility. A pan we are initially inclined to associate with "Nichetti"'s point of view (especially when it appears to be motivated by the movement of an attractive young woman) suddenly discovers "Nichetti" himself in the frame. As if the subject with whom the film's rhetoric has invited the spectator to identify had suddenly leaped to the other side of the lens, "Nichetti" then becomes the object of a gaze that is not now anchored by any character in the film. Spectators suddenly are on their own.

The way the image of the young woman works changes accordingly. This image now foregrounds and, in a sense, delegitimates *our* voyeurism by inviting our gaze to catch itself in the act of creating a striated, Oedipal visual field out of an accidental conjunction of figure and frame. From linchpin of reality, the female figure is transformed into the wild card of contingency. With our discovery of "Nichetti" where and when we least expect him, the film's temporality thus also changes. Unlike the homogeneous empty time that, like striated space, anchors a voyeuristic, Oedipally identified subject, in one moment (or generation), as well as one place, the topologically complex time produced here puts us back within the heterogeneity of rhetorical process that, as we saw earlier, the homogeneous, empty time of Andersonian nationhood camouflages.

Within a few more moments, even before the opening credits roll for the black-and-white film called *Ladri di saponette*, the ontologies of image and spectator and their respective spaces and times are further confounded. Suddenly we are hurtled from one end of the televisual process to the other by a cut from the technical director's order for "Silenzio" to what we retrospectively figure out are images on a TV and an image of the channel-zapping little girl who is watching them. Yet, because all these images, including that of the little girl, are framed the same way, and because they succeed each other so quickly, we can distinguish between "live" and video images only retrospectively. The sequence, that is, reads first as a montage of equivalent elements. As the rest of the film will elaborate, the apparently different times and spaces juxtaposed to each other in the fractally organized rhizome of media production and consumption all share the same (non)ontological status, while the multiplication of reflections with no origin all ironize one another. Conversely, making something of a hash of theories of spectatorship, each of the (non)exemplary spectators in this one middle-class family sees a different film (if they see a film at all). The images, narratives, and relationships organized by the director are no more powerful than the images, narratives, and relationships within which these figures are themselves enmeshed, and the latter factors are hardly stable or predictably interrelated. The first of our many stand-ins, little "Anna," for example, can play omnipotent

Picassobrain with her zapper one moment, and be sent to bed by her mother the next.

The pompous TV film critic's attempt to taxonomize films and codify their history (he parrots French auteur theory, predictably privileging classic Hollywood and New Wave French films over Italian films of any era; he has never heard of "Nichetti") is, consequently, ludicrous, and not the most serious threat to "Italian" cinema. His improvised comments on a film he has not seen by a filmmaker he has never heard of are actually not completely stupid, but no one is listening to him anyway. The pregnant housewife literally "mutes" him because she does not want him to spoil the plot for her. A hilariously profound reaction shot of little Anna, imitating both the muted film critic now silently mouthing his commentary, and a goldfish swimming placidly in its bowl on a table next to the television set, further deprivileges— literally decenters—the TV image. By implication, it also deprivileges the image of television *and* goldfish bowl that we are watching— especially, if we ourselves are watching them on a television monitor, which is quite likely given the fact that the film was financed by television mogul Silvio Berlusconi and broadcast on his network. (Or, if the spectator is in the United States, given the fact that Italian films have been poorly distributed there, we are probably watching a videotape.) But if Anna's wonderfully deflationary linking of critic and goldfish thus disestablishes the centrality of the TV screen, it simultaneously suggests a sort of equivalence between the fishbowl and the monitor—a suggestion repeated throughout the film at provocative junctures. The critic, no less than the fish, has been glassed in, so to speak, subsumed in a commodification process that collapses the distance and differences between public and private, knowledge and object, perhaps even human and animal. None of these readings, of course, precludes our also registering the image as satire. Critic and goldfish are probably equally knowledgeable about how this film will be received via the television monitor by its eight million viewers.

More threatening to the survival of "Italian" filmmaking than some massively unself-reflexive critic's pontifications is the work of "Nichetti" himself. The film director's impulse is to rebel against "materialism" or commodification (or whatever one chooses to call the complex mediation of desire characteristic of late capital, consumerist, bourgeois society) in a way that threatens to reproduce exactly the Oedipal agon so carefully deconstructed by De Sica. In his reading of

Italian film history, and in the opposition he would set up between his
film and the commercials that punctuate it, "Nichetti" is oblivious
to the relationship between his form of criticism and what he thinks
he stands against. The reading of *Ladri di biciclette*, for instance, to
be inferred from the original plot of the black-and-white *Ladri di
saponette* hyperbolically exemplifies the phallocentric reading of De
Sica's film as politically pure and/but castrated. Antonio, a working-
class father, is supposed to be paralyzed in an accident on his way
home, with a "borrowed" chandelier, from his first day of work at a
lamp-manufacturing plant after two years of unemployment (figure 2).
His wife Maria is then forced to turn to prostitution. Bruno, the little
son, has to use the wheels of the family bicycle to make a wheelchair
for his father. Both Bruno and his little brother Paolo are seen, under
the closing credits, entering an orphanage. For "Nichetti" to assume
that this story would be corrupted by the consumer wet dreams that
punctuate it during the broadcast, he must ignore the continuity, made
dramatically explicit once the "power" is interrupted, between his
own economic and sexual investments and those of the ads. When
Antonio lands his job at the light-fixture factory, "La Lux," he and
Maria get the same sexual charge that the commercials play to out of
their entry into capital. As they roll off their bed in a heap of consumer arousal, murmuring to each other, "You're lovely," "You're
lovelier," Maria recounts the dream she cherished through the darkest
hours of the war—to own a house with big rooms and a chandelier
"like the one she saw in the cinema." Antonio's unintentionally apt reaction to the medical benefits attached to the job is "Now we can all
get sick!" As the film was supposed to go on, the congruence between
"Nichetti"'s film and consumer culture would have been disguised by
the scapegoating of the woman and the martyrdom of the worker. The
working-class protagonist would lose everything, due to fate in league
with his wife's excessive desires. She would be fittingly punished for
her unseemly ambitions, particularly unfitting in a woman of the working class. The audience would be tenderly affected, especially by the
concluding orphanage scene, which would send people out of the
theater feeling righteously indignant on behalf of those unlucky
enough not to have a job with medical benefits. Nowhere would the
complex circuitry of patriarchy, consumerism, class hierarchy, and
sexism be made accessible, or emotionally decathected.

The intervention of the commercials and the director's loss of con-

Fig. 2. Maurizio Nichetti's *Ladri di saponette* (*The Icicle Thief*). Antonio Piermattei (Maurizio Nichetti), a working-class husband and father, "borrows" a chandelier on his first day at work at a lamp-manufacturing plant, La Lux, after two years of unemployment.

trol thankfully make this a very different film. After the priest, Don Italo, shames Maria out of performing in a mildly sexually exploitative musical review, the better to perform the church's version of patriarchal sexploitation at home, for example, her excessively cheerful preparations for Antonio's return from work are visually linked to the work Heidi's image is performing in the commercial that punctuates her floor scrubbing, pasta cooking, and dressing up. There is a perfect eyeline match across the cut from film to commercial, between the dark-haired Italian housewife on the left side of the screen and the blonde model driving a convertible, screen right, in the next frame. (Further confounding the opposition between the two women, Heidi in "real" life is considerably more maternal than Maria and "adores" old black-and-white Italian films.) The ridiculous analogies made between bodies like Heidi's and whatever is being sold in her commercial, moreover, could work only within an already masculinist, capitalist cultural context, with, in the case of Italy, self-minoritizing tendencies toward an Oedipal identification with Nordic power (namely, Don Italo's immediate assumption that Antonio really would kill his wife for a creature like Heidi). The supposed safety and sanctity of the Italian family look equally dubious whether little Bruno is being casually exploited by his parents and the priest (not to mention "the director") and baby Paolo's Keatonesque near misses with gruesome injury are being ignored, or women strip, children gorge on "Big Big" candy bars, and adolescents consume soft drinks every eleven minutes in people's living rooms.

One could go on. *Ladri di saponette* is as tightly constructed as its illustrious predecessor and was, according to Nichetti, edited literally frame by frame. But one image cross-referencing the "film" with the "commercials" intersects particularly powerfully with De Sica's use of Rita Hayworth, and will serve by comparison to exemplify Nichetti's postarboreal approach to decolonizing the screen. Maria, having mistaken Heidi for her husband's mistress, tries to drown herself in the river and emerges into the sudsy world of commercials from which Heidi came. There she gets a job in a chorus of women dressed as Gypsies, singing in praise of a detergent cleaning agent. Specifically, they sing to the music of Bizet's opera *Carmen*, the detergent substituting for the matador Escamillo, with whom, in the opera, Carmen has fallen in love. The new hero/phallus, in other words, is not a person at all, and not even a durable good like a bicycle or a chandelier, but something that breaks up in water and disappears as you use it—soap.

Nichetti, needless to say, is not opposing "good" opera to "bad" commercials. As Susan McClary has eloquently noted in her Foreword to Catherine Clément's *Opera, or the Undoing of Women*, Bizet's opera celebrates racism, imperialism, and a politics of gender unapologetically fatal to the proletarian, artistic, erotically independent heroine (Clément 1988, xii). Carmen the Gypsy, Clément herself argues, is a smuggler, a foreigner on Spanish soil, trailing traces of India, Egypt, the Maghreb, who fits nowhere and suffers the wrath of state-form society in the person of her lover/murderer, the policeman José (49–51). Maria, on the other hand, is delighted finally to be singing professionally and strenuously resists "Nichetti"'s attempts to drag her back to his depressing black-and-white film, whose treatment of the heroine suspiciously resembles that of Bizet's opera. As Heidi, announcing her own intention to decamp from "*Ladri di saponette*," informs Antonio, "you suffer too much in films."

What, then, is one to do with this commercial, mass-media Italian cannibalization, or theft, of an opera, a *French* opera, about a woman who is also a Gypsy, who challenges and is punished by Spanish patriarchy? Should not the fact of the theft itself empty out or dissipate the authority of the phallic configuration of meaning and power that is being appropriated? If one can simply excerpt the song of the chorus in praise of Escamillo, substitute soap for the matador, substitute an Italian piazza for Spain as the setting, Italian for French as the language, and a happy outcome for tragedy, then whom shall we say is the colonizer and whom the colonized? Are these terms even applicable? Can the Oedipal phallus and the Oedipalization of desire, in whatever form they take, survive the massive fun being made of male physiology by repeated evocations of the universalizing principle of foamy white soapsuds?

Walter Benjamin's enduringly relevant "The Work of Art in the Age of Mechanical Reproduction" exemplifies the kind of complexity with which I think we need to entertain these questions. In discussing the potential loss of the "aura" of presence, uniqueness, and originality involved in the invention of such technologies as photography and cinema, he plays both the critic and the visionary. The visionary sees the transformative possibilities of these new technologies, their creative role in the formation of a "mass" culture that is not organized hierarchically and centripetally, that gives birth, in fact, to a new sense of culture in which "art" itself dematerializes as a category and activity separable from politics and cognition. The critic, more pessimistically, foresees the reterritorialization of the technologies of mechanical reproduction. Grim parodies of the classical aura—the star system, fascist spectacle, modern, mechanized, and aestheticized nationalistic warfare—are equally likely historical readings of the "meaning" of mechanical reproduction. But does the historical reading invalidate the visionary reading? Benjamin's essay remains constantly in motion, itself highly resistant to decisions about its "meaning." Not Oedipally "exploding the constellation in which his conceptual terms are deployed," as Susan Buck-Morss has argued (Buck-Morss 1992, 5), Benjamin more subtly resists the reterritorialization of his argument by the stabilizing historiographies and ontologies he can envision being challenged. In this sense his essay incarnates, and therefore *does* make historical, the cognitive and conceptual transformation he theorizes.

Similarly, one does not witness in Nichetti's *Ladri di saponette* the withering away of the structure of the Oedipal desire that a rhizomatic flow of commercial media production and consumption might appear to indicate. The husband in the family of middle-class spectators ogles Heidi voyeuristically, the wife identifies happily with the moment Antonio and Maria kiss, precisely while, on-screen, Heidi and Bruno look forward to consuming their breakfast cornflakes. The endless proliferation of trivial Oedipalizations is enough to make one long for a good old nineteenth-century misogynist, tragic opera. Only the "director" is unhappy, appealing desperately through the television screen to the housewife (who cannot hear him), "Don't leave me in here. Let me out!"—as if her well-upholstered living room offered an avenue of escape. But, like Benjamin's essay, the film resists reterritorialization as either vision or nightmare. If the faux rhizome of capitalist television reduces "Nichetti" (last seen juxtaposed to the indifferent goldfish) to despair, it has also performed as a mapping of a differently experienced time/space in which the three Carmens become contemporaries and collaborators in evoking a non-state-form global village. That there be no phallic (or castrated) characters with whom we can identify is, as in De Sica's film, a prerequisite to this map's becoming visible. The film's circus atmosphere is conducive instead to the improvisational, to the postarboreal, contingent subjectivizing that, as Appadurai importantly notes, is *both* enabled and impeded by uneven flows of people, politics, money, and media around the world (Appadurai 1990, 17). Perhaps darker and less utopian than *Ladri di biciclette*, *Ladri di saponette* richly and relentlessly calls attention to the constitutive force of "contexts," joining much of the rest of contemporary Europe in the fear that designing "Italy," or any other reference point, as a rhizome may be more difficult the more urgent it becomes.

## Notes

1. Henri Lefebvre's critique of the fetishization of a certain "philosophico-epistemological notion of space," complements Deleuze and Guattari's project. By way of introducing his study, he expresses his concern that theory produces an only apparently extraideological mental space within which it then (re)produces ideas only too compatible with the ideas of a dominant class (Lefebvre 1991, 5–6).

2. The experience of Italian fascism and imperialism is, of course, also a referent here.

3. Altman's film is also, of course, satirizing the screenwriter. The reference to *Ladri*

*di biciclette* here signifies the character's sense of both purity and integrity and, I think, the filmmaker's sense of the character's fatuousness and profound cinematic illiteracy.

4. A recurring image in *Ladri di saponette* has Francesco, the son in the family, watching television, constructing a perfect replica of Saint Basil's Cathedral in the Kremlin out of an elaborate Lego set. Lego is, of course, manufactured by a Danish company. The potential polyvalence of this image is daunting or exhilarating, depending on the viewer's hermeneutic proclivities. The sixteenth-century cathedral itself, with its heterogeneous chapels, is something of an architectural analog for this film, and Nichetti went to architecture school. As an index of the Kremlin, it is also an image made familiar by the Cold War, whose hostilities are here commodified for market consumption, Communism thus ironically feeding capitalism. An Italian child using a Danish toy to create a similacrum of a Russian/Soviet cultural icon also brings home the rhizomatic globalization of the various mediascapes, ethnoscapes, technoscapes, ideoscapes, and finanscapes theorized by Appadurai. And so on.

5. Appadurai's description of the "fetishization" of production, "which masks translocal capital, transnational earning-flows, global mangement and often faraway workers . . . in the idiom and spectacle of local . . . control, national productivity and territorial sovereignty" (16) seems to me particularly relevant here—as does his "fetishism of the consumer," about which he writes, "I mean to indicate here that the consumer has been transformed, through commodity flows (and the mediascapes, especially of advertising, that accompany them), into a sign, both in Baudrillard's sense of a simulacrum which only asymptotically approaches the form of a real social agent; and in the sense of a mask for the real seat of agency, which is not the consumer but the producer and the many forces that constitute production. Global advertising is the key technology for the worldwide dissemination of a plethora of creative, and culturally well-chosen, ideas of consumer agency. These images of agency are increasingly distortions of a world of merchandising so subtle that the consumer is consistently helped to believe that he or she is an actor, where in fact he or she is at best a consumer" (ibid.).

6. As in *Capitol*, the soap opera that the pregnant, middle-class wife in the family of spectators wants to watch. She is apparently unaware that virtually everything she watches *is* a representation of "capital" in one form or another.

## Works Cited

I would like to acknowledge here the profound influence on my thinking about nationality and subjectivity of the women's art-making collective, Las Comadres, of the San Diego/Tijuana border region, with whom I have been working since 1988. Emily Hicks has been a particularly astute guide, and her book, *Border Writing*, a provocative example.

Anderson, Benedict. 1991. *Imagined Communities: Reflections on the Origin and Spread of Nationalism.* London and New York: Verso.

Appadurai, Arjun. 1990. "Disjuncture and Difference in the Global Cultural Economy." *Public Culture: Bulletin for the Center for Transnational Cultural Studies* 2: 1–24.

Benjamin, Walter. 1969. "The Work of Art in the Age of Mechanical Reproduction." In *Illuminations.* Trans. Harry Zohn. New York: Schocken Books.

Bhabha, Homi K. 1990. "DissemiNation: Time, Narrative, and the Margins of the Modern Nation." In *Nation and Narration*, ed. Homi K. Bhabha. London: Routledge. 292–322.

———. 1992. "Freedom's Basis in the Indeterminate." *October* 61: 46–57.

Bondanella, Peter. 1983. *Italian Cinema: From Neorealism to the Present*. New York: Frederick Unger.

Buck-Morss, Susan. 1992. "Aesthetics and Anaesthetics: Walter Benjamin's Artwork Essay Reconsidered." *October* 62: 3–41.

Clément, Catherine. 1988. *Opera, or the Undoing of Women*. Trans. Betsy Wing. Foreword by Susan McClary. Minneapolis: University of Minnesota Press.

de Lauretis, Teresa. 1984. "Desire in Narrative." *Alice Doesn't*. Bloomington: Indiana University Press. 103–57.

Deleuze, Gilles, and Felix Guattari. 1983. *Anti-Oedipus: Capitalism and Schizophrenia*. Trans. Robert Hurley et al. Minneapolis: University of Minnesota Press.

———. 1987. *A Thousand Plateaus: Capitalism and Schizophrenia*. Trans. Brian Massumi. Minneapolis: University of Minnesota Press.

Derrida, Jacques. 1972. "La Différance." In *Marges de la philosophie*. Paris: Minuit.

Doane, Mary Ann. 1985. "The Voice in the Cinema: The Articulation of Body and Space." In *Movies and Methods*, vol. 2, ed. Bill Nichols. Berkeley, Los Angeles, and London: University of California Press. 565–76.

Dratch, Howard, and Allen Frankovich. 1980. *On Company Business*. PBS documentary.

Fanon, Frantz. 1968. *The Wretched of the Earth*. New York: Grove Press.

Guattari, Felix. 1980. "Why Italy?" *Semiotext(e)* 3: 234–37.

Haraway, Donna. 1991. "Situated Knowledges." In *Simians, Cyborgs, and Women: The Reinvention of Nature*. New York: Routledge. 183–201.

Hay, James. 1987. *Popular Film Culture in Fascist Italy: The Passing of the Rex*. Bloomington and Indianapolis: Indiana University Press.

———. 1993. "Invisible Cities/Visible Geographies: Toward a Cultural Geography of Italian Television in the 90s." *Quarterly Review of Film and Video* 14:3: 35–48.

Hicks, Emily. 1991. *Border Writing: The Multidimensional Text*. Minneapolis: University of Minnesota Press.

Lefebvre, Henri. 1991. *The Production of Space*. Trans. Donald Nicholson-Smith. Oxford, U.K., and Cambridge, Mass.: Blackwell.

Marcus, Millicent. 1986. *Italian Film in the Light of Neorealism*. Princeton, N.J.: Princeton University Press.

Memmi, Albert. 1967. *The Colonizer and the Colonized*. Boston: Beacon Press.

Molineaux, Gerard. 1988. "The Bicycle Thieves." Paper delivered at Florida State University, January.

Mulvey, Laura. 1989. "Visual Pleasure and Narrative Cinema." In *Visual and Other Pleasures*. Bloomington: Indiana University Press. 14–26.

Nericcio, William. 1992. "Sordid Meditations on What Might Occur if Frantz Fanon, Rosario Castellanos, Jacques Derrida, Gayatri Spivak and Sandra Cisneros Asked Rita Hayworth Her Name: THEORYCELEBRITYSHAME." *Romance Languages Annual* 3: 531–40.

Parker, Andrew, et. al., eds. 1992. *Nationalisms and Sexualities*. New York and London: Routledge.

# If the Japanese Are Samurai, the Italians Are *Baka*: The Multiple Play of Stereotypes

*Antonio Marazzi*

Stereotypes, as a kind of negative discourse on the Other, can illuminate the complex elaboration of cultural identity through the construction of difference as the distorted, often reversed, projection of values on outsiders, be they individuals or groups. Each culture has its own internal processes for creating the exotic, the barbarian, and the savage, and an awareness of these processes can stimulate a critique of one's own reactions to the encounter with a real or imagined outsider.

Sometimes, however, the Other sends us back a mirror image of Us in which we fail to recognize ourselves. So great is the inaccuracy or even the forgery used in the Other's depiction of Us that—since we think we know how *we* really are—we find better evidence in this reverse case of the perversity of the stereotyping process than we do in the stereotypes of the Other we ourselves create. This process generally results in our rejection of the returned image of Us as seen from the outside; thus we lose a good opportunity for self-analysis through an alien eye.

Such mirror play becomes increasingly complex when we recognize in our exotic stereotypes our own dreams or obsessions staged in another culture's set, and when we recognize in the returned images of ourselves the use of some of our own cultural values as interpreted in a different ideological context.[1]

As regards Italian identity, Japan appears as the ideal counterpart for these kinds of multiple mirrorlike stereotyping processes, which, tied as they are to Japan's reciprocal historical development of social, political, economic, scientific, aesthetic, and intellectual relationships with other nations, offer rich but neglected occasions for intercultural

275

analysis. In fact, studies venturing outside the boundaries of Western culture—as mainstream anthropology has done—have been increasingly concerned about orientalizing the Other. In an effort to exorcise this danger, scholars often perform rituals of self-affliction. But no matter how much avoiding orientalizing can be considered a positive ethical concern and an invitation to more controlled analyses, it is also still another instance of a rigid dichotomizing process.

If we consider a more intricate web of interactions that move back and forth from one culture to another not only as a two-way street but as a highly stratified process where each level influences all the others, it becomes no more clear than in the dichotomizing model who is orientalizing whom.[2] Looking at the orientalization of a Western culture from a geographically oriental culture can be a cathartic exercise in cultural displacement for a European like myself.

However we are situated, a critique not in terms of our own cultural relativism but of our recognition of others' power of representing us can be a lively exercise in intersubjectivity, a double negation of objectivism. Reflexivity, instead of being turned inward, as now usually happens, can be stimulated by our interpretation of another culture's interpretation of our own culture, which is in itself the product of both social facts and their interpretations.

In the case I consider here, Italian culture becomes "Italian culture" as a Japanese construct to be looked at from an Italian standpoint— against the light, so to speak. From this perspective, in turn, we find a culturally specific construct of "the Japanese."

Americans have coined the term "workaholic" to express the characteristic of the contemporary Japanese that most obsesses Americans, but Italians seem to be more concerned about the physical appearance of Japanese persons. Importing few Eastern-built cars, and suffering from no embargo on their own exported goods, Italians seem to look with a kind of snobbish detachment at the seasonal, pacific invasion of tourists and consumers from the Land of the Rising Sun; they limit themselves to finding these visitors "ugly," as some newspapers have recently reported, in a dispute to which I shall soon refer.

If until the 1960s, Americans seemed to be more interested in importing from the Far East Zen and martial arts than cars and electronics, the historical first report on the Japanese from an Italian, Marco Polo, sounds strikingly aesthetic: "La gente sono bianche, di bella maniera e belli" (the people are white, well-mannered, and handsome)

(Marco Polo 1975, 154). Yellow and ugly they were seen to be later. Things change.

## The Baka Dispute

In order to follow our cultural mirror play, we must now shift to the Japanese perception of the stereotypical Italian. For this purpose, we have to discern significant elements believed to have contributed to an accepted, shared image of this subspecies of foreigner as they have been overtly expressed in local popular culture.

In November 1986, a Tokyo magazine with an American title, *Dime* (pronounced *daimu*), read by young executives and local yuppies with presumed contacts in the West, submitted its readers to a poll, asking who, in their opinion, are the stupidest people in the world, and why. Italians easily won this little-flattering contest, over the Australians (whose main drawback, in the opinion of the *Dime* readers, appeared to be a too-close contact with sheep and an excessive familiarity with nature) and the French (too concerned with their own traditions and grandeur); Americans fell lower on the list.

Logically enough, value judgments are translated from one language into another with much greater difficulty than terms of reference for objects, people, and actions, the more so if one ventures outside a major linguistic area such as Indo-European. In our case, the word used in the poll to connote the qualities attributed, to a greater or lesser extent, to the inhabitants of some foreign countries, was *baka*. For an appropriate translation of this term, I refer to one of the leading Yamatologists in Italy, Professor Adriana Boscaro of the University of Venice at Ca' Foscari. In her article on the contrast between "hero" and *baka* in the last play of Endo Shusaku, she writes: "The literal translation of *baka* could be 'idiot,' but this latter term evokes such strong Dostoyevskian echoes that one runs into the danger of deviating from [Shusaku's] idea" (Boscaro 1976, 141; my translation).

She continues, in a note: "I think that an appropriate translation in a Western language is the English 'fool,' and better still the expression 'wonderful fool,' used by Francis Mathy for his translation of Obakasan" (ibid.).

Unfortunately, we cannot apply this elegant attribution to the term as *Dime* uses it. The opinions of the Japanese readers were widely reported in the Italian press. The *Dime* columnist Ichiro Enokido, promoter of the poll, was interviewed about its results. From this published interview, we see that the shared accepted translation in Italian of *baka* was *stupido*. We can therefore rely on a fairly clear meaning of that value judgment. Let us now consider the motivations that led to the Italian first-place ranking in forty-two out of sixty answers in the *baka* poll.

Italians are too cheerful, too interested in running after women (a clear indication that the stereotyped image is that of a male), and too ready to go on strike: these are the first reasons given. Others are added: Italians always eat without working enough; they interrupt their working hours with a long nap; they are too concerned with the clothes they wear. Some simply gave this explanation: I had some Italian friends, and I never knew what to talk about; they were stupid.

Remedies? Some suggested greater use of reason (Japanese *risei*), shorter naps, and more work, more reading, being more serious. For many Japanese respondents, however, it seems that nothing can be done to improve the situation because the Italian climate is too mild. Their suggestion is for Italians to emigrate and try a hard life in a land with a more severe climate.

When asked why he launched such a poll in his magazine, *Dime*'s editor, Shigeru Nakamura, answered that he was more interested in criticizing the Japanese than in condemning the Italian way of life and that his frugal compatriots should learn how to live a more leisurely and luxurious life themselves. The poll was nothing more than a joke and, to stress its ironic mood, Nakamura proposed a counterpoll among Italians, asking why they find the Japanese to be so ugly.

The promoters' absurd intentions in asking such questions as the poll put forward should have aroused self-criticism among the silent majority of Japanese who in the autumn of 1986 were giving their approval to Prime Minister Nakasone's statements even when, in a world-famous diplomatic incident, he stated that the IQ of U.S. citizens was falling due to increases in the black and Latino populations. That same Nakasone had once proposed, in a semi-ironic mood, to increase internal consumption and vacations in the new Japanese tourist resorts by encouraging the immigration of some Neapolitans as experts in the fine art of hanging out, the *dolce far niente*, and consumerism.

No matter how serious, ironic, or provocative the intentions of the promoters of the *Dime* poll, the answers were faithfully reported by Renata Pisu, the Tokyo correspondent of the influential Turin newspaper *La Stampa* (Pisu 1986a, 1), and commented on by some of Italy's leading columnists. The Italian reaction was reported, in turn, in the *Asahi Journal*, which has a larger reading public than does *Dime*. And there was much talk in the corridors of the Italian embassy in Tokyo about whether grounds had been established for a diplomatic incident.

After teasing her readers for awhile, Pisu invites them not to be too touchy about the poll but to take it in with a sense of humor (Pisu 1986b, 1). She adds that she has read such reactions as: "We may be fatter than they are, but we are definitely better-looking," or "The reason the Japanese are yellow is because they envy our *sole mio*."

But let us examine in detail the arguments of the three Italian columnists whose remarks on the incident were later summarized in the *Asahi Journal* article (Takeyama 1987, 22). On the front page of the prestigious *Corriere della Sera*, Francesco Alberoni gives his opinion. Not a journalist but a sociologist at the University of Milan, a popular writer, and a public figure, Alberoni gives way to his usual moralistic mood. First he condemns the main vices of contemporary Italian society, where "a showy and vulgar race to success is emerging" and "power is again becoming arrogant without sensing any need to justify itself." Then he severely criticizes the Japanese of today, who he says are in the process of shifting "from an attitude of great humility to one of pride," which "is always very dangerous." He goes so far as to refer to a preceding analogous attitude in the "psychological error" of Pearl Harbor (Alberoni 1986, 1).

Ferdinando Camon, whose article appears on the front page of *Il Giorno*, is an internationally known writer of novels and essays. Until a couple of decades ago, he writes, the very same reasons that make us so stupid in the eyes of the Japanese of today would have been considered proof of our international reputation for shrewdness. Shrewdness is not pure, but applied, intelligence; the shrewd person is one who never forgets his own interest. Foreigners have always considered us shrewd because of our ability to live a good, enviable life. But something has happened, Camon writes, that has turned the image of Italians with a special talent for good living into an image of Italians as stupid people. A comparison of the Italian life model with the Japanese life model has produced, according to Camon, this radical change of opinion.

The crucial, and most interesting, point in Camon's argument is that there has been a sudden but precisely motivated reversal in the Japanese view of the Italian way of life. To go on strike, to take long naps, to make love, to enjoy a great cuisine, to be cheerful, to be undisciplined—these characteristics were enviable mirages for the Japanese of yesterday (Camon 1986, 1).

By contrast, the Japanese model has been a "sacrificial" one, to use Camon's term: some generations should simply be sacrificed to hard work, the fruits of which they would never enjoy. After having visited Japan, some Italians reported to their friends in Italy that Japanese workers would gather together to sing their company's song. This, and other such tales, contributed to the Italian image of Japan as having a forced, coercive, and alienated economic recovery certainly inapplicable in our own country. By comparison, then, the Italian dolce vita is a positive value; it is the condition of a people that is not losing its own life. But the sacrificial way has proven to be successful much more rapidly than expected, and the wealthy new Japanese of today have reversed the earlier Japanese judgment of the Italian lifestyle. They now consider themselves a mirage for the Italians.

Some points in Camon's analysis are worth further consideration. The opposition between the two models, the Japanese and the Italian, derives from an opposition between social behavior ruled by ethical principles and one where the political ideal is free from ethical obligations. Each has a long cultural history, one from Confucius, the other from Machiavelli and Guicciardini. There is much more at stake here than the choice of living like a workaholic or like a Latin lover.

Surprisingly, even such a silly dispute as the one triggered by the *baka* poll has resuscitated some basic guidelines for individual behavior in each of the two cultures. Even more surprisingly, each side ended up praising some of the other culture's opposite aspects.

In his commentary on the Italian commentators' reactions to the *Dime* poll, Hakuei Takeyama, the *Asahi Journal* writer, maintains that the Italians, far from being the most *baka*, are the most interesting people. He bases his opinion on arguments that at times are serious and at times odd. Among the latter, he cites the example of the policemen.

At some of Japan's cities' most dangerous intersections, a dummy policeman is erected. Seeing him from afar, Japanese drivers have a conditioned reflex to slow down, drive carefully, and behave correctly. In Italian cities, on the contrary, says Takeyama, street safety does not depend on real or fake policemen but on the drivers themselves.

Pedestrians cross streets at any point in the block without causing traffic problems, knowing that the drivers will spontaneously give way. Italians are not afraid of the policemen who, in turn, are there not to control but to facilitate traffic flow. This is a sign of freedom (and a warning about personal safety, might be my comment as an Italian).

Furthermore, unlike Japan, Italy has train stations, each of which is different from the others (where people wait for ever-late trains: second "Italian" comment). This is only one small sign, says Takeyama, of the extreme diversity of the Italian nation, from the north to the south. Italian society accepts all these peculiarities. Italy is a nonauthoritarian, noncentralistic country that has achieved freedom and democracy after hard-fought battles. In some respects, Italian history is similar to that of the Japanese, continues Takeyama. Both emerged as modern nations at about the same time during the past century, with the Meiji restoration and the Risorgimento independence movement, respectively. Both nations had a fascist experience, lost the last world war, and made tremendous efforts at national reconstruction. Unlike Japan and Germany, however, Italy overturned its authoritarian regime.

Contemporary Japanese show little interest in Italy, says Takeyama, because they are concerned only with the economy, but they could profitably study these aspects of the Italian situation. It is wrong to consider only one side of such a highly diversified country as Italy. Italians are very different one from another; the fact that they appear to us Japanese as rich and elegant, living in large homes and enjoying long vacations, is one of the many mysteries of a complexity that we find difficult to grasp.

## The Dark Shadow of Fascism

The image of a decadent contemporary Italian society is sometimes compared to that of the fascist era, when Italians were feeling strong and seemed inebriated by their own sense of power, as the Tokyo magazine *Brutus* notes in a rather ambiguous commentary on the present-day Japanese image of the Italians.

In the most bitter of the articles written in reaction to the *Dime* poll, Paolo Granzotto admits that the Japanese portrait of the average Italian is not far off the mark. He asks, nonetheless, why respondents to the poll consider such traits of the Italian national character as they noted to be those of a *stupido*. He goes on, certainly not nostalgically, to recall fascist lifestyles, thus commenting on one of the supposedly negative qualities of contemporary Italians: "Undisciplined? We were once disciplined (or we pretended to be), and this fact, which our Eastern friends liked so much that they decided to stipulate treaties and Axes, was not a lucky one for us" (Granzotto 1986, 1).

Here it is possible to find a link between three dimensions of responses (which also suggest three possible levels of analysis): (1) abstract stereotypes as frozen representations of consensus about certain positive or negative qualities; (2) the process with which, within the social history of ideas of a nation or group, certain ideals emerge to form something not dissimilar from the Weberian ideal types; and (3) the historical flow of events, where diverse modes of individual behavior are intertwined in a network of social relations.

In Italy, the reaction to the fascist era, when it is seen as the last episode in a long series of local events reinforced by a historical tradition of political pragmatism as a positive ideology, has resulted in a widely accepted oppositional model for individual behavior and value judgments of the social actions of others. The discipline and passive acceptance of social rules that characterized Italy under Mussolini are now generally considered dangerous for the individual and, in the end, for society at large. Simultaneously, a critical awareness of social and political realities is seen as an indication of a mature participation in the political sphere of the social arena.

We can easily find an opposition between this stereotypical behavioral guideline and the Japanese model of a social ethic, based as it is on cohesion and the uncritical acceptance of one's role within a collective, and on the positive value of unanimity and the negative one of dialectics within one's group and between groups within one's own society (though approving strong competition with the outside).

We could then conclude that to reinforce internal models of behavior and to confirm one's own value judgments, both sides would concentrate on some aspects of the other society's diffused behavior, as opposed to one's own, and form specific stereotypes of the "other" (in Japanese, *gaijin*, "the man outside") based on those peculiarities.

I would argue, however, that this is too simple an opposition. The history of modern Japan is made up not only of a series of military, economic, and political events focused on that country's encounter with the West. Even the concept of cultural influence, no matter how broad and vague, is insufficient to express some crucial but hidden aspects of the Japanese "cultural revolution" that began with the Meiji restoration.[3] When political power passed from the hands of the traditional military leader, the shogun, to the emperor and his young, open-minded supporters, the whole nation was literally opened to the West. One of the main concerns of the Japanese at that time, both consciously from the political leaders' side and unconsciously on the part of the entire population, was to make a good impression on foreigners, since foreigners seemed to be both powerful and sophisticated. To these so very "civilized" interlocutors, who appeared to be familiar with good manners as well as with astonishing inventions, the Japanese did not want to seem barbaric.

In fact, before this modern encounter, the reputation of the Japanese in the West was one of the highest among the people of non-European origin, as even Marco Polo's sentence quoted earlier shows. Nonetheless, we have much evidence that making a favorable impression on foreigners, particularly Western foreigners, became a strong, almost obsessive, concern for the Japanese during the final decades of the nineteenth century. There are many present-day indications that such a concern still endures.

## Two Meiji-Period Strategies

One of the strategies adopted by the Japanese to protect themselves from the criticism of Westerners was to assimilate their basic rules of moral conduct to Western standards while avoiding converting to Christianity. Ethics, then, severed from any transcendental link, was considered simply a set of principles guiding the behavior of the Western bourgeoisie, whose ultimate expression was considered to be— and not by the Japanese alone—the German family and state.

The second strategy, which became another official guideline for the Meiji reformers, was to adopt as the national cultural tradition that of its highest social class, the samurai. Samurai behavior, and also samurai sentiments, ideals, and emotions, had to become the invented inheritance of the entire population. Among the many Buddhist traditions that had arrived from the Asian continent, the samurai had adopted the most austere, most aesthetically refined version, the Chinese Ch'an, called Zen in Japanese. The rigid Ch'an ethical principles for private and public conduct molded the Bushido, the ethical code of the samurai. But the young samurai who were leading the modernization of Japan also relied heavily on another tradition of Chinese origin, Confucianism, which was a more explicit guide to proper conduct in all roles within the family and within the state at large as an extension of the family.

The combination of these two strategies produced a strong new code that formed the foundations of the social contract of modern Japan, which has been efficaciously called "bourgeois Confucianism."

Social relations between sexes and sexual behavior itself were the focus of modern Japanese ethics, which departed from traditional behavior patterns of the majority of the population. The majority was a rural one, whose "free" behavior is testified to by contemporary literary and other historical sources. Repressed behavior in this and other areas of conduct was now considered virtuous, not in the religious Christian sense, but as a Confucian social (or even filial) virtue; repressed sexuality was thus seen as contributing to the internal harmony of the group and a positive external image.

## Bourgeois Respectability, Confucian-Style

These are the historical premises of the present-day negative value judgments many Japanese hold regarding supposedly typical Italian behavior. This goes for Italian men's conduct toward women in particular and, in general, any distinctly individualistic form of expression. In the framework of Confucianism, individualism is a social sin in itself, since it is a refusal to repress personal desires and goals for the sake of collective harmony and strength. By contrast, the cult of the individual had its highest aesthetic, political, and philosophical investiture much before the European Enlightenment, and under many diverse forms, during the Italian Renaissance.

The rules of bourgeois respectability set up during the Meiji period still remain the guidelines for what is considered proper behavior in Japan; they are also the guidelines for disapproval of other kinds of behavior. In particular, the negative judgments given by the *Dime* readers regarding what they considered typical expressions of the Italian character are a precise expression of those Meiji rules.

But bourgeois respectability, European and Confucian alike, allows a special status to artists—provided they are recognized as such according to certain accepted activities, genres, and modes of expression. Although artists are not particularly high in the social ranks, they are somehow privileged. This privilege consists mainly in the limited social acceptance of deviant individual behavior. Behavior patterns other than the average are considered somehow expedient to the expression of the artist's ideas and sentiments, the bizarre side of qualities that may also contain great social value.

## The "Good" Individualism of the Italian Renaissance

Italians enjoy a worldwide reputation for artistic creativity, especially in music and in the visual arts. In terms of intercultural communication, these particular cultural productions have the great advantage that, although they obviously depend on culture-specific references, they do not need to be translated. As far as Japanese culture in particular is concerned, painting, sculpture, music, and even architecture are not considered its major traditional artistic expressions; such an honor goes instead to pottery, calligraphy, and flower arrangement. With the advent of Meiji modernization, the Japanese felt themselves free to appreciate Western artistic production without placing an appreciation of their own traditional art forms—which could not tolerate comparisons with foreign ones—at risk.

The first Japanese visitors to Europe, being fearful both of foreigners and of making a bad impression, did not dare to move about in the countryside in search of the monuments of the ancient past. Thus limiting their observations to what they could see in metropolitan museums, these travelers were astonished to see what for them were very strange subjects: nudes and religious figures. They were surprised to notice the great importance given to three-dimensionality in European statuary. They admired enormously the technical virtuosity they found in European art. Since then, Japanese people have never stopped visiting Italian museums, except during the years of World War II.

By looking at the travel guides they use and by listening to their comments, I find that Japanese visitors to Italy generally have a clear preference for a single period of Italian art history: the Renaissance. This preference is obviously one they share with many other tourists. Nonetheless, I think that the Japanese see the Italian Renaissance as being connected in a particular way with their own cultural values: it is the good side, so to speak, of individualism.

A Japanese person may easily get lost in the enormous diversity of artistic schools and cultural worlds expressed in the fourteenth and fifteenth centuries by the sociopolitical units that were the Italian cities, often but a few miles one from another: Florence, Siena, Urbino, Perugia. . . . But she or he sees expressed in these schools the work of extraordinarily talented people in the service of their own closely knit social group, which is a Confucian ideal. She or he also sees the importance given to handicraft as not separated from art and to the *signore*, who, like some of the shogun, is simultaneously a military man, an enlightened leader, and a lover and patron of the arts.

In order to accelerate Japanese assimilation of some Western social values, the Meiji leaders sent missions abroad with the task of studying social institutions and arts and sciences in different Western countries. The information thus acquired was to be used in deciding which society excelled in one institution or another and subsequently in adopting this or that foreign system. Meiji modernization thus included the adoption of French school districts, the American university system, German civil law, and British naval organization and public transportation systems. Italy, the Meiji leaders decided, was good for art.

The Iwakura Mission went to Europe between 1871 and 1873. In May 1873, their representatives visited Florence, where they admired the monuments and showed a marked interest in the production of mosaics, marbles, pottery and porcelain (at the famous Ginori factory, in particular), and silkworms and the silk industry. The Iwakura mission's visit increased Japanese interest in Italian art and artists. Some Italian artists, in fact, were invited to exhibit their work in Japan and to teach in some of Japan's best art schools. The painter Antonio Fontanesi, the sculptor Vincenzo Ragusa, and the engraver Edoardo Chiossone (who later became a noted collector of Eastern art), for example, thus spent significant periods of time in Japan.

## A Champion of Exotic Voyeurism

Probably the most prominent, and simultaneously the most mysterious, Italian figure in the Japanese visual arts world of the nineteenth century was Felice Beato—who changed his first name to Felix when he became a British citizen (Zannier 1986, 73). In 1863, several years before Japan officially became open to foreigners, Beato already had a photography studio in Yokohama. There he pursued an intense activity as a portraitist and documentary photographer, founding a school whose style and technical skills influenced early Japanese photographers such as Kusakabe Kimbei and Uyeno Kikoma.

Beato is the author of two albums of photographs: *Views of Japan* and *Native Types*, published in Yokohama in 1868. The first is an exemplary genre documentation of landscapes, houses, temples, rural life, and city life; the second is a visual taxonomy of what Beato found to be exotic human specimens, classified according to their social roles.

Beato would bring these "human types," as he called them, into his studio and photograph them in stylized postures, according to his own taste, in front of painted screens suggesting the interiors of various homes—those of a craftsman, for example, a landlord, or a geisha. One of his Japanese collaborators—immortalized as "our painter" in one of Beato's photographs—later tinted the prints with delicate watercolors.

The portraits are a remarkable example of exoticism, both in the sense of an anthropological fake and in that of a sophisticated European aesthetic fashion. They are simultaneously the forerunners of kitsch and the heirs of a Venetian tradition of portraits and domestic scenes (we do not know exactly where and when Felice and his brother Antonio—also an avid traveler and a pioneer of the art of photography—were born, but certainly it was somewhere in the Veneto region, if not in Venice itself).

Felice was also a daring photoreporter, taking shots of public executions, for example. In 1864, he managed to get what was a thrillingly dangerous scoop: he photographed the shogun, in spite of a severe prohibition against doing so, shortly before the shogun's fall from power. For twenty years thereafter, Beato was busy determining the images of Japan that were to become the lenses through which Italians and Westerners in general would build a stereotypical, exotic idea of that country and its culture.

## Those "Wonderful Fools"

Symmetrically enough, the Japanese perception of Italy and the Italians is constructed in similar ways, through stereotyped, artfully colored portraits of Italian artists and villains. A voyeuristic attraction, we might say, exists on both sides.

In both past and present history, it is well known that consumer goods have to be presented to the Japanese public with special care so as to look particularly desirable. Such care includes a sophisticated art of wrapping and displaying. Most of all, however, attention must be given to labels. There is a craze for labels in Japan. Foreign labels in particular are extremely attractive because of their exotic flavor and even more because signs of foreign style and ways of life mark a person as educated in Western cultural values.

This labelmania has its own European champions, many of whom are Italians. Fashion and industrial design have expanded the scope of expression of individual talent beyond the classical categories of art, where the Italians had already acquired a strong reputation. Armani and Versace for clothes, and Giugiaro and Pininfarina for cars, are, in the eyes of the Japanese, the Renaissance artists of today. To wear or to drive something designed—and signed—by these modern artists is a way to participate in something at the height of creative sophistication, something special, something worth bringing home from abroad.

In Japanese stereotypes of Italians, this is the accepted "good" side of Italian individualism. It constitutes the positive aspects of the reputation of Italians in Japan. Because of this, the Japanese image of an idealized inhabitant of Italy as a *baka* works, not in the sense of "stupid," but in that of "wonderful fool." "Wonderful fool," in fact, is a brilliant translation of an ambiguous Japanese term. The translator may never have realized how her talent would resolve the *baka* poll intercultural misunderstanding, and prevent it from becoming even a diplomatic incident.

## The Unbalanced Anthropologist

Anthropology has recurrently based its attempt to acquire scientific status as a cultural translator on a careful reference to firsthand collected data. Accurate ethnography is thus the necessary guarantee for any theoretical construction; the anthropologist follows an inductive process from the observation of single events to their generalization as social facts. But inside this heuristic path from fieldwork to analysis and interpretation there is often tension, if not conflict, between a tendency to stick cautiously to the "facts" and a desire to move toward the "meaning" of human social expressions. At one extreme, the anthropologist runs into the danger of empiristic reification; at the other, of rationalistic or idealistic abstractions unconnected from any culturally specific context (Sollors 1989).

In the case in which we look for our own culture's images in another cultural context, we cannot confidently rely on the objective power of evidence; the "facts" are elsewhere, and we are confronted with an image that cannot but appear to us as a shadow of our culture seen from afar. In this healthy imbalanced position, having before us a hardly recognizable, displaced image of something with which we are linked through an alien eye, we are doubly free from cultural reification. Here it becomes evident that we cannot always easily superimpose facts and their interpretations, that images can cross cultural boundaries to acquire elsewhere a different status and a different meaning.

At the same time, from our imbalanced, displaced position, we are not considering only the play, or interplay, of mental processes, however carefully culturally referred; we thus do not lose touch with the "hard facts." What is at stake is not confined to the ethic or aesthetic domain but directly influences the centers of social power. Japanese stereotypes about Italians not only lead to the moral condemnation of the latter as poor workers and overly enthusiastic lovers; they also make Italians desirable as designers of the bodies of Toyotas and Hondas. Thanks to Italian design, sales of these cars increase both in the West and in Japan. Here, then, we see the synthesizing power of the stereotyping processes at work: an image conventionally thought to condense qualities characteristic of another culture acquires a strong exchange value, superimposing meaning on the circulation of ideas as well as of commodities.

We see, therefore, that crossing boundaries in multiple ways can help Western thought to free itself from one of its obsessions, that of being trapped inside its own processes of knowledge and interpretation. Intercultural, intersubjective play is now increasingly open at a global level. The Western observer—the anthropologist in particular, as a specialist of intercultural relations—having left behind her or his past imperialist attitude, finds herself or himself in the position of the Other, the Exotic. The Westerner is no longer a detached "butterfly collector," as Westerners were sarcastically defined by Edmund Leach, nor a seduced seducer of a faraway culture like Pinkerton in Puccini's *Madama Butterfly*. And the Japanese are no longer, if ever they were, passive subjects of our Italian orientalism, looking West for the unlikely rise of a *fil di fumo*.[4]

Translated by Beverly Allen

## Notes

1. For other instances of such cultural refraction, see Elaine Chang and Mary Russo in this volume.—*Ed.*

2. While finding his analysis extremely stimulating, I take a different stand here from that of Edward Said when he writes, "To speak of scholarly specialization as a geographical 'field' is, in the case of Orientalism, fairly revealing since *no one is likely to imagine a field symmetrical to it called Occidentalism*" (Said 1979, 50; my emphasis). This is not a matter of disagreement; it is, rather, a question of different historical, geographical, and social facts taken into consideration under the same referential terms.

3. The Meiji revolution is referred to as both a restoration and a modernization, a fact that may seem contradictory to a Westerner. Historically, this is simple to explain. The first term refers to the reconquest of the political leadership of the nation by the emperor after a long period of military rule by the shogun. It was the emperor, then, who opened the doors of "traditional" Japan to the "modern" (Western) world. We should also take into account, however, that this opening was the result not only of an internal political confrontation under enormous pressure from the outside by the Westerners (the famous black warships of the American Commodore Perry). There was, at the same time, a cultural debate among Japanese intellectuals who subscribed to the *joi* theses ("barbarians, go home") and those who subscribed to the *kaikoku* ("open the country") thesis. The *joi* faction supported the shogun, while the *kaikoku* faction supported the emperor (Morishima). When the fifteen-year-old emperor came to power in 1868, the accompanying social changes in Japan were both a (political) restoration and a (cultural) modernization. In order to most rapidly achieve this second goal, Japan followed the road of Westernization with notable determination. At the same time, however, the new imperial regime wanted to appear as the legitimate restorer of national traditions. In order to accommodate both goals, the regime engaged in a process of cultural engineering and a careful invention of tradition (Hobsbawm and Ranger 1983).

4. "Ribbon of smoke," what Madame Butterfly yearns to see in the homonymous opera: a sign of the Western ship and Pinkerton's return.—*Trans.*

## Works Cited

Alberoni, Francesco. 1986. "Ma i Giapponesi sono davvero diventati perfetti?" (But have the Japanese really become perfect?). *Corriere della Sera*, December 1, 1.

Boscaro, Adriana. 1976. "Sul contrasto tra 'eroe' e 'baka' nell'ultimo dramma di Endo Shusaku" (On the contrast between "hero" and "baka" in the late theater of Endo Shusaku). *Annali della facoltà di lingue e letterature straniere di Ca' Foscari* 15:3: 141–57.

Camon, Ferdinando. 1986. "L'italiano stupido 'made in Japan'" (The stupid Italian made in Japan). *Il Giorno*, November 23, 1.

Granzotto, Paolo. 1986. "Buona la predica, discutibile il pubblico" (The sermon was good, the public, debatable). *Il Giornale*, November 23, 1.

Hobsbawm, E. J., and Terence Ranger, eds. 1983. *The Invention of Tradition.* Cambridge: Cambridge University Press.

Maraini, Fosco. 1992. *Italia e Giappone. Incontri e reincontri attraverso i secoli. Prolusione per il conferimento della laurea honoris causa.* University of Siena, May 23.

Mathy, Francis. 1974. *Wonderful Fool.* London: Peter Owen.

Morishima, Michio. 1982. *Why Has Japan Succeeded? Western Technology and the Japanese Ethos.* Cambridge: Cambridge University Press.

Pisu, Renata. 1986a. "Ci guasta il clima troppo dolce" (The too-good climate spoils us). *La Stampa*, November 22.

———. 1986b. "Tokyo–Roma andata e ritorno con un Jumbo di luoghi comuni" (Tokyo–Rome round trip with a jumbo of commonplaces). *La Stampa*, December 5.

Polo, Marco. *Il Milione* (The million). 1975. Ed. V. B. Pizorusso. Milan: Adelphi. 154–55.

Said, Edward W. 1979. *Orientalism.* New York: Vintage Books.

Sollors, Werner, ed. 1989. *The Invention of Ethnicity.* Oxford: Oxford University Press.

Takeyama, Hakuei. 1987. "Itariajin wa Hontoni Sekai ichi Baka Nanoka." *Asahi Journal*, January 23, 22–24.

Zannier, Italo. 1986. *Verso Oriente. Fotografie di Antonio e Felice Beato* (Toward the East: photographs by Antonio and Felice Beato). Ed. Paolo Costantini. Florence: Alinari.

# Spaghetti Eastern: Mutating Mass Culture, Transforming Ethnicity

*Elaine K. Chang*

## The Greening of the "All-American" Child

To borrow one of *Sesame Street*'s trademark devices, this essay is brought to you by several pasta products made in the USA, and by the color green. Chef Boyardee, Spaghetti-o's, and the "heroes on the half shell" after whom a turtle-shaped macaroni and cheese dish has been named reveal much about the processes of mass culture—particularly those by which ethnicity is remade and merchandised as something millions of Americans might want to eat. Artificial flavors and colors play a critical role in these processes; and recent history offers green as the most recognized and serviceable multipurpose signifier for human(oid) "otherness." Rubbery of mouth, malleable of body, and uniformly brilliant from misshapen head to foot, Gumby got the ball rolling in the 1960s: "He was once a little green blob of clay, but you should see what Gumby can do today." *Sesame Street*'s Kermit the Frog and his message—"it's not easy being green"—have spoken to at least two generations of children struggling for acceptance and distinction in a less than tolerant world. And in the early 1990s, the popularity of the Teenage Mutant Ninja Turtles (or call them macaroni) across four continents has been bruited as a triumph in color-blind multiculturalism: "they're not black, or white; they're green!"

The green evolution suggested by these three productions calls attention to processes of transformation and mutation, and not merely in terms of the technologies (claymation, animation, and animatronics) that have brought them to "life." Like Donna Haraway's "cyborg," Gumby, Kermit, and the Turtles embody a number of boundary con-

292

fusions, and call into question a multiplicity of determining categories,[1] "green-washing" them into irrelevance or irreverence—or, alternatively, into new forms and combinations possibly better adapted to the shifting demographics of the contemporary world. This essay asks how ethnicity in particular fares in such a wash, and focuses on the hybrid merger of "Italian" and "Japanese" ethnic identities represented by America's most celebrated green teens: Leonardo, Donatello, Michelangelo, and Raphael. The mutation of the Ninja Turtles from other cultural forms, from the waste products of late twentieth-century consumer society, and from the profusion of effects that have come to signify ethnic difference suggests a surprisingly complex allegory of multiculturalism—and one that may be seen both to collude with and to resist the exigencies of the latter-day culture industry.

By one definition, "mutation" may well be synonymous with profit capitalization, reinvestment in proven market successes, minor variations on the old resold to captivated consumers under the imprimatur of the new. As Max Horkheimer and Theodor Adorno described this "mass deception": "the conformism of the buyers and the effrontery of the producers who supply them prevail. The result is a constant reproduction of the same thing."[2] The reproduction of the pizza-loving, freedom-fighting, sewer-inhabiting, postnuclear, semiamphibian foursome has been not only constant, but explosive. The Teenage Mutant Ninja Turtles have mutated beyond their 1983 origins in comic books to spawn replications of themselves in toys, a cartoon series, and three motion pictures (the third, released in 1993 and which I will not discuss here, transports the Turtles to feudal Japan). They have also cut an album (which went gold in one week, selling only at Pizza Hut locations), and made televised appearances with Oprah Winfrey, Barbara Walters, Joan Rivers, and Robin Leach. Their names and likenesses have launched more than five thousand licensed products: action figures (of which 90 percent of American boys between the ages of three and eight in the 1980s purchased at least one, according to industry estimates),[3] clothing, school supplies, bedclothes, bath products, training toilets, and food items that—in addition to the aforementioned macaroni and cheese—include breakfast cereal, cream pies, flavored ices, and crunchy snacks. By November 1991, gross receipts from the Turtles had exceeded $2.5 billion.

"Turtle Power," in other words, has meant big green for corporations such as New Line Cinema, Playmates Toys, and Ralston-Purina.

And "freak" commercial success has had the aftereffect of conferring mythical status on the monied potentates who took their chances with an unlikely product. Paeans to these business mavericks are intriguing for their rhetoric, which reproduces Turtles iconology but with money doing most of the talking. Golden Harvest International's Raymond Chow has, for example, become an entrepreneurial legend, owing to his decision to finance the blockbuster *Turtles I* after all U.S. film studios had rejected it. Like the Turtles' own benefactor, Splinter the rat, the president of the Hong Kong–based company is cast repeatedly as a kindly, wise, and unassuming Asian male—a stereotype we will have reason and occasion to examine further—who came to the rescue of an orphan project and nurtured it to prosperity. The exotic and charitable qualities projected onto this "soft-spoken and modest mogul" are nevertheless reanchored in the familiar ideologies of global big business: "Everyone wants to do something wonderful that will be praised by the critics," Chow has said, "but first and foremost it is our duty to please the man on the street."[4]

Paternalism and opportunism work hand in hand, hand over fist, in the culture industry's sworn duty to please the man (more accurately, the boy) on the street and remain true to the character of its product.[5] The circularity of these posturings, and the effrontery of the process, is perhaps nowhere more conspicuous than in the ongoing commodification of ethnicity as "newness" and "difference." The Turtles' pizza-shaped marshmallows—the distinguishing ingredient of a cereal otherwise not all that different from the vaguely Irish-identified, "magically delicious" Frosted Lucky Charms—and pizza-flavored Crunchabungas are characteristic stylizations of ethnicity: "differences" reduced and repackaged as interchangeable simulacra of cultural groups, practices, and traditions. The food chain and the simulacral chain intertwine, each the engine for the other in one tautological process of deferred significations: in shape and in flavor, processed edibles resemble pizza; pizza evokes "Italian food"; Italian food represents the orientation of the American palate toward a variety of "different" taste sensations; different taste sensations demand different shapes and flavors. And so "difference" continually defers, reproduces, and cannibalizes itself within the same standardized economy of reference.

And yet, in supplanting the "All-American" hot dog as the nation's democratizing food, pizza (in all of its "real" and simulated shapes and flavors) does signify a historic shift in American sensibilities about race and ethnicity. The Fordist dream of total ethnic assimilation into the American "melting pot" has given way, according to Werner Sollors, to a national celebration of individual and collective differences: "In America, casting oneself as an outsider may in fact be considered a dominant cultural trait. . . . Every American is now considered a potential ethnic."[6] No longer derived exclusively from the processes of *descent*—heredity, kinship, affiliations with authentic or organic communities and groups—ethnic and cultural identity is now transformed by mechanisms and freedoms of *consent*, which stress "our abilities as mature free agents and 'architects of our fates' to choose our spouses, our destinies, and our political systems."[7]

Somewhat less willing to embrace these developments, Vivian Sobchack has located and analyzed the implications of Sollors's "consensual" model of ethnic identity and representation in the specific context of American consumer culture: "We can put ourselves together in almost any fashion we like—and our self-consciousness about so inventing ourselves tends to be reflected in the fact that the fashion we like asserts this 'right of representation' through pastiche or parody."[8] The Teenage Mutant Ninja Turtles are (hyper)active participants in the processes that Sobchack describes, scavenging and ironizing a varied range of ethnically marked "fashions": pizza, martial-arts movies, Godzilla and Gamera movies, the beat boxes and gang colors of inner-city youth culture, rap music, heavy metal chains, the skateboards and surfer-speak of the young southern California middle class. Differentiation by consent renders particularized identities, histories, and communities literally inessential from the perspectives both of an industry that has plenty of cultural effects it recycles and recombines to its profit and of consumers eager to remake themselves beyond confining biological and cultural determinations.

## Mutation and Surrogacy: Identities by Choice?

Whereas the former perspective suggests the expropriation, manipulation and denial of ethnic specificity under capitalist social conditions, the latter may posit mutation as the reinscription of ethnicity as a category more "user-friendly" to multiply constituted, contradictorily identified subjects. As both approaches continue to inform my interpretation of four overdetermined teenagers and one equally overdetermined adult, I will also pursue a third, related line of questioning: a reading whereby "free-floating" ethnic signifiers, detached from their original roots and nominal human constituencies, ultimately refer only to one another, and are marshaled, precisely in their capacity as free-floating and interchangeable signifiers, toward old and new mythologies of identity and difference, of insiders and outsiders. These mythologies can be seen to serve a range of social, cultural, and economic interests at given historical moments.

A process mystified from its "inception" or "discovery" in scientific discourses, mutation in the postmodern cultural context suggests innumerable fantastic possibilities for the (re)generation of new life-forms through nonconventional means. Among the many avenues offered by mutation, both the Teenage Mutant Ninja Turtles and one of their most significant intertexts, *The Karate Kid*, seize upon the possibility of reproduction by accident or coincidence as the structural premise for their stories, as well as a powerful cultural metaphor authorizing the realignment or abandonment of biologically and historically given determinations. A preferred figure or vehicle for mutation-as-reproduction in both cases is surrogacy—a term that generally serves to name the act of substituting one thing, person, or attribute for another, and that acquires particular reproductive connotations when applied to these two cultural events. Even before a displaced white ethnic teenager first meets his Asian mentor on-screen—and well before four helpless mutant turtles are discovered, adopted, and christened by a humanoid rat—crucial substitutions have taken place; ethnic and other "identities" have been established, determined in advance, more in adherence to well-known and well-worn Hollywood formulas than to anything else.

Amputated of their "real-life" contexts and associations, ethnicity, nationality, class, and sexuality are furthermore made to operate as surrogate categories for one another; each category is at stake, or elided, in every other category. Surrogacy also helps to describe the often complicated relationships between hybrid texts and intertexts that have helped bring the Turtles and the Karate Kid into being and on the screen, where both have demonstrated an astonishing capacity to reproduce themselves as film sequels. As its interwoven ethnic, class, and gender politics would suggest, *The Karate Kid* intertextually derives from such late 1970s Hollywood hits as *Saturday Night Fever*, *Rocky*, and *Breaking Away*.[9] And characteristics of these films can be seen to manifest themselves, as if phenotypically, in the sons of the Karate Kid: they who have been also called the "bastard progeny of E.T."[10] From their several cinematic grandfathers, or godfathers, the Teenage Mutant Ninja Turtles have derived some important affectations and distinguishing marks. Raphael's film accent (as distinct from his cartoon accent) is recognizable as "New York Italian" by its diluted resemblance to that of Rocky Balboa (i.e., Sylvester Stallone); and screen legacies of fighting, dancing, and competition in general have apparently been assimilated or inherited by all four Turtles as ready-made means by which to express and reconcile emotions, conflicts, and differences.

To *The Karate Kid*, the Ninja Turtles owe additional allusions they rework into their teenage mutant pastiche of pop culture references. "Wax on, wax off," for instance, is a code phrase from *The Karate Kid* quoted during a housecleaning scene in *Teenage Mutant Ninja Turtles II: The Secret of the Ooze* (1991). As may be the case with a multitude of "postmodernist" gestures toward "blank parody,"[11] including most of the Turtles' allusions, the ironic humor consists exclusively in the phrase's capacity as a quotation out of context, which a viewer either "gets" or does not. But far and away the most significant legacy *The Karate Kid* has passed on to the Turtles is a literal model of surrogate parenthood, one that crosses ethnic, national, and (in the case of the Turtles) species affiliations and boundaries. Both cultural productions feature close relations between biologically unrelated father and son figures; the men are Japanese-identified martial-arts masters, the boys adopted and tutored by them are free-wheeling teenagers endowed with (for the most part, residual or attenuated) Italian American characteristics. Within the immediate context of these father-son relationships, and the wider context of mass cultural mutation and surrogacy, culture industry machinations, consensual ideologies of ethnic identification and representation, and the "free play" of ethnic signifiers can all be seen to converge.

## *The Karate Kid* as "Master Text"

With the last of the opening credits to *The Karate Kid* (1984), Danny LaRusso (Ralph Macchio) and his widowed mother, Lucille (Randee Heller), are in the process of leaving their neighborhood in Newark, New Jersey. The beat-up station wagon that will serve as a shorthand sign of their class status throughout the film is loaded up with all their worldly possessions. The first dialogue of the movie belongs to Mrs. LaRusso: through the car window, she asks a female relative to "Tell Uncle Louie the red wine's in the refrigerator," before she and Danny wave good-bye to the relatives who have gathered to see them off. Although the presence of red wine in a refrigerator may be unfamiliar to some viewers, the codes contributing to the movie's opening are not. A mother, surrounded by extended family, assumes supervisory responsibility over food and drink; she is thus and in a matter of seconds cast specifically as an Italian mother.

Among Danny's first acquaintances upon arrival in the at once menacing and promising brave new world (i.e., the San Fernando Valley) is Mr. Miyagi (Noriyuki "Pat" Morita), fix-it man for the South Seas apartment complex. Wanting to arrange the repair of a leaky faucet, Danny peeks into a dimly lit area cluttered with tools; a white-haired man, his back to the door and a scarf tied around his head, is seated cross-legged on the floor, snapping at the air with a pair of chopsticks and an attitude of silent concentration. This concatenation of effects, accompanied by the sound track's austere pan-flute melody, ensures Danny's, and the audience's, identification of Morita's character as some kind of (not very assimilated) Asian immigrant. If his head scarf—similar to that worn by sushi chefs and Mickey Rooney (in his bucktoothed, overblown portrayal of the caricatured Mr. Yunioshi in Blake Edwards's *Breakfast at Tiffany's* [1961])—fails to jog further associations, Miyagi's work on bonsai trees helps to specify what kind of Asian he is. ("Are you from Japan?" Danny asks. "No. Okinawa," replies Miyagi, punctuating the difference with reference to a map he devises in the air. The distinction Miyagi makes, as well as the bonsai trees, will prove additionally significant in several respects.)

The close relationship that develops between the fatherless boy and childless man—facilitated by Danny's intense, if heretofore untutored, interest in karate and Miyagi's considerable prowess in the martial arts—exploits stereotypical representations of Italian American and Japanese males, setting up and undoing oppositions between the two types. A softer, more impressionable variation on Rocky Balboa and Tony Manero, Danny has nevertheless also been socialized to equate masculinity with physical strength and force, and shows passion and stubborn persistence in his emotions and his loyalties. As such, Danny fulfills, at least initially and in miniature, the sociocultural function allocated to the Italian American working-class hero who emerged in late 1970s movies.[12]

In contrast to the characteristics projected onto Danny, Miyagi (known to us, and to Danny, by his patronym only—and even that proves a pronunciational challenge for Danny and other white characters) is a paragon of the virtues attributed to the so-called model minority: gentleness, silence, modesty, self-discipline, respect for all things and all people, and a capacity to accept hardships as they come with grace. He also represents the not so prized stereotypical traits: his inscrutability and ability to bark orders recall the Japanese generals portrayed and demonized in World War II propaganda films. That Miyagi has created, with his own hands, an architectural and botanical wonder of a private residence, far from the South Seas and behind an abandoned oil derrick, speaks to the contradictory admirations and anxieties that generate the stereotypes. On the one hand, the Japanese can create paradise and prosperity wherever they are, even in concentration camps. On the other hand, they're so sneaky and subtle about it that their activities should be scrutinized at all times. Miyagi's litany, "Not everything is as seem," seems coined to support both perceptions.

Across the Italian American and the Japanese types Danny and Miyagi represent, the kind of balance to which Miyagi continually refers is, in a sense, achieved: Miyagi's lessons and examples in self-control, sensitivity, and interior strength serve to temper Danny's hotheaded side, and his more openly combative approach to big problems; Miyagi also prompts Danny to remember his mother. Danny, on the other hand, can bring a smile to Miyagi's poker face, move the composed sensei to raucous laughter, and even (by the end of *The Karate Kid III* [1989]) encourage him to forsake his habitual polite bow in favor of a big hug. Together, they create a spectacle of love, American family-style, that synthesizes the coziest and most desirable elements of Italian and Japanese personalities as they have been perceived and received through popular film.

## The Teenage Mutant Ninja Turtles: Bastard Genealogies

If the relationship between Danny LaRusso and Mr. Miyagi distills ostensibly incompatible Italian and Japanese ethnic stereotypes into a "new" and "cool" hybrid version, the newer, cooler ninja turtle mutation renders the troublesome implications of the "original" formula grossly explicit. Problematics arise not simply or straightforwardly owing to the fact that the paternal Asian sensei figure in the Turtles mythology happens to be a rat. The Turtles' history is dauntingly complex—not only because they derive from so many, often invisible, pop culture referents, but also because the movies, cartoons, and comic books offer conflicting accounts. A key variation involves Splinter the rat. The cartoon series alleges that he is originally a human ninja master who mutates during a nuclear explosion into rodent form. In the movies, he starts out as a rat, the devoted pet of Japan's most accomplished ninja master (from whom he learns the art); together with the turtles, Splinter grows incredibly in size and intelligence after contact with radioactive ooze, carelessly dumped into a sewer. The comic book offers the most complicated genesis story of the three: a former samurai, wrongfully banished from his clan and compelled to take residence in a New York sewer, is transformed by "a powerful mutagen—one that caused whoever touched it to take on the form of whatever creature they had most recently been in contact with." He had been playing with rats, while four turtles had been playing with him.

Although I omit full details, what seems to matter is not whether Splinter has his origins in the human or the animal world, but rather that he be qualified to perform his Miyagi-like function: to play surrogate father and instructor of "true ninja" to his four sons, "straight man" to their wisecracks, and example in the arts of balanced living. Also consistent across all accounts is that Splinter christens the turtles after four artists in a Renaissance art book he finds in a storm drain. The names are themselves a by-product of surrogacy and a parable for the noninnocent "origins" and permutations of ethnicized mass culture. On the mythified night in 1983 when struggling comic book artists Peter Laird and Kevin Eastman "accidentally" came up with the inspiration to conflate a "slowpokey turtle" and a "swift and wily ninja," the two originally found themselves at a loss for names. As to why they finally hit upon Leonardo, Donatello, Raphael, and Michelangelo, Eastman explains: "The characters should have Japanese names, but we knew we couldn't come up with convincing ones, so we decided to go way in the other direction."[13]

"Convincing" is no doubt a relative term in the restricted economy of ethnic signifiers, as are the possibilities of either achieving ethnic appropriateness or going "way in the other direction." The comic and exotic resonance of Italian(ish) names ending in the letter "o" enjoys an extensive history in American popular culture, which provisionally originates, intriguingly enough, in comic-strip form.[14] Whether or not their creators were aware of this genealogy—and although, or perhaps because, the Turtles' passion for pizza was added in the crossover to television—Leonardo, Donatello, Raphael, and Michelangelo play largely predetermined roles in what are ultimately minimal adjustments to mass culture's repertory of ethnic cultural effects. The vowel "o" is made to spin out some of its metoynymic associations, ostensibly by happenstance, by the one who lacks the appendage: Raphael is the designated rebel of the foursome, the one who leaves the group to brood or get into scrapes. After one such departure in *Turtles II*, Donatello remarks that "all the good ones end in 'o'!"[15]

Apart from Raphael's occasional defections, the four Turtles and their mentor manage to patch together family life in the sewer, and later in an abandoned yet fully equipped subway station. They are initially unknown to humans living above ground in New York City— and their reticence to reveal themselves and mix numbers among Splinter's prescriptions for modest and unassuming living. An exception to this code is all five's friendship with April O'Neil, a TV news reporter and the only woman to figure in the Turtles' adventures and intermittent, highly qualified sexual fantasies (apart, that is, from the supermodel, Paulina Porizkova, whose pinup poster—the commodified surrogate for the commodified female body—appears in *Turtles II* with her permission). The Turtles spend most of their time watching television, playing games like Trivial Pursuit, swapping witticisms and hip locutions, eating pizza—and fighting the forces of evil whenever and wherever possible.

## Good and Evil: Masculinity Meets Technology

The stark confrontations that are staged between "the forces of good" and "the forces of evil" in both *The Karate Kid* and *Teenage Mutant Ninja Turtles* are fairly typical of their genres; such confrontations are frequent, and there is never any doubt as to who's good, and rarely any doubt as to who's not good. The Manichaean opposition traditionally associated with superhero comic books, their surrogates, and their legatees proves quite slippery, however, in both cases. As if in anticipation or acknowledgment of the end of the Cold War, the movies (which span the period from 1984 to 1990) conspicuously lack ideological or political megavillains. In other words, there are no Nazis or Communists. Yet, in continuing to devise formally mandated representatives of absolute evil, both *The Karate Kid* and the *Teenage Mutant Ninja Turtles* cycle are actively involved in the production and reproduction of national, and global, enemies. The movies' quite frenzied, at times fractured, interpenetration of militarism, technology, and economic activity, for instance, manages to provide a remarkably consistent gloss to U.S. relations with Japan, past and present.

In *The Karate Kid I*, the opposition between good and evil is developed through various contrasts. Miyagi, who preaches karate as the art of the "empty hand," to be used against an opponent only in self-defense, is juxtaposed with another sensei figure, Kreese (Martin Kove) of the Cobra Kai dojo. Kreese's doctrine is one of "no mercy"; his dojo is run like boot camp; he trains his affluent students in flamboyant, commodified karate (at rates prohibitively expensive for Danny LaRusso), and expects them to win tournaments at any cost. Danny and the upper-middle-class Cobras contrasted with him faithfully replicate their teachers' philosophies in typically teenage form: although Danny avoids physical confrontation at school and elsewhere, the Cobras (who always move in a pack) are motiveless thugs, relentless in their persecution of the scrawny foreigner (i.e., New York ethnic), and by degrees his "pet Nip."[16] This type of opposition, between good and evil martial-arts instructors, desirable and undesirable role models for male youth, is central to all three Karate Kid movies and both Ninja Turtles movies. The extended contrasts between good and bad father figures, and all their good and bad sons, neatly frame the choice the films extend to their viewers: what is genuine masculinity, and what sort of man is a boy to become?[17]

*The Karate Kid* sets its contest over "authentic" masculinity in part against a backdrop of military service. Kreese is a Vietnam War veteran, and as his shrine of photographs and medals would suggest, proud of it; his service in a lost or dishonorable war is simultaneously blamed upon and responsible for his sham version of masculinity. By scapegoating discrete veterans—including Kreese's army buddy in *Kid III*—for their projected pathological traits, *The Karate Kid* clearly encourages a mass disowning of U.S. participation in the Vietnam War, so effectively "deglamorized" (and reconstituted) in advance by such late 1970s Hollywood movies as *The Deer Hunter*, *Coming Home*, and *Apocalypse Now*.

Miyagi, in contrast, served in the U.S. Army during World War II: a member of the most-decorated unit in that war, the all-Japanese American 442d regiment. About his stature as a war hero, Miyagi is characteristically modest and tight-lipped; and so it devolves upon Danny to mediate and translate the significance of Miyagi's past. While poring through his teacher's cache of effects and newspaper articles, Danny educates himself, and his audience, in world history and its personal inflections and tolls. Danny learns not only of Miyagi's distinguished service, but also of the deaths of his wife and son in the Manzanar "relocation center" during his assignment abroad. Bowing in awe before Miyagi's sleeping form, Danny manages to pay appropriate respects to "valor" (which does not discriminate, or so it is implied, according to race or nationality), and to sympathize with the human tragedy disclosed to him. This latter is represented as an "accident" of nature, inasmuch as Miyagi's wife and child are reported to have died during childbirth. If this sounds like another kind of national absolution, we must stay tuned for *The Karate Kid II* (1986).

Absolute good/evil distinctions are further played out through the representation of technology in all five films. Miyagi may be a technical wizard when it comes to tools and materials, but he prefers to do things simply, with his bare, and empty, hands. It would not occur to Miyagi to create anything sheerly for profit, and he shows no interest in the most fashionable and up-to-date commodities. Flashy cars abound in *The Karate Kid I*, but they belong mainly to the Cobras, also owners of fully loaded motorbikes that make for dramatic clashes with the solitary Danny on bicycle. Miyagi does, however, happen to own several automobiles, manufactured before the 1960s, which he keeps in mint condition. Impressed by the array, Danny asks, "Where did these cars come from?" Miyagi responds, "From Detroit."

Both Turtles movies help to clarify the message. Whereas Splinter is Miyagi's Asian ascetic to an extreme—his coat is in tatters, and despite the abundance of pizza, we never see him eating—his archrival, Shredder, represents the bad logics of capitalism gone totally out of control. Shredder's raison d'être in the first movie is to deploy his ranks of adopted sons ("juvenile delinquents" abandoned by everybody else, known under the collective rubric "The Foot") toward the theft of anything and everything. The illicit gains are stored and supervised in a labyrinthine underground lair, a dungeon-like setting also equipped with the video games and skateboard ramps by which

Shredder secures his teeming teenagers' acquiescence to his authority. "Your empire is growing, master," observes Shredder's henchman, the growling Tatsu, with obvious but inexplicable relish. Surveying the impressive stockpiles of televisions, stereos, and other high technological commodities, the adult viewer may well marvel that this accumulation makes no sense.

It makes too much sense, of course, in a broader economy of ethnic and national conflicts. With his chrome prongs and armor cybernetically fused to his face and body—Darth Vader, regurgitated, with a particularly samurai aftertaste—Shredder conflates and personifies the manifold evils of hypertechnological, globalizing capitalism. Like Kreese, Shredder represents commodified, and therefore contaminated, martial artistry, deployed for purposes of intimidation and conquest. Thus he serves as "other" to the Turtles' own techno-euphoria, posited, in contrast, as good. When Shredder's minions go out into the world to wreak their acts of terror and burglary, those teenagers—otherwise and visibly of all races, shapes, and sizes—wear depersonalizing, insect-like masks, equipped with almond-shaped mesh screens over the eyes. If there is any doubt as to what is being evoked by this spectacle, April O'Neil makes it explicit; accosted by the thugs in a subway station, she asks, "What, did I forget to make my Sony payment?"

As is suggested by Splinter's asceticism and Miyagi's admiration for American cars that predate the "Japanese Miracle," the Japanese male is an attractive type so long as he is shown to engage technology and capital in nonaggressive ways—ways that threaten neither American economic interests nor, by extension, white male egos. In the *Teenage Mutant Ninja Turtles* movies, the threatening Japanese "types" outnumber the good to the extent that Splinter comes off, really and truly, as a token or "pet." Distilling the model representative of the Asian minority and the Japanese nation in contradistinction to the "bad" ones is the project of *The Karate Kid II*, which takes Miyagi and Danny to Okinawa. In this locale, the heroes and their audiences face off against the evil Sato, an opponent armed with limousines, Italian suits, dark sunglasses, technologically enhanced karate moves, and a personal grudge against Miyagi that has not abated in the decades since his emigration to America. Sato is a proto-Shredder, not merely in his layered overaccumulation of expensive commodities and technologies, but in his revenge motives as well.[18]

Through Sato, we are, moreover, presented with the next installment of *The Karate Kid*'s re-visionary history of postwar relations between the United States and Japan. The transformation of Miyagi's home, Tomin Village, from a peaceful and picturesque seaside community to an American military base and commercial fishing and farming district is blamed squarely and by all concerned on the profit-seeking Sato, who subjugates the natives, destroys sacred landmarks, and prohibits the observance of ancestral rituals according to his whims. The (de facto) occupation and purchase of Okinawa by U.S. military interests ("returned" in 1972) is thereby circumvented through recourse, once again, to the scapegoat mechanism, by Sato's exemplary incarnation of capitalist ruthlessness and greed. Miyagi's self-identification as Okinawan, and not Japanese, is never as emphatic and ideologically saturated as it is in this context, when expressed as nostalgia for the simple village he has lost. The pastoral, highly traditional subsistence-level society whose passing Miyagi mourns is implicitly a white American fantasy projection of "the way they were"—perhaps the way "they" should be once again: not modernizing corporate giants, like Sato, but those of the quaint and decent Miyagi "type."

The story of good and evil does not quite end, however, with this crude exercise in mass cultural anthropology. To the incredulous Danny, Miyagi explains that Sato's sadistic cruelties and intense hatreds are symptomatic of a dedication to honor gone unhinged, unbalanced: "In Okinawa, honor has no time limit. In Okinawa, honor very serious." Okinawa is thus inserted into a recognizable space in the popular imaginary, into a cul-de-sac carved out by Hollywood for myths of timeless honor among men: *The Godfather*'s Sicily, the setting par excellence for cross-generational vendettas and revenge plots, and the place where mafiosi operate among a people out of step with the advanced industrial world. The transposition of Okinawa for Sicily may be facilitated by some sociogeographical similarities between the two regions; both are discrete islands off the national mainland, or main island, with distinctive cultural and economic identities. Perhaps the legacy of American occupation further renders the Okinawan setting familiar or "friendly" to creative annexation by Hollywood.

## Ethnic and Political Currencies; Defenders of the Planet

At any rate "Sicilianized" in *The Karate Kid II*, Okinawa is remade as a site for additional permutations of Italian cultural effects. The gangsterism of the Sato family is delivered to audiences replete with the sleek hairstyles, sunglasses, and double-breasted suits to which consumers of American Mafia movies may well have grown accustomed. Sato's excruciatingly evil nephew (and Danny's archrival) is distinguished from the pack by his large medallions, clinging shirts unbuttoned to the waist, and very tight pants—a peculiar invocation of the disco look that may "work" precisely by virtue of its noncorrespondence to any identity in particular. To add a polyester sheen to his inauthentic masculinity—revealed by his extortion of protection money from meek farmers, his vandalism of the Miyagi family dojo, and his cowardice in the face of natural disaster—the teenager is shockingly out of style. In *The Karate Kid II*, then, clothing functions as a marker less of "real-life" ethnic and class identifications, by either descent or consent, than of the portability and mutability of ethnicized signifiers.[19] "Italianness" and "Japaneseness" are in this way mobilized as surrogates for one another, twin commodities mediated by mass culture's version of ethnicity as a standardized currency of exchange.

Alongside ethnicity, the environment also figures as a recognized "currency" in both film series. And with this rather abrupt transition to "green politics," I have occasion to return to the color code for appealing "difference" with which I began. Since their emergence as the political issue of recent times, environmental concerns have served to locate yet another potential alliance, and real distance, between corporate producers and consumers in North America. To map the opposition with the help of extreme examples, we are presented with the audacity of the environmental disaster's worst perpetrators representing themselves as the earth's most dedicated human caretakers: "the people" who "really care" (Chevron Oil), who "bring good things to life" (General Electric), and who "help you do great things" (Dow Chemical). On the other hand, many individual consumers have adjusted their habits to include recycling, conservation, purchasing ecologically friendly products, and generally assuming personal responsibility where and when industry does not. I would venture that, in moving toward mutual impersonation in these ways, self-popularizing corporations and "globally thinking, locally acting" individuals engage in processes of surrogacy similar to those under discussion in this essay—and thereby risk incurring similar results: namely, the depoliticization of green politics and the concomitant release of "floating environmental signifiers" into the commodity atmosphere, where they become available as yet more advertising slogans and "lifestyle choices."

Into yet another breach between corporations and consumers, into the crossed purposes and the literal mess, tumble the Ninja Turtles and the Karate Kid: mass cultural manifestations that, as already discussed, have a propensity to switch roles and hybridize continually into new forms in such a way that both resolves and regenerates old contradictions. In the context of the current environmental crisis, the superheroic transformative abilities of our principal characters are put to an especially challenging test. Both the Turtles and the Karate Kid "give a hoot" about pollution, toxic waste, and the orphaned garbage barges of the world. And they treat these issues with much the same arsenal of gestures that they deploy toward ethnicity, nationality, and class—to what we can track as much the same effects.

By the late 1980s, Danny, Miyagi, and their requisite literal enemies mutate with the times into what is probably their most confused and confusing outing thus far, *The Karate Kid III* (1989). At the same time that environmental consciousness is being awakened, the rosy economic/Reaganomic picture of the previous two *Kid* films has collapsed. *Kid III* begins with Miyagi losing his job with the South Seas apartment complex and embarking on a new career as the owner of a bonsai tree shop. Bonsai trees come to signify both the emergence of the small-business entrepreneur on the revised horizon of American economic opportunity and—already a metonymic stand-in, or surrogate, for the Okinawan's native roots in an authentic, precapitalist society—Miyagi's ethnically flavored contribution to environmental correctness. Bonsai trees thus partake of two natures simultaneously: a commodity nature and a "natural nature" that becomes the material for *Kid III*'s most sumptuous and striking visual spectacles. Sensei and student perform kato moves (relatively more slow and deliberate, and by implication more "natural," than those of karate) by the Pacific Ocean, on mountaintops and beaches, against sunsets, and amid rising mists. Arrestingly steep camera angles and wide pan shots help to locate Danny and Miyagi, so exercised, always within close proximity of the most precious (personally, culturally, and commercially) of all bonsai trees: one Miyagi had originally brought with him to America, and transplanted in a concealed mountain niche, its preferred environment. The bonsai also furnishes yet another metaphor for Danny's development as a martial artist and as a man; as Miyagi tells him, "Tree have strong root . . . same same you . . . so must you choose how you grow."

Miyagi's characteristically elliptical lesson (a quality Splinter shares and takes to an extreme) proves, also characteristically, canny and well founded; for the villain of *Kid III* not only is responsible for the destruction of Miyagi's most cherished tree but also threatens to "uproot" young Danny and take over both his spiritual care and his martial-arts instruction, destroying him in the process. Above and beyond this villain's unsavory affiliations with *Kid I*'s Kreese, and his own uniquely unreedemable qualities, Terry Silver is president of Dynatox Industries: a company whose sole marketable service is the indiscriminate dumping of toxic waste. Thankfully, as Miyagi had prophesized, the strongly rooted Danny eventually comes to his senses and makes a choice; he just says no to the wily villain, and his relationship with Miyagi, the bonsai tree, and by extension the environment is restored to health. To resist Silver's toxic charms, therefore, is to foil the very forces of pollution, or so the film weakly concludes.

Pollution and toxic waste are the founding conditions for the Ninja Turtles, and are perhaps for this reason submitted to comparatively more ambitious, and ambiguous, decipherings and elaborations. In *Teenage Mutant Ninja Turtles* (1990), the origins story of Chernobylization into superhuman form is represented as cause for collective celebration. *The Secret of the Ooze* (1991) enlists the Turtles' usual antics, somewhat erratically, toward a more sobering parable on the state of the hyperindustrialized environment. Designated "role models" for real children, the Turtles come not only to choose what they scavenge and consume of mass culture, but also to say yes to the environmental cause; a sign, presumably handmade, in their converted subway station reads "Recycle, dudes." Within such a project of (consensual) environmentalism, the issue of waste disposal demands revisitation, and becomes problematized in the film by reference to the Turtles' "real" authors: the scientists who spearhead the unspecified product output of Techno-Global Research Institute (TGRI), and the corporate principals who have to this point successfully concealed from the public their mismanagement of radioactive ooze.

True to teenage mutant ninja turtle logic, however, the original villains behind this fictive nuclear accident mutate into the good guys by the film's end. Not only does a TGRI scientist come to see the errors of the industry's ways, but his social irresponsibility, after all, has given rise to Splinter and the Turtles in their current "bodacious" form. Yet to claim the Turtles as the "positive" effects of improperly handled toxic waste is an untenable contradiction in a film dedicated to environmental consciousness-raising. And so Shredder once again takes the place of a deferred, otherwise undisclosable other, this time as archenemy to the environment, who steals the last remaining canister of radioactive "ooze" for his own purposes of world conquest. Shredder attempts to produce his own counterparts to the Turtles; needless to say, his experiment fails. The two infantile, imbecilic, and short-lived creatures he produces have as their pop culture referents Godzilla and Gamera—the monsters of post-Hiroshima Japanese horror films who, however ironized in their present reincarnations, may serve to remind someone that nuclear holocaust is under no real circumstances redeemable.

These vestigial historical and cultural associations notwithstanding, the "secret of the ooze" is the true significance of the Turtles' mutational origins, which the film both reveals and occludes. In cryptic language meant to convey the simultaneous coldness and uncoolness of the contemporary scientific enterprise, the TGRI professor tries to explain how the "mutagenic properties" of the "green colloidal gel" had interacted with the Turtles' original genetic makeup. Donatello reacts to the news as might a human child upon hearing that he was an "accident": "I thought there'd be more to it . . . to us. I thought we were special." And with this plaintive reaction, Donatello sets up this essay's final observations about correspondences between the mutation of mass culture and the transformation of ethnicity.

## Specters of Origins and Ends

In response to Donatello's disappointment, Splinter says: "The specter of origin not be confused with your present worth." The wise old rat with the pathologically broken English then advises his charges to put their reflections about origins on hold, and to attend for the time being to "more urgent matters." The truncated quest for the secret of the ooze is, thereafter, never resumed as such. The "specter of origin" instead gives way, yields its place, to the "birth of ninja rap": courtesy of an end-all interethnic, intercultural, interspecies collaboration between the Turtles—who hip and hop until the actors inside the latex costumes literally drop—and the white rapper, Vanilla Ice, who at the time of production was at the apex of his popularity. The unambiguously human teenagers assembled in the film to bear witness to this spectacle are the empirical viewers' surrogates in the Turtles' fantasy world: and by approving so thoroughly of this "accidental" entertainment, the movie's rainbow coalition of youngsters disposes audiences, "like them," to salivate for more Turtles and more Ice.

From the perspective of the culture industry, the "birth of ninja rap" may register little more than an amalgamation of commercially successful performers employed by the same record label and parent company, and an economy of effort and expense that nevertheless can be sold as something "new and different." From the perspective of young consumers, however, the dissociation of "present worth" from "the specter of origins" may offer untold utopian possibilities. A child's desire to leave the adult world and remake himself or herself as a monster or animal (or cyborg) may encode a clear antihumanist impulse—perhaps a rejection of "the law of the father," patrilineage, and inheritance compatible with or serviceable toward more egalitarian visions of how the world should be organized. To dream of retreating underground with the Turtles, to a haven in which all material needs are (miraculously) satisfied, in which there is unconditional approval and friendship, may be to wage protest against a "real world" where these needs are not always and uniformly met. If anything, the Turtles may help to allay and cathect a child's anxieties about the impending destruction of the world's ecosystem, extending as they do the fantastic promise of (better) life after nuclear holocaust and environmental doom.

Although I, too, share the fantasy (of Channel Number 4, or is it 6?—April O'Neil reports to different stations on the large and small screens), I am compelled to end this essay by reinvoking the "specter of origin," and with some more somber reflections. The first regards the "specter" of gender. The models of mutational reproduction and surrogacy at work in all of the cultural productions discussed here require, and may derive their appeal from, the evaporation of mothers from the picture—leaving us, instead, with variations on conventional fantasies of masculine birth. Apart from the cycle's opening, Lucille LaRusso is a virtual nonentity in all three *Karate Kid* features, to an extent that suggests that Miyagi functions also a maternal surrogate. The mother of the Turtles is, similarly, a nonissue—except insofar as advertisements interpellate the mothers of Turtles-identified consumers as the adults to coerce into buying for one this or that new product. A world in which a child's needs for food, shelter, and warmth can be taken for granted—the Turtles' world—is, implicitly, one in which "women's work" is devalued or invisible. During an interview with the latex creations, Barbara Walters did ask one of the Turtles to talk about their mother, and this request, well rehearsed in advance, prompted yet another mass culture "accident" along the lines of "ninja rap": the remote-controlled device that would have enabled the designated Turtle to ooze out one sentimental tear refused to work during the actual taping, and instead released a torrent that soaked Walters to the skin. And in the ensuing, spontaneous hilarity, both question and potential answer were forgotten.

Furthermore, although ethnic cultural effects prove highly elastic and portable, their "free play" is by no means unrestricted. The engineers of mass culture surrogacy have their orders and their limits. The same dominant class interests that posit the Italian American male as popular cinema's "universal" hero deny other "hyphenated Americans" entry to this (already problematic) mass culture niche. Substitute African American children and white, middle-class adoptive parents into the equation posed by *The Karate Kid* and the *Teenage Mutant Ninja Turtles*, and we are presented with quite a different mutational story: *Diff'rent Strokes* and *Webster*, whose boy protagonists enjoy little of the license and autonomy accorded to their "Italian American" counterparts. In America, it is still not easy being not-white; and Hollywood continues to respond to this reality by recycling myths of white paternalism.

The "real world" from which ethnic signifiers are abstracted and detached reflects back at mass culture contradictions like these. And try as they might, mass culture and its consumers simply cannot mutate fast or effectively enough to keep up, not even with their own contradictions. The Teenage Mutant Ninja Turtles encourage children to "become defenders of the planet," and at the same time to digest "junk" food: an advertisement enclosed with the *Secret of the Ooze* videotape juxtaposes an application to join "Kids for Saving Earth" with a coupon for a Royal "OOZE Gelatin" mold. Anticipating the waning of the Turtles' popularity, Playmates Toys launched a "new" and "different" line of teenage mutants in 1991–92 that continues to capitalize on children's environmental nightmares: the "grime-fighting" Toxic Crusaders, who derive both their vocations and their superhuman strength from toxic waste. And when sales trends for the Turtles and their surrogates do fall off, as they invariably and inevitably will, there may be not enough room left in the world's landfills to contain the mutations that no one will want anymore, or their packages.

## Notes

1. Donna Haraway, "A Cyborg Manifesto: Science, Technology, and Socialist-Feminism in the Late Twentieth Century," in *Simians, Cyborgs and Women: The Reinvention of Nature* (New York: Routledge, 1991), 149–81.

2. Max Horkheimer and Theodor W. Adorno, "The Culture Industry: Enlightenment as Mass Deception" (1944), in *Dialectic of Enlightenment*, trans. John Cumming (New York: Continuum, 1986), 120–67, 134.

3. Andrew Tanzer, "Heroes in a Half Shell," *Forbes* 148:10 (October 28, 1991): 49–51.

4. Lisa Gubernick, "Turtle Power," *Forbes* 145:11 (May 28, 1990): 52–58, 52.

5. Culture industry mavens responsible for the Ninja Turtles and other products geared to juvenile audiences willingly admit to their designs on young consumers, cultivated during difficult economic times. "In a soft economy . . . you don't want to give a kid a choice between spending three dollars or eight dollars. You want to build a career." Or so explains the vice president of sales for SBK Records: the label that released the platinum sound track for the first Turtles film and accelerated the career of white rapper Vanilla Ice, who appears in *Turtles II* ("Sold on Ice," *Rolling Stone* [January 10, 1991], 41). In 1990, spending in the four- to twelve-year-old category increased to more than $60 billion in the United States ("Don't Believe the Hype," *Rolling Stone* [December 13–27, 1990], 70).

6. Werner Sollors, *Beyond Ethnicity: Consent and Descent in American Culture* (New York: Oxford University Press, 1986), 31 and 33; quoted in Vivian Sobchack, "Postmodern Modes of Ethnicity," in *Unspeakable Images*, ed. Lester Friedman (Urbana and Chicago: University of Illinois Press, 1991), 329–52, 330.

7. Sollors, *Beyond Ethnicity*, 6; quoted in Sobchack, "Postmodern Modes of Ethnicity," 332.

8. Sobchack, "Postmodern Modes of Ethnicity," 333.

9. For an insightful discussion of the boundary permeability among categories of ethnicity, class, and gender devised and exploited by these and other films, see Peter Biskind and Barbara Ehrenreich, "Machismo and Hollywood's Working Class," in *American Media and Mass Culture: Left Perspectives*, ed. Donald Lazere (Berkeley, Los Angeles, and London: University of California Press, 1987), 201–15.

10. Tom Engelhardt, "The Primal Screen," *Mother Jones* (May–June 1991): 68–71, 69.

11. Fredric Jameson, "Postmodernism; or, the Cultural Logic of Late Capitalism," *New Left Review* 146 (July–August 1988): 53–92, 65.

12. Peter Biskind and Barbara Ehrenreich have identified the white ethnic, working-class hero as the cultural repository of the "'old-fashioned' male virtues . . . no longer socially acceptable or professionally useful within the middle-class" ("Machismo and Hollywood's Working Class," 206).

13. Janice C. Simpson, "Lean, Green and on the Screen: The Teenage Mutant Ninja Turtles Go Hollywood," *Time* 155:14 (April 2, 1990): 59.

14. Gus Mager's first comic strip for Hearst newspapers (1904) featured four differ-

ent principal characters, all with simian features, on alternate days: Knocko the Monk on Mondays, Tightwaddo the Monk on Tuesdays, Henpecko the Monk on Wednesdays, and Groucho the Monk on Saturdays. The strip exploited the stereotypical image of an organ-grinder with a monkey (or "monk," in the popular parlance of the day) toward what may be among the first mass culture renderings of the Italian ethnic as mutant. By popular demand, the process of adaptation continued, and in 1910, Mager introduced Sherlocko the Monk and Dr. Watso to a roster that had also grown to include Yanko the Dentist and Beefo the Butcher. In turn, Mager's characters inspired the renaming of the Marx Brothers, although only one of the vaudevillians cum film stars, Chico, was to consistently play the part of an Italian throughout his career. See Luciano J. Iorizzo and Salvatore Mondello, *The Italian Americans*, rev. ed. (Boston: Twayne Publishers, 1980), 266–67.

15. I am not able to account adequately for the proliferation of names and words ending in vowel sounds in Ninja Turtles culture. Nevertheless, the sheer number of them, and potential categories by which to organize them, seem worth at least a passing mention. In addition to the letter "o," multisyllabic words ending in "a" appear to have a special cachet in (male) children's culture: the Turtles' signature interjection, "Cowabunga," that awakens and expresses irrepressible joy, bears similarities to the epithet favored by Bart Simpson of animated sit-com fame. Bart's "Ay, Caramba," like "Cowabunga," seems both to evoke and to elide ethnic otherness, in reassuringly anglicized form.

16. The overtly racist epithets—"slope" and "your little Jap" in *Kid III*—used by the films' literal enemies help to demarcate a backdrop against which the films' more subtle or generalized forms of racism (e.g., Japan bashing) can be politically and culturally vindicated. Together with other calculated devices, Danny's ("adoptive") legitimation and the audience's approval of the likable Miyagi serve more to designate a "special" (Okinawan) exception to the (Japanese) rule than to challenge the blatantly offensive terms and images.

17. For a related discussion of the role of generations in identity construction and legitimation, see the Beverly Allen essay in this volume.—*Ed.*

18. Miyagi, or so the story goes, had earned the affections of the lovely Yukia over Sato's designs, and familial claims, on her. Likewise, Shredder's animosity toward Splinter derives from the former's having lost the woman he coveted, Tang Shin (the Chinese name at once surprising, in a Japanese context, and not surprising, as a conflation of all that is Asian), to the latter's master. The formulaic pairing of love-and-war rivalries furnishes yet another example of an ethnicized mass culture code, informing ongoing amalgamations of Eastern and Western cinematic effects.

19. One episode of the Ninja Turtles' cartoon series is also noteworthy as a demonstration of the kinds of comic and ironic possibilities opened once cultural types become portable. "The Great Cuff Link Caper" inverts a presupposed, ethnically marked opposition between inherited wealth and gangster wealth, by juxtaposing Calzone the pizza magnate (art collector and upper-class snob) with Baby Face "The Beaver" Cleaver.

# Contributors

*Mohamed Aden* is a physician and political activist in Italy. He is the former minister of culture, education, and public health in Somalia.

*John Agnew* is professor of geography at the University of California at Los Angeles. A frequent visitor to Italy, Agnew is working on a study of the geography of political change in Italy since World War II.

*Beverly Allen* is professor of Italian, Comparative Literature, and Women's Studies and faculty affiliate of the Global Affairs Institute, the Maxwell School, Syracuse University. Her most recent book is *Rape Warfare: The Hidden Genocide in Bosnia-Herzegovina and Croatia* (Minnesota, 1996).

*Ayele Bekerie* is a visiting assistant professor at the African Studies and Research Center of Cornell University. Formerly a professional agronomist, Bekerie holds a Ph.D. in African American Studies from Temple University and an MSC in agronomy and an MPS in African Studies from Cornell University.

*Elaine K. Chang* is assistant professor of English at Rutgers University.

*Antonio Marazzi* is professor of cultural anthropology, University of Padua, Italy. He also serves as chairman of the Commission on Visual Anthropology of the International Union of Anthropological and Ethnological Sciences (IUAES). Marazzi has done extensive fieldwork in Japan and has published two books on Japanese culture.

*Francesca Miller* is a Faculty Fellow in history at the University of California, Davis Washington Center, Washington D.C. She is the author of *Latin American Women and the Search for Social Justice.*

*Antonio Negri*, political philosopher and activist, is professor of the Theory of the State at the University of Paris VIII. He also directs a prestigious weekly seminar in Rue Descartes and is a member of the editorial board of *Futur Antérieur.* Negri lived in exile in France from 1983 to 1997.

*Graziella Parati* is an associate professor in the department of French and Italian, Dartmouth College. She is the author of *Public History, Private Stories: Italian Women's Autobiography* (Minnesota, 1996).

*Karen Pinkus* is associate professor at the University of Southern California in the departments of French and Italian, and Comparative Literature. She is the author of *Bodily Regimes: Italian Advertising under Fascism* (Minnesota, 1995) and *Picturing Silence: Emblem, Language, Counter-Reformation Morality.*

*Paul Robinson* is the Richard W. Lyman Professor in the Humanities at Stanford University. His books include *Opera and Ideas* and *Freud and His Critics.* Robinson is also a regular contributor to the *New York Times Book Review* and is a Fellow of the American Academy of Arts and Sciences.

*Mary Russo* is dean of humanities and arts and professor in literature and critical theory at Hampshire College. She is the author of *The Female Grotesque: Risk, Excess, and Modernity* and coeditor of *Nationalisms and Sexualities.*

*Pasquale Verdicchio* is an associate professor in the Department of Literature, University of California, San Diego. His critical writings on film, poetry, Italian, and Italian expatriate culture and literature have been published in journals in Italy and North America. Verdicchio is also a well-known poet and translator of Antonio Porta, Giorgio Caproni, and other contemporary Italian authors.

*Marguerite R. Waller* is professor of English and chair of Women's Studies at the University of California, Riverside. She is the author of *Petrarch's Poetics and Literary History* and articles on Dante, Petrarch, Wyatt, Surrey, and Shakespeare. In cinema studies, she has published articles on George Lucas, Fellini, Wertmüller, Cavani, and Nichetti, among others. She has also written about the San Diego/Tijuana women's art-making collective, Las Comadres, in which she participated for several years.

*David Ward* is associate professor, Department of Italian, Wellesley College. He is the author of *A Poetics of Resistance: Narrative and the Writings of Pier Paolo Pasolini* and *Antifascisms: Cultural Politics in Italy, 1943–46. Benedetto Croce and the Liberals, Carlo Levi and the "Actionists."*

# Index

Abdille Hassan, Seyid M., 105–6
Abdulmajid, Iman, 151–52
Abyssinian Baptist Church, 130
Achille Lauro, 157
Action Party, 86, 88
actualism, 114n. 4
Adams, John, 157
Aden, Mohamed, 12, 101–13
adoption: and national identity, 2
Adorno, Theodor, 243, 293
advertising, 265, 306–7; antiracism and, 88; Benetton, 5, 148–49; blackness in, 13, 134–53; global, 273n. 5
Adwa, Battle of, 8, 37, 103, 117
AFIS (Amministrazione Fiduciaria Italiana in Somalia [Italian Trusteeship in Somalia]), 110
Africa, 9, 15, 32, 101–2, 124–25, 127, 138, 148, 152; immigrants from, 15, 169, 171, 174, 183; India and, 201; Italian colonization in, 7–8, 215; Italian studies in, 10
L'Africaine (Meyerbeer), 161
The African: A Journal of African Affairs, 126
African American(s), 13, 192, 206, 311; intellectuals, 119–25; and Italo-Ethiopian War, 116–31; press, 125–27
African authors, 170–71
African-Italian authors, 171, 172–87
Agig, Majuba, 182
Agnew, John, 11, 23–42
aid: humanitarian, 152; military, 128
Aida, 13–14, 156–65

Aksum stele, 130
Alberdi, Juan Bautista, 215
Alberoni, Francesco, 279
Allen, Beverly, 11, 50, 52–75, 113
Al-Mukhtar, Omar, 104
Altan, 93
Althusser, Louis, 55
Altman, Robert, 257
Amato, Giuliano, 83–85
amoral familism, 27, 29
Amsterdam News, 126
Anarquistas, graças a Deus! (Anarchists, thank the Lord!), 213–30
Anderson, Benedict, 3–4, 196, 241–42, 253–54
Anderson, Perry, 193
"Andiamo a spasso?" (Shall we go for a walk?), 180
Andreotti, Giuliano, 83
Angioni, Giulio, 172
anni di piombo (years of lead), 12, 52–54, 59–64, 67, 72–73, 75, 76n. 8
anthropology, 288–89
anticlericalism, 165
anticolonialism, 126
anticorruption campaign, 83–84
antifascism, 12, 25, 35, 81–82, 86, 88, 91–92; African Americans and, 126, 130
anti-imperialism, 159
Anti-Oedipus (Deleuze and Guattari), 263
antiracism, 86, 88, 92, 106, 186, 190n. 24; ad, 150 fig. 4

anti-Semitism, 86, 95n. 8
"A parlamento" (At the parliament),
    95n. 4
Apocalypse Now, 302
Appadurai, Arjun, 242, 254, 272, 273n. 4
Arbore, Renzo, 140
Archaeology of Knowledge (Foucault),
    237–38
architecture: and genre, 55
Arenol, Joseph C., 121
Argentina, 213–15, 232n. 33
Arnoldi, Charles, 248
Aronowitz, Stanley, 7
art movements, 136–37
art nègre, 136–37, 142
Asahi Journal, 279–80
Asia, 8, 9, 16; Europe and, 32; immi-
    grants from, 15, 169, 171, 174; Italian
    studies in, 10
Assimilação e Mobilidade (Ribeiro
    Durham), 221–22
Association of Italian Canadian Writers,
    209n. 1
Attila, 165
Australia, 8, 44
Austria, 35, 165, 197
Autonomy, 48, 49, 50n. 1
Azikiwe, Nnamidi, 124
Azpadu, Dodici, 205–8
Azzi, Riolando, 228

Ba, Saidou Moussa, 171–72, 175,
    178–79, 183, 190n. 24
Bach, Johann Sebastian, 160
backwardness, 23–40; as myth, 29–30;
    Europe and, 30–34; metaphors of,
    24–30; spaces and, 30–34
Badinter, Elizabeth, 93
baka, 277–81, 288
Baker, Josephine, 136–37, 143
Bakhtin, Mikhail, 55
Balbo, Italo, 114
Balbo, Laura, 170, 186
Balla, Giocomo, 136
Baltimore Afro-American, 126
"Banda Bassotti," 87
banditry, 2, 67, 77n. 18
Banfield, Edward, 27, 29
Barolini, Helen, 205–6
Baudrillard, Jean, 59, 242–44
Bayen, Melaku E., 126–28

Bazin, André, 256
Bearden, Romare, 120
"The Beast of Rome" (Garvey), 123
Beato, Felice (Felix), 286–87
Bekerie, Ayele, 13, 116–31
Belgium, 8
Bellochio, Mario, 53
Benetton, 5, 88, 148–49
Benigni, Roberto, 264
Benjamin, Walter, 60, 271
Ben Jelloun, Tahar, 175–78
ben Jochannan, Yosef, 121
Berardi, Franco, 92–93
Bergson, Henri, 135
Berlin Conference of 1884–86, 117
Berlusconi, Silvio, 2, 250n. 1, 267
Bernal, Martin, 32
The Betrothed (I promessi sposi), 35,
    56–57
Bhabha, Homi, 241, 254, 256
Bianchi, Michele, 114
The Bicycle Thief (Ladri di biciclette), 47,
    253–72; Maggiorani in, 261 fig. 1
Bifo, 92
Bikini Island, 259
Bixio, Nino, 198
Bizet, Georges, 270
Black Athena, 32
Black Jacobins (James), 124
The Blackman, 122–23, 126
blackness: in advertising, 13, 134–53
Black Power, 124
black style, 135–37
Black Tongue (D'Alfonso), 205
Bobbio, Norberto, 84
Boccasile, Gino, 144, 146, 148–49; ads
    by, 145 fig. 2, 147 fig. 3
Boine, Alberto, 36
Bokri, Mohamad, 186
Bologna, 92; bombings in, 60, 67,
    77n. 12
bombings, 1, 52, 60, 62, 67, 75n. 2,
    77n. 12. See also terrorism; violence
Borsellino, Paolo, 81
Boscaro, Adriana, 277
Bossi, Umberto, 83
Bouchane, Mohamed, 171–75, 177, 185
Bourbons, 35, 198
bourgeoisie, 28–29, 56; ethics and,
    283–85; fascism and, 86; in novels,

64–67, 73; unification and, 198; violence and, 53, 60, 67
Boutang, Yann Moulier, 48
Bowie, David, 151–52
Bowles, Paul, 178
Brandt, Willi, 94
Brazil, 14; immigrants in, 5, 213–30
*Breakfast at Tiffany's,* 298
*Breaking Away,* 296
Brecht, Bertolt, 243
Britain. *See* Great Britain
*Brutus,* 281
Bruno, Giordano, 43
Buck-Morss, Susan, 271
Budden, Julian, 163
Buddhism, 283–84
Burke, Kenneth, 54, 60
Burton, Tim, 257
Bush, Mary (Bucci), 206
Bushido, 284
Butler, Judith, 255

Caffé Bricco: ad, 145 fig. 2, 146
California, 242–43. *See also* Los Angeles; Venice (California)
Calvinism, 29
Calvino, Italo, 243
Camon, Ferdinando, 63, 279–80
Canada: immigrants in, 5–6, 192, 204–5, 208, 210n. 12
Cansino, Margarita Carmen, 259. *See also* Hayworth, Rita
*Canzoniere* (Petrarca), 196
capitalism, 33, 44, 49, 60, 243–44, 273n. 4; Hollywood and, 258–59; monogamy and, 143; print, 4; Teenage Mutant Ninja Turtles and, 303–4
capitalists, 38
*Capitol,* 273n. 6
Carducci, Giosu, 95n. 4
Caribbean, 124–25, 127
Carlini, Giuliano, 182
*Carmen,* 161, 270–71
Carnera, Primo, 130
*Caro Michele* (dear Michael), 63–68
Caroselli, Francesco Saverio, 102
cartoons, 87, 89 fig. 1, 90 fig. 2, 93, 94 fig. 4
Case del Popolo, 38
Castellaneta, Carlo, 53, 63, 68–73

Catholic(s), 35, 46, 56; immigrants, 185, 214; in Brazil, 228
Catholic church, 48; Brazilian, 220; Roman, 129, 229
Catholicism, 59, 129
Chang, Elaine, 16, 292–312
Cheney, Lynn, 236–37
*Chiamatemi Alì* (Call me Alì), 173, 185
*Chicago Defender,* 126
China, 38
Chiossone, Edoardo, 286
Chohra, Nassera, 175, 177, 181, 188n. 5; 189n. 9
Choukri, Mohamed, 177
Chow, Raymond, 294
Christian(s), 56, 129–30
Christian Democratic Party, 26, 35, 60, 73, 83
Christianity, 121, 283; Ethiopian Orthodox, 129
citizenship, 4, 38; Brazilian, 215
*City of Quartz: Excavating the Future in Los Angeles* (Davis), 243
city-states, 34, 195
civil order, 59
civil rights, 53
civil society, 81, 83, 86
civil unrest, 59
civil war, 45, 73, 91
Cixous, Hélène, 67
clandestine political groups, 59, 67, 73, 76n. 4
clandestine political violence, 53–54, 59–67, 71; perpetrators of, 74. *See also* violence
clandestinity, 71
Clarke, John Henrik, 121, 124–26
class, 5, 10, 148–49, 203, 236, 296, 307; immigrants and, 14; in Brazil, 224–25; in films, 311; in Japan, 283; in Los Angeles, 245; Italian Americans and, 7
*Classe operaia* (the working class), 48
class struggle, 38
Clément, Catherine, 270
clergy: in Brazil, 228
*Cleveland Gazette,* 126
clientalism, 28–29, 37, 39
coalition movements, 128
Cold War, 33, 39, 273n. 4, 301–2
Collodi, Carlo, 36
Colonia Cecilia, 14, 214, 219–20

colonialism, 14, 106, 116, 191–93; economic, 189n. 13; emigration and, 201;
European, 117; Italian, 8, 199–200,
202–5
colonization, 12–14, 191; blackness and,
148; demographic, 215; European, 6;
films and, 253–72; in Africa, 7–8,
102–8, 215; Italian, 3, 15, 199
Columbus, Christopher, 30, 40, 235–36,
242, 253, 259
Come si cura il Nazi (How to cure the
Nazi), 92–93
Coming Home, 302
"Coming Out Olive in the Lesbian Community: Big Sister Is Watching You"
(Romano), 206–7
commercials: in films, 263–65, 268–70
Il Commune in Riva al Mare (Rossi), 218
communism, 33, 45, 49, 273n. 4
Communist Party, 26; Cuban, 240;
Italian, 59, 67, 84, 192
Communists, 128
Comune di Milano, 182
concentration camps, 105
Confucianism, 284–85
Confucius, 280
conscientization, 204, 210n. 13
consciousness: novels and, 56
conscription: forced, 203, 220
consumer agency, 273n. 5
consumer culture, 295
consumer economy, 257
consumerism, 278; in the United states,
7; Italian, 13, 135; Japanese, 288
Contee, Clarence G., 129
Contropiano (counterplan), 48
cooperation, 111–13
Coordinamento donne 8 marzo, 182
Cornell, Drusilla, 67
Corradini, Enrico, 194, 200–203
Corriere della Sera, 38–39, 279
corruption, 23, 112–13; political, 81
Council of Chalcedon, 129
Covolo, Domenick, 248
Craxi, Bettino, 26, 83, 87–88, 94n. 3;
cartoons of, 89 fig. 1, 90 fig. 2
Crisantino, Amelia, 182
The Crisis, 118, 126
Crispi, Francesco, 36–37, 199
"Critique of Violence" (Benjamin), 60

Croce, Bendetto, 37, 83, 86–87, 93,
114n. 4
Cubism, 136
cultural difference, 250
cultural geography, 242
cultural history, 280
cultural influence, 283
cultural productions, 4, 53, 58, 61,
74–75, 285
cultural repetition, 235–50
cultural shifts, 250
culture, 11–12, 92–93, 289; authors and,
172, 175, 178; Brazilian, 229; colonization and, 107; European, 157–58;
Italian, 276; Japanese, 285; language
as, 173; mass, 16, 271, 292–312;
Western, 172
Culture and Imperialism (Said), 157
culture industry, 293–94, 297, 310
culture wars, 235
Cuore (Heart), 87, 92–93
Curcio, Renato, 26, 63, 181, 190n. 27
Cyrenaica, 104

Da Col family, 217–18, 220, 223, 227
da Giussano, Alberto, 82
Dagli aiuti mi guardi Iddito (God save
me from aid), 112
D'Alfonso, Antonio, 205
Dalla Chiesa, Nando, 81
Danane, 105
D'Annunzio, Gabriele, 83, 108
Dante, 9–10, 43, 45, 47, 195–96
Darwinism, 215
Davis, Mike, 243
Dear Diego (Poniatowska), 239–40
Death in Venice (Mann), 244
The Death of Klinghoffer (Adams), 157
de Bono, Emilio, 114
Decolonising the Mind (Ngugi), 173
Decree of the Duke of Aosta, 107
De Crescenzo, Luciano, 138, 140–42
The Deer Hunter, 302
deformation, 136, 142
De Girolamo, Carla, 173
Del Boca, A., 104
Deleuze, Gilles, 93, 253–55, 257, 262–63
Dell'Oro, Erminia, 172
De Martino, Ernesto, 194
De Mita, Ciriaco, 26

democracy, 11, 12, 25, 44, 84, 113;
  parliamentary, 83; revolutionary, 59
Democratic Party of the Left, 84
demographic changes, 16, 61, 293
de Morais, Prudente, 221
Depero, Fortunato, 136–37
De Renzi, S., 193–94
Derrida, Jacques, 258
*Description de l'Égypte* (Napoléon), 158
*deserto*, 231n. 16; Brazil as, 213–15,
  220, 228, 230
De Sica, Vittorio, 253, 256–59, 262–63,
  267, 270
determinism, 36
De Vecchi, Cesare M., 108, 114n. 10
development, 34, 112; national, 24; of
  Italy, 36
*Devil in the Flesh*, 53
*De Vulgari Eloquentia* (Dante), 195
*La Difesa*, 226
*La difesa della razza*, 136
*Diff'rent Strokes*, 311
Dilthey, Wilhelm, 48
*Dime*, 277–82, 284
Di Pietro, Antonio, 81, 84
di Sarro, Alessandra Atti, 177
*The Distant Fatherland* (*La patria
  lontana*), 200–203
*Dominion and Sabotage* (Negri), 49
*Do the Right Thing*, 210n. 17
*Dove lo stato non c'è. Racconti Italiani*
  (Where the state does not exist: Italian
  tales), 176
*The Dream Book: An Anthology of
  Writings by Italian American Women*
  (Barolini), 205
Du Bois, W. E. B., 13, 120, 124, 126
du Locle, Camille, 158
Dyer, Richard, 134–35

Eagleburger, L. Scott, 50
Eagleton, Terry, 30
Eastern Europe: immigrants from, 169,
  171, 174
Eastman, Kevin, 300
*Ecce Homo* (Nietzsche), 243
Eco, Umberto, 47, 244
economy, 260; cultural, 237, 254; Italian,
  8, 12, 23, 25, 37–38, 60
Edinger, Claudio, 248
Edwards, Blake, 298

Egypt: in *Aida*, 13, 157–65
electronic communication, 263–72
elites: cultural, 3; Italian, 29; South
  American, 214–15, 225
Ellison, Ralph, 130
emigrants, 45. *See also* immigrants
emigration, 5, 8, 187n. 1, 191; Italian, 8,
  37, 44–45, 60–61, 183, 200–204, 227.
  *See also* immigration; migration
empire building, 32
England, 8, 24, 28, 36, 40; immigrants
  from, 6; myths and, 30. *See also* Great
  Britain
Enlightenment: European, 284
Enokido, Ichiro, 277–78
environment, 306–9
Enzensberger, Hans Magnus, 39–40
Eritrea, 8, 109, 180, 187n. 1, 200, 202
*L'Espresso*, 83, 85
*Essay on the Inequality of the Human
  Races* (Gobineau), 114
Essien-Udom, E. U., 120
*o Estado de São Paulo*, 227
Esteva, Gustavo, 33
ethics, 283–84
Ethiopia, 8, 13–14, 36–37, 104–6, 108,
  112, 152, 180; colonialism and black-
  ness, 137–46; in *Aida*, 159, 161–62,
  165; war with Italy, 116–31
Ethiopian Orthodox Church, 129
*Ethiopian Voice*, 126
Ethiopian World Federation, 127–28
ethnic differences, 187, 259, 293; in
  *Aida*, 162
ethnicity, 4–7, 36, 237, 292–312;
  Gramsci and, 193; identity and, 239;
  Southern Italy and, 193–97
ethnocentrism, 10
ethnoscapes, 239, 242, 254, 273n. 4
Eurocentrism, 116, 175, 242
Europe, 9; Africa and, 125; Asia and, 32;
  backwardness and, 30–34; economies
  of, 25; Egypt and, 157–61; immigrants
  from, 15; immigrants in, 5; Italian emigration to, 44, 183; Italian studies in,
  10; Italy and, 11–12, 23–42; myths
  and, 30; racism in, 86; United States
  and, 242–43. *See also* Eastern Europe
European Community, 88
Eurotrash, 241–42
exceptionalism, 24

exile, 3–4, 64, 74–75, 174; Negri and,
43–50; Pedro II and, 219
exoticism, 287
Expo 2000, 249

*faccetta nera,* 103, 138, 139 fig. 1, 146,
152
"Faccetta nera" (song), 140–41
*Faccia da turco* (Turkish face), 178
Facta, Luigi, 83
Falcone, Giovanni, 81
*Falstaff,* 165
Fanon, Frantz, 259
Farinacci, Roberto, 83
Fasci, 199–200
fascism, 24–25, 35, 37–38, 81–88, 103,
120, 146, 195, 272n. 2, 281–83; black-
ness and, 13; capitalism and, 44; defor-
mation and, 136; ethnicity and, 5; male
sexuality and, 141; Mussolini and, 8,
53, 61; violence and, 52, 59
Fascist Party, 83–84
feminism, 59, 78n. 22
feminized nations, 197, 205, 209n. 4
Ferrera, Maurizio, 38
films, 15–16, 53, 253–72, 296–97
Fioravanti, Valerio, 77n. 12
First Republic, 84–85
flags, 7, 131; Ethiopian, 130–31,
133n. 61
Florence (Italy): bombings, 1
Flores d'Arcais, Paolo, 87
Fo, Dario, 53
Fontanesi, Antonio, 286
Forattini, Giorgio, 87; cartoons by,
89 fig. 1, 90 fig. 2
forced labor, 105
Forgacs, David, 35
Forti, Francesco, 112
"Fortress Europe," 88
Foucault, Michel, 15, 237–38, 241, 244
France, 8, 24, 28–29, 36–37, 109, 111,
171; blackness and, 138; Brazil and,
222; fascism and, 86; immigration to,
183, 189n. 13; Negri and, 46, 50n;
racism of, 93, 170
*francophonie,* 176
Frederick I, 82
free love, 220
Freud, Sigmund, 143, 146
Fuentes, Carlos, 239

*Futur Antérieur* (future past), 50n. 1
Futurism, 136–37, 142

Gallino, Luciano, 25
*Ganz Unten* (Wallraff), 178
Garboli, Cesare, 63
Garibaldi, Giuseppe, 82, 197–98
Garvey, Marcus, 13, 120, 122–25, 127
Gattai, Zelia, 14, 214, 216–30
gender, 5–7, 10, 14, 179–84, 236,
310–11; division, 138; in advertising,
148; in *Carmen,* 270
gender differences: in *Aida,* 162–63
genocide, 105
genre, 54–56, 71; terrorism and, 61
Gentili, Giovanni, 103
geography, 32, 40
Germany, 24, 28–29, 34, 36, 85, 94, 111,
281; *art nègre* and, 136; racism of, 93
*Geschichte und Klassenbewußtsein*
(Lukács), 48
Ghana, 121, 124
Ghirardelli, Massimo, 169
*Gilda,* 259–60
Ginsborg, Paul, 25–27
Ginzburg, Natalia, 64–67, 72–73, 75
Giolitti, Giovanni, 83
*Il Giorno,* 279
global markets, 3, 15–17
"Gloria all'Egitto," 160, 164
Gnisci, Armando, 189n. 17
Gobineau, Joseph Arthur, 104
*The Godfather,* 305
Goering, Hermann, 52
Gramsci, Antonio, 5, 28, 43, 47, 57, 73,
192–93, 198–99, 210n. 11
"Gramsci's Relevance for the Study of
Race and Ethnicity" (Hall), 193
Grande, Adriano, 105
"La grande proletaria si è mossa" (The
great proletarian nation has moved),
200–203
*Grand Street,* 157
Grant, Cary, 256, 262
Granzotto, Paolo, 281–82
Graziani, Rodolfo, 108
Great Britain, 27, 37, 95n. 10, 109;
racism of, 93. *See also* England
Greece, 32
*Il grido d'acquila* (The eagle's cry), 82
Guanahani, 259

Guattari, Félix, 93, 253–55, 257, 262–63
*La guerra lontana* (The distant war), 201
Guha, Ranajit, 33
Guicciardini, Francesco, 280
Guisti, Angelo, 229
Gumby, 292

Habermas, Jürgen, 33
Haiti, 117
Hall, Stuart, 193
Hapsburg dynasty, 14, 165
Haraway, Donna, 254–55, 292
Harlem, 13, 117, 119, 122, 127–28, 130
Harlem History Club, 121, 127
Harrison, Hubert, 127
Hayworth, Rita, 256–63, 270
Hegel, G. W. F., 32, 34, 37, 55, 105;
  Negri and, 48
Helms, Mary W., 31
Herman, Pee-Wee, 257
Hicks, Emily, 255
Hill, Robert, 122–23
Hispanic Americans, 236
historical blocs, 204
*The History of Florence* (Machiavelli), 35
Hobsbawm, E. J., 58, 72
Holocaust, 95n. 8
Horkheimer, Max, 293
*Ho trovato l'Occidente: Storie di donne
  immigrate a Palermo* (I discovered the
  West: stories of women immigrants in
  Palermo), 182
Huggins, Willis N., 121–22, 126–27, 129
Hughes, Langston, 13, 119–20
Hurston, Zora Neale, 205
Hutter, Lucy Maffei, 222–23

identity: class, 74–75, 306; communal,
  45, 57; cultural, 45, 101–13, 215, 235,
  250, 254, 275, 295, 305; economic,
  305; ethnic, 6, 185, 207, 236, 293,
  295, 306; gendered, 181, 256; historical, 241; local, 34; personal, 179, 181,
  184, 186–87, 238–29; political, 14, 35,
  37; racial, 122, 144–45, 148, 172, 179,
  206; regional, 237; religious, 184–86.
  *See also* national identity
identity politics, 4, 16
imagined communities, 3–4, 196, 229,
  241–42; time and, 253–54
Iman. *See* Abdulmajid, Iman

immigrants, 3, 5–6, 235; as authors,
  169–87, 204–8; from Africa, 15, 169,
  171, 174, 183; from Asia, 15, 169,
  171, 174; from Italy, 191, 205,
  213–30, 236; in Brazil, 5, 213–30;
  in Canada, 5–6, 192, 204–5, 208,
  210n. 12; in Italy, 93, 170–72, 174,
  182–87, 201; national identity and, 2,
  8; Portuguese, 216, 225; racism and,
  88, 91–92; to South America, 213–30
immigration, 3–4, 7, 9, 14–15, 169–71,
  174, 182, 241, 278; cultural, 15, 250;
  Italian, 236, 239; laws, 170; policies,
  88; race and, 5; racism and, 91; to
  South America, 213–30. *See also*
  emigration; migration
*Imperial Eyes* (Pratt), 214
imperialism, 14, 237; cultural, 196, 242;
  European, 157; fascist, 138; Gramsci
  and, 193; Hapsburg, 165; in *Carmen,*
  270; Italian, 5, 15, 123, 199–203,
  272n. 2; postcolonialism and, 191;
  Roman, 32
imperialist expansion, 8, 12
"The Imperial Spectacle" (Said), 157
impositions, 12–14
individualism, 284–86, 288
industrialization, 37
integration, 185
interculturalism, 235, 241, 250, 285,
  289. *See also* multiculturalism
Interlendi, 104
International Council of Friends of
  Ethiopia, 121
interpellation, 146
intolerance, 86, 93
*Invisible Cities* (Calvino), 243
*Invisible Man* (Ellison), 130–31
*Io venditore di elefanti* (I, an elephant
  salesman), 173, 183–84
*I promessi sposi* (The betrothed), 35,
  56–57
Islam, 85, 130
Ismail, Viceroy, 157–58, 160
Italian-African writers. *See* African-
  Italian authors
Italian American(s), 6–7, 13, 183,
  235–36; identity, 236, 238, 250; in
  films, 311; Italo-Ethiopian War and,
  118, 128; Karate Kid and, 299; south-
  ern, 192, 205–9; Teenage Mutant

Ninja Turtles as, 297; women writers, 205–8
Italianicity, 1, 235; in the United States, 6–7, 237, 244
*italianidade*, 228–29
*italianità* (Italianness), 206, 211n. 19, 257, 306
"The Italian Protocols," 228
Italian Social Movement (Movimento Sociale Italiano), 87
Italian studies, 9–11, 235
Italian Trusteeship in Somalia (AFIS [Amministrazione Fiduciaria Italiana in Somalia]), 110
Italo-Ethiopian War: advertising and, 137–48; African Americans and, 116–31
*italophonie*, 176
"Italy" (poem), 200–201
Iwakura Mission, 286

Jackson, John G., 127
Jacobitti, Edmund E., 37
Jacobs, Virginia Lee, 117
James, C. L. R., 124
Jameson, Fredric, 55, 58, 67
Japanese, 16, 275–89
Johnson, James Weldon, 126
"Josephine Backer [*sic*] on the Champs-Élysées and Experimental Theater at Montmarte" (Depero), 136–37
*Journal of Negro History*, 126
*Jungle Fever*, 210n. 17

*The Karate Kid* (films), 16, 296–312
Kenya, 124
Kenyatta, Jomo, 124
Kerman, Joseph, 158
Kermit the Frog, 292
Kermode, Frank, 29–30
Khan, Kubla, 16
Khouma, Pap, 171–73, 175, 178, 183–87, 189n. 13
Kikoma, Uyeno, 287
Kimbei, Kusakabe, 287
Kinney, Abbott, 245, 247
kinship, 4, 57, 121, 225, 295
Knights of Columbus, 6
Kremlin, 273n. 4

labels: in Japan, 288
labor unions, 60
*Ladri di biciclette* (*The Bicycle Thief*), 47, 253–72; Maggiorani in, 261 fig. 1
*Ladri di saponette* (*The Icicle Thief*), 253–72; Piermattei in, 269 fig. 2
Laird, Peter, 300
Lama, Luciano, 84
La Malfa, Giorgio, 92, 95n. 5
Lanaro, Silvio, 35–39
land, 198–99, 202–3; in Brazil, 219–22, 225
language, 173–74
*La Laterna*, 226
Lapponi, Paolo, 52
*L.A. Story*, 252n. 30
Latouche, Daniel, 61
Leach, Edmund, 289
League of Nations, 121, 125–26, 129, 138
League of Young Somalis, 109
Lefebvre, Henri, 243, 272n. 1
Lee, Spike, 7, 210n. 17
Lega del Nord, 170
Lega lombarda (Lombard League), 82–83, 92, 208; racism of, 91
*legge Martelli* (Martelli law), 170–71
Legnano, 82
Lembo, Rosario, 28
*Lenta ginestra* (the slow broomhedge), 50n. 1
Leoni, Andrea, 52
Leopardi, Giacomo, 43, 46–47, 50n. 1
lesbians, 206–8
Lessona, Alessandro, 138
*Lettere garibaldine* (Garibaldine letters), 197
Libya, 8, 104, 109, 114n. 12, 203
*Linea d'ombra*, 180
literary texts, 54
literature, 15, 47–48; French, 176; Italian, 9, 43, 47–48, 57, 169–87, 197. *See also* novels
Lockwood, Charles, 248
Lodoli, Marco, 172
I Lombardi, 165
Lombard League (Lega lombarda), 82–83, 92, 208; racism of, 91
Lombroso, Cesare, 142, 194
Los Angeles, 242–50

Louis, Joe, 130
Lugard, F.D., 32
Lukács, Georg, 48, 54–55
Lyotard, Jean-François, 251n. 12
lyric, 54

"Macchia nera" (Black stain), 87
Machiavelli, Niccolò, 9, 35, 43–45, 47, 280
*Madama Butterfly,* 289
Mafia, 23, 44, 73, 113; bombings and, 1; films, 6
Maggiorani, Lamberto, 257, 261 fig. 1
Magubane, Bernard, 118
Maier, Charles J., 29
Mambro, Francesca, 77n. 12
Manconi, Luigi, 170, 186
Mandrou, Robert, 31
"Mani pulite," 83–84
Mann, Thomas, 243–44
Manzoni, Alessandro, 35, 56–58, 67, 73, 78n. 23
"Manzoni and His Humble Characters" (Gramsci), 57
Marazzi, Antonio, 16, 275–89
Mariette, Auguste, 158, 163
marketing, 6
Marley, Bob, 128
Martelli, Claudio, 170–71
Martinazzoli, Mino, 83
Marx, Karl, 48
*Marx Beyond Marx* (Negri), 49, 50n. 1
Marxism, 86, 204
Marxists, 243
masculinity, 301–6
Mason, Tim, 24, 27–28
Masonic organizations, 73, 113
Masslo, Jerry, 169, 171, 176
mass media, 6, 13
Mathy, Francis, 277
Mauss, Marcel, 38
Mazzini, Giuseppe, 27–28
McClary, Susan, 270
McKay, Claude, 120
Meiji restoration, 281–86
Mella, Julio Antonio, 240
Melliti, Moshen, 171, 175
Memmi, Albert, 259
Menelik, Emperor, 117
"La 'Merica," 230

mestizos, 6, 106
metaphors: of backwardness, 24–30
Methnani, Salah, 171–72, 175, 177–78, 184
*métissage,* 174, 176, 179, 187
Mexico, 238–40
Meyerbeer, Giacomo, 161
Mezzogiorno, 28
*Mezzogiorno tra riforme e rivoluzione* (Villani), 194–95
Micheletti, Alessandro, 172, 190n. 24
middle class, 38
Miglio, Gianfranco, 83
migration, 5, 173–74, 182, 200, 214, 232n. 33; in Brazil, 220; Italian, 237; seasonal, 216; to Los Angeles, 243. *See also* emigration; immigration
Milan, 81; bombings, 52, 60, 75n. 2
*Milano-Palermo: La nuova Resistenza* (Milan-Palermo, the new resistance), 81
military government, 59, 62
military intervention, 194
*Le mille e una donna. Donne migranti: incontri di culture* (A thousand and one women: migrating women: the intersection of cultures), 182
Miller, Francesca, 14, 213–30
Minculpop, 103, 114n. 5
Ministry of Foreign Affairs, 111
miscegenation, 263
Mitchell, Loften, 130
mobility, 242; class, 12; social, 225
*Moda,* 151
modernism, 11, 13
modernity, 24–30, 33–34, 36, 38–40, 243
modernization, 24–26, 30, 33, 39
Modotti, Tina, 237, 238–42, 250
monogamy, 143
Monroe, Marilyn, 251n. 12
Montanelli, Indro, 106
*The Moral Basis of a Backward Society* (Banfield), 27
Moretti, Nanni, 264
Moro, Aldo, 49, 50n. 1, 60, 67, 73, 75n. 2
Morocco, 171, 174, 178, 186
Morucci, Valerio, 52
Moschino Jeans: ad, 150 fig. 4

Movimento Sociale Italiano (Italian Social Movement), 87, 170
multiculturalism, 16, 237, 292–93. See also interculturalism
Mulvey, Laura, 258–59
Mura, David, 209
music, 2–3; in Aida, 159–65; oriental, 161, 163–64; reggae, 128
Musical Elaborations (Said), 156
Muslims, 185
Mussolini, Benito, 36, 102, 114n. 4, 114n. 10, 123, 282; Africa and, 8, 103, 116, 118–19, 129–30, 155n. 25; in cartoons, 87–88; fascism and, 8, 53, 61; Fascist Party and, 83; Italian Americans and, 128; Vatican and, 129
mutation, 293, 295–97
myth: of backwardness, 29–30

Nabucco, 165
Naison, Mark, 128
Nakamura, Shigeru, 278
Nakasone, Prime Minister, 278
Napoléon, 117, 158
Nation, 156–57
National Association for the Advancement of Colored People, 118
national difference, 259
National Endowment for the Humanities, 236
national identity, 2–4, 9–17, 34–35, 38, 43, 45–47, 52, 73, 75, 92, 172, 194; authors', 177; blackness and, 135; immigrants and, 8, 14; in novels, 66, 71; novels and, 53–59, 61, 73–74; Oedipal behavior and, 256; race and, 5, 148; religion and, 35; southern Italians and, 204–9. See also identity
nationalism, 3–4, 14, 56, 75, 93, 152, 191–92, 235, 241; African, 120–21, 125; African Americans and, 118–19, 126; Brazilian, 229; cultural, 229; Ethiopian, 155n. 25; films and, 260, 264; Italian, 36, 196, 201, 203, 215; religious, 130
nationalist organizations, 128
nationalization, 27, 39
nation-race, 13, 134
Nations and Nationalism since 1780 (Hobsbawm), 72
nation-states, 9, 12, 13, 17, 28, 75, 110,

257; blackness and, 134; novels and, 55–58, 71, 73
Native Types (Beato), 287
Nazi(s), 86, 91, 92–93, 95n. 10; art movements and, 137; fascism, 87
Naziskins, 85, 93
Negri, Antonio, 11, 43–50, 60, 64, 74–75
Negro Liberator, 126
neocolonialism, 111
neofascism, 76n. 3
neorealism, 47
Nericcio, William, 259
Neruda, Pablo, 240
New Order, 53
New York Age, 126
Ngugi Wa Thiong'o, 173
Niceforo, Alfredo, 209n. 2
Nichetti, Maurizio, 253, 259, 263–72
Nietzsche, Friedrich, 243
Nievo, Ippolito, 194–95, 197–98, 205
Nigeria, 32, 117, 124
Nkrumah, Kwame, 111, 121–22, 124, 127
"noble expenditures," 38
"Il nome di Maria Fresu" (Maria Fresu's name), 53
nonviolence, 93
North America, 9; immigrants in, 6; Italian Americans in, 206; Italian emigration to, 8, 14, 191–92; Italian studies in, 10
Northern Exposure, 257
northern Italy: versus southern, 5, 9, 23, 27–28, 92, 148, 193, 198–99, 205, 208
Northern League, 2, 5, 148
novels, 11–12, 52–75, 172. See also literature

Occhetto, Achille, 83; cartoon of, 90 fig. 2
Occidente (Camon), 63
Oedipal behavior: in films, 256–57, 263, 266–67, 270–72
Okinawa, 304–5, 313n. 16
Ombre (Castellaneta), 68–72
On Laughter (Bergson), 135
opera, 156–65

*Opera, or the Undoing of Women* (Clément), 270
Opéra-Comique, 158
opportunism, 294
*Opportunity,* 126
oppression, 116
*Orchids in the Moonlight* (Fuentes), 239
organ donors: and national identity, 2
organized crime, 81
Orient, 32
orientalism, 276, 289; *Aida* and, 156–65
*Otello,* 165
Ottieri, Maria Pace, 172
Ottley, Roy, 117–18, 126
Ottomans, 32
Ottone, Piero, 83
overpopulation, 199–200, 203

*Pacific Wall* (Lyotard), 251n. 12
Padmore, George, 124
Palermo, 81
Pan-African Conference, 125
Pan-Africanism, 13, 116–17, 120–22, 124–25, 127–28
*Pan-Africanism or Communism?* (Padmore), 124
*Panorama,* 171
Pantanella, 181
*Pantanella. Canto lungo la strada* (Pantanella: a song along the road), 175
Parati, Graziella, 15, 169–87
Parsons, Talcott, 33, 37–38
Partisans, 81–82, 92
Partito d'azione, 86
Partito Repubblicano, 170
Pascoli, Giovanni, 194, 200–203
Pasolini, Pier Paolo, 3
paternalism, 294, 311
*La patria lontana* (The distant fatherland), 200–203
patriotism, 56, 125; Brazilian, 215, 225, 228
patronage, 152
"paulista," 215–16
Pearl Harbor, 279
Pedro II, 218–19
*Pee-Wee's Big Adventure,* 257
Pena, Afonso, 232n. 34
Petrarca, Francesco, 196
*The Philosophy of Literary Form* (Burke), 60

*Philosophy of Right* (Hegel), 32
photography, 287
*Phylon,* 126
Picasso, Pablo, 287
"Piccoli equivoci senza importanza" (Little misunderstandings of no consequence), 53, 72
pickaninnies, 137, 141, 153n. 5
Piermattei, Antonio, 269 fig. 2
Pinkus, Karen, 13, 134–53
*Pinocchio* (Collodi), 36
Pintacuda, Father Ennio, 113
*Pipe-line* (Negri), 48
Pisacane, Carlo, 194
Pisu, Renata, 278–79
*Pittsburgh Courier,* 126
Pivetta, Oreste, 173
*The Player,* 257
Pletsch, C. E., 33
*Poemas de um Imigrante Italiano* (Guisti), 229
poetry, 53, 93
political society, 86
politics, 23, 28, 93
*The Politics of Identity* (Aronowitz), 7
*The Politics of Subversion* (Negri), 48
Polo, Marco, 16, 276–77, 283
polygamy, 186
Poniatowska, Elena, 239–40
*The Post-Colonial Critic* (Spivak), 173
postcolonialism, 191–209, 253
postmodernity, 15–17, 235, 244, 250, 259, 296
*Il potere costituente* (constituent power), 50n. 1
Potere Operaio (workers' power), 48
Powell, Adam Clayton, Jr., 128, 130
Powell, C. B., 126
Pratt, Mary Louise, 30, 214
*The Prince* (Machiavelli), 35
"The Problem of Political Direction in the Formation and Development of the Nation and State of Modern Italy" (Gramsci), 198–99
*The Production of Space* (Lefebvre), 243
*La promessa di Hamadi* (Hamadi's promise), 172, 178–79
*I promessi sposi* (The betrothed), 35, 56–57
propaganda, 135–36, 138, 140, 142, 144; Egypt and, 158

"La prova del fuoco" (Trial by fire), 53
Prussia, 36
public opinion, 63, 125
purges, 88

*Quaderni rossi* (red notebooks), 48
quadrumvirate, 106

race, 5–7, 12–14, 93, 135, 191, 237, 295;
    gender and, 184; Gramsci and, 193;
    southern Italy and, 193–97, 205; war,
    117
racial difference, 179, 187, 192, 194, 225
racism, 3, 6, 12, 81–94, 106, 113,
    169–70, 191; deformation and, 136;
    Gramsci and, 193; in *Carmen*, 270; in
    *The Karate Kid*, 313n. 16
Radical Party, 49, 50n. 1, 112
Ragusa, Vincenzo, 286
Ramazzotti: ads for, 146, 147 fig. 3
rape, 77n. 17
Rapisardi, Mario, 194
Ras Tafari movement, 128
rationalization, 33
*La Razza* (The race), 104, 114n. 6
*I razzismi reali* (Real racisms), 170
*The Real Facts about Ethiopia* (Rogers),
    122
Red Brigades (Brigate Rosse), 26, 49,
    50n. 1, 53, 59–60, 67, 75n. 2, 190n. 27
Reed, Ishmael, 129
Reformation: Protestant, 29, 38
religion: Italo-Ethiopian War and,
    129–31; national identity and, 35
religious wars, 32
Renaissance, 31–32, 34; individualism
    and, 284–86
repeatable materiality, 237–38
reproduction: and national identity, 2
*La Repubblica*, 138, 151
Republican Party, 92, 95n. 5
Resistance, 73, 81–86, 91–92, 94, 109
La Rete (the network), 81
Revolution of 1789, 38
Ribeiro Durham, Eunice, 221–22, 225
*Rigoletto*, 165
Ringling Museum, 244
Risorgimento, 14, 35–36, 73, 81–82,
    103, 165, 194–98, 281. *See also*
    unification
Rivera, Diego, 239–40

Robeson, Paul, 13, 120–21
Robinson, Paul, 13–14, 156–65
*Rocky*, 296
Rogers, J. A., 122, 126
    *Le Roi de Lahore*, 161
Romano, Rose, 205–6
Rome, 87, 102
Ronchey, Alberto, 83
*Roots of Ras Tafari* (Jacobs), 117
Rosa, Alberto Asor, 26
"Roses, Mexico," 240
Rossi, Giovanni, 218–19, 231
Rossi, Nicola, 25
Ruocco, Monica, 175
Russell, John, 249
Russo, Mary, 15, 235–50
Ryan, Michael T., 31

Sahlins, Marshall, 38
Said, Edward, 13, 32, 156–65, 290n. 2
Saint Basil's Cathedral, 273n. 4
Salvemini, Gaetano, 203
*Samson et Dalila*, 161
samurai, 283–84
*sanatoria*, 170
Sanusy, 109
Sarasota (Florida), 244–45
Sassoon, Anne Showstack, 204
*Saturday Night Fever*, 296
*Saturday Night in the Prime of Life*
    (Azpadu), 207–8
*The Savage Anomaly: The Power of
    Spinoza's Metaphysics and Politics*
    (Negri), 49, 50n. 1
Scalfaro, Oscar Luigi, 83
Schmidt-Brümmer, Horst, 247–48
Schoenberg, Arnold, 243
Schomburg, Arthur, 121, 127
Schuyler, George L., 126–27
Schwoebel, Robert, 32
Scott, William R., 125, 127, 129
segregation, 105
Selassie, Haile, 109, 121–22, 128, 138,
    152; *Aida* and, 159
"Se la storia fa la faccia feroce" (If
    history pulls a ferocious face), 85
self-image, 93–94
Selznick, David O., 256
Senegal, 171, 178–79, 183–84
Sereni, Emilio, 200
Serra, Michele, 92–93

Settembrini, Domenico, 25
"Settimanale di Resistenza Umana"
(Weekly of human resistance), 87
sexual difference, 256, 259
sexuality, 93, 296; blackness and,
137–38, 140–44; female, 144,
231n. 16; in films, 257, 259–60; in
novels, 68–72, 207; integration and,
185; Japan and, 284; male, 140–41,
144; stockings and, 142–43
Sforza, Count Carlo, 109
*Shish Mahal* (Curcio), 181
short stories, 53–54, 73, 75
Shusaku, Endo, 277
Sicily, 199, 205–6
*sinister wisdom*, 206
Sobchack, Vivian, 295
social change, 33, 59–60
socialism, 49, 229
Socialist Party, 83, 87, 94n. 3
Socialists, 26
social models, 33
social movements, 119
social order, 33, 38
social organization, 17, 55
social structure, 182
social text, 54, 62, 72, 74–75
Socini, Fausto, 51n. 2
Socini, Lelio, 51n. 2
Socinians, 43
Sollors, Werner, 295
Somalia, 8, 12, 102–8, 112, 151–52;
Italian trusteeship in, 108–11
Somalis, 138, 141–42, 144
Somali Youth League (SYL), 110
South Africa, 106, 117, 169
South America, 9; immigrants and, 6;
Italian emigration to, 8, 213–30;
Italian studies in, 10
southern Italy, 191–209, 228; versus
northern, 5, 9, 23, 27–28, 92, 148,
193, 198–99, 205, 208
sovereignty, 32–33, 117
Soviet Union, 38, 109, 128
space, 254–55, 257, 263, 265–66;
cultural, 260, 262
spaces, 10; and backwardness, 30–34
Spain, 36; immigrants from, 6
*Spinoza sovversivo* (Spinoza as subver-
sive), 50n. 1
Spivak, Gayatri, 173

Springborg, Patricia, 32
*La Stampa*, 85, 279
stereotypes, 12, 16, 102–5, 113, 294,
298–99; Japanese and, 275–89,
298–99; in literature, 206; of immigrants, 171, 183–84; of men, 259–60,
298; of women, 260
stockings, 142–43
*strage dello stato*, 59, 73, 75n. 2
Stravinsky, Igor, 243
strikes, 84
Sturzo, Don Luigi, 83
"Su! del Nilo," 160
Suez Canal, 157
surrogacy, 295–97, 300, 306, 311

"The Taboo of Virginity" (Freud), 143
Tabucchi, Antonio, 53, 72
Takeyama, Hakuei, 280–81
Tana Beles, 112
Tanner, Tony, 249
Tasso, Torquato, 43
Taubate Convention, 232n. 34
Taviani Brothers, 53
Taytu, Empress, 117
technology, 303–4
Teenage Mutant Ninja Turtles, 16,
292–312
*Teenage Mutant Ninja Turtles II: The
Secret of the Ooze,* 297, 301, 308,
311, 312n. 5
television, 84, 255, 257, 263–67, 301
*La terra in faccia: Gli immigrati raccon-
tano* (Dirt in your face: immigrants
narrate), 182
*The Terrible Twos* (Reed), 129
terrorism, 75n. 1; fascist, 62–63, 74,
77n. 12; in novels, 11–12, 52–75; left,
62–63, 74. *See also* bombings; violence
Third World, 14, 33–34, 39, 171, 191,
241
*A Thousand Plateaus* (Deleuze and
Guattari), 253
*Three Brothers,* 53
Tiecher, Bartolomeu, 228
time, 253–54, 257, 265–66
Tipps, Dean, 33
Titone, Virgilio, 194
Tonioli, Gianni, 25
Toscano, Mario, 114
Toure, Kwame, 124

tourism, 3, 12, 60, 285
Transnational Radical Party, 115n. 19
*trasformismo*, 28–29
*Travels in Hyperreality* (Eco), 244
*La Traviata*, 165
Triennale d'Oltremare, 140
Trudeau, Pierre, 61
Tullio-Altan, Carlo, 25–29
Tunisia, 171, 175
Turati, Filippo, 83
Turin, 84
Turkey, 203

Uffizi Museum, 1
*Uguali e diversi: Il mondo culturale, le reti di rapporti, i lavori degli immigrati non europei a Torino* (Equal and different: the cultural world, the network of relations, the occupations of non-European immigrants in Turin), 181
unification, 28, 35, 44, 82, 165, 191, 193–95, 197–200, 204, 208; novels and, 57–59. *See also* Risorgimento
*L'Unità*, 92
United Nations, 101, 109–10
United States, 24, 36, 109, 256; African Americans and, 124; blackness in, 13, 134; demographic changes in, 16; ethnic identities and, 236; Garvey and, 122; immigrants in, 5–6, 192, 204; Italian Americans in, 13, 206, 208, 235; Italian emigration to, 6, 44, 183, 232n. 33; Italianicity in, 7; Italian migration to, 237; Italians as slaves in, 5; Italian studies in, 9–10; Italo-Ethiopian War and, 128; Japan and, 302, 305; modernity and, 33, 39–40; myths and, 30; racism of, 93
United States Immigration Act of 1924, 18n. 19
United States of Africa, 122
Universal Negro Improvement Association, 122
universal state, 34

"Va, pensiero," 165
Valpredo affair, 60
Vanilla Ice, 309, 312n. 5
Vatican, 73, 125; and Mussolini, 129–30
Vattimo, Gianni, 47, 85
"Vediamo se Bossi è un altro Mussolini"
(Let's see if Bossi is another Mussolini), 83
*Vendetta* (Romano), 205
Venice (California), 237, 239–50; trompe l'oeil, 245, 246 fig. 1
*Venice, California: An Urban Fantasy* (Schmidt-Brümmer), 247
Venice (Florida), 244–45
Venice (Italy), 243–45, 248–49
*Venice Beach* (Edinger), 248
Verdi, Giuseppe, 13–14, 157–65
Verdicchio, Pasquale, 14, 191–209
Veyne, Paul, 37
Viarengo, Maria, 179–81
victimization, 247
Vidor, Charles, 259
Vietnam War, 39, 302
*Views of Japan* (Beato), 287
"Villa Literno" (Ben Jelloun), 176
Villani, Pasquale, 194–95
violence, 1–3, 52–53, 60, 75n.1, 83, 85–86, 169; domestic, 4; in novels, 71; political, 12, 75; racist, 86, 88, 93; women as objects of, 107. *See also* bombings; clandestine political violence; terrorism
Vittorio Emanuele III, 83
Vivarelli, Roberto, 25
*Voice of Ethiopia*, 128
*Volevo diventare bianca* (I wanted to become white), 177
Volterrani, Egi, 176
von Humboldt, Alexander, 214–15

Wagner, Wieland, 162
Waldner, Francesco, 39
Waller, Marguerite R., 15, 253–72
Wallraff, Günter, 178
Ward, David, 12, 81–94
Watt, Ian, 55
Weber, Max, 33, 38
*Webster*, 311
The Week of Modern Art, 229
welfare state, 38; Britain and, 27
Weston, Edward, 239–40, 251n. 16
white supremacy, 121, 123, 130
Winter, Aaron, 91
*WKHY* (Curcio), 63
Wolin, Sheldon, 30
women, 106–7, 141–44, 186, 259; bodies as landscape, 251n. 12; education of,

227; films and, 259; immigrant, 181–84, 223; in *Aida,* 162–64; southern Italian, 206; Teenage Mutant Ninja Turtles and, 301; writers, 180, 205–8
Woodson, Carter G., 120
Work, F. Ernest, 118
workers, 38, 43, 45, 60
working class, 257–58, 299
"The Work of Art in the Age of Mechanical Reproduction" (Benjamin), 271
World Court, 228
World Cup, 250n. 1
World War I, 8, 200–201

World War II, 8, 45, 87, 95n. 10, 109, 148, 303

xenophobia, 9, 12, 113, 170; Brazilian, 225; films and, 260; Northern League and, 2

years of lead (*anni di piombo*), 12, 52–54, 59–64, 72–73, 75, 76n. 8
youth movement, 59
Yugoslavia, 85

Zanzotto, Andrea, 53